NATIONAL GALLERY CATALOGUES

THE EARLY NETHERLANDISH SCHOOL

BY

MARTIN DAVIES

The first series of major catalogues of the various Schools of Painting in the National Gallery Collection was launched in 1945. The series is now being extensively revised and the initial volumes of the second series, *The Dutch School* and *The Early Italian Schools*, are in preparation.

Meanwhile five of the original text volumes have been reprinted. Each has been reissued without alteration to the text, but a list of paintings in the relevant school acquired since the publication of the last edition is added as an appendix. For further details about these paintings the reader is referred to the *Illustrated General Catalogue* (2nd edition, 1987) and successive volumes of the *National Gallery Report*.

NATIONAL GALLERY CATALOGUES
First series reprints

The Earlier Italian Schools by Martin Davies
The Sixteenth-Century Italian Schools by Cecil Gould
The Seventeenth and Eighteenth Century Italian Schools
by Michael Levey
The Flemish School 1600–1900 by Gregory Martin
The Early Netherlandish School by Martin Davies

National Gallery Publications
The National Gallery
London

Published by order of the Trustees

First published 1945
2nd edition 1955
3rd edition 1968
Reprinted 1987

ISBN 0 947645 23 3

Printed and bound in Great Britain by
William Clowes Limited, Beccles and London

Cover
Rogier van der Weyden, *The Magdalen Reading* (detail)

NOTE

It would be hopeless to try to define precisely the frontiers of the Early Netherlandish School; two lists at the end of this book, of the inventory numbers of the pictures, and of the attributions changed from the catalogue of 1929, will be a guide to what is included.

The biographical notices of the painters need a brief explanation; they omit many facts to be found in the Dictionaries, and are largely definitions of why certain pictures are associated with certain names. Some facts concerning the painter's life are given, if relevant to attribution; the status of key-works is discussed at some length, if these are few and doubtful. The definition of a nucleus of more or less documented work is in general all that is attempted. It is assumed that the student can see reproductions of ascribed pictures; and that he can decide for himself which of these are important, which trivial. Sometimes brief indications are given of a painter's place in the history of the School; no attempt has been made to estimate his merits or defects.

As for the attributions of the pictures themselves, nothing is either signed or documented unless explicitly so described. Some caution in the *expertise* has been observed; no attempt has been made to quote all opinions, though there is sufficient matter to start the student of ascriptions on his way, and some space is used in explaining the statements of the 1929 catalogue. Some opinions on dating are usually quoted, though as likely as not the reasons for them are subjective.

Description of the pictures has been largely omitted; reference to a reproduction is given instead. Inscriptions on the fronts and (if they too are pictures) on the backs are recorded; iconographical identifications and any details hard to see are stated. If elucidation of these statements is needed, it has been made lower down, in the commentary; but explanation of the commoner points of iconography, such as the emblems of Saints, will be found in the iconographical index. The reader is assumed to have a working knowledge of Latin and the chief languages of Western Europe.

In the difficult matter of condition, some suggestions are given in almost every case. If the condition is marked as fair or better than fair, the student need not bother about it unless he wishes. The compiler has had exceptional opportunities for studying the condition, opportunities that could probably not be granted to students wishing to dispute his statements. The compiler feels this to be an additional disadvantage in a subject already difficult, in which he freely admits that he is likely sometimes to be wrong; but unless there is a statement of the condition such as is provisionally attempted here, the field of attribution is mined ground. The notes on condition are more elaborate for the better pictures, and are concerned chiefly with the more important parts; thus the condition may be called good even if fairly large areas of no particular interest have been repainted.

The condition above the paint film, i.e. dirtiness, is seldom referred to; but the word 'undercleaning' may here be explained. The surface of a picture is not a plane, but is made up of ridges and hollows, sometimes more, sometimes less; partial cleaning often removes all dirt and varnish from the ridges and none from the hollows. The spotty texture thus achieved is referred to in this catalogue as an effect of undercleaning.

The allied subject of *pentimenti* has been treated fairly fully, but with no attempt at completeness.

Some of the Indices have been already referred to; a few words may be added about the *Index of Religious Subjects*. It was felt that brief explanations, with any chance points of general interest added, would be more useful than a mere list, and it is hoped that what is said is reasonably exact.

Authorities are cited in the text; but I would wish here to thank, first my colleagues (past and present), then the staffs of the National Portrait Gallery, the British Museum (especially the Print Room) and the Victoria and Albert Museum (especially the Library). Messrs. Christie, Manson and Woods have been unfailingly helpful in matters relating to their sales.

MARTIN DAVIES

NOTE TO THE SECOND EDITION

THE FIRST EDITION of this catalogue was published in 1945. It has been partially revised for the present issue; entries for three recent acquisitions have been added.

Much of the work for the first edition was done during the war, when I could not travel on the Continent. I have now checked various points, seeing pictures or consulting manuscripts and books; but the revision is uneven.

The entries for the Flemish pictures in fifteenth-century style have been fairly fully reconsidered. I have been privileged to write on these pictures for the series *Les Primitifs Flamands* (*Corpus*); and I am greatly indebted for help to Dr. Paul Coremans, M. René Sneyers, Mlle. Nicole Verhaegen and others in Belgium. The present catalogue was, and remains, less elaborate in treatment than the *Corpus* volumes; but I have (with Dr. Coremans' permission) inserted here the corrections and amplifications that seemed to me desirable. In the *Corpus* volumes, the *Laboratoire Central des Musées de Belgique* gave a full and valuable account of the structure and condition of the pictures, but this would be beyond the scope of the present catalogue, where the notes on condition are on the same principles as in the first edition. The sizes are recorded in the *Corpus* volumes with more minuteness than is done here. Some references are given here to points there discussed at greater length, but references are usually not given to the copious illustrations.

The biographies of the painters, and the entries in the present volume for pictures not in the *Corpus*, have been less thoroughly revised.

In preparing this volume, I have received help of various kinds in the National Gallery. I am particularly indebted to the Scientific and Photographic Staffs for infra-red, ultra-violet and X-ray photographs. Some scientific photographs had indeed been available to me during the war; many more have been taken since. I am further greatly indebted to Mrs. Newton for notes on costume, many of which are acknowledged in their place.

I wish also to thank Dr. Ludwig Baldass, who kindly sent me some notes about the pictures; Dr. H. K. Röthel and Dr. O. Bock von Wülfingen of the Ältere Pinakothek at Munich, for photostats of Œttingen-Wallerstein catalogues and for other help; and the Librarian of Dr. Williams's Library, for permission to consult some unpublished parts of H. Crabb Robinson's diary. I have further received much valuable help from the authorities of the Witt Library at the Courtauld Institute, the Rijksbureau voor Kunsthistorische Documentatie at The Hague, and the Cabinet des Estampes in the Bibliothèque Nationale at Paris.

M.D.

NOTE TO THE THIRD EDITION

The first edition is now more than twenty years old. Perhaps it is becoming due to be rewritten entirely. I have not attempted that; I have inserted corrections and amplifications as well as I could. Matters of taste have been less attended to than matters of fact. The latter are indeed considerable since the second edition of 1955. First, the cleaning of many pictures, some of great importance. Secondly, research since 1955, particularly significant for the main production of the sixteenth century, also for a noticeable number of volumes on the fifteenth century in the *Corpus* series from Brussels. Several new acquisitions, some of very great importance, have been made since the 2nd edition, and are recorded here. An index of collections has been added.

While revising the present catalogue, I have also been preparing a supplementary volume for the *Corpus des Primitifs Flamands;* Mlle. Micheline Sonkes in particular has been unfailingly patient in helping me for the pictures there included. Mr. Robert A. Koch has been kind enough to send proof sheets of some pages of his book on Patenier, due to be published in 1968; some notice of his studies in that field could thus be incorporated here. M.D.

EXPLANATIONS

Painters' Names: Often no standard spelling exists; the forms chosen could be justified, and some cross-references are given from other spellings.

Attribution: A picture labelled as *by* a painter or from his *Studio* is presumed to have been produced as his in his shop. If doubt needs emphasis, *Ascribed to* is prefixed. If there seems to be a connection of style but not of hand, *Follower of*, *After* or *Style of* is prefixed. *Follower* replaces the word *School*, here reserved for a town or district; *After* may indicate a posthumous continuation of the workshop, or an independent copy of any date; *Style of* indicates a vague relation.

Condition: All canvases are relined unless the contrary is stated; cradling of panels is not noted. Damages in the supports, such as cracks in panels or waviness in canvases, are usually not noted.

Measurements: These are given in inches, followed by metres in brackets. Height precedes width. The size of the painted surface, not of the supporting canvas or panel, is given. When the painted area has been extended in recent times up to the edges of the support, the size of the original only is given; doubtful cases are noted as such.

Medium: This is assumed to be oil, or whatever is meant by the technique of the van Eycks, unless otherwise stated.

Right and Left: These terms indicate the spectator's right and left, unless the context clearly implies the contrary.

Jan van AMSTEL

active 1527, died not later than 1543 (?)

This painter, from Amsterdam, is recorded at Antwerp in 1527. He became Master there in 1528, and a citizen there in 1536; he apparently (Jan de Hollandere) had a pupil there in 1538. He seems to be identical with a Jan de Hollander, recorded by van Mander as a landscape painter. The latest possible date of his death is deduced from evidence given by van den Branden, who uses both van Mander and documents at Antwerp. The two key-documents for this matter seemed to be those of 1527 and 1544, cited by van den Branden on pp. 288 and 307; the compiler is much indebted to P. Coremans and F. Van Molle for photostats and transcriptions of them, and for comments on them. The date claimed for Jan van Amstel's death depends upon the identity of his wife in 1527, 'Adriane Martens alias van Doernicke, Jans dochtere,' and Gillis van Coninxloo's widow in 1544, 'Adriana Hermans, alias van Doernicke.' On the evidence of these two documents alone, the identity seems doubtful; the compiler does not know if other documents establish the identity, or if it is admitted because of what van Mander says. Hoogewerff thinks than Jan van Amstel was a brother of Pieter Aertsen.

He is often identified with the Brunswick Monogrammist. A picture at Brunswick carries a monogram, in which Genaille claims to read all the letters J. v. Amstel (*Revue Belge d'Archéologie et d'Histoire de l'Art*, 1950, pp. 150 ff., with plate; L. v. Puyvelde in the same periodical, 1951, pp. 68/9, disputes the reading). Simone Bergmans suggests that the monogram refers to a person who was not the painter, Jan van der Meere (1490–1562). See particularly the catalogue *Le Siècle de Bruegel*, Brussels, 1963, no. 253, and her article in the *Bulletin des Musées Royaux des Beaux-Arts de Belgique*, Vol. XIV, 1965, pp. 143 ff. She also claims that a picture of different style representing *The Deluge* is the work of Jan van Amstel, finding his portrait there on comparison with the features recorded in D. Lampson, *Les Effigies Des Peintres Célèbres des Pays-Bas* (1572), ed. J. Puraye, 1956, pp. 44–5; see particularly S. Bergmans in the *Revue Belge d'Archéologie et d'Histoire de l'Art*, Vol. XXVI, 1957, pp. 25 ff.

Friedländer, Vol. XII, pp. 87 ff., inclines to accept a different identification for the Brunswick Monogrammist, Jan van (or rather de) Hemessen. It appears impossible to read in the monogram letters to indicate Hemessen's name, and Friedländer's other arguments for the identification are not convincing. See further Vitale Bloch in *The Burlington Magazine*, 1956, pp. 445 f. and Simone Bergmans in the *Revue Belge d'Archéologie et d'Histoire de l'Art*, 1958, pp. 77 ff.

Simone Bergmans thinks that the painter of the Brunswick picture is Meyken Verhulst, wife of Pieter Coecke van Aelst; see particularly the *Revue Belge d'Archéologie et d'Histoire de l'Art*, Vol. XXIV, 1955, pp. 133 ff. Meyken Verhulst was still alive in 1580; see Georges Marlier, *Pierre Coeck d'Alost*, 1966, p. 47.

A second monogrammed picture is mentioned by Friedländer, p. 87. It seems irrelevant; it appeared in the Exhibition *Le Siècle de Bruegel*, Brussels, 1963, no. 151, as by Jan Mandijn.

After JAN VAN AMSTEL (?)

5577 ITINERANT ENTERTAINERS IN A BROTHEL

Various marks on the wall may not be intended to make words. A picture on the wall is inscribed: *Hier sit ic als printer*(?) | *van der Hooghe* . . . | *Siet het is enich*(?) | *met eenre* | *muts*. . . .

Oak, $18 \times 23\frac{7}{8}$ (0·455 × 0·607); painted up to the edges all round.

Rather rubbed. Many *pentimenti*. In particular, the headdresses of the women, 3rd and 5th from the left in the main group, were once different; the man second from the left had his right hand a little higher, a platter(?) on the table was intended instead of the taller glass (these two variations only drawn in), etc.

This composition, with variations, is known in several versions; two, at Antwerp[1] and in the Lanckoroński Collection, once at Vienna,[2] are recorded by Friedländer as copies after the Brunswick Monogrammist.

The style of execution of No. 5577 differs from that of the Brunswick Monogrammist. It is further improbable that it is the original of the design. The Antwerp and Lanckoroński versions correspond with the first form of No. 5577, in the details where *pentimenti* are recorded above; this seems to imply another version, from which both No. 5577 and the other pictures would have been copied.

The Antwerp and Lanckoroński versions, in a rough way, correspond much better in style with the Brunswick Monogrammist than does No. 5577. Yet it remains uncertain if they are copies after a lost picture by that painter; the length of the men's tunics, the size of their caps and the angle at which these are worn would accord with a date in the 1550's, and it is unlikely that these details of costume could be from Jan van Amstel's life-time, if he died before 1544.[3] It may be that the two pictures are copies after the Brunswick Monogrammist, slightly modernized in the costume; or they may be copies after a follower of the Brunswick Monogrammist; or the Brunswick Monogrammist may not be identical with Jan van Amstel (as indeed is indicated in the biography above)[4].

The costume of No. 5577 differs in various details from the costume of the Antwerp and Lanckoroński versions, but its very probable date, the 1550's, is not different.

The inscription on the picture on the wall is very difficult to decipher; the parts of the text given above are not clear.[5]

VERSIONS: See above.

PROVENANCE: Probably Sir Theodore F. Brinckman Sale, St. Leonards, Windsor, 20 March, 1919 (lot 1093), bt. Parsons.[6] H. P. Cunliffe Sale, 30 April, 1920 (lot 2), bt. by Lowinsky.[7] Presented by Thomas Esmond Lowinsky, in memory of Lt. T. M. F. E. Lowinsky, 1945.

REPRODUCTION: *Plates, Early Netherlandish School*, 1947, Plate 45.

REFERENCES: **(1)** Antwerp, 1948 Catalogue in French, p. 27, No. 875; reproduced by Pol de Mont, *La Peinture Ancienne au Musée des Beaux-Arts d'Anvers*, 1914, Plate 43. Friedländer, Vol. XII, No. 238a, as copy. **(2)** Reproduced in *Ausgewählte Kunstwerke der Sammlung Lanckoroński*, 1918, Plate III; Friedländer, Vol. XII, No. 238b, as copy. Probably identical with the version engraved in Lebrun's *Galerie des Peintres Flamands*, Vol. I, 1792, p. 5, as Massys. **(3)** Notes on the costume, by Mrs. Newton, are in the Gallery archives. **(4)** The costume of the Brunswick picture itself indicates *ca.* 1535/40. The two brothel scenes at Berlin and Frankfort, considered to be by the same hand, could well be of this date also. **(5)** The transcription was kindly made at the Rijksbureau voor Kunsthistorische Documentatie at The Hague. **(6)** German School, An Interior, with Figures of Montebanks (*sic*), etc., Woman receiving Money, and Man playing the Bagpipes, panel, 17½ × 23½. *Brinkman* is written on the back of No. 5577. **(7)** Christie's stencil is on the back, kindly identified by E. V. Heather. As P. Aertsen.

DIRCK BARENDSZ.

1534–1592

Son and probably pupil of Barend Dircksz. Van Mander gives the date of birth, and says that he became a pupil of Titian in Venice *ca.* 1555, returning to Amsterdam *ca.* 1562. His study under Titian is confirmed from other sources. His most certain picture is a large triptych of the *Nativity* and other scenes in the Gouda Museum; reproductions in Hoogewerff, *De Noord-Nederlandsche Schilderkunst*, IV, 1941/2, figs. 299–302.

Van Mander records three corporation pieces, of which one is identified with a picture dated 1566 in the Rijksmuseum, No. 429. Another, No. 428 of the same museum, dated 1562, is attributed to Dirck Barendsz. For further details, see A. D. de Vries in Taurel's *Art Chrétien*, 1881, II, pp. 175 ff.; Alois Riegl, *Das Holländische Gruppenporträt*, 1931 (with reproductions); Hoogewerff, *op. cit.*, pp. 626 ff.; and J. R. Judson in the *Bulletin de Musées Royaux des Beaux-Arts de Belgique*, 1962, pp. 77 ff.

Ascribed to DIRCK BARENDSZ.

2597 THREE MEN AND A LITTLE GIRL

Canvas. The size of the original canvas is approximately 33 × 27½ (0·84 × 0·70).

The picture has been very much repainted round the edges; but the main part is in excellent condition except for a slight spottiness due to undercleaning.

Formerly called *Three Venetians and a Child.* The child is recognizable as a girl from the dress; the dress of the men could be, but is not necessarily, the dress of Venetians.[1]

Ascribed by A. B. de Vries [2] to Dirck Barendsz., as a work of his Venetian period (i.e. *ca.* 1555/60). The attribution depends on comparison with the attributed picture of 1562 at Amsterdam; it seems to be quite likely on stylistic grounds.[3]

It was ascribed by Sir Claude Phillips[4] to Johannes Stephan von Calcar (q.v.). There are no sure pictures by Calcar; all attributions depend on the traditional attribution of a male portrait of 1540 in the Louvre, which does not seem to be by the same hand as No. 2597.

PROVENANCE: Given by Urban VIII (i.e. Maffeo Barberini, Pope 1623) to the Barberini Collection, Rome, where in an inventory of 1631.[5] Seen in Palazzo Barberini by Ramdohr[6]; seen in February 1815 by Samuel Rogers[7] in Palazzo Sciarra. May safely be supposed to have been included in the Sciarra Sale of 1891/2.[8] In the Salting Collection by 1904[9]; George Salting Bequest, 1910.

REPRODUCTION: *Illustrations, Continental Schools*, 1937, p. 42. *Plates, Early Netherlandish School*, 1947, Plate 1.

REFERENCES: **(1)** Notes on the costume by Mrs. Newton in the Gallery archives. **(2)** A. B. de Vries, *Het Noord-Nederlandsch Portret*, 1934, p. 50. **(3)** There is, nevertheless, a difficulty in the child's costume, which indicates fairly clearly a date of *ca.* 1540; a time-lag of 15 years is difficult to accept. **(4)** Claude Phillips in *The Burlington Magazine*, XVII (1910), pp. 21/2. **(5)** J. A. F. Orbaan, *Documenti sul Barocco in Roma*, 1920, p. 505, as Titian. **(6)** Ramdohr, *Ueber Malerei in Rom*, etc., 1787, ii, p. 287, as Venetian School. **(7)** *The Italian Journal of Samuel Rogers*, ed. J. R. Hale, 1956, p. 244. A division of the Barberini pictures, by which some passed to the Sciarra Colonna, took place in 1812; cf. J. Lavalleye, *Juste de Gand*, 1936, p. 105. **(8)** For the lawsuit about the Sciarra Sale, see *La Chronique des Arts*, 1893, pp. 91, 100 and 108, and 1895, p. 195. **(9)** Salting MSS., as Mor.

JEAN BELLEGAMBE

active 1504—died not later than 1540

Active at Douai; usually classed in the Early Netherlandish School. The bases for attribution to him are sufficiently surely established. His son Martin was a painter.

See NETHERLANDISH SCHOOL, No. 265.

AMBROSIUS BENSON

active 1518(?), died 1550

Several spellings of the name are known. He came from Lombardy: Thieme-Becker records the names Benzone, Benzoni of other artists working in Milan and Ferrara. Master in Bruges, 1519, where active.

Reasonably supposed to be the author of a group of works at one time classed as by the *Master of the Deipara Virgo of Antwerp*, after a picture in the Museum there; or the *Master of Segovia*, with which town several principal pictures in the group are associated (see Justi in the *Zeitschrift für bildende Kunst*, 1886, pp. 139 ff.). Some pictures in this group were wrongly ascribed to Mostaert, being wrongly associated with others that came to be assigned to the pseudo- or Waagen'sche Mostaert (see under 'Ysenbrandt').

The ascription to Benson is due to Hulin (*Catalogue Critique*, 1902, p. xxvii); it is based on the fact that a picture at Brussels is signed AB, and another once at Nuremberg AB 1527 (Friedländer, Vol. XI, Plates LXXXIII and LXXXV). Georges Marlier, *Ambrosius Benson*, 1957, pp. 74 ff., has shown that the latter is compositionally related to Andrea del Sarto (cf. John Shearman, *Andrea del Sarto*, 1965, Vol. II, pp. 290 f.; also S. J. Freedberg, *Andrea del Sarto*, volume subtitled *Catalogue Raisonné*, 1963, p. 187). Any Italian element of style, nevertheless, in this picture or in others assigned to Benson is not recognizably due to Andrea del Sarto, and is perhaps due to Milanese painters (cf. Marlier, *op. cit.*, pp. 78 f.). For dates on compositions, see Marlier, *op. cit.*, nos. 7 (1538), 37 (1528), 74 (1533); several of the portraits assigned to Benson are dated.

The chief Netherlandish influence in his style is that of David, with whom Benson is known to have been associated. See Georges Marlier, *Ambrosius Benson*, 1957; also the Marqués de Lozoya in the *Archivo Español de Arte*, Vol. XXXIII (1960), pp. 1 ff.

655 THE MAGDALEN READING

Oak, original painted surface, $16\frac{1}{8} \times 14\frac{1}{4}$ (0·41 × 0·365).

Cracked on the red dress, but otherwise apparently in good condition. Several *pentimenti.*

One of many versions, or variants. Marlier[1] thinks it autograph, and dates it *ca.* 1525, as the earliest of a series of four closely connected examples.

The design occurs also in pictures by 'Ysenbrandt' and the Master of the Female Half-Lengths; it goes back ultimately to some such figure as in Rogier van der Weyden, No. 654 in this catalogue.

VERSIONS: See Friedländer's list.[2]

PROVENANCE: On the back is branded G C within a circle; also a seal. Sale of Pictures from Stoke Court, Bucks, at Christie's (collection owned by Granville John Penn), 10 July, 1851 (lot 11),[3] bt. by Nieuwenhuys. Purchased[4] with the rest of the Edmond Beaucousin Collection, Paris, 1860.

REPRODUCTION: *Illustrations, Continental Schools*, 1937, p. 17. *Plates, Early Netherlandish School*, 1947, Plate 2.

REFERENCES: (1) Georges Marlier, *Ambrosius Benson*, 1957, pp. 197 ff. and p. 310, No. 105. The compiler has classed it as from the studio, dating it as probably late; but Marlier seems to be right in calling it autograph (whatever exactly that means for Benson). Dating of such works is most difficult, but Marlier gives some reasons for putting No. 655 quite early. Bodenhausen, *Gerard David*, 1905, No. 60, as replica of Benson; No. 275g of Friedländer's list, Vol. XI. (2) Friedländer's Vol. XI, No. 275. (3) As Mabuse. (4) As Bernaert van Orley.

HIERONYMUS BOSCH

living 1474, died 1516

Also called Jerome or Hieronymus van Aken (presumably Aix-la-Chapelle originally). Recorded at 's-Hertogenbosch (Bois-le-Duc) from

1474: see P. Gerlach, O. F. M. Cap., *Jeronimus van Aken alias Bosch en de Onze Lieve Vrouwe-Broederschap*, in *Jheronimus Bosch, Bijdragen* (supplement to the catalogue of the Bosch Exhibition at 's-Hertogenbosch), 1967, p. 51. According to van Mander, born at 's-Hertogenbosch. Several signed works exist; none dated. His most characteristic pictures (e.g. at Madrid, the Escorial, Lisbon) contain numerous small and often fantastic figures.

His teacher is unknown; his work is in any case detached from the main tradition of Netherlandish painting under the dominance of Rogier van der Weyden.

Some of the pictures ascribed to him, even if they bear 'signatures,' are by imitators; see on this subject some curious remarks in the *Comentarios de la Pintura* of Felipe de Guevara, who died in 1563.

4744 CHRIST MOCKED (THE CROWNING WITH THORNS)

The dress of the Jew in profile on the left is ornamented with a crescent and a star.

Oak, painted surface, 29 × 23¼ (0·735 × 0·59).

Many *pentimenti*, especially in the hands; Christ's hands were once intended to be lower down, and the neck of His robe was once intended to have a different form. The condition is good; but the painting is very thin, so that the ground has come to show through in the half-shadows, and some of the *pentimenti* are disturbing.

Christ is in white. At the Crowning with Thorns, a scarlet robe was put on Him, according to Matthew xxvii, 28 (other Gospel accounts have variations). The treatment of the subject in No. 4744 seems to be devotional more than historical. According to Luke xxiii, 11 (no mention in Luke of the Crown of Thorns) Christ at His mocking by Herod was clad in a *veste alba*, following the text of the Vulgate, not of the authorized or revised versions.

The picture seems certainly autograph, and is generally accepted as such.[1] Probably early work.

VERSIONS: There are a number of versions of this subject by Bosch or of his following; none repeat this, and most of them vary considerably from one another[2]

PROVENANCE: Coll. Hollingworth Magniac, Colworth; exhibited at the R.A. 1882 (No. 198),[3] lent by his son, Charles Magniac; Sale, London, 4 July, 1892 (lot 134),[4] bt. (Robert) Crawshay, an English Collector living in Rome. Purchased, Temple-West Fund, from the Sangiorgi Gallery, Rome, 1934. Bosch Exhibition at 's-Hertogenbosch, 1967 (No. 22).

REPRODUCTION: *Illustrations, Continental Schools*, 1937, p. 24. *Plates, Early Netherlandish School*, 1947, Plate 3.

REFERENCES: (1) See Friedländer's Vol. XIV, p. 101, and Tolnay's *Bosch*, 1937, No. 33. It is rejected by Conway, *The Van Eycks*, 1921, p. 344. (2) See Friedländer, Vol. V, Nos. 79, 80. (3) As Holbein (?). (4) As Early Flemish School.

AELBRECHT BOUTS

living 1473, died 1549

Second son of Dieric Bouts. Active at Louvain. First mentioned in 1473; a minor (i.e. under 25) in December, 1476; married by May, 1481. For the documents, see E. van Even in the *Messager des Sciences Historiques*, 1866, pp. 329 ff., or W. Schoene, *Dieric Bouts*, 1938.

An *Assumption of the Virgin* at Brussels, No. 534, around which some works of a *Master of the Assumption* had already been grouped, was ascribed without proof to Aelbrecht Bouts by van Even, *loc. cit.* Strong confirmation of this attribution is given by Hulin in the *Catalogue Critique* of the Bruges Exhibition, 1902, pp. xviii ff.; see further Marguerite Wéra in the *Revue Belge d'Archéologie et d'Histoire de 'lArt*, Vol. XX, 1951, pp. 139 ff.

A very large number of pictures has been grouped round the Brussels *Assumption*. Many are merely repetitions; as Friedländer admits, it is the work of a factory. There are no dates: the style is under the influence of Dieric Bouts and more particularly of Hugo van der Goes.

Style of AELBRECHT BOUTS

1083 CHRIST CROWNED WITH THORNS

Wood, much reduced in thickness, and mounted on canvas, $17\frac{1}{8} \times 14\frac{1}{2}$ ($0{\cdot}435 \times 0{\cdot}37$).

Damaged on the lower part.

One of the very many varying versions, associated in style with A. Bouts; a list is given by Friedländer,[1] another more complete by Schoene.[2] Schoene remarks that No. 1083 differs from all the other known versions and that it is certainly by Aelbrecht. Certainty is a strong word for such a vague derivative. The composition comes ultimately from Dieric Bouts (cf. the studio piece, No. 712 in this catalogue), but it has been a good deal modified.

VERSIONS: See the lists in Friedländer[1] and Schoene.[2]

PROVENANCE: Noted, with description sufficient to identify, and an attribution to Rogier, in the collection of Karl Aders, a German merchant living in London, by Henry Crabb Robinson.[3] Seen by Passavant, 1831, in this collection.[4] Aders Exhibition, No. 29[5]; Aders Sale, 1 August, 1835 (lot 100), bt. Dr. Wilis. Anon. (H. C. Robinson, or rather Aders Trust) Sale, London, 26 April, 1839 (lot 57), bt. Green; coll. J. H. Green, Hadley.[6] Exhibited at Manchester, 1857 (Provisional Catalogue, No. 481; Definitive Catalogue, No. 388). Bequeathed by Mrs. Joseph H. Green, 1880.

REPRODUCTION: *Illustrations, Continental Schools*, 1937, p. 30. *Plates, Early Netherlandish School*, 1947, Plate 4.

REFERENCES: **(1)** Friedländer's list is in Vol. III, No. 63; the present picture under the letter o. **(2)** Schoene's list is in his *Dieric Bouts*, 1938, No. 107; the present picture the 27th of the list. **(3)** Diary, 10 November, 1817, from a transcript of the original in Dr. Williams's Library. **(4)** Passavant, *Kunstreise*, 1833,

p. 96, as Rogier van der Weyden. (5) This is from an undated catalogue, of which by the kindness of Mr. Frank Simpson a copy has been made for the National Gallery library; the exhibition was at No. 10 Warwick Street, Golden Square. A different exhibition of Aders' pictures was held at the Gallery of the British Artists, Pall Mall East; no catalogue has been found, but an account of it is given in *The Gentleman's Magazine*, February 1832, pp. 153 f. On p. 154 it is stated that Aders was from Holland, believed to be from near Geldorp; Waagen, *Ueber Hubert und Johann van Eyck*, 1822, pp. 229 f., says Aders was German and, whatever his birthplace may have been, it seems reasonable in the references in this catalogue to call him a German merchant. (6) As Rogier van der Weyden the Younger; see Waagen, *Treasures of Art*, 1854, ii, p. 459.

Dieric BOUTS

living *ca.* 1448, died 1475

The christian name is also spelt Dierick, Dirk, etc.; in French Thierry, in Latin Theodoricus. Active at Louvain, though not born there. First mentioned 1457, but his marriage at Louvain *ca.* 1448 or earlier has been deduced. On the strength of an obscure passage in Molanus (*ca.* 1575), sometimes said to have been born in 1400, which is probably a good deal too early.

The documents are rather confusing: not only were both his sons, Dieric and Aelbrecht (q.v.), painters, but there was another family of painters at Louvain at the time, Hubrecht Stuerbout and his three sons, Hubrecht, Gillis and Frans (Frissen). Even the documents, it seems, sometimes confuse Dieric Bouts with Hubrecht Stuerbout: a clear exposition is in Arnold Goffin's *Bouts*, 1907, though for the complete documents E. van Even in the *Messager des Sciences Historiques*, 1866, pp. 290 ff., or W. Schoene, *Dieric Bouts und seine Schule*, 1938, must be consulted.

It is in any case certain that Dieric Bouts painted (1) a large triptych, of which the central panel represents the *Last Supper*, in S. Peter's, Louvain (1464–*ca.* 1468); (2) two large panels representing the *Justice of Otho*, now at Brussels; one of these was not finished at his death in 1475 (begun *ca.* 1470(?); cf. the catalogue of the Bouts Exhibition, Brussels–Delft, 1957–8, nos. 30, 31, and the *Bulletin de l'Institut Royal du Patrimoine Artistique*, I, 1958, pp. 7 ff.). Further, Molanus' mention of a second triptych (*The Martyrdom of S. Erasmus*) in S. Peter's, Louvain, makes this work semi-documented; it is datable probably from before 1466.

From these three pictures, several others can with confidence be ascribed; the earliest date on any of these is 1462 on No. 943 below. Some works clearly of an earlier style can also be reasonably ascribed; No. 664 is an example.

Bouts is most probably identical with Dirck van Haarlem, mentioned in various source-books; especially by van Mander (1604), who is more explicit and probably more trustworthy than usual. Little is known of early painting at Haarlem, but there seems to be some stylistic connection between Bouts and a *Raising of Lazarus* at Berlin, which there is some reason for ascribing to the Haarlem painter, Aelbert van Ouwater.

Bouts reflects strongly the style of Rogier van der Weyden. On a triptych in S. Sauveur, Bruges, usually admitted as Bouts but rejected by Schoene, the portraits at least are recognizably by Hugo van der Goes; several different explanations are possible, especially as the extent of van der Goes' participation is disputed (cf. Friedländer, Vol. XIV, p. 90, Schoene, and F. Winkler, *Das Werk des Hugo van der Goes*, 1964, pp. 51 ff.).

Bouts has suffered the contrary of what has often happened to others; there has been a reluctance to ascribe pictures to his hand. Schoene demands not one *Doppelgänger*, but two, whom he refers to as the *Meister der Perle von Brabant* (or *Dieric Bouts the Younger*, q.v.), and the *Meister der Münchner Gefangennahme*.

664 THE ENTOMBMENT

The Virgin, supported by S. John, and two Holy Women are standing behind the tomb. Joseph of Arimathaea (?) supports the body of Christ; Nicodemus (?) stands at His feet. In front of the tomb, S. Mary Magdalene.

Tempera on flax[1], painted surface, $35\frac{1}{2} \times 29\frac{1}{4}$ (0·90 × 0·74). A little of the painted surface continues turned over the edges of the present stretcher; this is not included in the above measurements.

The condition is good for a picture of this kind; very thin in parts, but in most places pure. *Pentimenti* in the back of Nicodemus (?) and elsewhere.

The technique is usually described as tempera, sometimes as watercolour, on linen; another example is Massys, No. 3664[2].

The types recur in the Granada-Valencia triptychs, which must be fairly early[3]; Friedländer doubtfully dates the present picture *ca.* 1455.[4] The design is possibly derived from Rogier van der Weyden; cf. the small imitation relief in the framing of the central panel of the Marienaltar (studio version at Berlin, No. 534A).

It has been claimed that this is a side picture, from an ensemble of which the central picture is a *Crucifixion*, in private possession in Italy[5]; but the association of No. 664 with this *Crucifixion* seems to the compiler dubious.

DERIVATION: In the von Bolin *et al.* Sale, Munich, 14/5 December, 1934 (lot 300), reproduced in the catalogue.

PROVENANCE: With three others (?), formerly in the Foscari Collection; purchased in Vienna at the beginning of the nineteenth century by Guicciardi, an envoy from Milan (Conte Diego Guicciardi, 1814/5 ?).[6] Bought from the Guicciardi family, Milan, 1860.

REPRODUCTION: *Illustrations, Continental Schools*, 1937, p. 31. *Plates, Early Netherlandish School*, 1947, Plate 5.

REFERENCES: *General:* Friedländer, Vol. III, No. 3. Baldass in the Vienna *Jahrbuch*, 1932, pp. 87 f. Schoene, *Dieric Bouts und seine Schule*, 1938, No. 4.

In text: (1) Letters from Professor W. T. Astbury, 9 and 14 October, 1958, in the Gallery archives. (2) From the literature on early pictures on fabric, it is to be recorded that a list of such pictures is given by Schoene, *Dieric Bouts und seine Schule*, 1938, pp. 82–3. See also some comments by K. Arndt, *Zum Werk des Hugo van der Goes*, in the Munich *Jahrbuch*, 1964, p. 93 (note 24). Dr. K. G. Boon kindly called the compiler's attention to a record of paintings on canvas illustrating the life and passion of S. Peter for a chapel at Tournai, to be executed by Henry de Beaumetiel on designs by Campin, carrying out a testamentary disposition of 1438; see A. Pinchart, *Quelques Artistes et Quelques Artisans de Tournai*, in the *Bulletin de l'Académie Royale de Belgique*, 3rd Series, Vol. IV, No. 12, 1882 (pp. 55–6 of the offprint, 1883). (3) See the elaborate entry and plates in Roger van Schoute, *La Chapelle Royale de Grenade* (Corpus de la Peinture des Anciens Pays-Bas Méridionaux), 1963, No. 95. (4) Friedländer, Vol. III, p. 38. (5) Florence, Flemish Exhibition at Palazzo Strozzi, 1947, *Catalogo* (p. 34, No. 6), and Fig. 29. For the association, see E. Panofsky, *Early Netherlandish Painting*, 1953, Vol. I, p. 536 (on the suggestion of J. G. van Gelder). The picture was No. 1 of the Bouts Exhibition, Brussels-Delft, 1957; elaborating and partly correcting what he wrote in the catalogue, F. Baudouin specifies his reserves about the association with No. 664 in the *Bulletin des Musées Royaux des Beaux-Arts*, VII, 1958, pp. 121 ff. See also K. G. Boon in *The Burlington Magazine*, Vol. C, 1958, p. 11. (6) Eastlake note-books, 1858 and 1860. Eastlake actually saw the *Adoration of the Kings*, which he described as a pendant but not so good nor so well preserved. The other subjects were said to be the *Presentation* (or *Crucifixion*) and *Annunciation*. They were called Lucas van Leyden, and were ascribed to Rogier van der Weyden by Eastlake. A *Resurrection*, at one time belonging to Matthiesen's, has also been associated; recorded and reproduced in M. J. Friedländer *Early Netherlandish Painters*, 1968, Vol. III, Add. no. 116.

774 THE VIRGIN AND CHILD WITH S. PETER AND S. PAUL

S. Peter kneels on the Virgin's right, S. Paul on her left. God and a Saint are depicted in the stained glass behind.

Oak, painted surface, 27 × 20¼ (0·685 × 0·515).

Cleaned in 1956–7. Somewhat worn and otherwise damaged, but the condition on the whole is good. The Child's feet had been repainted in a different form; His right foot is a good deal damaged.

The original attribution to Bouts is due to Conway,[1] and is accepted by Friedländer.[2]

Pächt[3] rejects it on compositional grounds. Baldass,[4] dismissing this objection, at one time rejected it, grouping No. 774 with several other madonnas apparently by different hands; but in 1949 (MS. communication) he inclined to accept the picture as by Bouts. An old attribution to the Master of the Pearl of Brabant[5] has been taken up again recently by Schoene.[6] A close connection between this picture and the Pearl of Brabant is denied by Baldass.[7]

A principal reason for the variations of criticism concerning the picture is obviously the unsatisfactory condition before the cleaning of 1956–7. Though rather soft, it seems to be an authentic Bouts, not far in date from No. 943.

The rich decoration (e.g. the glass roundels, which also appear in No. 943, and the pillars of the throne) is characteristic of Bouts and his followers; it appears to be an Eyckish rather than a Rogieresque reminiscence. The heads of the two saints in No. 774 correspond fairly closely with those of S. Peter and the apostle to the left of S. Peter in Dieric Bouts' *Last Supper* at Louvain. The legs and feet of the Child, with the feet as now revealed in their original position, correspond quite closely with those in a *Virgin and Child* in the Louvre, usually accepted as by Dieric Bouts.[8]

VARIANT: A variant is reproduced in *L'Arte*, 1908, p. 289 (then Coll. Castellaci, now Coll. Barone Arezzo, at Ragusa Ibla, Sicily).

PROVENANCE: From the Zambeccari Collection, Bologna; No. 36 of a catalogue there[9]; purchased[10] from the Eastlake Collection, 1867.

REPRODUCTION: *Illustrations, Continental Schools*, 1937, p. 30. *Plates, Early Netherlandish School*, 1947, Plate 6.

REFERENCES: **(1)** Conway in *The Academy*, 25 March, 1882, p. 213. **(2)** Friedländer, Vol. III, No. 21 (as *ca.* 1465). **(3)** Pächt in *Kritische Berichte zur Kunstgeschichtlichen Literatur*, 1927, pp. 46/7. **(4)** Baldass in the Vienna *Jahrbuch*, 1932, pp. 111/2, 114. **(5)** The Pearl of Brabant is a picture at Munich admitted as Bouts by Friedländer, Vol. III, Plates XXXIII-XXXIV. **(6)** W. Schoene, *Dieric Bouts*, 1938, No. 70. Schoene thinks the 'Master of the Pearl of Brabant' may be Dieric Bouts the Younger (q.v.). **(7)** Baldass in the Vienna *Jahrbuch*, 1932, p. 100, and in *Pantheon*, 1940, p. 96. **(8)** See H. Adhémar, *Le Musée National du Louvre* (Les Primitifs Flamands, Corpus), Vol. I, 1962, Plates LI, LII. Cf. also the *S. Luke Painting the Virgin*, in the Penrhyn Castle Collection (Friedländer, Vol. III, Plate 84). **(9)** Eastlake note books, 1857 (as perhaps van der Goes). **(10)** As van der Goes.

943 PORTRAIT OF A MAN

Dated, .1462.

Oak, painted surface, $12\frac{1}{2} \times 8$ (0·315 × 0·205).

Very good condition. Cleaned in 1952. Small *pentimenti* in the outlines of the shoulder and cap.

The earliest dated work of Bouts; the attribution is due to Crowe and Cavalcaselle.[1] Friedländer[2] says it is perhaps the earliest example of a portrait in a room with a view out of the window. It would not appear to be part of a diptych or triptych, nor has it the air of a self-portrait.

PROVENANCE: Sometimes identified with a picture of 1462, called a self-portrait of Rogier van der Weyden, seen by Marcantonio Michiel in the house of Zuan Ram, Venice, 1530/1.[3] Was seen by Passavant[4] in 1831 in coll. Karl Aders, a German merchant living in London. Aders Exhibition, No. 2.[5] Sale, 1 August, 1835 (lot 111), bt. Solly. Coll. Samuel Rogers, London, by 1844[6]; exhibited at the British Institution, 1848 (No. 61), and 1850 (No. 11); Sale, 2 May, 1856 (lot 599), bt. Pearce. Coll. Wynn Ellis, London; exhibited at Manchester, 1857 (Provisional Catalogue, No. 496; Definitive Catalogue, No. 400); at the British Institution, 1860 (No. 38); at Leeds, 1868 (No. 524). Wynn Ellis Bequest, 1876.

REPRODUCTION: *Illustrations, Continental Schools*, 1937, p. 32. *Plates, Early Netherlandish School*, 1947, Plate 7 (both before cleaning). Reproduced after cleaning in the compiler's *The National Gallery* (*Les Primitifs Flamands, Corpus*), Vol. I, 1953, Plates XCVII, sqq.

REFERENCES: *General:* Friedländer, Vol. III, No. 12. Schoene, *Dieric Bouts*, 1938, No. 6.

In text: **(1)** Crowe and Cavalcaselle, *The Early Flemish Painters*, 1857, pp. 239/40, 294/5, 365. **(2)** Friedländer, Vol. III, p. 43. See further E. Panofsky, *Early Netherlandish Painting*, 1953, Vol. I, p. 316. In the first edition of this catalogue, it was pointed out that Christus, No. 2593, shows an arrangement nearly the same. Panofsky criticizes this, partly on the ground that the original size and shape of the Christus portrait cannot be stated for sure; following on his remarks, the compiler satisfied himself, by means of cleaning tests and X-radiographs, that No. 2593 is not a fragment of a large portrait or devotional picture. **(3)** The Anonimo, ed. Frimmel, 1888, p. 104. **(4)** Passavant, *Kunstreise*, 1833, p. 94, as Memlinc by himself. **(5)** For this exhibition, see *Style of Aelbrecht Bouts*, No. 1083, note 5. **(6)** Mrs. Jameson, *Companion to the most celebrated Private Galleries of Art in London*, 1844, p. 405, No. 43.

2595 THE VIRGIN AND CHILD

Oak, painted surface, 14⅝ × 10⅞ (0·37 × 0·275).

The condition of the Virgin is good, the Child is considerably repainted. The picture suffers slightly from overcleaning in places. There is a *pentimento* in the Virgin's drapery against the window; a few other small changes.

The attitudes make it unlikely that it was the wing of a diptych or triptych.[1]

PROVENANCE: A Spanish inscription on the back says that it was cradled in 1863. Coll. Frédéric Spitzer (died 1890) in Paris; Sale, Paris,[2] 30 May–12 June, 1893 (lot 3308). Coll. George Salting, London; on loan to the Gallery from 1895; Salting Bequest, 1910.

REPRODUCTION: *Illustrations, Continental Schools*, 1937, p. 32. *Plates, Early Netherlandish School*, 1947, Plate 8.

REFERENCES: *General:* Friedländer, Vol. III, No. 14. Schoene, *Dieric Bouts*, 1938, No. 9.

In text: **(1)** For some comments on the composition, see E. Panofsky, *Early Netherlandish Painting*, 1953, Vol. I, p. 317. **(2)** As Flemish School.

Studio of DIERIC BOUTS

711 'MATER DOLOROSA'

712 CHRIST CROWNED WITH THORNS

Oak, each, painted surface, 14½ × 10¾ (0·365 × 0·275).

Very good state.

There are many versions. Formerly catalogued as from the School of Rogier van der Weyden, but these designs derive more directly from Bouts, Friedländer[1] says that Nos. 711, 712 are by a follower of Bouts. Schoene[2] says, probably of the last quarter of the fifteenth century; he does not admit any known versions as originals by Bouts. Baldass thinks the original of the *Virgin*, No. 711, is in the collection of Baron van der Elst.[3] If, as is not impossible, Nos. 711, 712 date from after Bouts' death in 1475, a more accurate label for them would be 'After Bouts.'

Compare the *Christ* on the back of No. 1433, from the Studio of Rogier van der Weyden, and the *Christ* and the *Virgin*, No. 295, after Massys.

VERSIONS: Numerous.[4]

PROVENANCE: Apparently passed from Frf. von Welden at Laupheim to Johann Georg Deuringer at Augsburg (by 1813),[5] from whom acquired in 1816 by Prince Ludwig Kraft Ernst von Œttingen-Wallerstein.[6] At Schloss Wallerstein.[7] Exhibited at Kensington Palace (for sale), 1848 (Nos. 58, 57),[8] bought with the rest of the collection by the Prince Consort. At Kensington Palace.[9] Exhibited at Manchester, 1857 (Provisional Catalogue, Nos. 480, 479; Definitive Catalogue, Nos. 389, 387), lent by Prince Albert. Presented by Queen Victoria at the Prince Consort's wish, 1863.

REPRODUCTIONS: *Illustrations, Continental Schools*, 1937, p. 403. *Plates, Early Netherlandish School*, 1947, Plates 9, 10.

REFERENCES: *General:* Friedländer, Vol. III, No. 83. Schoene, *Dieric Bouts*, 1938, No. 19A(2).

In text: (1) Friedländer, Vol. III, No. 83, and titles to Plates LXIX and LXX. (2) See Section No. 19 of Schoene's Catalogue. (3) Baldass in the Vienna *Jahrbuch*, 1932, p. 86. (4) See the lists in Friedländer, Vol. III, No. 83 and in Schoene, No. 19; an annotated selection was published by the compiler in *The National Gallery* (*Les Primitifs Flamands, Corpus*), Vol. I, 1953, pp. 34 ff. For yet further information, see the Corpus volumes *New England Museums* by Colin T. Eisler, 1961, pp. 58 ff.; the *Louvre* by Hélène Adhémar, Vol. I, 1962, pp. 54 ff.; *Leningrad* by V. Loewinson-Lessing and N. Nicouline, 1965, pp. 1 ff. Also K. Arndt in the *Zeitschrift für Kunstgeschichte*, 1964, p. 177; Vienna, *Gemäldegalerie der Akademie der Bildenden Künste*, XIV Sonderausstellung, 1966, No. 1, fig. 2. (5) Deuringer Catalogue, January, 1813 (Nos. 141, 142) as Lucas van Leyden. (6) According to Georg Grupp in the *Jahrbuch des Historischen Vereins für Nördlingen und Umgebung*, 1917, p. 95, as Lucas van Leyden or Jan van Eyck. In the first edition of this catalogue, from information supplied to H. I. Kay, the Prince was stated to have acquired them 'from Prince Georg Œttingen, Augsburg' in 1813, which seems to be a corruption of the provenance given above. One may indeed wonder, in spite of Grupp, whether 1813 is not right, since the pictures are lacking from Deuringer catalogues of 1814 and 1816 (in the National Gallery library). The Prince himself, *ca.* 1844/7, told Alfred Michiels (*Histoire de la Peinture Flamande*, 2nd edition, Vol. III, 1866, p. 96) that the pictures came from the Fugger Collection. For further discussion of the provenance, see the compiler's *The National Gallery*, *cit.* in note 4, pp. 34 ff. See also Norbert Lieb, *Die Fugger und die Kunst im Zeitalter der Hohen Renaissance*, 1958, pp. 306, 471; he records a Fugger-Welden marriage some time before 1803. (7) Cf. *Kunst-Blatt*, 1824, p. 318. Nos. 39, 40, as Jan van Eyck, of Wallerstein Catalogues of *ca.* 1826 and 1827 (originals at Munich; photostats in the National Gallery). The collection was moved from Schloss Wallerstein after a time. (8) As Roger of Bruges. (9) Waagen's *Catalogue*, 1854 (No. 37), as Rogier van der Weyden the Younger; cf. Waagen, *Treasures*, IV, 1857, p. 227.

Follower of DIERIC BOUTS

708 THE VIRGIN AND CHILD

Oak, painted surface, $8 \times 5\frac{3}{4}$ (0·20 × 0·145).

The character of the flesh parts has been seriously altered by repairs.

The condition is far too untrustworthy for any exact attribution to be made, but the picture is rightly associated by Baldass[1] and Schoene[2] with the following of Bouts.

The note in the 1929 Catalogue that it is possibly by the Master of the S. Lucy Legend is due to Lippmann.[3]

PROVENANCE: On the back are inscriptions, including an attribution to Dürer and (separately) *BP/cōprato dal Sig*r (?) *Ange(lo ?)*. Stated to be from the Coll. Count Joseph von Rechberg, Mindelheim, and bought in 1815 by Prince Ludwig Kraft Ernst von Œttingen-Wallerstein.[4] At Schloss Wallerstein.[5] Exhibited at Kensington Palace (for sale), 1848 (No. 54),[6] bought with the rest of the collection by the Prince Consort. At Kensington Palace.[7] Exhibited at Manchester, 1857 (Provisional Catalogue, No. 476; Definitive Catalogue, No. 395), lent by Prince Albert. Presented by Queen Victoria at the Prince Consort's wish, 1863.

REPRODUCTION: *Illustrations, Continental Schools*, 1937, p. 117. *Plates, Early Netherlandish School*, 1947, Plate 11.

REFERENCES: (1) Baldass in the Vienna *Jahrbuch*, 1932, pp. 112, 114. Baldass boldly called it (as *Meister der farbenfreudigen Madonnen*) by the same hand as three madonnas reproduced by Friedländer, Vol. III, Plates LXXII, LXXIV, LXXV. In 1949, Baldass maintained the association with the second and third of these. The pattern of the embroidered hanging of the second corresponds closely with the pattern of the hanging in No. 708. (2) Schoene, *Dieric Bouts*, 1938, No. 148. (3) Lippmann in *The Burlington Magazine*, Vol. XII (1907/8), p. 108. (4) Cf. *Kunst-Blatt*, 1824, p. 353. Details concerning the formation of the Œttingen-Wallerstein Collection were given orally to H. I. Kay. (5) Probably No. 35, as Jan van Eyck, of Wallerstein Catalogues of *ca.* 1826 and 1827 (originals at Munich; photostats in the National Gallery). The collection was moved from Schloss Wallerstein after a time. (6) As Margaret van Eyck. (7) Waagen's *Catalogue*, 1854 (No. 35), as possibly G. v. d. Meire; see also Waagen, *Treasures*, IV, 1857, p. 226.

DIERIC BOUTS THE YOUNGER

ca. 1448–1490/1

Elder son of Dieric Bouts. His birth *ca.* 1448 is deduced from his emancipation (i.e. at the age of 25) in 1473: for the known facts of his life, see W. Schoene, *Dieric Bouts*, 1938. No documented works exist. Schoene thinks he is the author of a group of pictures, sometimes labelled as by the *Master of the Pearl of Brabant* after a picture at Munich. No. 774 of this catalogue is included by Schoene among pictures he ascribes to the younger Dieric Bouts; it is ascribed in the present catalogue to his father.

See DIERIC BOUTS, No. 774

PIETER BRUEGEL THE ELDER

active 1551, died 1569

Other spellings Brueghel, Breughel: formerly called 'Peasant Bruegel' or 'Bruegel the Droll.' His place of birth is uncertain. He was, according to van Mander, a pupil of Pieter Coecke van Aelst; in any case, Master at Antwerp, 1551. There is good evidence that he journeyed to Rome and elsewhere, *ca.* 1552/3: *ca.* 1563, he removed from Antwerp to Brussels.

Much of his early work seems to have been for engravings published by Hieronymus Cock. There are many signed and dated drawings from

1552, pictures (many at Vienna) from 1553. There is an apparently reliable record of painted wings of 1550/1 once at Malines; see A. Monballieu in the *Handelingen van de Koninklijke Kring voor Oudheidkunde, Letteren en Kunst van Mechelen*, 1964, pp. 92 ff., or the reference to this by G. Marlier in the *Bulletin des Musées Royaux des Beaux-Arts de Belgique*, 1965, p. 141.

Hieronymus Bosch was a formative influence on his style. His landscapes are from early times personal, under slight influence of Patenier and Titian. His mature and most original work partakes of genre and satire, the subject being often recondite.

There exist many copies and derivations by one of his sons, Pieter Brueghel the Younger.

3556 THE ADORATION OF THE KINGS

Signed: BRVEGEL M.D.LXIIII.

Oak, painted surface, $43\frac{3}{4} \times 32\frac{3}{4}$ (1·11 × 0·835).

The bottom is a true edge; the picture may have been cut on the other three sides.

Condition good. The shadows are very thin and have here and there been made up; this is especially sensible on the Virgin's face and bust, where the character is much softened. There is a little obvious damage at the sides, especially left. Some of the underdrawing has come to show through; and there are several *pentimenti*, the most prominent being on the Child and on the Moorish King's left foot. The profile of the kneeling King was at first drawn in a little further to the right. The sky at the top left corner seems to be unfinished. The end of the date has been retouched, but the reading is certain.

The picture is not certainly mentioned in old sources (see under *Provenance*), but its authenticity is unquestioned.

The treatment *en hauteur* with comparatively few actors is odd for Bruegel. He may have been attempting a work in the traditional Netherlandish style; but caricature has broken in. There is a more natural play of his originality in both his other designs of this subject.[1]

The figure of Balthazar, the Moorish King, might perhaps be a vague reminiscence from the Bosch in the Prado, No. 2048; the arrow in the crossbowman's hat is perhaps also borrowed from Bosch (cf. No. 4744 in this catalogue). A straw hat for St. Joseph was one of the 'properties' of the Master of the Death of the Virgin (see No. 2603). The soldiery takes in this picture a remarkably prominent place. The picture shows an ass, but the ox associated with the ass at the Nativity is lacking. Various explanations could be made; yet it may be no more than an example of painters' vagaries, but with the remark that the ox and ass can be considered less proper in *The Adoration of the Kings* than in *The Adoration of the Shepherds* or *The Nativity* itself.[2] Münz[3] claims that the border of the robe of the most prominent King shows the four elements, but this seems not clearly established.

COPIES: Jan Brueghel I, a son of Pieter, used some figures in No. 3556 for three pictures, No. 3547 in this Gallery, No. 908 in the Gallery at Vienna, and No. 497 in the Musée Mayer van den Bergh, Antwerp. The figures repeated are the black King; St. Joseph and the man whispering to him; and the soldier looking downwards in the centre.

PROVENANCE: Probably in the Imperial Collection at Vienna *ca.* 1619[4]. According to Glück,[5] it turned up in a Viennese private collection soon after 1890: according to a MS. note,[6] the owner was a nobleman living in Prague. It had passed to the Collection of Georg Roth, Vienna, by 1898.[7] Exhibited at Bruges, 1902 (No. 356). Bought from the Roth Collection by Guido Arnot, from whom purchased out of the Temple-West and Florence Funds and the Grant-in-Aid, with donations from the N.A.-C.F., and Arthur Serena through the N.A.-C.F., 1920. Exhibited at the National Gallery, N.A.-C.F. Exhibition, 1945/6 (No. 7).

REPRODUCTION: *Illustrations, Continental Schools,* 1937, p. 38. *Plates, Early Netherlandish School,* 1947, Plate 12.

REFERENCES: *General: P. Bruegel* by René van Bastelaer and Georges H. de Loo, 1907, p. 288, No. A9. Friedländer, Vol. XIV, No. 24.

In text: **(1)** Friedländer, Vol. XIV, Nos. 2 and 39. **(2)** In two pictures by the Master of S. Bartholomew, *The Adoration of the Kings* at Munich and an *Adoration with Shepherds* in the Petit Palais at Paris, claimed to be from a single series, the former shows an ass but no ox, the latter both ass and ox. Several other examples of *The Adoration of the Kings* with ass and no ox are known; in the central panel of an 'Ysenbrandt' triptych at Birmingham (*The Adoration of the Kings*) there is an ox and no ass. There does seem to be a definite meaning for ass and no ox in Bosch's *Adoration of the Kings* in the Prado; see Lotte Brand Philip in *The Art Bulletin,* 1953, pp. 267 ff. For comment on the ox and the ass, see E. Panofsky, *Early Netherlandish Painting,* 1953, p. 470; for an ox in the *Flight into Egypt,* the same, *Albrecht Dürer,* 1945, Vol. II, p. 38, No. 309. **(3)** Ludwig Münz, *Bruegel, The Drawings,* 1961, p. 25 (cf. his fig. 23). **(4)** F. Grossmann, *Bruegel, The Paintings, ca.* 1955, p. 196, says that it was probably in the inventory of the Archduke Ernst, 1594, and in an inventory of the Imperial Collection at Vienna, 1619. The first statement seems to be a mistake; the picture of *Les Trois Rois* bought in Brussels by the Archduke in July 1594 is not specified to be by Bruegel, nor is any Bruegel of the subject recorded in the inventory of 17 July, 1595 after the Archduke's death. See Dr. Coremans, *L'archiduc Ernest,* etc., in *Compte-Rendu des Séances de la Commission Royale d'Histoire ou Recueil de ses Bulletins,* Vol. XIII, 1847, pp. 102, 140 ff.; the inventory after death better in Marcel De Maeyer, *Albrecht en Isabella en de Schilderkunst,* 1955, pp. 259 ff.; cf. S. Speth-Holterhoff, *Les Peintres Flamands de Cabinets d'Amateurs au XVIIe Siècle,* 1957, pp. 35–6. See De Maeyer, p. 52, for what happened to the Archduke's pictures after his death; the claim for No. 3556 is made by Gert Adriani in A. Lhotsky, *Kunsthistorisches Museum, Wien, Die Geschichte der Sammlungen,* Part I, 1941–5, p. 218. On the other hand, No. 3556 may indeed be referred to in an inventory of the collection at Vienna of *ca.* 1619, 'Ein taffel auf holz, die heiligen drei Khönig, gar altfrenkhisch sauber gemalt vom alten Prigel' (Vienna *Jahrbuch,* Vol. XXVI, 1906–7, Supplement, p. IX, No. 45; cf. the entry in an inventory of *ca.* 1610–19, 'N° 29 et 30. 2 Stuckh vom Prügl, also n° 29 die heiligen drei Khönig . . .', *ib.,* p. VII). **(5)** Glück, *Bruegels Gemälde,* 1932, p. 50. **(6)** MS. note from Guido Arnot in the Gallery archives. **(7)** See Hermann Dollmayr in the Vienna *Jahrbuch,* 1898, p. 290.

See also NETHERLANDISH SCHOOL, No. 1298

BRUGES MASTER OF 1500

See MASTER OF THE BRUGES PASSION SCENES

BRUNSWICK Monogrammist

See Jan van AMSTEL

Johannes Stephan von CALCAR

active *ca.* 1536/7, died *ca.* 1546

His birth date is generally given as 1499, the evidence not being forthcoming. According to van Mander, born at Calcar; *ca.* 1536/7 at Venice, where a pupil of Titian; died *ca.* 1546. Vasari met him in 1545 at Naples; according to a note in Milanesi's Vasari, VII, pp. 460/1, he perfectly imitated the style, first of Titian, then of Raphael. Some anatomical engravings exist by him.

The identification of his pictures is most uncertain. The key work for attribution is a male portrait of 1540 in the Louvre, mentioned as by Calcar in an inventory of the French Royal Collections in 1683. As an inventory of the Austrian Imperial Collections of 1659 records, also as by Calcar, a portrait of comparable type now held to be by Moroni (Vienna, 1928 Catalogue, No. 217), there is no good ground for supposing that the Louvre picture is actually by Calcar; but it is the style of the Louvre picture that is meant when modern attributions to Calcar are made. See Seymour de Ricci, Catalogue of the Louvre, *Ecoles Etrangères, Italie et Espagne*, 1913, and the Berlin Catalogue, 1931, in each case s.v. Calcar.

See Ascribed to Dirck BARENDSZ., No. 2597

Robert CAMPIN

1378/9–1444

Active at Tournai from 1406, but not born there. For the date of birth, see M. Houtart in *XXIIIe Congrès Archéologique et Historique de Belgique*, Ghent, 1913, Vol. III, p. 88. Some pictures are assigned to him, but none of these is documented (for mural work, see Paul Rolland, *La Peinture Murale à Tournai*, 1946, pp. 42 ff. and plates). Some pictures are known by a pupil, Jacques Daret, documented and dated *ca.* 1434. Campin had another pupil at the same time as Daret (between 1427 and 1432), Rogier de le Pasture; he is often identified with the famous painter of the same name (in Flemish), Rogier van der Weyden (q.v.).

Campin has been supposed to be the author of a group of works, perhaps not all by the same hand, that show a near relationship to pictures reasonably ascribed to Rogier but are earlier in style. This group was formerly labelled as by the *Maître à la Souricière*: then more commonly *Master of Merode* (after an *Annunciation* once owned by the Merode family, now in the Cloisters, New York) or *of 'Flémalle'* (after some pictures at Frankfort, wrongly supposed to come from a castle (?) or abbey (?) at Flémalle). There have also been attempts to identify him with Nabur Martins (Maeterlinck) and with Roger of Bruges (supposed distinct from Rogier van der Weyden: Hasse). All these names are misleading and another is desirable.

The argument for the use of 'Campin' depends on a consideration of the pictures by Daret, taken in conjunction with pictures ascribed to Rogier van der Weyden. A definition of what is meant by the work of Rogier is too complicated for this place; it will be found under his biography. It must suffice here to state that the pictures of *ca.* 1434 by Daret show close stylistic analogies with some pictures in the group called Master of 'Flémalle,' and with others ascribed to Rogier van der Weyden. As Daret was, in point of fact, fellow-pupil of Campin with a Rogier de le Pasture, the Master of 'Flémalle' may reasonably be claimed to be identical with the former and van der Weyden with the latter.

In the 'Campin' group (assuming that they really belong) the Werl wings in the Prado are dated 1438. Hulin has given a reason for supposing that a *Deposition*, of which a fragment is at Frankfort, was in existence before 1430 (*Heures de Milan*, 1911, p. 48); the dating is probable, but the reason given is invalid (cf. Kees de Witt, *Das Horarium der Katharina von Kleve, etc.*, in the Prussian *Jahrbuch*, 1937, pp. 114 ff.).

As the subject is very obscure, it may be said that the core of the group consists of the 'Flémalle' panels, the Merode *Annunciation*, and No. 2609 below.

The pictures ascribed to 'Campin' have been sometimes called youthful works of Rogier van der Weyden (q.v.): recently by E. Renders (*La Solution du Problème van der Weyden Flémalle Campin*, 1931). The documentary evidence is indecisive, no valid reasons against the possibility of Campin's authorship have been adduced, and the attributions are in the present state of knowledge a matter of stylistic evidence. The difficulty of making these attributions to 'Campin,' particularly in the case of pictures near in style to others reasonably ascribed to Rogier, has been stressed by all competent scholars. It seems likely that the group 'Campin' is not altogether homogeneous, and the whole subject (including the works of Rogier) needs revision.

Friedländer, in his Vol. XIV, 1937, pp. 81 ff., seems inclined to ascribe some or all of the pictures called 'Campin' to Rogier; but his text is obscure and incomplete. Hulin's latest statement appears in the *Biographie Nationale . . . de Belgique*, XXVII (1938), cols. 243/4; it is against the identification of 'Campin' and Rogier. Winkler's recent statements, also against this identification, appear in *Pantheon*, 1941, pp. 145 ff., and in Thieme-Becker, Vols. XXXV (Weyden) and XXXVII (Flémalle). Cf. also Paul Rolland, *Les Primitifs Tournaisiens*, 1932, *La Peinture Murale à Tournai*, 1946, and in the *Revue Belge d'Archéologie et d'Histoire de l'Art*, 1949, pp. 145 ff.; Martin Davies in *The Burlington Magazine*, September, 1937, pp. 140 ff.; W. Schoene, *Dieric Bouts*, 1938, pp. 58 ff.; Charles de Tolnay, *Le Maître de Flémalle et les Frères van Eyck*, 1939, especially pp. 41/4, note 13; and E. Panofsky, *Early Netherlandish*

Painting, 1953. A summary of the views is given in the Editor's note in the second edition of Friedländer, *Early Netherlandish Painting*, Vol. II, *Rogier van Weyden and the Master of Flémalle*, 1967, pp. 95 ff. A minor argument for identity is given by Valentin Denis from a copy of the Merode *Annunciation* bearing the remains of an inscription with Rogier's name; see the *Annales de la Fédération Historique et Archéologique de Belgique*, 35ᵉ Congrès, Courtrai 1953, 1955, pp. 541 ff. Some earlier works are referred to in the biography of Rogier van der Weyden.

'Campin' is important for historians of the change of style from 'International Gothic' (e.g. the Wilton Diptych) to 'Realism.' He seems more primitive than Jan van Eyck (q.v.), but the priority of one or the other has not been established. Some earlier cases of a greater or less reaction against 'Gothic' on French soil are the sculptures of Sluter and his followers at Dijon (from *ca.* 1390); the *Martyrdom of S. Denis* in the Louvre assigned to Henri Bellechose (*ca.* 1415 (?)); the de Limbourg miniatures at Chantilly (not later than 1416). It is impossible here to treat properly of this elaborate question, but it may be said that nothing of earlier date shows near relations with 'Campin' or Jan van Eyck, who further appear to be largely independent of each other: their origins are thus obscure. Besides the works of these two Netherlanders, some pictures of importance in the 'realistic' movement elsewhere in Europe are the Tiefenbronn Altar-piece of Moser (1431); the works of Conrad Witz at Basel and Geneva (*ca.* 1435/45); an *Annunciation* in the Church of the Madeleine, Aix-en-Provence (after 1442 (?)). Whether or not 'Campin' was a founder of this movement, his influence was strong on contemporary and subsequent painting, not only in the Netherlands, either directly or through Rogier van der Weyden.

'Robert CAMPIN'

2609 THE VIRGIN AND CHILD BEFORE A FIRE-SCREEN

Oak, painted surface, 25 × 19¼ (0·635 × 0·49).

The left-hand side is a true edge; the picture may have been cut along the bottom. A space of about 1¼ in. (*ca.* 3 cm.) along the top, and of 3¾ in. (*ca.* 9·5 cm.) along the right-hand side is entirely of modern fabrication (modern paint on modern additions to the panel); this includes the whole of the cupboard and the chalice. The original fragment without the additions has been reproduced.[1]

The condition of the original is good on the whole, though it suffers slightly from uneven cleaning; the shadow of the Virgin's right cheek has been strengthened somewhat. The X-ray reveals several *pentimenti*, e.g. in the draperies centre, the Child's right knee, the Virgin's hair.[2] The Child's eyes were originally turned the other way.

The picture would seem to be by the same hand as the 'Flémalle' panels at Frankfort, and (to judge from reproductions) the Merode *Annunciation*;

on the other hand it is difficult to ascribe it to Rogier.[3] It is near in style to Nos. 653A and B below. It is obviously early; there are no sure means of dating it, but it is generally agreed that it is from before 1430.

As Bouchot[4] pointed out, a similar fire-screen appears in the de Limbourg miniature for January at Chantilly, not later than 1416; here it is used as a naturalistic substitute for a halo. The Virgin is wearing a ring on the third finger of her right hand, like the *Virgins* at Frankfort ('from Flémalle') and in the doubtful picture at Berlin, No. 1835. The drapery under the book is a book-cover, as a comparison with Rogier van der Weyden, No. 654 makes clear; such book-covers are common in 'Campin's' works and not rare elsewhere. The shop shown in the background here has been claimed to recur in other pictures; this is inexact, but some similarities can be found.[5]

M. Meiss[6] published the picture as a *Madonna of Humility*, but the Virgin appears to be sitting well above the ground.

VERSION: The derivation published by Destrée is referred to in note 1.

PROVENANCE: On the back in a hardly legible XVIII (?) Century hand, 'conte balviano' (?). Falsely stated to come from Palazzo Chigi, Rome.[7] According to Bode,[8] from the collection of Conte de Bardi, Parma; Bode obtained an option on it from Riblet, Florence (commission-agent) *ca.* 1875/6 for the Berlin Museum, but the purchase was not ratified. According to Wurzbach,[9] said to be from the ducal family of Parma, and certainly bought in Venice by Léon Somzée in 1875 (this seems in fair accord with Bode's statement). Tschudi[10] says that the picture was long on the art market, and was bought by Somzée about ten years before his article (i.e. *ca.* 1888). It was certainly lent by Léon Somzée[11] to the Exposition Néerlandaise de Beaux-Arts at Brussels, 1882, *Tableaux Anciens* (No. 75); exhibited at the Burlington Fine Arts Club, 1892 (No. 29), at the New Gallery, 1899/1900 (No. 48) and at Paris, Exposition Universelle, Pavillon de la Belgique, 1900 (No. 6). Exhibited at Bruges 1902 (No. 23), lent by C. and G. de Somzée. Acquired by Agnew's with several other Somzée pictures, 1902; passed to George Salting, 1903.[12] Exhibited at the R.A., 1904 (No. 4) and at the Primitifs Français, Paris, 1904 (No. 31); on loan to the Gallery from 1907. George Salting Bequest, 1910.

REPRODUCTION: *Illustrations, Continental Schools*, 1937, p. 45. *Plates, Early Netherlandish School*, 1947, Plate 13.

REFERENCES: *General:* Friedländer, Vol. II, No. 58. The picture is a key-piece in the 'Campin' group; very few particular references are given here, and the reader should consult the biographies of Campin (above) and Rogier van der Weyden.

In text: **(1)** *The Burlington Magazine*, September, 1937, p. 142. Joseph Destrée published in *The Connoisseur*, April, 1926, p. 209 (and elsewhere) a derivation of the later fifteenth century, which shows a possible original design for the cupboard. **(2)** Cf. A. Burroughs in *Metropolitan Museum Studies*, 1933, pp. 140 ff. **(3)** The attribution to the group here referred to as 'Campin' was first made by Bode in the *Gazette des Beaux-Arts*, 1887, I p. 218. Friedländer accepts the attribution in his Vol. II, No. 58; in his Vol. XIV, where he seems to try and telescope 'Campin' and Rogier, he does not refer to this picture. Weale in *The Burlington Magazine*, Vol. I (1903), p. 205, separated it from all the other pictures grouped as 'Campin' except one of the pictures at Leningrad, and dubitatively ascribed it to Daniel Daret (of whom no works are known). **(4)** Bouchot in the Catalogue of the *Exposition des Primitifs Français*, Paris, 1904. **(5)** Colin T. Eisler, *New England Museums* (Corpus series), 1961, p. 75; his Plate XCIV, the *Gazette* *des Beaux-Arts*, February 1959, p. 74, fig. 10 (the Merode *Annunciation*) and H. Beenken, *Roger van der Weyden*, 1951, Plate 87 (Berlin, the Bladelin altar-piece). **(6)** M. Meiss in *The Art Bulletin*, 1936, p. 451. His view is supported by E. Panofsky, *Early Netherlandish Painting*, 1953, Vol. I, p. 422 (note 2 to p. 163). **(7)** The Chigi provenance is given in the Salting MS.; a letter from E. K. Waterhouse settling this point is in the Gallery Archives. **(8)** Bode, *Mein Leben*, 1930, I, p. 138. The collector referred to may be Enrico Carlo Lodovico di Borbone, Conte di Bardi (1851–1905), brother of Robert, the last reigning Duke of Parma. **(9)** Wurzbach, *Niederländisches Künstler-Lexikon*, III, p. 73. **(10)** Tschudi in the Prussian *Jahrbuch*, 1898, p. 89. **(11)** Bode in the *Gazette des Beaux-Arts*, 1887, I, p. 218, says it was bought by Somzée in Italy. **(12)** Geoffrey Agnew, *Agnew's, 1817–1967*. 1967, p. 42 and lettering of the plate of No. 2609.

6377 PORTRAIT OF A MAN

Oak, painted surface, $7\frac{3}{8} \times 4\frac{5}{8}$ (0·187 × 0·117); including the frame, which is on all four sides in one piece with the picture, 9 × 6 (0·227 × 0·152).

Very good condition, though the shadows of the face are somewhat worn. Several *pentimenti* are to be seen in an X-radiograph; the sitter seems at first to have held a book, not the present scroll; the neckline of the dress was rather higher at the left; there has been a slight change in the position of the ear.

It seems clearly an individual portrait; there is, indeed, no trace of hinge marks on the frame to indicate that it did not originally stand alone. The sitter may be a member of a religious order; perhaps a Benedictine or an Augustinian hermit, if the colour of the dress is meant for black rather than very dark grey.

The picture is clearly by 'Campin', being close in style to the Merode triptych in the Cloisters at New York.[1]

PROVENANCE[2]: From the Collection of W. H. Nicholson. Acquired by Messrs. Agnew at a sale room. Purchased from Messrs. Agnew, Grant-in-Aid and Colnaghi Fund, 1966.

REPRODUCTION: In the Report of *The National Gallery, January 1965–December 1966*, opp. p. 80; in the article mentioned in note 1; and in the second edition of Friedländer, *Early Netherlandish Painting*, Vol. II, *Rogier van der Weyden and the Master of Flémalle*, 1967, Plate 141.

REFERENCES: **(1)** No. 6377 was published by the compiler in *The Burlington Magazine*, December, 1966, p. 622. **(2)** Information kindly given by Mr. Geoffrey Agnew.

Ascribed to 'CAMPIN'

653a A MAN

653b A WOMAN

Each, oak, painted surface, 16 × 11 (0·407 × 0·279).

Companion portraits, presumably of man and wife.

The woman in very good condition. The shadows of the man's face are messed, the turban heavily cracked, the dress seems blocked up and is perhaps repainted. The X-ray shows some small *pentimenti* on the woman's head-dress and the line of her lower right eyelid.

The pictures are obviously early, without being exactly datable. The style is not unlike that of the pictures classed as by Rogier, e.g. the *Portrait of a Woman* at Berlin,[1] but the likeness is less in the original than in reproduction. They are clearly not far from No. 2609 above. Winkler[2] contrasts the style with that of No. 1433 of this Gallery, here catalogued as by Rogier.[3] Frinta[4] accepts No. 653b as by Campin, but rejects No. 653a, thinking it rather in the Eyckian tradition, or an early sixteenth century copy.

PROVENANCE: Seen by S. Boisserée in the Campe Collection at Nuremberg, 1832,[5] Dr. Frederick Campe Sale, London, 18 May, 1849 (lots 37, 38). Purchased with the rest of the Edmond Beaucousin Collection, Paris, 1860.[6]

REPRODUCTIONS: *Illustrations, Continental Schools*, 1937, p. 44. *Plates, Early Netherlandish School*, 1947, Plates 15, 16.

REFERENCES: *General:* Friedländer, Vol. II, No. 55. Like No. 2609 above, these are key-pieces in the general 'Campin' problem, and the reader is referred to the biographies of Campin (above) and Rogier van der Weyden.

In text: (1) Friedländer, Vol. II, Plate VII. (2) Winkler, *Der Meister von Flémalle*, 1913, pp. 52 ff. (3) The attribution to 'Campin' was first dubiously made by Bode in the *Gazette des Beaux-Arts*, 1887, I, pp. 218/9. The pictures appear as of *ca.* 1425/9 in Friedländer's sketchy list, Vol. XIV, p. 84, of works that might (he apparently does not say should) be ascribed to Rogier. (4) Mojmír S. Frinta, *The Genius of Robert Campin*, 1966, pp. 57 ff. (5) E. Firmenich-Richartz, *Sulpiz und Melchior Boisserée als Kunstsammler*, Vol. I, 1916, p. 514. Campe called them Massys. (6) As by Rogier van der Weyden the Younger.

After 'CAMPIN' (?)

2608 THE VIRGIN AND CHILD WITH TWO ANGELS

Oak, painted surface, $22\frac{1}{8} \times 17\frac{3}{8}$ (0·56 × 0·44).

Suffers from undercleaning, and a little from overcleaning. There have been some retouchings on the features and some repairs on the dress of the angel right, but the quality is not seriously affected by these.

Numerous versions exist,[1] continuing down to the time of Bernaert van Orley, etc.; the composition is sometimes known as the *Virgin in the Apse* or the *Virgin of Salamanca.*[2] They are supposed to be derived from a lost original by 'Campin.' This version is one of the less bad ones: although the design is obviously of early date, no original recognizably by 'Campin' has been discovered.

VERSIONS: Numerous.[3]

PROVENANCE: Félix Ravaisson-Mollien Decd. Sale, Paris, 23 November 1903 (lot 67),[4] bt. Christian de Marinitsch.[5] Coll. George Salting, London; exhibited at the Burlington Fine Arts Club, 1904 (No. 3); Salting Bequest, 1910.

REPRODUCTION: *Illustrations, Continental Schools*, 1937, p. 43. *Plates, Early Netherlandish School*, 1947, Plate 17.

REFERENCES: (1) This picture is Friedländer, Vol. II, Nos. 74 f and g. There is a misprinted reference to the identity of these two in his Vol. XIV, p. 88. (2) Cf. *The Burlington Magazine*, Vol. VII (1905), pp. 238 and 387. The apse shown in these pictures is not that of the Old Cathedral of Salamanca; see the compiler's *The National Gallery* (*Les Primitifs Flamands, Corpus*), Vol. I, 1953, p. 61. (3) See

Friedländer, Vol. II, No. 74; VI, No. 217; VIII, No. 125. Also Germain Bazin in *L'Amour de l'Art*, December, 1931, pp. 495 ff., and the compiler's *The National Gallery*, as in previous note, pp. 62 ff. Further to what is recorded in the last reference, see the second edition of Friedländer, *Early Netherlandish Painting*, Vol. II, *Rogier van der Weyden and the Master of Flémalle*, 1967, pp. 74/5: it may here be noted that No. 1 on p. 62 is no longer at Minneapolis; see the entry in *Flanders in the Fifteenth Century*, exhibition catalogue, Detroit, 1960 (No. 6). Friedländer, Vol. II, No. 74i, is probably a picture now at Toledo, U.S.A. An additional variant suggestive of Gerard David was in the Mme. K. L. Sale, Paris, 30 November, 1954 (lot 23), Plate X. For p. 63, item C, a better reference for the Cadiz picture is the 1964 catalogue, pp. 92 f., No. 95, repr. A further Orleyish example is at Poznán; catalogue of the Early Netherlandish Exhibition at Warsaw, 1960, No. 47, Plate 53. For p. 64, item a, the Madrid picture was doubtfully ascribed to Provoost by S. Sulzberger in *Oud-Holland* (*Mededelingen* . . .), 1961, p. 107. A varied picture was published and associated with Provoost by Julius Held in *The Art Bulletin*, 1955, p. 233 and p. 208, fig. 1. Item c, Petri sale, was associated with Coecke by G. Marlier, *Pierre Coeck d'Alost*, 1966, fig. 182. **(4)** As Dürer. **(5)** A letter from Mme. Bouchot-Saupique, 21 January, 1948 (in the Gallery archives for Correggio, No. 2512) refers to this purchaser. It should not be doubted that he is identical with the painter, born 1868.

Imitator of 'CAMPIN'

early sixteenth century (?)

658 THE DEATH OF THE VIRGIN

The Virgin is lying on a bed; the twelve Apostles around. God or Christ in a gloriole accompanied by four angels above her head. On a book on the floor are apparently the remains of a short inscription, perhaps beginning *di*.

Oak, top corners cut, painted surface, 15 × 13¾ (0·38 × 0·35) approx. The paint has partly been made up to the edges. The top was originally of a flattened rounded form.[1] The picture is not cut at the bottom or at the left; the right side has probably been trimmed.

The main part of the picture is in very good state; the damage along the edges comes furthest in right and bottom. The Virgin's drapery and the shadow of the dress of the Apostle reading have darkened and cracked to some extent.

What little damage there is to important parts of the picture is partly due to the painter's *pentimenti*; but these have been in general extremely well done and are hardly visible in normal light. In considering them, we shall refer to another version of the picture at Berlin[2]; there the Apostles and the Virgin (but not her head) are very nearly on the same design, the rest being different.

No. 658 had originally a tester to the bed, as at Berlin, instead of God in a gloriole and an arch, window and view of a town in the background.[3] Lines of the falling bed-curtain pass through and near the right-hand angel; there are traces of a horizontal line to the bedhead, perhaps corresponding to the line dividing the two sets of its panels at Berlin. The tester itself was about level with the spring of the arch; its pelmet or valance in front is fairly clear, and it appears to have been supported from above, perhaps by cords, at intervals. The bunched curtain at the left end of the tester descended nearly to the candlestick. Further, there was a window to the left, just as at Berlin, instead of a table with bottles and candlestick. Even some of the minor *pentimenti* correspond with the Berlin version; thus, the right hand of the youthful Apostle holding a candle seems to have been originally as or nearly as at Berlin, and the cover of the book on the ground originally had five studs connected with tooled lines, just as at Berlin. There are further faint indications of changes in the Virgin's head, apparently not clear enough to be interpreted.

These *pentimenti* should all be compared with the corresponding details in the Berlin version. Doubtful suggestions in the first edition of this catalogue concerning changes in the size and location of the group of God and the Angels have not been confirmed.

The above remarks are important for the attribution of the picture, which on account of its high quality has been much discussed. It seems clear that the group of God and the angels is by the same hand as the principal figures in No. 658. But this group is an addition. If the nearly corresponding pictures in Berlin (and Prague) do not themselves contain a bewildering series of *pentimenti*, the Berlin/Prague design is the earlier one and should be discussed first.

Both the Berlin and the Prague pictures correspond very nearly with No. 658 in the principal figures; with the notable exception that there the style of the heads, the hands and the feet is in poor imitation of Hugo van der Goes. This has led to the supposition that these pictures derive from a lost van der Goes [4]; but most probably they do not. Van der Goes' authentic picture of the *Death of the Virgin* is in the museum at Bruges[5]; it could be claimed as the origin of the Berlin/Prague pictures. The curtain and lamp [6] to the right and several of the Apostles (rearranged) are fairly similar; and the idea of putting the Virgin not in but on the bed is a point in common. This suggests that the Berlin/Prague design may be derived in part from the picture at Bruges, and need not be an original design by van der Goes. It is further true that the known versions suffer from poor psychology and the intrusion of caricature; and the bed, by a somewhat strange conceit, has been shifted round, so that its back is not against the back curtains, but against the side curtains. Van der Goes, then, may have left a few indications,[7] but the evidence is not convincing that the Berlin and Prague pictures truly reflect a work of his.

As for No. 658 as it stands now, the principal variations from the versions at Berlin and Prague are the head of the Virgin, God and the angels, and the view of the town; these suggest the style of 'Campin.'[8] The idea that No. 658 is a faithful copy of a lost 'Campin,'[9] the Berlin and Prague versions being derivations from the following of van der Goes, is rendered unlikely by its *pentimenti*. There are two further arguments of some weight against its being a *faithful* copy: (1) the bed has no tester, which is very unusual in the Netherlands in the fifteenth century—and even later; (2) the flattened round arch, with hollow mouldings and no capitals, is unlikely before about 1500.[10]

The best hypothesis, then, seems to be that it is by a *pasticheur*, directly of 'Campin,' indirectly of van der Goes (whose style does not appear at all in this version). Hulin argues that such *pastiches* were not done in the early sixteenth century; but painters such as Colijn de Coter and the Master of St. Giles in their different ways did reproduce earlier works of art in a fairly accurate style. The possibility that No. 658 is not purely Netherlandish may be borne in mind.[11]

VERSIONS: See Friedländer, Vol. IV, No. 25 (Berlin, Prague, and another, of later date). Other pictures may be thought connected, though loosely.[12] For drawings, one precisely connected, see note 7.

PROVENANCE: Said by Nieuwenhuys[13] to have been in Charles I's Collection; this may be due to a misreading of a label once on the back, Cte R. | N. 6 | Marten Schoen.[14] Sir Thomas Lawrence Sale, London, 15 May, 1830 (lot 123),[15] bt. Zachary; M. M. Zachary Decd. Sale, London, 31 March, 1838 (lot 21), bt. Fuller. King William II of Holland Coll., The Hague; 1843 Catalogue (No. 41);[16] Sale, 12, etc., August, 1850 (lot 52),[17] bt. Nieuwenhuys. Coll. Edmond Beaucousin, Paris, by 1857[18]; purchased with the rest of the collection, 1860.

REPRODUCTION: *Plates, Early Netherlandish School*, 1947, Plate 18; not in the *Illustrations, Continental Schools*, 1937.

REFERENCES: *General:* Friedländer, Vol. IV, No. 25c.

In text: (1) For this, and for further details about the *pentimenti*, with plates, see the compiler's *The National Gallery* (*Les Primitifs Flamands, Corpus*), Vol. I, 1953, pp. 52 ff. (2) Berlin, 1931 Catalogue, p. 195, No. 538B, size, 0·39 × 0·37 (ex-Palazzo Sciarra); reproduced, Berlin Illustrations, *Die Deutschen und Altniederländischen Meister*, 1929, p. 194. A version offering only very minor variations from the Berlin example is at Prague; 1912 Catalogue, pp. 149/50, No. 452; size, 0·35 × 0·365; reproduced in the Catalogue, Plate 27. (3) To be strictly accurate, there do not seem to be any *pentimenti* lines across the *lower* part of the window, where is now the view of the town; but a glance at the Berlin version shows that the town could not have been there originally. (4) This view is held by Winkler, *Der Meister von Flémalle*, 1913, pp. 14/5, and *Das Werk des Hugo van der Goes*, 1964, pp. 134 ff., and by Friedländer, Vol. II, No. 77, and Vol. IV, p. 69, and No. 25. (5) Reproduced by Friedländer, Vol. IV, Plate XXI, etc. (6) The lamp would have been behind the gloriole in No. 658; it is now seen, with little alteration, in the right background. (7) Friedländer, Vol. IV, pp. 69/70, mentions three drawings more or less in van der Goes' style, one (Berlin Print Room, No. 780) with six figures corresponding quite closely with the Berlin version; they do not prove that van der Goes himself is responsible for more than one *Death of the Virgin* (at Bruges). (8) E.g. the Dijon *Nativity*; compare also the view of a town in the *Virgin and Child before a Fire-Screen*, No. 2609. (9) This view is held by Hulin; letter of 1936 in the Gallery Archives, giving a résumé of his courses at the University of Ghent. J. Bruyn, *De Levensbron*, 1957, p. 112, argues in favour of a Campin original of the design. (10) In his Bruges picture, van der Goes is not very clear about the tester; even if it is assumed that it is absent from there (an unjustifiable assumption), it would be impossible to prove that its absence from our picture is due to van der Goes. Testerless beds occur in series such as the *Sacraments*: e.g. Destrée, *Roger de la Pasture*, 1930, Plates 75, 77, 82; Friedländer, Vol. II, Plate LXVII, and Vol. X, Plate XXIX. Whereas it was normal in the Netherlands for the bed to have a tester, this does not seem to have been the case in Germany and Austria. A *Death of the Virgin* without tester by the Master of the Life is at Nuremberg; reproduced by Aldenhoven, *Geschichte der Kölner Malerschule*, 1902, Plate 65. Another, also of the fifteenth century, is in St. Nicholas', Kalkar; reproduced by Clemen, *Die Kunstdenkmäler der Rheinprovinz, Kreis Kleve*, 1892, Plate V. One dated 1439 is at Kremsmünster; this and others of later date are reproduced by Benesch in the Vienna *Jahrbuch*, 1928, pp. 76 ff., figs. 131, 132, 144, 145, 149. It should be stated that the two arguments in the text do not exclude fifteenth-century Netherlandish execution; see for instance the two miniatures assigned to the Mansel Master, reproduced by Winkler, *Die Flämische Buchmalerei*, 1925, Plate 9. **(11)** It is suggested in the text above that the execution of No. 658 is of the early sixteenth century, and that the main part of the design may have been invented by a follower of van der Goes, perhaps with some indications from van der Goes himself. Notes on the costume, by Mrs. Newton, are in the Gallery archives. The costume of the various versions was not intended to reflect the fashion current when they were painted, but to some extent it does. Certain points where No. 658 differs from the Berlin and Prague versions may be held to confirm the dating suggested for No. 658. The dating of the Berlin and Prague versions themselves, on the evidence of costume, is not easy. It is probable that some details are misunderstood, e.g. the coif with chin-strap of the apostle standing furthest to the right, which appears more reasonably without a chin-strap in the drawing mentioned in note 7. Two figures in the Berlin and Prague versions show a costume difficult to reconcile with the time of van der Goes, the hooded apostle standing left centre behind the bed, and the kneeling apostle right centre; so far as their costume can be interpreted, it suggests the time of Rogier or even 'Campin.' If this is exact, it would still be legitimate to suppose that some follower of van der Goes picked up ideas for these two figures from a source earlier than van der Goes. Some critics might prefer to derive the whole composition from a *Death of the Virgin* of the second quarter of the fifteenth century, but it would not follow that the 'Campinesque' elements found in No. 658 appeared there. Further study of the Berlin and Prague versions, which the compiler cannot undertake for the present entry, is desirable. **(12)** For one, see Friedländer, Vol. X, pp. 114/5, Plate XC; a clearer reproduction in F. Winkler, *Das Werk des Hugo van der Goes*, 1964, fig. 104. A picture mentioned in connection with No. 658, as at Douai (J. Lavalleye, *Hugo van der Goes*, 1962, p. 69; cf. Winkler, *op. cit.*, p. 139) is a derivation from van der Goes' *Death of the Virgin* at Bruges; it is at Valencieunes, and is recorded in various writings. **(13)** Nieuwenhuys, Catalogue of William II of Holland Collection, 1843, No. 41. **(14)** The attribution to Schongauer was no doubt due to his engraving of the subject. The design is only vaguely similar; how far it may have inspired van der Goes in his Bruges picture is another matter. Another label, formerly on the back of the picture, has *A Pétersbourg chez* ALI(C?) . . ., perhaps cut from the cover of a book. **(15)** As Memlinc. **(16)** As Holbein. **(17)** As Schongauer. **(18)** Crowe and Cavalcaselle, *The Early Flemish Painters*, 1857, pp. 324/5.

Petrus CHRISTUS

active 1442 (?), died 1472/3

The signatures are in an abbreviated form, in semi-Greek lettering perhaps in imitation of Jan van Eyck; they imply a name Christi. Sometimes called Cristus, and formerly (wrongly) Christophori or Christophsen. The last form, by the misuse of a document, was applied to a different group of pictures, by the Cologne Master of S. Bartholomew.

Christus was born at Baerle (the identity of this place is uncertain; cf. Hoogewerff, *De Noord-Nederlandsche Schilderkunst*, II, 1937, p. 14). Bruges 1444, where active. There are several signed pictures. Dated works, 1446–1457(?); reproduction of the signature with the latter date in the *Bulletin des Musées Royaux des Beaux-Arts*, Brussels, *Miscellanea Erwin Panofsky*, 1955, p. 152. A picture at Detroit is dated 1442 (Friedländer, Vol. XIV, p. 79); but the attribution is disputed (see L.

Baldass, *Jan van Eyck*, 1952, p. 276 and E. Panofsky, *Early Netherlandish Painting*, 1953, Vol. I, pp. 189 f.).

He copied several compositions by or ascribed to Jan van Eyck (died 1441), whose pupil (probably wrongly) he is supposed to have been. He shows some connections with Rogier and Bouts; an elaborate attempt to work out his stylistic development was made by Pächt in *Belvedere*, 1926, pp. 155 ff.

It is often said, on inadequate evidence, that he influenced the style or technique of Antonello da Messina; cf. F. Malaguzzi Valeri, *I Pittori Lombardi del '400*, 1902, p. 89. He may, nevertheless, have travelled; a picture assigned to him once at Dessau is stated to be on fir, a support rarely used in the Netherlands.

2593 PORTRAIT OF A YOUNG MAN (LEFT WING OF A TRIPTYCH?)

He holds an open prayer-book. The inscription begins *Bedice* (for Benedice: most of the rest merely marks on the page, not meant to be read as words); the clasp carries an inscription that looks like *mai*. On the wall behind hangs an illuminated scroll, with the Head of Christ in a cruciform aureole between Āω̄, and a hymn as follows:

Incipit or̄o ad scām V̄onicā

Salue sācta facies	*Salue o sudariū*
Nostri redeporis	*Nobile iocale*
In q' (ni ?)*tet* (species ?)	*Es nr̄m solaciu*
Dīni splendoris	*Et memoriale*
Impēssa pāniculo	*Non depicta maībus*
Niuei coloris	*Scolpta vel polita*
Data q: Veronice	*Hoc scit sū' Artifex*
Si(gnū ?) *ob* (amo)*ris*	*Qui te fecit ita*
Salue nr̄a gloria	*Esto nobis q̄sim'*
In hac vita dura	*Tutū adiuuamē*
Labili qz fragili	*Dulce refrigeriū*
Cito transitura	*Atq: osolamen*
Nos ꝑduc ad pr̄iam	*Ut nobis nō noceat*
O felix figura	*Hostile grauamen*
Ad videndū faciem	*Sz fruamur requie*
Que est xp̄i pura	*Dicam' ōnes ame'*

Explicit

Oak, painted surface, 14 × 10⅜ (0·355 × 0·263). Surrounded by a band of new gold, which very slightly encroaches upon the original painted surface.

Considerably overcleaned in the flesh, mended and stippled. The hair is in very bad condition; the outline of the brown hair is considerably within the present black and ill-defined outer circumference, which has been increased by retouches not meant for hair. The quality of the flesh is somewhat changed, but the landscape is characteristic of Christus.

Possibly the left wing of a triptych.[1]

Formerly supposed to represent Philip the Good, Duke of Burgundy, but the resemblance is merely general. Datable from the style *ca.* 1450/60.[2]

The hymn was popular in the fifteenth century.[3] A transcription with some slight differences was given by Weale in the Northbrook Catalogue, 1889; the one above is as far as possible literal. It is to be noted that the abbreviation for *Christi* at the bottom of the first column is similar to the form of Christus' signatures. Dr. de Bruin[4] reads the mark on the clasp in a way unacceptable to the compiler, and interprets it as being IHαωM (Iesus, alpha and omega, Maria).

A bag rather similar to the one visible here appears in a picture by Christus at Copenhagen[5]; another of a not dissimilar design is in a fragment by a follower of Rogier van der Weyden at Petworth.[6]

PROVENANCE: On the back, 257/*Luca d'Olanda*. Bought from Farrer, 1863, by Thomas Baring, who died in 1873 and bequeathed it with other pictures to his nephew, Lord Northbrook.[7] Exhibited, R.A. 1880 (No. 194)[8]; Northbrook Catalogue, 1889 (No. 16); exhibited at the Burlington Fine Arts Club, 1892 (No. 10). Still in the Northbrook Collection in August, 1894.[9] Lent by Salting to the National Gallery from 1895, and to Bruges, 1902 (No. 18); George Salting Bequest, 1910.

REPRODUCTION: *Illustrations, Continental Schools*, 1937, p. 54. *Plates, Early Netherlandish School*, 1947, Plate 19.

REFERENCES: **(1)** Cf. E. Panofsky, *Early Netherlandish Painting*, 1953, Vol. I, pp. 490/1 (note 5 to p. 313); following on this, cleaning tests and X-ray photographs satisfied the compiler that No. 2593 is not a fragment. **(2)** Friedländer, Vol. I, pp. 155/6 and Pächt in *Belvedere*, 1926, p. 158, date it near the Berlin Altarwings of 1452; Hulin, *Catalogue Critique*, 1902, No. 18, associates it in date with the pictures at Berlin, Frankfort and Copenhagen. The costume would suit a date 1450/5 (note by Mrs. Newton, in the Gallery archives). No one rejects the attribution. **(3)** See Karl Pearson, *Die Fronica, Ein Beitrag zur Geschichte des Christusbildes im Mittelalter*, 1887, pp. 22 ff.,70 (for indulgences in connection). He gives from a MS. at the British Museum of the second half of the fifteenth century a text of twelve eight-line verses, including all the lines on our picture with a few verbal alterations and some differences of order. On p. 25, he gives another, shorter text from an earlier MS., also at the British Museum, which he considers to approximate to the original form of the hymn. The hymn with variants appears on the wings of a version of *Christ* associated with van Eyck (Baldass, type of No. 35), lent by Dr. H. Wetzlar to Delft, *Prisma der Bijbelse Kunst*, 1952, No. 231, Plate 1. **(4)** T. L. de Bruin in *Das Münster*, 1966, pp. 402, 404. **(5)** M. J. Friedländer, *Early Netherlandish Painting*, Vol. I, 1967, Plate 90A; cf. *The Burlington Magazine*, 1928, ii, p. 49. **(6)** Petworth Catalogue by C. H. Collins Baker, 1920, No. 122, as 'Burgundian School'; Friedländer, Vol. XIV, p. 88, as Rogier; H. Beenken, *Rogier van der Weyden*, 1951, Plate 82. **(7)** As Rogier van der Weyden (?). **(8)** As Christus (?). **(9)** Minute at the National Gallery.

CLEVE *See* JOOS VAN CLEVE (biographical note): the pictures are listed under the MASTER OF THE DEATH OF THE VIRGIN

Pieter COECKE van AELST

1502–1550

Pieter Coecke, Cock, Koecke (there are yet other spellings) van Aelst (Alost); his son of the same name was also a painter.

The dates of birth and death are from an inscription on his funeral monument, given by Sweertius, *Monumenta Sepulcralia*, 1613, p. 293; Rombouts and van Lerius (*De Liggeren*, p. 108) wrongly make the birth date 1507. Van Mander says that he was a pupil of Bernaert van Orley, and that he visited Rome. Master at Antwerp, 1527, where active chiefly. 1533, Constantinople. He was painter to Mary of Hungary and the Emperor Charles V; he also designed or executed buildings, sculptures, stained glass, tapestries, and translated Vitruvius and Serlio.

His work as a draughtsman is tolerably well known. Some Turkish designs, certainly his, were published in engraving by his widow, 1553. Further, a good many drawings carry his name in old writing; see Popham, *Catalogue of Dutch and Flemish Drawings in the British Museum*, V, 1932, p. 21. See further Marlier, pp. 88 ff.

These are of little help towards identifying his pictures. Marlier, pp. 75 ff., points out that a triptych at Lisbon is well established as his by testimony of 1585; apparently late work (see also Luís Reis-Santos, *Masterpieces of Flemish Painting . . . in Portugal*, 1962, pp. 115 f.). Till recently, attributions were based on a series of repetitions of the *Last Supper* (cf. Marlier, pp. 50 f.), many of which bear dates, the earliest recorded to be 1525 (Christie's, 1 April, 1960, lot 127), up to his death (and later). This composition was engraved by H. Goltzius, 1585; one copy (not two; the Prussian *Jahrbuch*, 1917, p. 73) has an old manuscript inscription that the engraving is after Pieter van Aelst. Further, an Antwerp painter in 1544 is recorded to have owned a small *Last Supper* by Coecke (van den Branden, *Antwerpsche Schilderschool*, 1883, p. 154). See Marlier, pp. 93 ff.

These *Last Suppers* were at one time labelled as by Lambert Lombard (the traditional name), the Pseudo-Lombard and the *Maître des Saintes Cènes*; there seems to be some connection with Coecke, although the grouping of them all together may depend rather on an identity of design than of execution. Friedländer, Vol. XII, p. 62, associated them with Coecke, but explicitly says that none of the versions are autograph. It seems that Coecke was the overseer of a factory, and that attributions to him should indicate this by being marked with the prefix 'Studio'.

The *Last Suppers* are influenced by Leonardo's design, and by the taste of the High Renaissance (Raphael). Friedländer (Vol. XI, No. 103, and Vol. XII, p. 65) says that some of the compositions he connects with Coecke are carried over from his Antwerp *Master of 1518*.

His wife, Meyken Verhulst, has been claimed to be the painter known as the Brunswick Monogrammist; see under Jan van Amstel.

Literature: Georges Marlier, *Pierre Coeck d'Alost*, 1966.

Ascribed to the Studio of COECKE

2606 TRIPTYCH: THE VIRGIN AND CHILD ENTHRONED

A small altarpiece in its original frame.

Central panel: in the background, an angel and a figure possibly S. Joseph.

Right wing: S. Louis (?), with sceptre and necklace of cockle shells.

Left wing: a bishop Saint in white, holding a book; the Virgin and Child appear on his crozier.

Reverse, central panel: black paint with a brown edging and two brown horizontal bands, between which: RESPICE FINEM ET NON/PECCABIS IN ETERNVM (cf. *Ecclesiasticus,* VII, 40).

Reverse of right wing: S. Anthony of Padua standing before an archway; he holds in his left hand a Crucifix, in his right hand a book on which the Infant Christ is seated.

Reverse of left wing: S. James the Greater before a corresponding archway. He is represented as a pilgrim, with staff, wallet, hat with cockle shell; he holds a book.

The two saints on the reverse are not in grisaille.

Wood, irregular tops. The painted surfaces are: central panel, 10¼ × 7¼ (0·265 × 0·185); wings, obverses, 10¼ × 2¾ (0·265 × 0·07); wings, reverses, 10⅝ × 3½ (0·27 × 0·09). Including the frames, which are fixed to the pictures, the sizes are: central panel, 12⅝ × 9½ (0·32 × 0·24); wings, 12⅝ × 4¾ (0·32 × 0·12). The simple design on the reverse of the central panel has the measurements of the obverse including the frame.

As the support is entirely covered with paint or gold, it is not possible to say what the wood is.

The frame has been regilt. The design and inscription on the back of the central panel may not be contemporary. The picture has been a good deal worn and restored, especially in the flesh parts; the most trustworthy figure is S. James. There are *pentimenti* in his right arm.

The mystic fountain in the central panel may be compared with a more elaborate treatment in Netherlandish School, No. 1085 of this catalogue, painted probably at Antwerp a little earlier than this.

The name of Pieter Coecke for the present triptych has been brought forward by Friedländer, at first dubiously and as *ca.* 1530,[1] then more precisely and as before 1527.[2] The attribution is accepted by Winkler.[3] Marlier[4] accepts it with slight reserves as Coecke's, an early work. As explained in the biography above, all attributions of pictures to Coecke should be marked 'Studio'. The figures in No. 2606 have certainly some stylistic resemblance to those of the *Last Suppers*; the architecture is very different.[5] In the *Last Suppers* from 1525 onwards, it is in a fairly sober Renaissance style; here it is a semi-Renaissance continuation of the 'Antwerp Mannerism' that set in soon after 1500, and similar to certain backgrounds by Bernaert van Orley (Brussels).

The attributions of No. 2606 to the Coninxloos are as follows. It was ascribed by Tschudi[6] to Cornelis van Coninxloo. Of several painters recorded as of this name, one presumably painted the picture at Brussels, signed and dated 1526.[7] That picture is the origin of all association of No. 2606 with the name of Coninxloo; but Coecke is more justifiable.

The triptych appeared at the Bruges Exhibition, 1902, as by Gillis van Coninxloo.[8] There were at least four (?) painters of this name; the only one whose works are known is the 'Frankenthal' landscape-painter, 1544–1606/7, which will not do. Friedländer[9] pointed out that Cornelis van Coninxloo was a possibility. In the 1911 Gallery Catalogue[10] is a note that Sir Claude Phillips had suggested one of the Coninxloo. In the 1913 Gallery Catalogue,[11] the name appeared as Jan van Coninxloo. It is uncertain how many painters of this name there were. Signed pictures: two at Brussels (one dated 1530, one dated 1546), at Jäder (Sweden), and at Rouen. Friedländer[12] at one time said that but for the signatures, the Brussels, the Jäder and the Rouen pictures would not be grouped together; the curious may consult the reproductions of Jeanne Maquet-Tombu[13] and Friedländer's latest text.[14] No. 3650 of this catalogue (Netherlandish School) is somewhat in the style of an attributed altarpiece.

The 'picture by the same hand at Palermo' referred to in the 1929 Catalogue may be no other than Gossaert's *Malvagna Triptych*, which is *not* by the same hand.

VERSIONS: Friedländer notes a larger version of the central panel at Basel (Bachofen-Burchardt Gift). Wescher notes that the figure of S. James reappears in an altarpiece that shows the Virgin and Child in a Glory, once with the Spanish Art Gallery. Marlier notes that S. Anthony recurs in a picture in the museum at Evora.[15]

PROVENANCE: Owned by Benito Garriga, Madrid; Sale, Paris, 24 March, 1890 (lot 20).[16] In the Collection of Léon Somzée, Brussels. Lent to the Burlington Fine Arts Club (Private Rooms), 1892.[17] Exhibited at Bruges, 1902 (No. 366), lent by C. and G. de Somzée.[18] Acquired in 1902 by Agnew's with several other Somzée pictures.[19] George Salting Bequest, 1910. Exhibited at Brussels, *Le Siècle de Bruegel*, 1963 (No. 78).

REPRODUCTION: *Illustrations, Continental Schools*, 1937, p. 121 (obverse). *Plates, Early Netherlandish School*, 1947, Plate 20 (obverse). The reverse is reproduced in *Paintings and Drawings on the Backs of National Gallery Pictures*, 1946, Plate 31.

REFERENCES: **(1)** Friedländer, *Meisterwerke*, 1903, p. 29, or in the *Repertorium für Kunstwissenschaft*, 1903, p. 165. **(2)** Friedländer in the Prussian *Jahrbuch*, 1917, pp. 80 and 83, and his Vol. XII, pp. 62/3 and No. 145. **(3)** Winkler, *Die Alt-Niederländische Malerei*, 1924, p. 294, as perhaps only a 'repetition.' **(4)** Georges Marlier, *Pierre Coeck d'Alost*, 1966, pp. 177 ff. **(5)** Friedländer in the Prussian *Jahrbuch*, 1917, p. 83, thinks the architecture similar to that of an engraving of the *Triumph of Jakob Castricus*, reproduced in the Prussian *Jahrbuch*, 1894, p. 58; but there seems to be little or no connection. **(6)** Tschudi in the *Repertorium für Kunstwissenschaft*, 1893, p. 115. **(7)** Reproduced by Fierens-Gevaert, *Les Primitifs Flamands*, III, Plate CLXXXV. **(8)** Bruges Exhibition, 1902 (No. 366). **(9)** Friedländer, references as in note 1. **(10)** 1911 Catalogue, p. 110. **(11)** 1913 Catalogue, p. 258. **(12)** Friedländer in the Prussian *Jahrbuch*, 1909, p. 10. According to Johnny Roosval, *Schnitzaltäre in Schwedischen Kirchen*, etc., 1903, p. 35, the Jäder pictures are wings of a carved altarpiece unclearly dated 1514. **(13)** Jeanne Maquet-Tombu in the *Gazette des Beaux-Arts*, 1931, ii, pp. 148 ff. **(14)** Friedländer, Vol. VIII, pp. 148/9. **(15)** Friedländer, Vol. XII, No.

145a; P. Wescher in *Belvedere*, 1928, i, p. 27. See Marlier, *op. cit.*, figs. 108, 120, 121; also figs. 122, 123, for a related figure (S. John the Evangelist). (**16**) Reproduced in the Catalogue. (**17**) Tschudi in the *Repertorium für Kunstwissenschaft*, 1893, p. 115. (**18**) As Gillis van Coninxloo. (**19**) Geoffrey Agnew, *Agnew's, 1817–1967*, 1967, p. 42, for the purchase in 1902 of a group of Somzée pictures; No. 2606 is assumed to have been in the group.

Pieter van CONINXLOO

active 1479, died 1513 or later

In French, Pierre de Royalme. The name of this painter, who is not included in Thieme-Becker, was exhumed by Pinchart and published by A.-J. Wauters (*Bulletin des Musées royaux du Cinquantenaire*, 1914); their researches are summarized by Friedländer, Vol. VIII, pp. 146 ff., and Vol. XII, pp. 21 ff. He is mentioned from 1479 in Brussels and was active on various works for the court there. Last mentioned, 1513. On the grounds that his place and time are possible, he has been identified by Friedländer with the

MASTER of the MAGDALEN LEGEND (q.v.)

For connections with other painters surnamed Coninxloo, *see*
Ascribed to the Studio of COECKE, No. 2606
NETHERLANDISH SCHOOL, No. 3650

Aelbrecht CORNELIS

active 1513, died 1532

His entry into a guild is not recorded, but he is mentioned at Bruges from 1513. He appears to have been highly productive, although only one existing picture is established as his. Between 1517 and 1522 he produced an altarpiece, the central panel of which still exists at S. Jacques, Bruges. This picture was the subject of much bickering: the documents were published by Weale in *Le Beffroi*, I, pp. 1 ff. Friedländer, Vol. XI, pp. 91/6, misreads a date as January, 1519, instead of 1519 old style (i.e. 1520) and makes an erroneous deduction therefrom. The principal subject of dispute was that the picture was not delivered to time, not that it was painted partly by another hand. Cornelis agreed in the original contract to paint the flesh parts himself and it is unreasonable to suppose that he did not. These faces are rather like those of the group of paintings arbitrarily labelled 'Ysenbrandt,' so it is possible that he is the true author of some or all of these works. See Georges Marlier, *Ambrosius Benson*, 1957, pp. 50 ff., and cf. Bodenhausen, *Gerard David*, 1905, pp. 215/6. No. 657 of this catalogue (Follower of Gerard David) has also been ascribed to him.

See 'YSENBRANDT'

See Follower of GERARD DAVID, No. 657

PETRUS CRISTUS *See* PETRUS CHRISTUS

GERARD DAVID

active 1484, died 1523

Born at Oudewater, Holland; 1484, Bruges, where active. In 1515, 'Meester Gheraet van Brugghe, scildere' was admitted to the Antwerp Guild; presumably this is Gerard David, who in any case is again recorded at Bruges in 1519–1523. Documented altarpiece of 1509 at Rouen; date 1498 on the semi-documented *Judgement of Cambyses* at Bruges. Several other pictures grouped as by David can be approximately dated by other than stylistic evidence.

He was perhaps trained in Holland (some relationship with Geertgen); at Bruges he was influenced by van Eyck, Rogier, van der Goes (strongly), Memlinc. His style bears some not easily definable relationship to miniature painting at Bruges; a series of miniatures bearing the early date 1486 in the Escorial is attributed to David himself by Hulin (cf. W. Schoene in the Prussian *Jahrbuch*, 1937, pp. 170 ff.). For his latest style, see Nos. 1078, 1079 below. In addition to the other literature, the student should consult Georges Marlier, *Ambrosius Benson*, 1957, pp. 15 ff., 43 f.

710 AN ECCLESIASTIC PRAYING (RIGHT WING OF A DIPTYCH?)

Oak, painted surface, $13\frac{3}{8} \times 10\frac{1}{2}$ (0·34 × 0·267).

Much stippled on the face and hands; *pentimenti* in the hands, in the tower on the right, etc.

Presumably the right wing of a diptych for private devotion. The sitter could be either an Augustinian hermit or a Cistercian monk; it is claimed that the first alternative is the more probable, since a fold in his habit at the waist suggests the presence of the Augustinian belt.[1] He was at one time wrongly called Floreins van der Ryst.[2]

The tower in the background left is apparently meant for that of Notre-Dame, Bruges. The other was stated to be unidentifiable in the first edition of this catalogue; it has been claimed to be that of S. Sauveur at Bruges, which may be true, but is not quite convincing.[3]

Although the character of the picture is considerably altered by restoration, it seems to be an autograph David, and is admitted as such by Friedländer.[4]

VERSION: A similar portrait of a different sitter, apparently not by David himself, was in the Rodolphe Kann Collection, Paris; now Cleveland Museum.[5]

PROVENANCE: Stated to be from the Coll. Count Joseph von Rechberg, Mindelheim, and bought in 1815 by Prince Ludwig Kraft Ernst von Œttingen-Wallerstein.[6] At Schloss Wallerstein.[7] Exhibited at Kensington Palace (for sale) 1848 (No. 59),[8] bought with the rest of the collection by the Prince Consort. At

Kensington Palace.[9] Exhibited at Manchester, 1857 (Provisional Catalogue, No. 514; Definitive Catalogue, No. 438), lent by Prince Albert. Presented by Queen Victoria at the Prince Consort's wish, 1863.[10]

REPRODUCTION: *Illustrations, Continental Schools*, 1937, p. 84. *Plates, Early Netherlandish School*, 1947, Plate 21.

REFERENCES: (**1**) Dom Anselm Veys, O.S.B., '*Portrait of an Ecclesiastic*,' in the *Album English*, Bruges, 1952, pp. 430/1. (**2**) The picture was then supposed to be a Memlinc; see Crowe and Cavalcaselle, *Les Anciens Peintres Flamands*, 1862/3, ii, p. 43. (**3**) See Veys, *op. cit.*, p. 425, referring to a thesis by Th. van de Walle de Ghelcke; and the discussion of this point in the compiler's *The National Gallery* (*Les Primitifs Flamands, Corpus*), Vol. I, 1953, p. 77. There may be added to the pictures cited for comparison a portrait of Pierre Lootyns, 1557, in S. Sauveur at Bruges (No. 298 of the Bruges Exhibition, 1902); this does not make the identification in No. 710 more convincing. (**4**) Friedländer, Vol. VI, No. 223. Bodenhausen, *Gerard David*, 1905, No. 124, calls it influenced by David. (**5**) Rodolphe Kann *Catalogue*, 1907, ii, No. 111; 0·355 × 0·305. Cleveland Museum, Catalogue of the John L. Severance Collection, 1942, Plate II. (**6**) Details concerning the formation of the Œttingen-Wallerstein Collection were given orally to H. I. Kay. (**7**) See *Kunst-Blatt*, 1824, p. 318, as School of van Eyck; cf. also p. 353. No. 43, as Memlinc, of Wallerstein Catalogues of *ca.* 1826 and 1827 (originals at Munich; photostats in the National Gallery). The collection was moved from Schloss Wallerstein after a time. (**8**) As Memlinc. (**9**) Waagen's *Catalogue*, 1854 (No. 38); cf. Waagen, *Treasures*, IV, 1857, p. 227, with an attribution to Mabuse. (**10**) In the Gallery Catalogue, 1870, as van der Goes.

1045 CANON BERNARDINUS DE SALVIATIS AND THREE SAINTS (LEFT WING OF AN ALTARPIECE)

S. Donatian has on his morse the Virgin and Child and two angels; on his cross, the Virgin and Child and three other figures. S. Bernardino has 'ihs' on his book. S. Martin, with his beggar in the background, has on his cope the Adoration of the Magi, the Virgin and Child, SS. Donatian, Bernardino, Martin, the Baptist, the Magdalen; on his morse, S. Martin; on his crozier, the Virgin and Child with an angel.

Reverse, remains of what seems to be Christ at an open window.

Oak, painted surface, 40½ × 37¼ (1·03 × 0·945).

Cut at the top, which almost certainly had a curved form originally. A very little rubbed in the shadows, but on the whole in excellent state. A few *pentimenti*. The line of the hill on the horizon originally continued to the left nearly as far as S. Martin.

Bodenhausen notes that Weale refers to this picture as documented without in any of his writings on David quoting any document. According to Weale, this picture and another now lost were shutters to the reredos of the altar of SS. John the Baptist and Mary Magdalene in S. Donatian's, Bruges; he says that in 1501 Bernardinus de Salviatis, having obtained leave to restore this altar, commissioned Gerard David to paint the shutters.

The document concerning the restoration of the altar in 1501 has been found; the compiler does not know of the documents indicating that the altar was dedicated to the Magdalen as well as to S. John the Baptist, that No. 1045 was one wing of the altarpiece or that it was painted by Gerard David.[1] Nevertheless, there is strong internal evidence that the provenance is correct (presence of SS. Bernardino, Donatian, John the Baptist, even Mary Magdalene). The date in that case may be assumed to be 1501 or soon after. The authorship of Gerard David is generally admitted by modern critics.

Bernardinus (not Bernardus) de Salviatis was the illegitimate son of a Florentine merchant, born at Bruges, secretary to the Chapter of S. Donatian's from 1489, canon 1498; he died in 1519.

The subject of the reverse has not been interpreted; probably it is only the left half of a composition, the other part having been represented on the missing right wing[2].

Weale gives some notes about the vestments in this picture.

PROVENANCE: According to Weale[3] the wings remained *in situ* until 1787, when they were sold by order of the chapter. No. 1045 has HL (?) on the back.[4] Bought as by Gossaert in 1792 by Thomas Barrett of Lee Priory, Kent[5]; 1817 Catalogue, p. 42 (No. 65). Barrett Sale, London,[6] 28 May, 1859 (lot 154), bought by William Benoni White (dealer), who bequeathed it, 1878.

REPRODUCTION: *Illustrations, Continental Schools*, 1937, p. 84 (obverse). *Plates, Early Netherlandish School*, 1947, Plate 22 (obverse). The reverse is reproduced in the compiler's *The National Gallery* (*Les Primitifs Flamands, Corpus*), Vol. I, 1953, Plates CXCIV/VI.

REFERENCES: *General:* Weale, *Gerard David*, 1895, pp. 17 ff. Bodenhausen, *Gerard David*, 1905, No. 22. Friedländer, Vol. VI, No. 219.

In text: **(1)** For a fuller discussion of the documentation, see the compiler's *The National Gallery* (*Les Primitifs Flamands, Corpus*), Vol. I, 1953, pp. 82 ff. **(2)** Students may compare the back of two wings showing scenes of S. John the Baptist, associated with Bernaert van Orley. See Baldass in the Vienna *Jahrbuch*, 1944, pp. 151 ff., figs 132–5. Included on one back is Christ, on the other a donor. The latter has now been separated from its front (mostly representing the *Decollation*), and is reproduced, better than by Baldass, in the catalogue of the Arnold, Seligmann, Rey & Co. Sale, New York, 23 January, 1947 (lot 228). Christ and the donor on the backs might be thought to be represented as framed pictures; yet these perhaps poorly conceived figures are rather, it seems, to be thought of as at windows. These S. John wings are closely connected with two showing scenes of S. Martin, formerly in the Mortimer Schiff Collection (Friedländer, Vol. VIII, No. 92), one now at Kansas City. The backs of the Schiff pictures (photographs in the National Gallery) show the Virgin and Child, and a donor; owing to the cradling of two panels, only the inner parts of the framing of these figures are to be seen. It has been claimed by Baldass and others that the S. John and S. Martin pictures were originally together, the four forming the two wings of a single altarpiece; this idea should be considered on careful study and comparison of the originals, but there are various strong objections to it, one being the possibility that the two donor figures show the same man. Objections to the suggested arrangement are well made by Luís Reis-Santos, *Masterpieces of Flemish Painting . . . in Portugal*, 1962, pp. 99 f. Another work for comparison with the back of No. 1045 is the exterior of the outer wings of an altarpiece at Tallin (Reval), associated with Notke (W. Paatz, *Bernt Notke*, 1944, fig. 57). **(3)** Weale, *Gerard David*, 1895, p. 17. **(4)** This mark resembles the unidentified mark, No. 1331 of F. Lugt, *Les Marques de Collections de Dessins et d'Estampes*, 1921. **(5)** Cf. a note by Horace Walpole, printed by M. W. Brockwell, *The 'Adoration of the Magi' by Jan Mabuse*, 1911, Appendix B, p. 10, and Horace Walpole's *Letters*, edited by Mrs. Paget Toynbee, 1905, xv, p. 110 (1792), p. 327 (1794). **(6)** See the preface to the sale catalogue for a genealogical note of the ownerships.

1078 THE DEPOSITION

Christ is mourned by the Virgin, S. John, S. Anne (?), the Magdalen (M.A.M.A. on her headdress) and two Holy Women. In the background, SS. Joseph of Arimathaea and Nicodemus are leaving the Tomb.

Reasonably held to be one panel from an altarpiece.

Oak, painted surface, $24\frac{3}{4} \times 24\frac{1}{2}$ (0·63 × 0·62).

The picture has suffered somewhat from neglect; unskilful repairs on the figure of Christ, the faces of the Virgin and S. John, and elsewhere. The rubbed appearance of the whole is due partly to undercleaning; dirt left in the hollows accentuates the grainy look. Much of the gold round the Virgin's head is new.

For the attribution and dating, see the note to No. 1079. The figure of the Magdalen suggests the influence of Massys.

VERSIONS: Several designs are known, more or less related in whole or part, by David or his following; e.g. (inverted) in the *Virgin of Seven Sorrows* by 'Ysenbrandt' at Bruges, Notre Dame.[1]

PROVENANCE: A label with *King* (?) | *157* on the back.[2] Coll. Karl Aders, a German merchant living in London, 1831[3]; Aders Exhibition, No. 49[4]; Sale, 1 August, 1835 (lot 102), bt. Dr. Willis. Coll. J. H. Green, Hadley[5]; exhibited at Manchester, 1857 (Provisional Catalogue, No. 483; Definitive Catalogue, No. 449)[6]; bequeathed by Mrs. Joseph H. Green, 1880.

REPRODUCTION: *Illustrations, Continental Schools*, 1937, p. 86. *Plates, Early Netherlandish School*, 1947, Plate 23.

REFERENCES: *General:* Bodenhausen, *Gerard David*, 1905, No. 41, as not autograph and of *ca.* 1515/23. Friedländer, Vol. VI, No. 194.

In text: **(1)** See further in the compiler's *The National Gallery* (*Les Primitifs Flamands, Corpus*), Vol. I, 1953, p. 90; and V. Loewinson-Lessing and N. Nicouline, *Le Musée de l'Ermitage, Leningrad* (*Les Primitifs Flamands, Corpus*), 1965, pp. 21 ff., No. 109. **(2)** Cf. No. 1079, and Follower of Massys, No. 1081. The compiler has consulted the catalogues of several King sales (Lugt 12399, 14278, 14318, 14469, 20044), without identifying these pictures there. **(3)** Passavant, *Kunstreise*, 1833, p. 96, as School of van Eyck. **(4)** For this exhibition, see Style of Albrecht Bouts, No. 1083, note 5. **(5)** Waagen, *Treasures*, 1854, ii pp. 459/60, as Rogier van der Weyden the Younger, but connecting it in style with the Bruges *Baptism* (by David, at that time unknown). **(6)** As Rogier van der Weyden.

1079 THE ADORATION OF THE KINGS

Balthazar (the Moorish King) wears at his belt a purse with the letters AW. OUVVATER has been scratched into the paint at the left-hand bottom corner. Comment on these two points is made below.

Reasonably held to be one panel from an altarpiece.

Oak painted surface, $23\frac{1}{2} \times 23$ (0·595 × 0·585).

In similar condition to No. 1078, but the damage is on less important parts; chiefly in the foreground and on the dresses of the kneeling Kings, though there is some damage to their hair also. Further, the picture is hardly affected by undercleaning (the worst part is on the green cloak of Balthazar), so the appearance is rather different. The gold seems mostly original. There are *pentimenti* in the drapery on which Christ is sitting, and in the back of the stone seat.

Nos. 1078 and 1079 have been in the same collections since the first record of them in 1831, are very nearly of the same size, and very much in the same style; they are therefore probably parts of one altarpiece.[1] The attribution to David is accepted by Friedländer; it depends on the supposition that after joining the Antwerp Guild in 1515 (see the biography above), he clarified his palette in imitation of Massys. No certain works by David from after 1515 are known, but these have as a good a claim as any to be ascribed to him. Compare the style of Bodenhausen, No. 40.

The letters AW on Balthazar's wallet are probably mere ornament, perhaps a tasteless application of *AΩ*[2]; Hulin[3] considers them a signature, and somewhat fantastically connects this picture with a painter Arend Winne, mentioned in documents at Ghent in 1511. The same letters AW appear on the headdress of the principal temptress in an altarpiece of S. Anthony by the Master of Kappenberg.[4] The difficulty of accepting all letters on wallets as signatures is exemplified by the EV on the Oultremont Triptych, referred to in the biography of Mostaert. A genuine case is the L in an engraving by Lucas van Leyden.[5]

The word OUVVATER has been scratched into the paint in the left-hand bottom corner; this was done long after the paint was dry, perhaps *ca.* 1800 (?), though it is hard to see why.[6]

As Conway[7] remarks, the entrance to the town in the background reappears with variations in two *Nativities*, reproduced by Bodenhausen.[8]

VERSIONS: A larger copy, stated to be signed by Damianus Van der Goude (presumably Damiaen van Gouda), and dated 1555, exists in Spain.[9] Friedländer[10] mentions a workshop copy in Spain. Two differing designs of the subject by David are at Munich and Brussels.

PROVENANCE: A label with *King* (?) | *157* on the back.[11] Coll. Karl Aders, a German merchant living in London, 1831[12]; Aders Exhibition, No. 50[13]; Sale 1 August, 1835 (lot 103), bt. Dr. Willis. Coll. J. H. Green, Hadley,[14] exhibited at Manchester, 1857 (Provisional Catalogue, No. 482; Definitive Catalogue, No. 415); bequeathed by Mrs. Joseph H. Green, 1880.

REPRODUCTION: *Illustrations, Continental Schools*, 1937, p. 87. *Plates, Early Netherlandish School*, 1947, Plate 24.

REFERENCES: *General:* Bodenhausen, *Gerard David*, 1905, No. 38, as mostly not autograph and *ca.* 1515/23; Friedländer, Vol. VI, No. 182.

In text: **(1)** In the past, some doubts have been raised if No. 1078 and 1079 are by the same hand; see in the compiler's *The National Gallery* (*Les Primitifs Flamands, Corpus*), Vol. I, 1953, pp. 89 and 93/4. In infra-red photographs, the underdrawing of No. 1079 shows clearly, that of No. 1078 very little. **(2)** *AΩ* is properly used with the Head of Christ on Christus, No. 2593. **(3)** Hulin *Catalogue Critique*, 1902, No. 343. **(4)** In S. Victor's, Xanten; reproduced in the Düsseldorf Exhibition, 1904, Memorial Volume, Plate 43. The fact was pointed out by Crowe and Cavalcaselle, *Les Anciens Peintres Flamands*, 1862/3, ii, p. 64. **(5)** Reproduced by N. Beets, *Lucas de Leyde*, 1910, Plate IV. **(6)** Nevertheless, it is claimed to be a signature by Armstrong, *Notes on the National Gallery*, 1887, p. 29, and by Conway, *The Van Eycks*, 1921, p. 289. **(7)** Conway, *The Van Eycks*, 1921, p. 283. **(8)** Bodenhausen, Nos. 2 and 3; Budapest, and ex-Kaufmann, now Pannwitz Collection. **(9)** Owned by a friend of Eduardo Díaz, Huelva, 1924; photo in the Gallery archives. **(10)** Friedländer, Vol. VI, No. 182a. **(11)** Cf. No. 1078, and Follower of Massys, No. 1081. **(12)** Passavant, *Kunstreise*, 1833, p. 95. **(13)** For this exhibition, see Style of Albrecht Bouts, No. 1083, note 5. **(14)** Waagen, *Treasures*, 1854, ii, p. 459.

1432 THE VIRGIN AND CHILD WITH SAINTS AND DONOR

In a walled garden (the Hortus Conclusus) the Virgin and Child are seated centre. Right, S. Barbara with an ornament in the form of a tower on her forehead, an unfinished tower in the background; and the Magdalen with M(?)MA on her vase, MAGDALEN on her head-band. Left, S. Catherine, her wheel by the pillar behind, receives a ring from the Infant Christ. The donor (Richardus de Capella) kneels in front; a coat of arms on the collar of a dog on the ground before him; nearby, a staff with figures of the Trinity and two adorers. In the background (left) an angel gathering grapes (?), (right centre) S. Anthony Abbot.

Oak, painted surface, $41\frac{3}{4} \times 56\frac{3}{4}$ (1·06 × 1·44).

The damage to this picture, though considerable, has been exaggerated. It suffers all over, especially in the shadows, from heavy cracking. There is a good deal of repaint especially in the flesh: the disturbing parts are the Magdalen's head, the fingers of her right hand, the shadowed part of S. Barbara's head, the neck and chin of the Virgin and the eyes of the Child. The numerous brown points, especially on the donor's surplice, are small restorations which have changed colour with time. The Virgin's right hand and the drapery above are badly over-cleaned. Several *pentimenti*, especially towards the right; the fingers of the Magdalen's right hand were originally stretched upwards, changes in her collar and head-dress, S. Barbara's collar was once rounded at the neck, some changes in the outlines of the Child, etc.

This picture is stated to come from the altar of S. Catherine in the chapel of S. Anthony in S. Donatian's at Bruges; the donor is claimed to be Richardus de Capella (Richard de Visch de la Chapelle). This is not proved, but is almost certainly correct. Weale[1] says that No. 1432 remained on the altar of S. Catherine in S. Donatian's until 1793; this, if proved, would be decisive for the provenance. In the present state of knowledge, confirmation of the provenance is found in the identification of the donor, which is reasonably certain. The arms on the dog's collar in the picture correspond with those of de Visch.[2] That the donor is Richard, and not another member of the family, is indicated by the staff shown on the ground in No. 1432; this corresponds well with the description of a cantor's staff in inventories of S. Donatian's,[3] and Richard (still young in 1444, died 1511) became cantor of S. Donatian's in 1463.[4] He was associated with the chapel of S. Anthony there,[5] and the chaplaincy that he founded is stated to have been at the altar of S. Catherine in this chapel[6]; since there is no reasonable doubt that S. Catherine of Alexandria and S. Anthony Abbot are meant, the presence of these two saints in No. 1432 is confirmation of the provenance claimed.

On historical grounds, the date would be probably between 1500 (when Richard obtained leave to restore the chapel of S. Anthony[7]) and 1511 (date of his death). Bodenhausen[8] thinks the picture was probably not painted until *ca.* 1505/9. The style agrees well enough with that of the altarpiece of 1509 at Rouen.

There is no documentation for the attribution.

The emblematic ornament of S. Barbara may be compared with what David did on his altarpiece at Rouen.[9]

PROVENANCE: As already mentioned, stated to have remained on the altar of S. Catherine in S. Donatian's, Bruges, until 1793. Stated to have been in the chapel of the Marchese Giustiniani in Italy,[10] it appeared in the Edward O(utran) *et al.* Sale, Paris, 18 January, 1877 (lot 7), bought by a dealer who sold it to Lebrun. Coll. Baron de Beurnonville, Paris; exhibited at the Musée des Arts Décoratifs, August, 1878 (No. 116); Sale, Paris, 14–16 May, 1881 (lot 287). Coll. Mrs. Lyne Stephens,[11] Paris, by whom bequeathed, 1895.

REPRODUCTION: *Illustrations, Continental Schools*, 1937, p. 85. *Plates, Early Netherlandish School*, 1947, Plate 25.

REFERENCES: *General:* Weale, *Gerard David*, 1895, pp. 15 ff. Bodenhausen, *Gerard David* 1905, No. 27. Friedländer, Vol. VI, No. 216.

In text: **(1)** Weale in *The Academy*, 19 October, 1878, p. 391. **(2)** Weale, p. 16, says that the shield contains in chief the arms of van Axele; but this is a mistake. **(3)** See *Le Beffroi*, I, p. 337. **(4)** *Le Beffroi*, Vol. II, 1864/5, p. 121. **(5)** Cf. the compiler's *The National Gallery* (*Les Primitifs Flamands, Corpus*), Vol. I, 1953, p. 102. **(6)** Jacobus Beernaerts (?), *Compendium Chronologicum Episcoporum Brugensium*, 1731, p. 160. Details about Richard's devotion to S. Catherine of Alexandria may be found in the compiler's *The National Gallery, cit.*, pp. 99 ff. **(7)** The compiler's *The National Gallery, cit.*, p. 102. **(8)** Bodenhausen, No. 27. **(9)** The taste may further be compared in the picture by the Master of the Virgo inter Virgines at Amsterdam (Friedländer, Vol. V, plate XLI). **(10)** Cf. *L'Art*, Vol. I of 3rd year, 1877, pp. 113 ff. It seems probable that the picture was in the Giustiniani chapel for a time; but the claim in the sale catalogue that it was painted for it need not be taken seriously. **(11)** Mrs. Lyne Stephens had been a dancer, Yolande-Marie-Louise, known as Pauline, Duvernay; there is a short essay on her by C. W. Beaumont, *Three French Dancers of the 19th Century*, 1935. She is mentioned in *The Ingoldsby Legends*.

3067 CHRIST NAILED TO THE CROSS

A skull and bone in the foreground (to indicate Golgotha).

Oak, painted surface, 19 × 37 (0·485 × 0·94).

Much damaged, especially on the right-hand side, from flaking and wearing; unskilful repairs.

The picture is reasonably held to be the central panel of a small altarpiece, the wings of which are at Antwerp, Nos. 179, 180; on the new frame of one of these are the arms of Adolphe de Bourgogne, illegitimate great-grandson of Philip the Good, Golden Fleece 1516, died 1540.[1]

The subject is rather unusual, without being rare; it occurs in Memlinc's *Passion Scenes* at Turin and elsewhere. The dog sniffing a skull recurs without much variation in a picture in the Thyssen collection.[2]

The picture is generally accepted as a very early work of David with reminiscences of early 'Dutch' rather than Bruges style. The rather slight indications of the costume of the main figures are not in disaccord with a date in the early 1480's.[3] The costume of the small figures in the background is confused in style, and seems to be a partial modernization of something earlier; it is possible that the source freely used by David is the last row of figures, beneath and between Christ and the bad thief, in *The Crucifixion* ascribed to Hubert van Eyck at New York.[4] The picture is clearly less Davidian in style than the Escorial miniatures of 1486; presumably several years earlier.

PROVENANCE: On the back a seal with (LU)OGO. PIO. DI. N. S. D(I. L)ORETO. FIDEL. Bought by Sir Austen Henry Layard from Count (Ercole ?) di Thiene, Vicenza,[5] probably *ca.* 1860.[6] Exhibited at the British Institution, 1862 (No. 101)[7] and at the South Kensington Museum, 1869 (No. 17).[8] Thence transferred to Dublin for some years, and then to Venice, probably in 1875/6.[9] Layard Bequest, 1916. Exhibited at the R.A., 1927 (No. 95); David Exhibition, Arts Council, 1949 (No. 4).

REPRODUCTION: *Illustrations, Continental Schools*, 1937, p. 86. *Plates, Early Netherlandish School*, 1947, Plate 27.

REFERENCES: *General:* Bodenhausen, *Gerard David*, 1905, No. 1. Friedländer, Vol. VI, No. 162.

In text: **(1)** According to van Mander, Adolphe de Bourgogne was a patron of Gossaert, and the former ascription of the Antwerp panels to Gossaert is perhaps not unconnected with the presence of these arms. **(2)** Friedländer, Vol. VI, Plate LXXXIII. A comparable motive occurs in the name-piece of the Master of the Bruges Passion Scenes, in S. Sauveur, Bruges. **(3)** Notes on the costume, by Mrs. Newton, are in the Gallery Archives. **(4)** Reproduced in the New York Catalogue, *Early Flemish, Dutch and German Paintings*, 1947, p. 4. See further the *Bulletin des Musées Royaux des Beaux-Arts*, Brussels, *Miscellanea Erwin Panofsky*, 1955, pp. 173 ff. **(5)** Layard MSS. in the National Gallery. **(6)** Probably the picture referred to in a letter of 11 October, 1860, printed in *Sir A. Henry Layard Autobiography and Letters*, ed. W. N. Bruce, 1903, Vol. II, p. 228. **(7)** As *The Crucifixion*, painter not given. For the identification, see Mrs. Jameson and Lady Eastlake, *The History of Our Lord*, 4th Edition, 1881, II, p. 133. **(8)** As Flemish School. **(9)** From information in the Layard papers at the British Museum.

Studio of GERARD DAVID

2596 S. JEROME IN A LANDSCAPE

On the crucifix, *i n r i.*

Oak, painted surface, $13\frac{7}{8} \times 9\frac{1}{4}$ (0·35 × 0·23).

Much damaged and repaired: the right hand, though cracked, is fairly free from repaint.

Several small *S. Jeromes* of varying design by David or 'Ysenbrandt' or in their style are known.[1] The execution of No. 2596 is weak; it may be in part by David himself, to whom it is generally ascribed.[2]

There is little evidence for the dating. Hulin[3] and Bodenhausen[4] call it early; Friedländer[5] rather early. It would seem nearer in style to No. 1045 than to No. 3067 above.

PROVENANCE: Coll. Léon Somzée, Brussels: exhibited at Brussels, 1882 (No. 139 *bis*), apparently[6]; at the Burlington Fine Arts Club, 1892 (No. 37)[7]; and at the Exposition Universelle, Paris, Pavillon de la Belgique, 1900 (No. 7). Exhibited at Bruges 1902 (No. 172), lent by C. & G. de Somzée. Bought with several other Somzée pictures by Agnew's, 1902[8] Exhibited, R.A. 1904 (No. 5), lent by Salting. George Salting Bequest, 1910.

REPRODUCTION: *Illustrations, Continental Schools*, 1937, p. 85. *Plates, Early Netherlandish School*, 1947, Plate 28.

REFERENCES: (1) Compare, for instance, Friedländer, Vol. XI, Plates LIX, LX. (2) E.g. by Bodenhausen, *Gerard David*, 1905, No. 6 and *sub* No. 9; Friedländer, Vol. VI, No. 221. (3) Hulin, *Catalogue Critique*, 1902, p. 45. (4) Bodenhausen, *op. cit.*, No. 6. (5) Friedländer, Vol. VI, p. 91. (6) As Memlinc. For the probable identification, see the catalogue and the *Chronique des Arts*, 1882, p. 155. (7) As School of David. (8) Geoffrey Agnew, *Agnew's, 1817–1967*, 1967, p. 42, for the purchase in 1902 of a group of Somzée pictures; No. 2596 is assumed to have been in the group.

Studio of GERARD DAVID (After HUGO VAN DER GOES ?)

3066 THE VIRGIN AND CHILD

The Child holds a rosary. On the wings: *Aue* | *Sanctissima* | *Maria mr̄* | *Dei Regina* | *Celi porta* | *Paradisi* | *Domina* | *Mūdi pura* | *Singularis* | *tu es Virgo* | *Tu sine pecō* | *Concepta* | *concepisti* | *Jh̄m sine* | *ōni macula*; and, *Tu* | *Peperisti,* | *Creatorem* | *et saluatorē* | *Mundi* | *In quo non* | *Dubito* | *libera me* | *Ab omni* | *malo Et* | *Ora pro* | *Peccato* | *Meo* | *Amen.*

Oak, painted surface, $12\frac{3}{4} \times 8\frac{1}{4}$ (0·325 × 0·21); wings, $16 \times 4\frac{3}{4}$ (0·405 × 0·12); including the (original) frame, 19×15, $7\frac{1}{2}$ (0·48 × 0·38, 0·19).

Rather damaged by cracking, but on the whole good condition. Cleaned in 1957. Much of the gold on the frame is new. Several *pentimenti* are visible in the outlines and in the Virgin's left eye.

A small altarpiece, perhaps for private devotion.

The manner of painting is characteristic of Gerard David, though it seems too weak to be from his own hand. The design is reminiscent of Hugo van der Goes; this is particularly apparent in reproduction. Morelli[1] ascribed it doubtfully to van der Goes; but Friedländer[2] says it is perhaps a copy after him by David. This seems likely; but the execution can hardly be, as Friedländer says, by David himself, and it is not clear if a lost painting or a lost cartoon by van der Goes was used. Another Davidian copy after van der Goes is No. 20a of Friedländer's IVth Volume.

Winkler[3] thinks it an early David, perhaps following van der Goes. Arndt[4] believes that it is a copy with cut field of a van der Goes, executed in the circle of Gerard David.

If the execution by David or in his studio is admitted, the date is on stylistic grounds later than that of No. 3067 above; it cannot be more exactly stated.

The prayer to the Virgin Immaculate on the wings is known from other sources.[5]

PROVENANCE: Bought in the autumn of 1872 at Madrid by Sir Austen Henry Layard[6]; transferred to Venice almost certainly in 1875.[5] Layard Bequest, 1916.

REPRODUCTION: *Illustrations, Continental Schools* 1937, p. 122 (with the wings) *Plates, Early Netherlandish School*, 1947, Plate 29 (without the wings).

REFERENCES: (1) Morelli's opinion is quoted in the Layard MS. Catalogue. (2) Friedländer, Vol. IV, p. 72 and No. 27 as perhaps a copy by David after van der Goes, or a work in common (?); and Vol. VI, No. 210, under David. Bodenhausen, *Gerard David*, 1905, does not mention the picture. (3) F. Winkler, *Das Werk des Hugo van der Goes*, 1964, pp. 231 ff. (4) K. Arndt in the Munich *Jahrbuch*, 1964, p. 82. (5) See V. Leroquais, *Les Livres d'Heures manuscrits de la Bibliothèque Nationale*, 1927, Vol. I, pp. 299, 336, and Vol. II, pp. 32, 190; also S.

Ringbom in the Warburg *Journal*, Vol. XXV, 1962, pp. 326 ff. (6) Letter from Layard to Morelli, 26 October, 1872 (British Museum, Layard Papers, Vol. XXXVI, Add. MS. 38966). (7) Letter from Layard to Morelli, 6 June, 1875 (same volume as for note 6).

Follower of GERARD DAVID

657 WINGS OF AN ALTARPIECE

(A) S. Peter and a Male Donor. *Reverse:* in grisaille, in a niche, S. Jerome standing, with the lion.

(B) S. Paul and a Female Donor. *Reverse:* in grisaille, in a niche, S. Nicholas restoring three children to life.

Oak, each, painted surface (obverse and reverse), $32 \times 10\frac{1}{2}$ ($0{\cdot}815 \times 0{\cdot}265$).

The grisailles are in good condition. The obverses are in a fair state, but suffer from past flaking. Some of the shadows and outlines on the faces of S. Peter and the Male Donor have been slightly retouched.

It is a work by a poor follower of Gerard David *ca.* 1525 or later [1]: the patron saints differ somewhat from David's style, but the donors are characteristic of his manner. The *S. Nicholas restoring three children to life* has a vague relation to the design by Gerard David once in the Loyd Collection and now at Edinburgh.[2] A standing *S. Jerome*, mentioned by Friedländer,[3] is on a different design.

It was purchased as Jacob Cornelisz. van Oostsanen, with whom the style has nothing to do. This attribution was rejected by L. Scheibler,[4] who dubitatively assigned it to the region of David or of the young Mabuse. It was ascribed by P. Wescher [5] to Aelbrecht Cornelis (q.v. for biography).

COPY: A drawing after the donatrix by Degas was in the 4th Sale of Degas' Studio, Paris, 2–4 July, 1919 (lot 88a).[6]

PROVENANCE: From a collection at Bois-le-Duc.[7] Purchased with the rest of the Edmond Beaucousin Collection, Paris, 1860.

REPRODUCTIONS: *Illustrations, Continental Schools*, 1937, p. 72 (obverses). *Plates, Early Netherlandish School*, 1947, Plate 30 (obverses). The reverses are reproduced in *Paintings and Drawings on the Backs of National Gallery Pictures*, 1946, Plate 11.

REFERENCES: (1) This date is from the costume; note by Mrs. Newton in the Gallery Archives. The previously suggested date, soon after 1500, is too early. (2) Reproduced by Bodenhausen, *Gerard David*, 1905, p. 171; National Gallery of Scotland, *Illustrations*, 1965, p. 25. (3) Friedländer, Vol. VI, No. 174; reproduced in the van Diemen Sale, Berlin, 25 January, 1935 (lot 20). (4) Scheibler in the Prussian *Jahrbuch*, 1882, p. 28. (5) Wescher in *The Burlington Magazine*, 1931, i, p. 251. (6) Reproduced in the volume of illustrations. This was pointed out by T. Reff in *The Burlington Magazine*, Vol. CV (1963), p. 248. (7) N.G. MS. Catalogue.

JAN VAN EYCK

active 1422, died 1441

Perhaps born at Maaseyck, near Maastricht. 1422–4, working for John of Bavaria at The Hague; from 1425, for Philip (le Bon), Duke of Burgundy, chiefly at Bruges but with frequent absences.

An altarpiece in the Cathedral of Ghent was, according to an inscription on it, begun by Hubrecht van Eyck and completed by Jan in 1432. Hubrecht was (it seems) a brother of Jan and died in 1426. During the last century and a half, innumerable attempts have been made to distinguish the work of two hands on the Ghent altarpiece; none has received general acceptance. P. Coremans, L. Loose and J. Thissen in *L'Agneau Mystique au Laboratoire*, 1953, pp. 120/2, say that their technical examination of the inscription leaves a doubt if it was painted at the time of the picture. So far as the compiler can see, the non-originality of the present inscription would do little to reduce the authority of what it says.

There are no reasons except 'stylistic evidence' for attributing any other existing works to Hubrecht; from 1432 onwards there are many pictures signed and dated by Jan. The triptych at Dresden has fairly recently been found to be signed and dated; see the Dresden catalogue, *Niederländische Malerei 15. und 16. Jahrhundert*, 1966, pp. 29 ff.

Earlier Eyckish works are first and foremost a series of obscure problems. The most important (if they are earlier) are two groups of miniatures; some were burnt in 1904. Hulin, who had seen all the originals, attributes one group to Hubrecht, one to Jan, and dates them *ca.* 1416/7 (see *Les Heures de Milan*, 1911), but both attribution and dating are often disputed.

It is an exceptional characteristic of Jan's pictures that 'studio execution' is apparently unusual.

It is not certain in what way or to what extent Jan van Eyck's 'Realism' in reaction to the previous 'International Gothic' is original; see a brief note in the biography of Campin, whose attributed works are more primitive in style but not necessarily earlier.

For many centuries it has been repeated that Jan (or Hubrecht) van Eyck invented oil painting. This is literally untrue, but no doubt one or the other made some important change in technique.

Jan van Eyck has been famous from early times, but his style had less influence on his contemporaries and successors than might be expected.

The following books, usually with van Eyck in the title, may be consulted: Weale, 1908; Weale and Brockwell, 1912; Friedländer, Vol. I, 1924; M. Dvořák, 1925; L. Scheewe, 1933; E. Renders, 1933; Friedländer, Vol. XIV, 1937, pp. 73 ff.; Charles de Tolnay, 1939 (with bibliography); Ludwig Baldass, 1952.

186 THE MARRIAGE OF GIOVANNI (?) ARNOLFINI AND GIOVANNA CENAMI (?)

They stand side by side in a bedroom, her right hand in his left; he raises his right hand as for an oath. On a chairback by the bed, a statuette of S. Margaret (most probably); one candle burns in the chandelier. The room is reflected in a mirror on the back wall; the two figures are seen from behind, and between them are two very small figures in a doorway, one of these being presumably Jan van Eyck himself. The frame of the mirror is ornamented with designs illustrating the Passion; beginning at the bottom and going left, the Agony, the Capture, Christ before Pilate, the Flagellation, Christ carrying the Cross, the Crucifixion, the Deposition, the Entombment, Christ in Hell and the Resurrection. Signed: *Johannes de eyck fuit hic.* | . 1434.

Oak, painted surface, $32\frac{1}{4} \times 23\frac{1}{2}$ (0·818 × 0·597).

Excellent condition; small local damages. Many alterations in varying stages of completion, especially to Arnolfini himself; his raised right hand was intended in a different position, two fingers of his left hand have been drawn in to come forward over her right hand, there are probably three positions for each of his legs, etc. Among other changes, it may be noted that the mirror-frame was once intended to be octagonal.[1]

The picture is not to be considered as a work of pure portraiture. An elaborate account of the subject and its symbols is given by Panofsky.[2] Although no priest is present, he maintains that a marriage is really being performed; the statuette apparently of S. Margaret[3] and the single candle are symbols proper to a nuptial chamber. Panofsky interprets the peculiar inscription as 'Jan van Eyck was here (as a witness to the marriage).'[4] The gravid outline of Mme. Arnolfini is usually explained as an appearance due to the fashion of dress at the time; the mode would indeed explain the shape of her figure, but not perhaps the exact position of her left hand, which might however be a marriage symbol in the Renaissance taste.[5]

Giovanni di Arrigo Arnolfini, a Lucchese merchant, lived a great deal at Bruges; he seems to be first recorded in 1420, and he was buried at Bruges in 1472 (not 1470). His wife Giovanna Cenami (in French Cename) was a daughter of Guglielmo, a Lucchese merchant living at Paris from 1403; she seems to have died in 1480, though according to another record she was still alive in 1489/90.[6]

From time to time[7] it has been thought that the woman was Jan van Eyck's wife, on the grounds of a fancied resemblance to her portrait of 1439 at Bruges; this would make the man the painter himself, but numerous descriptions in inventories from 1516 onwards can hardly refer to any picture but this, and seem to settle the matter that he is Arnolfini.[8] They do not settle that he is Giovanni di Arrigo Arnolfini, no christian name being mentioned in the known inventories. Even in Bruges, other Arnolfinis are recorded in the fifteenth century. There was Michele, who was married and seems to have been Giovanni di Arrigo's brother; and there was Giovanni di Nicolao, perhaps too young to have a claim. It may be said that, in the present state of knowledge, Giovanni di Arrigo is the most likely man.[9]

Another portrait of Arnolfini is in the Berlin Gallery, No. 523A; the sitter was identified by comparison with No. 186. A portrait supposed to represent Bonne d'Artois, known in several versions, has been claimed to be derived from the lady seen in No. 186[10]; but the claim seems very dubious.

The picture seems to have some compositional relation to a *Lady at her Toilet* ascribed to van Eyck; a record of it is its representation, on the wall of Van der Geest's picture gallery at Antwerp, in a picture by W. v. Haecht, 1628.[11]

VERSIONS OR IMITATIONS: In the Aloisiuskolleg, Godesberg, there is a double portrait of the German School, assigned to the Meister der Aachener Schranktüren, *ca.* 1470; this is now covered with another painting, and is known only from a photograph taken from the back when the support had been (temporarily) removed. It is clearly derived in some way from No. 186.[12] Weale notes that an imitation, signed *Godefridus Johannis fecit anno 1581*, was owned by the Rev. James Beck.[13] A miniature of different subject by Loyset Liédet seems to show some reminiscences.[14]

PROVENANCE: Owned[15] by Don Diego de Guevara (died 1520), whose arms were on the shutters now lost; he gave it to Margaret of Austria, Regent of the Netherlands,[16] who died in 1530. Passed to Mary of Hungary, her great-niece and successor as Regent, who left the Netherlands for Spain in 1556;[17] she died in 1558.[18] In the Spanish Royal Collections, Madrid; in the Alcázar, inventory of 1700, with verses from Ovid on the frame; inventory of 1754; inventory of 1789, No. 871.[19] Claimed to have fallen into the hands of a French General (Gen. Belliard ?).[20] Stated to have been bought in Brussels in 1815 by Major-General James Hay, who brought it to England[21]; apparently on approval for the Prince Regent's collection at Carlton House, 1816/8[22]; from *ca.* 1828, housed for the owner by the grandfather of J. C. Wardrop;[23] exhibited at the British Institution, 1841 (No. 14); purchased from Major-General Hay, 1842. *Cleaned Pictures* Exhibition at the National Gallery, 1947 (No. 22).

REPRODUCTION: *Illustrations, Continental Schools*, 1937, frontispiece. *Plates, Early Netherlandish School*, 1947, Plate 31 (after cleaning).

REFERENCES: *General:* Weale, *Hubert and John van Eyck*, 1908, pp. 69 ff. Weale and Brockwell, *The Van Eycks and their Art*, 1912 (a revised edition of the preceding), pp. 114 ff. Friedländer, Vol. I, pp. 55/7.

In text: **(1)** See the reproductions (infra-red) and further comments in the compiler's *The National Gallery* (*Les Primitifs Flamands, Corpus*), Vol. II, 1954, pp. 117/8 and Plates CCLXXXII, CCXCVI, CCXCVIII. Also, in connection with infra-red photographs of other pictures by Jan van Eyck, J. Desneux in *The Art Bulletin*, 1958, pp. 13 ff. **(2)** Panofsky in *The Burlington Magazine*, Vol. LXIV (1934), pp. 117 ff.; see also his *Early Netherlandish Painting*, 1953, Vol. I, pp. 201 ff. Already claimed as a marriage picture by Karl von Tolnai in the Munich *Jahrbuch*, 1932, p. 334. **(3)** One cannot exclude that it is S. Martha. **(4)** Some criticism of Panofsky's view that a marriage is actually being performed has been made; but attempts to define the subject as something other than a marriage ceremony leave (apart from anything else) the peculiar inscription difficult to explain. P. T. A. Swillens, *In de Spiegel van Jan van Eyck*, in the *Nederlandsch Kunstshistorisch Jaarboek*, IV, 1952–3, pp. 70 ff., makes some restrictions. J. Desneux in the *Bulletin des Musées Royaux des Beaux-Arts*, Brussels, *Miscellanea Erwin Panofsky*, 1955, p. 133, goes no further than: 'du moins est-il clair qu'à l'occasion de ce sacrement, Jean (van Eyck) a exécuté le premier 'portrait-souvenir' du jour de l'union des époux'. J. De Baets, O.P., *Het Dubbelportret der Arnolfinis*, in *Schets*, 1956, pp. 332 ff., thinks that the subject is faithfulness in marriage; he says on p. 330 that the inscription might mean 'Jan van Eyck dwelt here,' which seems dubious for the Latin and of dubious significance. Maurice Nédoncelle in the *Revue d'Esthétique*, April-June, 1957, pp. 147/8, says that 'l'échange des consentements . . . détermine juridiquement le mariage des chrétiens'; while approving much of what Panofsky wrote, he denies that a marriage ceremony is depicted as taking place in No. 186, without a priest, not in a church. E Schiltz, *Van-Eyck-Studiën*, 1958, pp. 8 ff., thinks that the figures in the doorway in No. 186, shown in the mirror, are leaving and not entering the room (they are facing into the room): and that the subject of the picture is the evening following on the marriage, when Arnolfini and his wife are left alone with each other. **(5)** It may well be that, if she took away her left hand, there would be nothing to support the dress in its present position; there are many cases where it is clear that a dress is held off the ground by a hand alone. Yet it is perhaps not fantastic to suppose that the position of the hand is a marriage symbol; cf. the de Limbourg miniature for April at Chantilly. A less certain example is a double portrait, which may be a marriage portrait, in the style of Filippo Lippi at New York (reproduced in the 1941 Catalogue). Panofsky, *Early Netherlandish Painting*, Vol. I, note 3 to p. 201, supports this suggestion and adds an example from Rogier van der Weyden's *Seven Sacraments* at Antwerp. **(6)** See L. Mirot in the *Bibliothèque de l'Ecole des Chartes*, XCI, 1930, pp. 103 and 114; or better, L. Mirot and E. Lazzareschi, *Un Mercante di Lucca in Fiandra. Giovanni Arnolfini*, in the *Bollettino Storico Lucchese*, 1940 (offprint in the National Gallery Library). **(7)** E.g. by Dimier in the *Revue de l'Art Ancien et Moderne*, 1932, i, p. 187, and Jenkins in *Apollo*, 1934, ii, pp. 13 ff. M. W. Brockwell, *The Pseudo-Arnolfini Portrait*, 1952, also thinks the sitters are Jan van Eyck and his wife. This view is criticized in detail by J. Desneux in the *Miscellanea Erwin Panofsky*, 1955, pp. 129 ff. **(8)** For Dimier's very doubtful translation of the inscription ('Jan van Eyck was this man'), see the *Gazette des Beaux-Arts*, 1932, i, p. 423, and ii, p. 317 (Jirmounsky); and *The Burlington Magazine*, Vol. LXV (1934), p. 135 (Dimier), p. 189 (Sir George Hill) and p. 296 (Panofsky). **(9)** For more on these various Arnolfinis, see p. 120 of the compiler's book, referred to in note 1. **(10)** Cf. for instance L. Baldass, *Jan van Eyck*, 1952, p. 281, No. 22a. **(11)** See Weale and Brockwell, p. 197; reproduced by Weale, p. 176; Baldass, *op. cit.*, p. 284, No. 36, and figs. 79 and 80; *The van Berg Collection of Paintings*, New York, 1947, pp. 14 ff., with plates; S. Speth-Holterhoff, *Les Peintres Flamands de Cabinets d'Amateurs au XVIIe Siècle*, 1957, p. 103. For comments on the subject, see Julius S. Held in the *Gazette des Beaux-Arts*, 1957, II, pp. 74 ff. **(12)** See E. Buchner, *Das Deutsche Bildnis der Spätgotik und der frühen Dürerzeit*, 1953, Plate 196 and pp. 173 ff., or (with more detail) Eduard Syndikus, *Hochzeit und Tod-Ein Wiederentdecktes Bild*, in the *Zeitschrift für Kunstwissenschaft*, 1952, pp. 47 ff. **(13)** Not identified in the sale of 9–11 June, 1897, Lugt No. 55481. **(14)** This suggestion, made with reserves by the compiler in his *Corpus* publication, Vol. II, 1954, p. 122, is elaborated by J. De Baets in *Schets*, 1956, p. 328, his fig. 4 (with mistaken caption) being a reproduction of the miniature. It may be noted that the inscription on the wall in the miniature is a motto, but this can hardly be the case for the inscription on No. 186. **(15)** The provenance of No. 186 before it was owned by Major-General Hay in the nineteenth century has been disputed by M. W. Brockwell, *The Pseudo-Arnolfini Portrait*, 1952. In the compiler's opinion, however, it is beyond reasonable doubt. The evidence concerning the provenance has been dealt with at greater length by the compiler in his book (referred to in note 1), pp. 119 ff., where the texts of the documents are given. **(16)** In her inventories of 1516 and 1523/4. **(17)** In her inventory of 1556/8; it seems clear that she took the picture to Spain. **(18)** Vaernewyck, 1568, says she bought it from a barber; see Weale and Brockwell. **(19)** The descriptions in the Spanish inventories are short, but there is no reasonable doubt about the identity. Allende-Salazar in the *Archivo Español de Arte y Arqueología*, 1925, p. 191, suggests that the frame with verses from Ovid may have been burnt in 1734. **(20)** Weale, p. 70. This is a guess by Weale; it is likely enough that the removal of the picture from Spain to Flanders was due to the French army. **(21)** C. J. Nieuwenhuys, *Description de la Galerie des Tableaux de S. M. le Roi des Pay-Bas*, 1843, pp. 4/5. **(22)** See Oliver Millar in *The Burlington Magazine*, Vol. XCV (1953), pp. 97/8. **(23)** This information was printed in a letter from Lindo S. Myers in *The Morning Post*, 15 May, 1922.

222 A MAN IN A TURBAN

The original frame (cleaned in 1950) has the following inscriptions: on the top, . AAC . IXH . XAN., and along the lower edge the signature, . JOH̄ES . DE . EYCK . ME . FECIT . ĀNO . M°CCCC° . 33° . 2Ï . OCTOBRIS.

Oak, painted surface, $10\frac{1}{8} \times 7\frac{1}{2}$ (0·257 × 0·19); with the frame, $13\frac{1}{8} \times 10\frac{15}{16}$ (0·333 × 0·258). The frame is original, the sides being of one piece with the support; the top and bottom parts of the frame are separate, being fixed on from the front.

In pure condition, especially in the flesh. Rather marked craquelure.

Weale [1] and Christiane Aulanier [2] call the sitter van Eyck's father-in-law, on the grounds of a supposed resemblance in feature to Margaret his wife. E. Durand-Gréville and others [3] call it a self-portrait.

The words *Als ich can* in semi-Greek lettering occur on several of Jan van Eyck's works; they are said to refer to a Flemish proverb, *As I can, but not as I would.*

PROVENANCE: Inscribed on the back, *E Collectione Arundelia*(na); no doubt the picture in an inventory of that collection called van Eyck's self-portrait.[4] This inventory of *ca.* 1655 is a list of pictures taken abroad *ca.* 1643 by Lord and Lady Arundel; they were both dead in 1655. Their eldest son had died unmarried in 1624. Their second son was also dead, and had been succeeded by his son, later the 5th Duke of Norfolk; there may have been some division of property in favour of the last,[5] but all the pictures in the inventory were claimed by Lord Arundel's other son, William Howard, who apparently obtained them all on ceding his claims to another part of the Arundel Collection referred to as the Cabinet of Daniel Nys.[6] This William Howard was born in 1614, was created Baron and Viscount Stafford, and was attainted in 1678 and beheaded in 1680. Apart from any pictures, etc., Lord Stafford also inherited Lord Arundel's London house known as Tart Hall or Stafford House [7]; this house passed to Lord Stafford's son Henry, born in 1648, created Earl of Stafford in 1688, died in 1719. No. 222 is imprecisely mentioned at Stafford House by Vertue in 1720 [8]; there was a sale in 1720 (1721 ?),[9] and it is justifiable to assume that No. 222 was included in it. No. 222 is described in some detail, with a provenance from the Arundel Collection and from Lord Stafford, by Vertue in 1722/3.[10] It was then in the Collection of Mr. Broderick, M.P.; this was Thomas Brodrick, born in 1654, died in 1730, whose brother and heir Alan had been created Viscount Midleton in 1717. No. 222, together with most of the Brodrick pictures mentioned by Vertue, remained in the Midleton Collection until removed from Peper-harow for sale in London, 31 July, 1851 (lot 79), where bought by Farrer; purchased from H. Farrer, 1851.

REPRODUCTION: *Illustrations, Continental Schools*, 1937, p. 110. *Plates, Early Netherlandish School*, 1947, Plate 33 (both without the frame). The inscriptions on the frame reproduced by Martin Davies. *The National Gallery* (*Les Primitifs Flamands, Corpus*), Vol. II, 1954, Plate CCIV.

REFERENCES: *General:* Weale, *Hubert and John van Eyck*, 1908, pp. 68 ff. Weale and Brockwell, *The Van Eycks and their Art*, 1912 (a revised edition of the preceding), p. 112. Friedländer, Vol. I, pp. 52/3.

In text: **(1)** Weale in *The Burlington Magazine*, Vol. XVII (1910), p. 177. **(2)** Aulanier in the *Gazette des Beaux-Arts*, 1936, ii, p. 57. **(3)** E. Durand-Gréville, *Hubert et Jean van Eyck*, 1910, pp. 26/7, and in the *XXIIIe Congrès Archéologique et Historique de Belgique, 1913*, Ghent, Vol. III, pp. 67 ff. This appears to be the traditional identification. For further comment on this matter, and on the very doubtful claim that No. 222 was a pendant to Jan van Eyck's *Portrait of His Wife* at Bruges, see the compiler's *The National Gallery* (*Les Primitifs Flamands, Corpus*), Vol. II, 1954, pp. 130 f. See in addition E. Panofsky, *Early Netherlandish*

Painting, 1953, Vol. I, p. 198 and notes; Panofsky remarks upon the way in which the sitter's glance is turned towards the spectator, and inclines to accept the picture as a self-portrait. K. Bauch, *Bildnisse des Jan van Eyck* in the *Jahresheft 1961/2 der Heidelberger Akademie der Wissenschaften*, p. 114, favours the view that it is a self-portrait, particularly on the ground that Jan van Eyck's personal motto appears prominently on the frame, which might seem to imply that the portrait itself has a personal connection with the painter. **(4)** See the publication by Mary L. Cox in *The Burlington Magazine*, Vol. XIX (1911), p. 286, or Mary F. S. Hervey, *Life, Correspondence and Collections of Thomas Howard, Earl of Arundel*, 1921, p. 479, No. 129. **(5)** See Vertue's *Note-books*, V, published by The Walpole Society, Vol. XXVI (1937/8), p. 59. **(6)** Miss Hervey, *op. cit.*, p. 410; cf. also Miss Hervey's p. 473, and Mary L. Cox, *loc. cit.*, p. 282. The cabinet of Daniel Nys may have included the Arundel gems, which passed through the 7th Duke of Norfolk to Lady Betty Germain. **(7)** Vertue V (as in note 5), p. 26. **(8)** Vertue I, in The Walpole Society's Vol. XVIII (1929/30), p. 65. **(9)** Vertue II, in The Walpole Society's Vol. XX (1931/2), p. 84. **(10)** Vertue III, in The Walpole Society's Vol. XXII (1933/4), p. 9.

290 PORTRAIT OF A YOUNG MAN

He holds a roll of manuscript. On the stone parapet in front is inscribed, TYM. WΘEOC. and LEAL SOVVENIR, and the signature: *Actū ano dni . 1432 . 10 . die octobris . a . ioh de Eyck.*

Oak, painted surface, 13⅛ × 7½ (0·334 × 0·19).

Pentimenti in the outlines of the nose and cheek; the sitter's right eye was originally higher, and there are some changes in his right hand. Well preserved in general. Less dirty than would appear at first sight; the lack of transparency seems to be largely in the paint[1].

The sitter has been claimed not to be Flemish,[2] but there seems no doubt that he could be. Panofsky[3] claims that the inscription *Tymotheos* refers to the musician Timotheos of Miletus, and that the sitter is therefore a musician, Guillaume Dufay (*ca.* 1400–1474) or preferably Gilles Binchois (*ca.* 1400–1460). The student is referred to Panofsky's texts for the justification of this suggestion, which is attractive but is not proved[4]; it depends largely upon the claim that Timothy as a name does not occur in the Netherlands before the Reformation, which may well be true of Netherlandish citizens.[5] It should be added that Jan van Eyck for some unexplained reason adopted a sort of Greek lettering for his motto (see the commentary to No. 222 above); that Tymotheos (not Tymotheoi) is correct; and that Leal Souvenir in large letters had obviously some important meaning to sitter or painter. The peculiar form of the signature may also have had some special meaning.

COPIES: A copy on copper was in 1857 in the Lochis Collection at Bergamo.[6] Another copper copy was owned by Count Bertolazone d'Arache (presumably), and in 1857 by his nephew Count Castellani at Turin.[7]

PROVENANCE: A sign on the back, possibly the mark of a former owner, consists of a cross resting on a bar, at each end of which is a capital G, below and detached a spade-like outline; it was once wrongly read as containing three G's.[8] Bought from Karl Ross, Munich, 1857.[9]

REPRODUCTION: *Illustrations, Continental Schools*, 1937, p. 111. *Plates, Early Netherlandish School*, 1947, Plate 34.

REFERENCES: *General:* Weale, *Hubert and John van Eyck*, 1908, p. 63. Weale and Brockwell, *The Van Eycks and their Art*, 1912 (a revised edition of the preceding), p. 108. Friedländer, Vol. I, pp. 51/2.

In text: (**1**) A note on the technique, so far as it can be judged by means of X-rays, is given by A. Burroughs, *Art Criticism from a Laboratory*, 1938, pp. 178 f. (**2**) Weale, *Hubert and John van Eyck*, p. 64. (**3**) E. Panofsky in *The Warburg and Courtauld Journal*, 1949, pp. 80 ff. and *Early Netherlandish Painting*, 1953, Vol. I, pp. 196 f. (**4**) Some comments on it in the compiler's *The National Gallery* (*Les Primitifs Flamands, Corpus*), Vol. II, 1954, pp. 133 ff. (**5**) The possibility that the sitter was not Netherlandish has not been excluded. (**6**) Eastlake's note-book, Part I for 1857; see also the Lochis 1858 Catalogue, p. 247, No. CXLV, as Pontormo. (**7**) Mündler's Diary; inscribed Palma Vecchio on the back. It is possible, but unlikely, that the two copies recorded are identical. (**8**) It is reproduced not quite accurately by Weale and Brockwell. Brockwell in *The Connoisseur*, August 1955, pp. 12 ff., tries to prove that the mark (which he reproduces not quite correctly) was the personal cipher of Guglielmo Cenami. Guglielmo's trade-mark, which he reproduces, and which had been reproduced (perhaps better) by Mirot in the *Bibliothèque de l'Ecole des Chartes*, Vol. XCI, 1930, Plate I opp. p. 150, has some resemblance but is not the same. (**9**) Published by Foerster in *Kunst-Blatt*, 1854, p. 373, as Ross Collection, bought some time before. Karl Ross was a painter (1816–1858).

Follower of JAN VAN EYCK

696 MARCO BARBARIGO

In his right hand a letter inscribed: *Spetabilj et Egregio Dño | Marcho barbaricho q̄da Spe | tabillis dn̄j franzisẏ pº | churatoris S̄ti marzj | d̄d̄*; and lower down *Londonīs*, and in the bottom corners what seem to be the letters *f* and *n*.

Oak, painted surface, $9\frac{1}{2} \times 6\frac{1}{4}$ (0·24 × 0·16).

Cleaned in 1967. Somewhat damaged, but since cleaning the condition is not, as it was, untrustworthy.

Marco Barbarigo (*ca.* 1413–1486); he was Venetian Consul in London in 1449.[1] He became Doge in 1485; a medal of him as Doge seems to be posthumous, and in any case the difference of age is great.[2]

The inscription would make the date 1443 or later (Francesco Barbarigo became Procurator of S. Mark's 17 February, 1443 N.S.), and almost certainly 1448 or later (date of his death). It would naturally mean that the picture was painted in London,[3] where no follower of Jan van Eyck (*ca.* 1450 ?) is otherwise known to have worked. The letters f n are obscure.[4]

The style is near to that of Jan van Eyck (cf. the hand of No. 290). The picture was attributed in the National Gallery Catalogues 1911–1929 to Petrus Christus[5]; the style of Christus is known in 1446, 1449, and 1452 to have been different, and later on he seems to have become less Eyckian than before,[6] or at least not Eyckian as No. 696 is Eyckian.[7]

PROVENANCE: Seen in Venice by the dealer Sasso, 1791.[8] Venice, Manfrin Collection (being formed at the end of the eighteenth century); mentioned there by Eastlake, 1855/6[9]; purchased thence,[10] 1862.

REPRODUCTION: *Illustrations, Continental Schools*, 1937, p. 55. *Plates, Early Netherlandish School*, 1947, Plate 35.

REFERENCES: (**1**) See Rawdon Brown, *Calendar of State Papers and Manuscripts relating to English Affairs in the Archives and Collections of Venice*, Vol. I, 1864, pp. CXXX and l; Rawdon Brown thought that such appointments were only for one year. Dr. Ferruccio Zago of the Archives at Venice in 1955 kindly sent a photograph of the document; there is no suggestion that this document of 15 February, 1449, indicates the date of the appointment, or that the appointment was for only one year. (**2**) Hill, *Corpus of Italian Medals*, 1930, No. 449; reproduced Plate 84. (**3**) J. Duverger in the *Bulletin des Musées Royaux des Beaux-Arts*, Brussels (*Miscellanea Erwin Panofsky*), 1955, p. 104, objects to this, saying that London may merely indicate the sitter's dwelling-place. The compiler has been unable to discover any comparable example of a portrait, with the name of a town inscribed as the sitter's dwelling-place, painted in a different place. (**4**) Dr. Zago in 1955 suggested *fratri nostro*. (**5**)The attribution to Christus appears to be due to Crowe and Cavalcaselle, *The Early Flemish Painters*, 1872, p. 144; it is rejected by Friedländer (by letter). The picture is not mentioned in Cohen's article on Christus in Thieme-Becker. See also Martin Davies in *The Burlington Magazine*, Vol. LXX (1937), pp. 138 ff. (**6**) But Pächt gives a different account of his development; see *Belvedere*, 1926, pp. 155 ff. (**7**) Hulin de Loo, *Un portraitiste de style Eyckesque vers 1440*, in *Apollo* (Belgium), December 1941, pp. 8 ff., wrongly associated it with No. 2602 of this Catalogue (Netherlandish School). J. Bruyn, *De Levensbron*, 1957, pp. 129/30 (or 150), inclines to associate it with *The Fountain of Life* in the Prado and a portrait at Leipzig. (**8**) MS. letter to Sir Abraham Hume, copy in the Gallery archives. (**9**) Notes by Eastlake of 1855/6, in the National Gallery; presumably No. 353 of the 1856 Manfrin Catalogue. (**10**) As G. v. d. Meire.

GEERTGEN tot Sint Jans

late fifteenth century

There are no contemporary mentions of this painter. The source is van Mander (1604), who mentions an architectural painting of Haarlem Cathedral, and two pictures now at Vienna. There is also an engraving of one of the latter, with Geertgen's name, datable *ca.* 1621/30; see Hoogewerff, *De Noord-Nederlandsche Schilderkunst*, II, 1937, pp. 138 ff. The architectural picture at Haarlem is useless for stylistic criticism, and its status is uncertain; cf. E. Panofsky, *Early Netherlandish Painting*, 1953, Vol. I, p. 536, with further references; also the exhibition catalogue, *Middeleeuwse Kunst der Noordelijke Nederlanden*, Amsterdam, 1958, No. 94 (Pieter Gerritsz ?).

The name means the little Gerard, of the brethren of S. John (at Haarlem). He was born at Leyden; he died aged about 28; the approximate dates, born *ca.* 1455/65, died *ca.* 1485/95, have been deduced. The Vienna pictures have been connected with the gift of the right hand of the Baptist at Rhodes, 1484, by Bajazet to Pierre d'Aubusson, Grand Master of the Knights of Rhodes (Malta); cf. K. G. Boon, *Geertgen tot Sint Jans*, 1967, pp. 5/6. Pupil of Albert van Ouwater, whose only documented(?) work is at Berlin. Most of this rests on van Mander's sole authority: an anecdote he reports in his life of Geertgen is demonstrably false, but it is usual to accept his statements unless they are proved wrong. The possibility that he was an apprentice in Bruges in 1475/6 is claimed by Koch in *The Art Bulletin*, 1951, p. 259. See further J. Q. van Regteren Altena in *Oud-Holland*, 1966, pp. 76 ff.

The difficulties concerning Geertgen and in particular of ascribing to him No. 4081 below are indicated by Martin Davies in *The Burlington Magazine*, Vol. LXX (1937), pp. 88 ff.; but cf. Karl Œttinger in the Vienna *Jahrbuch*, 1938, p. 68, note 20.

Ascribed to GEERTGEN TOT SINT JANS

4081 THE NATIVITY, AT NIGHT

In the background, the Annunciation to the Shepherds.

Oak, painted surface, $13\frac{1}{2} \times 9\frac{7}{8}$ (0·34 × 0·25).

Painted up to the edge all round and probably cut slightly.

Cleaned in 1958. On the whole the lighter parts of the picture, which alone can be clearly seen, are in trustworthy condition. Leo Balet [1] says that it was somewhat damaged by fire in 1904; this seems by no means impossible.

The attribution to Geertgen is usually accepted,[2] but Geertgen's *œuvre* is difficult to define, and a comparison with the Vienna pictures affords no certainty.

It is an early but not the earliest treatment of the subject at night outside Italy. Meister Francke has obvious priority, but his treatment of the night is not naturalistic.[3] More nearly comparable, and indeed possibly connected, some pictures of the subject are reasonably held to be derived from a lost composition by Hugo van der Goes (died 1482).[4]

COPY: There is an old copy with a slightly larger field in a composite altarpiece, from Pedralbes, in the Diocesan Museum, Barcelona.[5]

PROVENANCE: Bought in Paris for the Richard von Kauffmann Coll., Berlin; 1901 Catalogue, No. 32[6]; exhibited at Utrecht, Sept./Oct. 1913 (No. 26), lent by Frau von Kauffmann; Sale, Berlin, 1 December 1917 (lot 106). Coll. Onnes (Castle of Nijenrode) by 1919[7]; Sale, Amsterdam, 10 July, 1923 (lot 6). Coll. Hans Tietje, Amsterdam, *ca.* 1923.[8] Purchased through Cassirer, 1925. Exhibited at Amsterdam, *Middleeuwse Kunst der Noordelijke Nederlanden*, 1958 (No. 21).

REPRODUCTION: *Illustrations, Continental Schools*, 1937, p. 134. *Plates, Early Netherlandish School*, 1947, Plate 36.

REFERENCES: **(1)** Leo Balet, *Geertgen*, 1910, p. 64. **(2)** E.g. by Friedländer, Vol. V, No. 1, Hoogewerff, *De Noord-Nederlandsche Schilderkunst*, II, 1937, pp. 176 ff., Ring in *The Burlington Magazine*, May, 1952, p. 147, E. Panofsky, *Early Netherlandish Painting*, 1953, Vol. I, p. 325, and K. G. Boon, *Geertgen tot Sint Jans*, 1967, p. 8. Baldass (MS. in the National Gallery) thinks No. 4081 is by a follower of Geertgen. There has been some tendency recently to associate it (within Geertgen's *œuvre*) with a *Tree of Jesse* at Amsterdam (ex-Pannwitz Collection); see A. van Schendel in the *Bulletin van het Rijksmuseum*, 1957, pp. 75 ff. This is not agreed by Boon, *op. cit.*, pp. 9/10. **(3)** Meister Francke's *Nativity* of *ca.* 1424 is at Hamburg; Catalogue, 1931 (No. 492) and Plate IV. **(4)** See particularly F. Winkler, *Das Werk des Hugo van der Goes*, 1964, pp. 141 ff., with a number of reproductions. Winkler thinks that No. 4081 is based, though with considerable variations from the other works he reproduces, on van der Goes. Cf. also K. Arndt in the Munich *Jahrbuch*, 1964, p. 98, note 92.

Also the commentary to No. 2159, After Hugo van der Goes (?); that picture is from a different series, with the Child lying on the ground. (5) Reproduced in *The Burlington Magazine*, Vol. LXX (1937), p. 89. Reproduced after cleaning in *Emporium*, November 1960, p. 219. (6) See also the Prussian *Jahrbuch*, 1903, p. 68. (7) See the Vienna *Jahrbuch*, Vol. XXXV (1920–1), Heft I dated 1919, p. 23. (8) Oral communication.

See also NETHERLANDISH SCHOOL, No. 1085

JUSTUS OF GHENT *See* JOOS VAN WASSENHOVE

HUGO VAN DER GOES

active 1467, died 1482

Probably born at Ghent, where active from 1467; in 1475, it has been claimed, he became a 'frater conversus' in the Rode Klooster, Brussels, but this seems rather to have been later, since he remained connected with Ghent until 1477 or even 1478 (see A. De Schryver in *Gentse Bijdragen*, Vol. XVI, 1955–6, pp. 193 ff.). He did not cease painting on entering the monastery. His teacher is unknown. Attributions are based on the Portinari Altarpiece in the Uffizi, mentioned as by Ugo d'Anversa in Vasari (1550), and on a composition of *David and Abigail* (known from copies), mentioned in van Mander, etc. (see Friedländer, Vol. IV, Plates XI–XVIII and XXX). The former is datable *ca.* 1475 or soon after, though there is some doubt about the exact year; a pair of wings on loan from Holyrood Palace to the National Gallery of Scotland are probably of towards 1480 (Friedländer, Vol. IV, No. 12).

The finest works of Hugo van der Goes are the altarpiece at Florence and an *Adoration of the Kings* at Berlin.

Literature: F. Winkler, *Das Werk des Hugo van der Goes*, 1964.

After HUGO VAN DER GOES(?)

2159 THE NATIVITY, AT NIGHT

In the background, the Annunciation to the Shepherds, and the Shepherds pointing to the Star.

Oak, top corners cut, original painted surface, $24\frac{1}{2} \times 18\frac{1}{4}$ ($0{\cdot}62 \times 0{\cdot}46$).

Cut at the top, where two triangular spandrels joined by a horizontal band *ca.* 1 in. across have been added to bring the panel to a rectangular form; the line of junction goes through the star. In bad condition.

The style cannot be accurately observed, but it is certainly of poor quality. It seems to derive from van der Goes (died 1482); but the execution seems later than 1500, perhaps considerably later.[1] Connection was van der Goes was claimed by Friedländer[2]; the picture was claimed with more detail by Winkler[3] to be a copy of a lost composition by van der

Goes, and this view seems likely. Winkler reproduces variants once on the Roman art market (now in the Galleria Nazionale, Palazzo Barberini, Rome—*Catalogo*, 1964, p. 26 and fig. 102) and at Evora, also a miniature and a drawing that may be connected.[4] Some parts of No. 2159 are less suggestive of van der Goes than others, so if it is derived from a composition by him, it is likely to be a varied copy; nevertheless, it may be the most accurate record known of a design of his.

The picture has some iconographical interest. For a note on Night *Nativities*, see No. 4081, ascribed to Geertgen; No. 2159 is from a different series, with the Child on the ground instead of in a crib. S. Joseph holding a candle appears frequently, e.g. in 'Campin's' *Nativity* at Dijon (by daylight). Panofsky[5] claims, and probably rightly, that this tradition is derived from S. Bridget. Mâle[6] says that it merely symbolizes the night time. The two women behind S. Joseph are presumably the midwives of the Virgin, Zelomi (Zebel) and Salome (S. Mary Salome); the hand of the latter withered on account of her unbelief.[7] These ladies are apparently rare in fifteenth- and sixteenth-century pictures, but they appear in 'Campin's' Dijon *Nativity*, in Daret's derivation of *ca.* 1434, and elsewhere.

PROVENANCE: Coll. Krüger, Minden[8]; purchased with most of the rest of the collection, 1854. Lent to the National Gallery, Dublin, 1857–1926.

REPRODUCTION: *Illustrations, Continental Schools*, 1937, p. 56. *Plates, Early Netherlandish School*, 1947, Plate 37.

REFERENCES: (1) A copy of a Bouts, perhaps of a somewhat similar style, is reproduced by Friedländer, Vol. III, Plate XXXVI. (2) M. J. Friedländer in the *Zeitschrift für bildende Kunst*, 1927–8, pp. 278/9, claimed that the prostrated angel seen from the back is a borrowed motive, he thought from van der Goes, and that the whole picture is reminiscent of van der Goes. (3) F. Winkler, *Das Werk des Hugo van der Goes*, 1964, pp. 119 ff. (4) Winkler, *op. cit.*, figs. 94, 230, 93 and 215. (5) E. Panofsky, *Early Netherlandish Painting*, 1953, Vol. I, p. 126 (with further references). (6) E. Mâle, *L'Art Religeux de la Fin du Moyen Age en France*, 2nd edition, 1922, p. 76. (7) Cf. E. Mâle, *L'Art Religieux du XIIIe Siècle en France*, 5th edition, 1923, pp. 210 ff., and Tolnay, *Le Maître de Flémalle et les Frères van Eyck*, 1939, note 17. See also the Religious Index to this Catalogue, Section 4, Nativity. (8) Catalogue, 1848, II, No. 19, as Claessen, at that time supposed to be the author of Gerard David's two Sisamnes pictures at Bruges. This explains why the 1929 Catalogue uses an impossible attribution to Antoon Claeissins, *ca.* 1536–1613. For biographical facts concerning Carl Wilhelm August Krüger (1797–1868), living at Aachen from 1830(?) until 1835, when he moved to Minden, see Wilhelm Karl Schmidt in *Mindener Heimatblätter*, June-August, 1953, pp. 62 ff.

See also Imitator of 'CAMPIN', No. 658

Studio of GERARD DAVID, No. 3066

JAN GOSSAERT called MABUSE

active 1503, died 1532

He or his family were from Maubeuge in Hainault. So far as is known, up to 1515 his signatures are some form of Jennin Gossart: from 1516,

Joannes Malbodius. He was probably the Jennyn van Henegouwe (Hainault), Master at Antwerp, 1503 and mentioned there in 1505 and 1507. 1508/9 (it is believed), journey to Italy, chiefly Rome. Then much at Middelburg. For the date of death, see J. K. Steppe in the catalogue of the Gossaert Exhibition, Rotterdam-Bruges, 1965, pp. 33 ff. In M. Gossart, *Jean Gossart de Maubeuge*, 1903, pp. 56, 143–4, there is what seemed to be reliable evidence that he was alive in 1533, probably dying that year; but this must be faulty.

His early style is an obscure problem. His principal early work is No. 2790 below: connections with van der Goes (?), David, Dürer's engravings and 'Antwerp Mannerism' are visible. There are a few more or less reliable signatures on other pictures and drawings supposed to be early works. Friedländer's theories on his formation are to be found in Vol. VIII, Vol. XI, pp. 73 ff., and Vol. XIV, pp. 111 f. Winkler's essay on the subject is in the Prussian *Jahrbuch*, xlii, pp. 5 ff.; he thinks the chief Italian influence at the time of his journey was that of Leonardo or the Milanese School, and he deals with a problematical signature in the Grimani Breviary. A further note by Winkler on early drawings appeared in *Old Master Drawings*, X, pp. 30/1.

There are many works dated from 1516 onwards; Gossaert was then one of the principal 'Romanists' in the Netherlands.

See the catalogue of the Gossaert Exhibition, Rotterdam-Bruges, 1965.

656 A MAN WITH A ROSARY (RIGHT WING OF A DIPTYCH)

Oak, painted surface, 27 × 19¼ (0·685 × 0·49).

Painted up to the edges of the panel except at the top.

Very slightly rubbed here and there, e.g. on the upper lip. *Pentimento* on the outline of the nose.

The right wing of a diptych: the design of what might have been the left wing, a *Virgin and Child* before similar architecture, is known in several versions.[1] Of these, a picture published by Bautier[2] seems to be of good quality; the size is not given. The version in the J. G. Johnson Collection, Philadelphia, No. 390,[3] is called by Friedländer a copy by an imitator, and in any case is on a reduced scale (21½ × 16⅛). The version at Nuremberg[4] (0·986 × 0·68) is a copy by Baldung, signed and dated 1530; the date might give a *terminus ante quem* for the date of No. 656. The version in the Prado, No. 1930 (0·63 × 0·50) is considered to be an original, but the background common to the above mentioned versions and to No. 656 is here of a different form. Unless therefore the background now visible is a later alteration, the Prado and the National Gallery pictures were not the parts of one diptych.

A. J. Wauters unconvincingly suggested that the sitter is Philippe de Bourgogne, amiral de Zélande and Bishop of Utrecht (1465–1524).[5]

Various rather late datings have been suggested.[6]

PROVENANCE: Purchased with the rest of the Edmond Beaucousin Collection, Paris, 1860. Gossaert Exhibition, Rotterdam–Bruges, 1965 (No. 24).

REPRODUCTION: *Illustrations, Continental Schools*, 1937, p. 198. *Plates, Early Netherlandish School*, 1947, Plate 38.

REFERENCES: *General:* Friedländer, Vol. VIII, No. 71.

In text: (1) Three of these are listed by Friedländer without a reference to the National Gallery portrait in his Vol. VIII, No. 35. A variant (not original) is at Bruges (H. Pauwels, *Musée Groeninge, Catalogue*, 1963, p. 67, No. 35, repr.); no attempt has been made to find other such derivatives. (2) P. Bautier in *La Revue d'Art*, 1925, i, pp. 89 and 91; the owner was at that time Baron de Terschueren, Brussels. (3) Reproduced in the second volume of the large Johnson Catalogue. (4) Nuremberg, 1937 Catalogue, No. 1000, Plate 241. See also E. Weisz in *Cicerone*, 1913, p. 536. (5) A. J. Wauters in *L'Indépendance Belge*, 21 September, 1902, *Supplément Littéraire*; cf. the entry for No. 656 in the catalogue of the Gossaert Exhibition, 1965, No. 24. The copper coin referred to, showing Philippe, is reproduced in *Oud-Holland*, 1922, p. 88, figs. 7a, 7b; the drawing in the Recueil d'Arras is Giraudon photo No. 11745. (6) See the catalogue of the Gossaert Exhibition, 1965.

946 PORTRAIT OF DAMIÃO DE GOES(?)

A number 788 (?) in the right-hand bottom corner.

Oak, painted surface, $9\frac{5}{8} \times 6\frac{5}{8}$ (0·245 × 0·165).

Good condition. *Pentimenti* in the knuckles of the left hand and on the tips of the glove.

Friedländer[1] calls it autograph; the hands are rather weak, but no better version is known, and it is justifiable to catalogue it as an original.

L. Reis-Santos[2] claims that the sitter is probably the Portuguese Damião de Goes, on comparison with his sculptured features on the stone with his epitaph in S. Maria de Varzea, Alenquer. Damião de Goes was a humanist and collector, 1502(?)–1574; he was often in the Netherlands and Northern Europe. Reis-Santos gives reasons for believing the date of the picture to be 1530–2.

PROVENANCE: In the collection of Charles I.[3] Coll. William Wells of Redleaf[4]; Sale, London, 12 May, 1848 (lot 40), bt. Evans for Scarisbrick. Charles Scarisbrick Decd. Sale, London, 18 May, 1861 (lot 456), bt. Emery.[4] Perhaps exhibited at the British Institution, 1863 (No. 88), lent Wynn Ellis[4]; Wynn Ellis Bequest, 1876.

REPRODUCTION: *Illustrations, Continental Schools*, 1937, p. 198. *Plates, Early Netherlandish School*, 1947, Plate 39.

REFERENCES: (1) Friedländer, Vol. VIII, No. 70. (2) Prof. Reis-Santos kindly sent the text of his communication on the subject to the XXIX Congress of the Fédération Archéologique et Historique de Belgique, at Bruges, 16 September, 1966. (3) His brand on the back; CR surmounted by a crown. This type of brand is reproduced in The Walpole Society's Volume XXXVII (1960), p. XIV, fig. 1. (4) As Holbein.

1689 AN ELDERLY COUPLE

On vellum (?), painted surface, $18 \times 26\frac{1}{2}$ (0·455 × 0·67).

Some slight damage to the woman's headdress in the shadows.

Friedländer[1] lists it as by Gossaert. The attribution was doubted in the 1929 catalogue of the National Gallery, but it cannot reasonably be questioned.

PROVENANCE: Possibly (C. Burrell) Sale, 21 May, 1808 (lot 120),[2] bt. Hill. Coll. William Wells of Redleaf; exhibited at the British Institution, 1824 (No. 28), 1837 (No. 50), 1839 (No. 22); Sale, London, 13 May, 1848 (lot 76), bt. Seguier. Exhibited at the British Institution, 1848 (No. 88), lent Mrs. Whyte. Derby, Midland Counties Exhibition, 1870 (No. 184), lent Capt. A. F. Dawson; R.A., 1879 (No. 219), lent Capt. A. F. Dawson, of Barrow Hill, Rocester[3]; purchased through A. H. Buttery, 1900. *Cleaned Pictures* Exhibition at the National Gallery, 1947 (No. 33). Gossaert Exhibition, Rotterdam-Bruges, 1965 (No. 28).

REPRODUCTION: *Illustrations, Continental Schools*, 1937, p. 201. *Plates, Early Netherlandish School*, 1947, Plate 40 (after cleaning).

REFERENCES: (1) Friedländer, Vol. VIII, No. 80. The attribution seems to have been first made by him, in the *Repertorium für Kunstwissenschaft*, 1900, p. 490. (2) In this and other sales and exhibitions as Massys. (3) Barrow Hill had passed by inheritance to Captain Dawson from Mrs. Mark Anthony Whyte; she had died without children, and left it to her niece, Louisa Jane Finch Simpson, who married Captain Dawson's father (information from Major Arthur Dawson, 1955).

2211 A LITTLE GIRL (JACQUELINE DE BOURGOGNE?)

She holds an armillary sphere, inscribed: I-I-I-A-A-N-N-R-R-R-P . . . . G–T-Y- (middle part rubbed away).

Oak, original painted surface, $14\frac{1}{4} \times 11\frac{1}{4}$ ($0{\cdot}375 \times 0{\cdot}285$). Complete painted surface at present, $15 \times 11\frac{3}{8}$ ($0{\cdot}38 \times 0{\cdot}29$).

The face is in fair condition, though some washes, e.g. on the lips, slightly alter the character of the modelling. The hair is mostly worn away. The neck, the headdress and the hands are much repainted.

Hulin,[1] without giving reasons, admitted the traditional identification of the sitter as Jacqueline, youngest daughter of Adolphe de Bourgogne, Lord of Beveren and Veere, and of Anne de Bergues. The date of her birth is unknown, but the parents married in 1509; if the picture represents her, it might therefore have been painted about 1520 or later, a date not discordant with the style and costume.[2] A further point is that, according to van Mander, Adolphe de Bourgogne was a patron of Gossaert's, and, in fact, two versions of a Gossaert portrait of Anne de Bergues exist, the identification of the sitter being certified by a drawing in the Recueil d'Arras. Though there is no real reason for accepting the identification of Jacqueline, it has on these grounds some plausibility. Jacqueline de Bourgogne married (1) in 1540, Jean II, Sieur de Paret, and (2) Jean de Cruninghem Vicomte de Zélande.

It may be mentioned that the armillary sphere seems to have been an emblem of King Manuel of Portugal.[3]

It has been suggested[4] that the pearls across the sitter's breast and shoulders are each placed on a letter A. The poor condition excludes certainty, but in the compiler's view it is extremely unlikely that A's were intended.

PROVENANCE: According to an old French inscription on the back, painted by 'Leonard de Vinsy.' Coll. Sir E. A. H. Lechmere, The Rhydd; Worcestershire Exhibition, 1882 (No. 87)[5]; (Lechmere) Sale, Christie's, 27 April, 1901 (lot 75), bt. Pottier. Toison d'Or Exhibition, Bruges, 1907 (No. 68); Paul Leroi (real name Léon Gauchez) Decd. Sale, Paris, 16 December, 1907 (lot 29), bt. Agnew. Purchased from Agnew's at cost price, Clarke Fund, 1908. Gossaert Exhibition, Rotterdam–Bruges, 1965 (No. 19).

REPRODUCTION: *Illustrations, Continental Schools*, 1937, p. 199. *Plates, Early Netherlandish School*, 1947, Plate 41.

REFERENCES: *General:* Friedländer, Vol. VIII, No. 75.

In text: **(1)** Hulin in *The Burlington Magazine*, Vol. XIII (1908), p. 100. **(2)** According to a note by Mrs. Newton in the Gallery archives, the costume is fairly precisely datable *ca.* 1522. **(3)** See, for example, the catalogue of the *Exhibition of Portuguese Art* at the Royal Academy, 1955/6, No. 83, 93, 103, etc. **(4)** Cf. the Catalogue of the Gossaert Exhibition, 1965. **(5)** As Jacqueline de Bourgogne by Gossaert.

2790 THE ADORATION OF THE KINGS

Gaspar kneels, Balthazar stands to the left and Melchior to the right; left centre, S. Joseph (with a stick). In the sky, God (in the form of the star), the Holy Ghost as a dove, and nine angels. Right centre middle-ground, the ox and the ass, and several shepherds; centre background, the Annunciation to the Shepherds (?).

On the lid of the chalice presented by Gaspar is inscribed (L)E ROII IASPAR. On Balthazar's crown, at the top, is inscribed BALTAZAR; lower down is a signature IENNI | GOSSART: |, the remaining marks, sometimes interpreted as DE MABV. . . . half hidden by the metal work of the crown, being probably decoration. Near the hem of the cloth Balthazar holds are inscribed: SALV(E) | REGINA, MIS, and VIT (see below). Round the neck of Balthazar's black follower is a second signature: IENNIN | GOS (   ). One of the angels holds a scroll inscribed *Gloria: in: excelsis: deo:* |. The capital of a column visible to the right of the Virgin is sculptured with the Sacrifice of Abraham: the other sculptures on the building are merely *putti*. On Gaspar's sceptre is a figure of Moses.

Oak, painted surface, $69\frac{3}{4} \times 63\frac{1}{2}$ ($1{\cdot}77 \times 1{\cdot}61$).

Excellent condition; some of the preparatory shading has come to show through the reds. The frame slightly covers the edges of the picture, but the picture itself has not been cut. There are *pentimenti* in each of Balthazar's feet and on some of the paving stones; a few small ones elsewhere.

As is usual in Epiphanies of the later fifteenth and earlier sixteenth centuries, the scene is a sumptuous ruin; nor is it uncommon for suggestions of the *Adoration of the Shepherds* to be mixed up with the subject. There can be little doubt that the star with its wide halation, from which rays and the Holy Ghost descend, symbolizes also God; the presence of the three Persons of the Trinity in an *Adoration of the Kings* seems to be an iconographical caprice. It may, however, be a throw-back to a rather unusual Gothic tradition. Thus, in an Antonio Vivarini at Berlin, God the Father, the Holy Ghost and the star separately appear, and an example without the Holy Ghost is reproduced by van Marle, *The Italian Schools*, vol. vii, fig. 122; but these forms are unusual. The nine angels are supposed to figure the celestial hierarchy, but Gossaert has not distinguished them by colours or inscriptions.[1] The column visible to the right of the Virgin appears frequently in Netherlandish *Nativities:* the explanation is given by Mâle.[2] The argument for identifying the young man standing behind Melchior as S. Adrian is not convincing.[3] It is supposed to be in the Netherlandish tradition for painters to represent themselves in odd corners of their compositions: it is therefore just possible that the small figure standing within a doorway behind the ox is Gossaert's own portrait.

As the picture is twice signed, there is no doubt about its attribution; but the date is disputed. The later placed marks on Balthazar's cloth are sometimes interpreted as a date MDVII. H. Pauwels,[4] however, has convincingly shown that they are parts of the *Salve Regina*, other parts being hidden by the folds of the cloth. The *Salve Regina* begins: *Salve regina*, mater *mis*ericordiae, *vit*a, dulcedo. . . . It may be mentioned that the *Ave regina cœlorum* (Timmers, No. 1037) decorates the edge of the Virgin's robe, with various parts hidden by the folds, in Daret's *Visitation* at Berlin (Friedländer, Vol. II, 1924, Plate LXV).

The painter after 1515 appears never to have used a signature Gossaert but always Malbodius; on the other hand, the dog to the right is clearly taken from Dürer's engraving of *S. Eustace*, which has been dated *ca.* 1500/1.[5] It is thus fairly safe to date the picture between 1500 and 1515. Some evidence is given under *Provenance* that it is not earlier than 1506. The legend that it took seven years to do may be neglected[6]; it is more useful to consider if it is likely to have been painted before or after Gossaert's Italian journey, presumed to be of *ca.* 1508/9.

The style is more primitive than in a characteristic Gossaert, such as the *Neptune and Amphitrite* of 1516 at Berlin. In spite of superficial differences, there is much in the picture that recalls Gerard David.[7] The larger angels are perhaps reminiscent of van der Goes (died 1482). The smaller angels are in the style of 'Antwerp Mannerism,' which seems to have set in very soon after 1500; Gossaert's relation to this movement is extremely obscure, but he is not likely to have undergone its influence late.[8] It is not surprising, therefore, that many authors have dated the picture *ca.* 1503/8, i.e. before the Italian journey.

Friedländer,[9] on the other hand, has dated it *ca.* 1512. The chief reason he gives is that the *Adam and Eve* on a small triptych at Palermo by Gossaert, which he says is in style very near to No. 2790, may seem to be taken from a design of the same subject in Dürer's *Small Passion* of 1510. Dürer's engraving is reproduced *inter al.* by Tietze and Tietze-Conrat[10]; the correspondence of the two designs is not very close. Further, several manneristic drawings and paintings, some apparently signed, have of recent years been brought forward as by the young Gossaert; if these attributions are to be accepted as earlier works, it might be difficult to date No. 2790 before 1508.[11]

Von der Osten[12] says that grisailles of *The Agony in the Garden* at Berlin and *S. Jerome* at Washington may well have been originally wings of No. 2790; this appears speculative.

COPIES: Several known.[13]

PROVENANCE: According to J. K. Steppe,[14] it is recorded in chronicles of S. Adrian's, Grammont, as the altarpiece of the Lady Chapel behind the choir; this is stated to have been built by Abbot Joannes de Broeder, alias van der Cruycen or van Coppenhole (1506–1525). Purchased in 1601 from Jérôme Monseau, Abbot of S. Adrian's, by the Governors of the Netherlands Albert and Isabella (following on their visit to the abbey in August 1600), and placed as an altarpiece in the Palace Chapel at Brussels, 25 March, 1603; it remained there until at least 1745.[15] It was removed by Prince Charles-Alexandre de Lorraine; in his inventory after death, 16 October, 1780 (No. 66); in his sale, Brussels, 21 etc. May, 1781 (lot 66), bt. de Cock (an Antwerp dealer).[16] Sale of van Fulens of The Hague at Greenwood's, Leicester Square, 26 April, 1788 (lot 111), probably bt. in.[17] On sale at Bryan's Gallery, 27 April etc., 1795 (No. 180).[18] Purchased by Lord Carlisle, and already at Castle Howard by August 1796[19]; Castle Howard Catalogue, 1805 (No. XVII). Exhibited, British Institution, 1851 (No. 1); Manchester, 1857 (Provisional Catalogue, No. 517; Definitive Catalogue, No. 436); R.A., 1885 (No. 230), after which transferred to Naworth Castle. Purchased from Rosalind, Countess of Carlisle out of the Temple-West and Loan Exhibitions Funds and the Grant-in-Aid, with donations from the N.A.-C.F., Lord Glenconner, Lord Iveagh and Alfred de Rothschild, and with the aid of a special grant, 1911. Exhibited at the National Gallery, N.A.-C.F. Exhibition, 1945/6 (No. 9).

REPRODUCTION: *Illustrations, Continental Schools*, 1937, p. 200. *Plates, Early Netherlandish School*, 1947, Plate 42.

REFERENCES: *General:* Friedländer, Vol. VIII, No. 12.

In text: **(1)** Contrast the picture by A. Cornelis in S. Jacques, Bruges, discussed from this point of view in *Le Beffroi*, I, pp. 1 ff. **(2)** E. Mâle, *L'Art Religieux de la Fin du Moyen Age en France*, 2nd edition, 1922, pp. 47/8. See further E. Panofsky, *Early Netherlandish Painting*, 1953, Vol. I, p. 277. **(3)** See Maurice Brockwell's monograph on our picture, 1911, pp. 8/9. The picture was at one time at S. Adrian's, Grammont; the object held by the rider behind has been called a hammer, to symbolize S. Adrian's martyrdom on an anvil. **(4)** Letter from H. Pauwels, 3 January, 1958. For the text of the *Salve Regina*, see for instance J. J. M. Timmers, *Symboliek en Iconographie der Christelijke Kunst*, 1947, No. 1035. **(5)** Tietze and Tietze-Conrat, *Kritisches Verzeichnis der Werke Albrecht Dürers*, Vol. I, No. 182. The architecture is said by E. Heidrich, *Alt-Niederländische Malerei*, 1910, p. 272, to be based on that of Dürer's engravings of the *Life of the Virgin*, one of which is dated 1504. This opinion is quoted with approval by Winkler in the Prussian *Jahrbuch*, XLII, p. 9; but the buildings are much more obviously connected with the style of Bruges, as seen in Gerard David's pictures. The dog in the centre is probably taken from an engraving of the *Adoration of the Kings* by Schongauer (died 1491). **(6)** This legend is referred to by Brockwell, *op. cit.* **(7)** Gerard David, No. 1079 of this catalogue, may be compared, provided that the irrelevance of its probable date, *ca.* 1515/23, is clearly seen. **(8)** See Friedländer, Vol. XI, pp. 73 ff. There is no characteristic example of 'Antwerp Mannerism' in this Gallery. **(9)** Friedländer, Vol. VIII, pp. 17 ff. More recently, Friedländer, *Jan Gossart* (*Mabuse*), *The Adoration of the Kings*, Gallery Books, No. 19, n.d., p. 12, says that a date shortly before 1508 or soon after cannot be decided with certainty, but inclines to the latter alternative. K. G. Boon inclines to *ca.* 1510 (see the catalogue of the Gossaert Exhibition, Rotterdam-Bruges, 1965, p. 23). **(10)** Tietze and Tietze-Conrat, *op. cit.*, Vol. II, Part i, p. 205. **(11)** Baldass, however, protests against Friedländer's dating for the picture, and puts forward arguments in favour of its preceding the manneristic drawings; see the Vienna *Jahrbuch*, 1937, pp. 120/1. **(12)** G. von der Osten, *Studien zu Jan Gossart*, in *De Artibus Opuscula XL*, Essays in Honor of Erwin Panofsky, 1961, p. 457. **(13)** See, for instance, Friedländer, Vol. VIII, sub No. 12; Bautier in *La Revue d'Art*, 1925, I, pp. 86/7, note 1. The copy in the church at Nethen is reproduced by Destrée in *Annales de la Société Royale d'Archéologie de Bruxelles*, 1930. For a copy in the Museo de San Carlos, Mexico, see the catalogue of the exhibition at Mexico, *Pintura Neerlandesa en Mexico*, 1964, No. 33, repr. For possibly yet another copy, see note 15. **(14)** J. K. Steppe in the catalogue of the Gossaert Exhibition, Rotterdam-Bruges, 1965, p. 40. **(15)** See Destrée, as in note 13, and Marcel De Maeyer, *Albrecht en Isabella en de Schilderkunst*, 1955, pp. 269–70, docs. 21, 22 (identity clear, although Gossaert's name is not stated); also Steppe, *loc. cit.* in note 14, pp. 43–4, with other references. De Maeyer, *op. cit.*, pp. 366–7, doc. 184, quotes a further reference to the picture of 1622, and gives another, later, on p. 117. On pp. 462–3, doc. 279, he gives the specific record that the picture was not destroyed in a fire of 1731 (document of Jan.–Feb. 1732, No. 25). For some description of the framework of 1603, see Léon Halkin, *L'Itinéraire de Belgique de Dubuisson-Aubenay* (1623–1628), in the *Revue Belge d'Archéologie et d'Histoire de l'Art*, 1946, p. 60. Dubuisson-Aubenay also mentions a copy of No. 2790, of reduced size, in Notre-Dame du Sablon at Brussels in his time. **(16)** In each case as Dürer. Cf. Maurice Brockwell's monograph, 1911. **(17)** See Brockwell's letter in *The Times*, 8 May, 1912. **(18)** Among pictures from the Calonne, Nagel, Reynolds and other collections. **(19)** See Whitley, *Artists and their Friends in England*, 1700–1799, ii, pp. 191/4. It would appear that Lord Carlisle acquired the picture early in 1796; 'Lord Carlisle has bought the large high finished picture by*,' at Bryan's implied in the context (*The Farington Diary*, unpublished passage of 20 March, 1796).

Follower of JAN GOSSAERT

2163 THE MAGDALEN

Oak, rounded top, painted surface, $8\frac{3}{4} \times 5\frac{3}{4}$ (0·22 × 0·145). Fixed to the original frame (regilt): overall size, $11\frac{1}{2} \times 8\frac{3}{4}$ (0·29 × 0·22).

In untrustworthy condition. There is a good deal of repaint on the face, and the hair is much worn. The mouth is in fair condition. The hands seem to be overcleaned rather than repainted. Several *pentimenti*, especially in the hands.

Formerly entitled *A Lady as S. Mary Magdalene*; but, as with several other sixteenth-century pictures in this Gallery, there is no reason to suppose it a portrait, especially as there is a halo.[1]

The picture is admitted as Gossaert by Friedländer.[2] The style is like, but the treatment is more *malerisch*, and both the colour and the drawing seem to be rather different. Kronig[3] made an unacceptable attribution to Scorel. The picture has an Hispano-Flemish air: but, as it seems to differ from all the known hands, this may be an effect of the condition. Perhaps it is the youthful work of a pupil of Gossaert.

PROVENANCE: Purchased from Thomas H. Mack, Lewis Fund, 1907.

REPRODUCTION: *Illustrations, Continental Schools*, 1937, p. 199. *Plates, Early Netherlandish School*, 1947, Plate 44.

REFERENCES: **(1)** Glück thinks it a portrait; Vienna *Jahrbuch*, 1933, p. 192. See also the commentary to No. 2615, Netherlandish School. **(2)** Friedländer, Vol. VIII, No. 25, as *ca.* 1515. **(3)** Kronig in *The Burlington Magazine*, Vol. XIII (1908), p. 227.

After GOSSAERT (LATE COPY)

1888 THE VIRGIN AND CHILD

In a niche with inscription: GE. 3. MVLIERIS SEMEN IHS̄. SERPENTIS CAPVT CONTRIVIT.

Oak, rounded top, painted surface, 12 × 9¼ (0·305 × 0·235).

The inscription refers to the words of God to the Serpent after the Fall (Genesis iii, 15). The Vulgate runs: *Inimicitias ponam inter te et mulierem, et semen tuum et semen illius: ipsa conteret caput tuum, et tu insidiaberis calcaneo ejus.*

The picture is a copy, perhaps of the seventeenth century, of a Gossaert design of 1527.[1]

VERSIONS: Among versions may be mentioned one with signature in the Munich Gallery; another is at Vienna.[1]

PROVENANCE: Purchased with the rest of the Edmond Beaucousin Collection, Paris, 1860.

REPRODUCTION: *Plates, Early Netherlandish School*, 1947, Plate 45. Not in the *Illustrations, Continental Schools*, 1937.

REFERENCE: (1) See Friedländer, Vol. VIII, No. 27.

JAN DE HEMESSEN *See* JAN VAN AMSTEL

KATHARINA DE HEMESSEN

1527/8–after 1566 (?)

Jan de Hemessen, a painter at Antwerp, was her father; she married in 1554. Guicciardini in his *Descrittione dei Paesi Bassi*, of which the preface is dated 1566, says that she went to Spain with Mary of Hungary (i.e. in 1556) and that she was still alive at the time of his writing. Several signed pictures exist. Mostly they are small female portraits; there is one of herself, 1548, aged 20; No. 1042 below has the latest date known. A signed *Rest on the Flight* is reproduced in the *Repertorium für Kunstwissenschaft*, 1928, p. 212.

1042 PORTRAIT OF A MAN

Inscribed: CATHARINA. FILIA | IOANNIS DE HEMES | SEN PINGEBAT | .1552., over another, apparently similar inscription or signature.

Oak, painted surface, 14¼ × 11½ (0·36 × 0·29).

Painted up to the edge all round.

A good deal damaged by overcleaning.

PROVENANCE: Purchased from James C. Wallace, Holloway, out of the Lewis Fund, 1878.

REPRODUCTION: *Illustrations, Continental Schools*, 1937, p. 155. *Plates, Early Netherlandish School*, 1947, Plate 46.

4732 PORTRAIT OF A LADY

Signed: CATHARINA DE | HEMESSEN | PINGEBAT | 1551.
Oak, painted surface, 9 × 7 (0·227 × 0·175).
Slightly worn, but the condition generally is very good.

PROVENANCE: Owned in 1901 by Lady Brooke[1] of Norton Priory, Cheshire, daughter of Sir Harry Mainwaring, of Over Peover, Cheshire; she died in 1911. Presented by her daughter, Mrs. D. E. Knollys, 1934.

REPRODUCTION: *Illustrations, Continental Schools*, 1937, p. 155. *Plates, Early Netherlandish School*, 1947, Plate 47.

REFERENCE: (1) Documents in the Gallery archives.

Ascribed to KATHARINA DE HEMESSEN

1860 A LADY WITH A ROSARY

Oak, painted surface, $9\frac{3}{8} \times 6\frac{7}{8}$ (0·235 × 0·175).

It is painted up to the edge all round, but the painted surface does not appear to have been cut. Condition good. The slightly rubbed appearance of the face is partly intended, partly due to undercleaning: but there are a few small retouches.

The costume agrees with a date within a few years of 1550 (cf. No. 4732 above). Wescher[1] is wrong in saying that the picture must be from before 1540.

The attribution is possible but not certain. E. Michel[2] thinks it probable on comparison with Katharina's earliest sure works of 1548. P. Wescher[3] ascribes it to her father Jan: this is unlikely. The picture is of a type characteristic of Katharina and not altogether unlike in execution. It has, however, some stylistic similarity to Netherlandish School, No. 622 of this catalogue, of *ca.* 1530: it may therefore be merely a work in an anonymous Antwerp tradition. Further, Simone Bergmans does not accept as authentic any unsigned picture.[4]

PROVENANCE: According to a label on the back, given by her mother to Julia E. Gordon; by whom bequeathed, 1896.[5]

REPRODUCTION: *Illustrations, Continental Schools*, 1937, p. 156. *Plates, Early Netherlandish School*, 1947, Plate 48.

REFERENCES: **(1)** P. Wescher in *Belvedere*, 1929, p. 41. **(2)** E. Michel, letter in the Gallery archives. **(3)** P. Wescher in *Belvedere*, 1929, p. 41; the attribution is not accepted by Baldass (*Städel-Jahrbuch*, 1930, p. 89). **(4)** Simone Bergmans in the catalogue of the exhibition *Le Siècle de Bruegel*, Brussels, 1963, p. 110. **(5)** As Anthonis Mor. Miss Julia Emily Gordon, who presented and bequeathed to the Nation various works by Wilkie and others, was a daughter of General Sir James Willoughby Gordon (who appears in the D.N.B.) and of Julia Lavinia *née* Bennet.

ISENBRANDT *See* 'YSENBRANDT'

JOOS VAN CLEVE

active 1511, died 1540/1

Master at Antwerp, 1511, where active: also called Joos van der Beke and Joos van Cleef. Confused by van Mander with his son Cornelis (1520–1567), who was known as 'sotte-Cleef' (mad Cleve).

Joos van Cleve is usually identified with the *Master of the Death of the Virgin*. The evidence (which is weak) is as follows:

(1) A publication of 1572 includes an engraving of a picture now at Windsor as a portrait of Joos van Cleve, painter not given; cf. L. Burchard in *Mélanges Hulin*, 1931, pp. 53 ff. It is not certain if this is a self-portrait, nor if the features are the same as in several presumed self-portraits by the *Master of the Death*, nor if the style of painting is the same as the latter's. As the subject is at best obscure, it may be remarked that L. van Puyvelde in *The Burlington Magazine*, Vol. LXXVIII (1941), pp. 151 ff., wrongly criticizes Burchard's notes on the engraving.

(2) Two altarpieces at Cologne and Warsaw (formerly at Danzig; for comment on this picture, see Jan Bialostocki in *Oud-Holland*, 1955, pp. 121 ff.), and a version of No. 2155 of this Gallery are supposed to include more or less clearly the initials J. B. (supposedly for Joos van der Beke). Drawings of the first two are reproduced in Wurzbach's *Niederländisches Künstler-Lexikon*, s.v. Scoreel; cf. also E. Firmenich-Richartz in the *Zeitschrift für bildende Kunst*, 1894, pp. 187 ff., or his edition of Merlo's *Kölnische Künstler*, 1895, Col. 1143 ff. For the third, see No. 2155.

(3) Friedländer, Vol. IX, pp. 25/6, makes a poor, strange argument from the appearance of the arms of Marck and Cleve on two of the versions of No. 2155 in this Gallery. Cf. Baldass, *Joos van Cleve*, 1925, note 76.

(4) Portraits of François Ier and his Queen exist, apparently originals or derivatives of the *Master of the Death*; and Guicciardini in his *Descrittione dei Paesi Bassi*, of which the preface is dated 1566, says that Joos van Cleve painted both these sitters.

(5) A further argument, but apparently not of great weight, is given by H. Gerson in *Oud-Holland*, 1955, pp. 129 f.

(6) The *Adam and Eve* in the Louvre by the *Master of the Death* is dated 1507, whereas the earliest sure mention so far discovered of Joos van Cleve is of 1511. (Valentiner in the *Gazette des Beaux-Arts*, January 1955, p. 5, suggests that he is identical with Joos van Wezele, a pupil at Antwerp in 1510.)

See the MASTER of the DEATH OF THE VIRGIN

JOOS VAN WASSENHOVE

active 1460–*ca.* 1480/5 (?)

The name is here applied to the author of a *Communion of the Apostles* (1473/4) at Urbino; the contractual documents and Vasari call him *Giusto da Guanto* (i.e. Justus of Ghent).

Although the Latin for Joos should be Jodocus and not Justus, it is difficult to believe that Giusto da Guanto is other than Joos van Wassenhove, Master at Antwerp in 1460, Master at Ghent in 1464, recorded at Ghent until 1469, recorded to have gone to Rome some time before 1475.

The essential books on this painter are: J. Lavalleye, *Juste de Gand*, 1936, with bibliography; the same, *Le Palais Ducal d'Urbin* (*Les Primitifs Flamands, Corpus*), 1964; and Friedländer, Vol. III (for stylistic criticism).

At Ghent, Joos was in contact with Hugo van der Goes, who may have been younger, but probably influenced his style. The few pictures associated with Joos in his Netherlandish period are all attributions, the principal being a *Crucifixion* in the Cathedral of Ghent; for this, see the *Bulletin de l'Institut Royal du Patrimoine Artistique*, Vol. IV, 1961, pp. 7 ff. The style of Bouts seems to have influenced these pictures at least as much as that of van der Goes did. There is some ground for attributing the *Crucifixion* to Daniel de Rijke; see A. De Schryver in the catalogue of the *Juste de Gand* Exhibition, Ghent, 1957, pp. 22 f.

The *Communion of the Apostles* at Urbino is a documented Giusto da Guanto (1473/4); the style shows a considerable difference from that of the pictures just referred to. The last known record of Giusto in the documents of Urbino is of 1475.

A group of paintings for Federico d'Urbino shows affinities with the *Communion.* Possibly the earliest piece of work in the group is Federico's praying hands on an altarpiece by Piero della Francesca in the Brera; the picture in which these hands are is well claimed to be not later than 1474, and it has been argued to be not earlier than 1472 (see M. Meiss in *Studies in Art and Literature for Belle da Costa Greene*, 1954, pp. 92 ff.). There are 28 *Heads of Famous Men* at Urbino and Paris (apparently finished 1476); a *Portrait of Federico in Armour*, most probably part of the same decorative scheme; and a portrait group of *Federico and others at a Lecture* in the Royal Collection.

Of these pictures, the *Portraits of Famous Men* and probably that of *Federico in Armour* (but not the others) are semi-documented. Vespasiano da Bisticci, 1421–1498, a Florentine bookseller in touch with Federico, and for a time his librarian, whose presence at Urbino is recorded in 1482, says that they are by a painter ('maestro solenne') brought from the Netherlands by Federico; his text is of weight, and presumably refers to Giusto, the only known Netherlandish painter at Urbino at the time.

Closely attached to the above group, but more Italian in style, are the two pictures, Nos. 755, 756 below, from a series to which two pictures formerly at Berlin also belong. As will be shown below, these probably date from the later 1470's or earlier 1480's.

It would appear that Joos is the only reasonable name as author, or at least production-overseer, of these pictures; but some others have been put forward. A recent attribution is (wholly or partly) to Pedro Berruguete, active (in Spain) 1483, died *ca.* 1503; first published by Gamba, it acquired some resonance from Longhi, was pursued (sometimes bitterly) by Allende-Salazar and Sánchez Cantón, and received the blessing of

Hulin and Berenson. It has been dealt with by Lavalleye, to whom the student is referred for the bibliography.

The *dossier* of the Berruguete case is as follows:

(1) According to a document referred to by Pungileoni in 1822, a *Pietro Spagnolo pittore* was in Urbino in 1477. The document cannot now be found.

(2) Pablo de Céspedes is sometimes said to have said that the *Heads of Famous Men* (Urbino and Paris) were by Berruguete. Céspedes was born in 1538 or 1548, and spent some years in Italy in the third quarter of the sixteenth century; he had a sporadic interest in the history of art, but on his own evidence not enough for him to read Vasari. The text in question is dated 1604. All this would render his authority poor, if he made an attribution to Berruguete; he does not, but says that the *Heads* are by a Spanish painter, 'other' than Berruguete.

(3) Some words on one of the leaves of a book held by Albertus Magnus, in the series of *Heads*, are (apparently) in Spanish. Sánchez Cantón, in the *Archivo Español*, 1933, pp. 146/8, lays some stress on this, without reaching any very coherent explanation; no definite conclusion may be drawn from it at present, but it is an argument for some Spanish intervention in the series.

(4) A *Beheading of S. John the Baptist* in Santa María del Campo has been ascribed to Berruguete (see Post, *History of Spanish Painting*, Vol. IX, Part I, pp. 101 ff. and Fig. 25). This picture certainly contains reminiscences of Montefeltrian architecture; it appears to be of unworthy quality.

(5) Finally, there is stylistic comparison; each must decide for himself. It may be remarked that pure stylistic criticism in this case is a good deal hampered by the bad condition of most of the pictures in the group.

In the present state of knowledge, Joos is seriously to be considered as the author of the group; Berruguete may be held to have assisted him. The critics who make attributions to Berruguete differ a good deal about which items they choose. Such uncertainty is not very surprising if the control was in the hands of a single painter; Bisticci clearly implies that this was so for the *Portraits of Famous Men.*

Lavalleye's conclusion in 1964 (p. 94) is that the *Famous Men* are by Joos with studio assistants including Berruguete. This volume contains much more on the subject than is included in the present catalogue, *inter al.* discussion of attributions to Melozzo, Giovanni Santi and Bramante.

755 RHETORIC(?) (FROM A SERIES OF THE LIBERAL ARTS?)

Inscribed across the background, DVX VRBINI MONTIS FERETRI AC (most of the D has been cut away).

Reverse: Drawings of a male torso seen from the front to the knees, part of the head visible; of the crupper and rear leg of a horse; and some unintelligible scribbles. They are in pigment on the unprimed wood, like some drawings published in *Dedalo*, and other examples in this Gallery[1]; they have been done across the breadth of the constituent panels, and are thus at right angles to the picture.

Poplar,[2] painted surface, 61¾ × 41½ (1·57 × 1·055). Painted up to the edges all round, but the top may be a true edge. Obviously cut at the left, where part of the D of the inscription is missing; possibly cut at the right, the C being very near the edge. It will, however, be shown below that the cut at the left side is slight nor is there any reason to suppose more than an inch or so missing from the right side.[3] A thin dark line under the bottom of the carpet corresponds with a wider space in the same place in No. 756; if a comparison were licit, a cut of a couple of inches could be inferred along the bottom of No. 755, but the original arrangement of the pictures, discussed below, makes the point doubtful.

Condition bad; the flesh in particular being much distorted by flaking, over-cleaning and (especially) repaint. The head of the kneeling youth has been changed slightly several times.

For *Provenance*, *Reproductions* and *References*, see No. 756 below.

756 MUSIC (FROM A SERIES OF THE LIBERAL ARTS?)

The kneeling youth may be Costanzo Sforza (see note 7 below). A spray of laurel hangs from the background wall; the top of the throne is ornamented with an eight-pointed star between marks suggesting lettering. Inscribed across the background, I(?) ECLESIE CONFALONERIVS. (the first I of dubious antiquity; it may have been originally an H).

Reverse: Drawings, similar to those on the back of No. 755, of a nude figure seen from behind blowing a trumpet, a standing nude figure, and unintelligible scribbles. As on No. 755, they have been made across the breadth of the constituent panels; but since these are here horizontal instead of vertical, the drawings are the same way up as the picture.

Poplar,[2] painted surface, 61¼ × 38¼ (1·555 × 0·97). Painted up to the edges all round. The top has the air of being a true edge, and the field of the picture at the bottom is greater than on No. 755, but the total height is less. The width is also less, and the foot of the kneeling youth is cut in two at the left; but the absence of an edge to the carpet on the upper steps (as on No. 755) is not an argument for cutting, as the original arrangement of the pictures, discussed below, makes clear.

Condition similar to that of No. 755, but slightly less bad; even on No. 756, however, there are hardly any pure places. The architectural rulings, incised across the ground, show a good deal at the top. There are several *pentimenti*. The head of the kneeling youth was originally intended to be a little further to the right, and slightly tipped downwards. Several changes in the outlines of Music's right hand; her dress was once a little further to the right near the top of the organ, which was intended to be wider. Some changes in the architecture, top right, are unclear (see note 17).

Nos. 755 (*Rhetoric* ?) and 756 (*Music*) are parts of a series, to which two other pictures formerly at Berlin, representing *Dialectic* (?) and *Astronomy*,[4] clearly belong. It is commonly said that the original series represented the *Seven Liberal Arts*; that it was painted for Federico di Montefeltro, and adorned his library at Urbino; and that the kneeling men and even the allegorical figures are portraits of members of the ducal family. The order of the pictures is said to have been *Grammar*, *Rhetoric*, *Dialectic*, *Geometry*, *Arithmetic*, *Music*, *Astronomy*; and an inscription across them is said to be recorded as follows: *Fridericus Montefeltrius | Dux Urbini Montis Feretri Ac | Durantis Comes. Serenissimi | Regis Siciliae Capitaneus Generalis | Sanctaeque Romanae | Hecclesie Gonfalonierus | M.CCCC.LXXVI.*[5]

A few of these points are, or may be, true; but the subject has been much confused by the statements of modern critics, passing for facts, and it is necessary to begin again at the beginning.

The parts of the inscription known are DVX VRBINI MONTIS FERETRI AC (on No. 755), DVRANTIS COMES SER. . . . (on the *Dialectic* (?) ex-Berlin), and I(?)ECLESIE CONFALONERIVS (on No. 756). The *Astronomy* ex-Berlin had no inscription; the picture had been cut down in the part where it should be, and a modern addition took its place.

The long text given above is not certainly or even probably the one formerly across the series of pictures. It is taken from Schrader (1592); but he was recording an inscription that still exists under the ceiling of the studio at Urbino.[6] The inscription across the pictures is, in the parts that remain, of similar form; the rest may have been utterly different. All that need be said for the moment is that *Rhetoric* (?) and *Dialectic* (?) must have been placed originally side by side, and that they were obviously preceded by one panel, on which the name was inscribed.

The kneeling figure on the *Dialectic* (?) ex-Berlin is Federico d'Urbino[7]; this is proved by the prominent position of his coat of arms as well as by a not very characteristic profile (in dubious state). It follows as probable that the other kneeling figures were also portraits, either of contemporaries or of 'famous men.'

Federico has been given the third place. No argument can be drawn from this subordination; for the loss of his right eye made it *de rigueur* to represent him in profile to the left, which could not have been conveniently done in the first picture of the series. But this first picture would have been, according to the theory commonly received, rather odd; someone—and it is generally supposed to have been Federico's son and successor, Guidobaldo—would have been kneeling before a wall prominently inscribed, FEDERICVS MONTEFELTRIVS.

The fragments of the inscription, most naturally applied to Federico, could also apparently be applied to Guidobaldo; and it cannot therefore be excluded that the words on the missing first panel were GVIDO VBALDVS MONTEFELTRIVS.

An argument against this would be that the kneeling figure on No. 755 is facing (more or less) towards Federico, and turning his back on the missing figure supposed to be Guidobaldo.

It would further be wrong to lay much stress on the oddity of Federico's name being inscribed above a different person; as will be shown presently, the first, second and third pictures formed a single pictorial unit.

The limits of date so far established are between August, 1474 (when Federico became Duke) and 1508 (when Guidobaldo died).

The subject of the pictures may now briefly be considered. *Rhetoric* (?) and *Dialectic* (?) are not identifiable on internal evidence. It is obvious enough that some series akin to the *Seven Liberal Arts* was represented; but the number of seven is not proved. In any case, the series of the *Liberal Arts* was sometimes (though not often) increased to nine, by the addition of *Medecine* and *Architecture*.[8]

The original location of the pictures is doubtful. As they are clearly of Montefeltrian *provenance*, it has been assumed that they come from Urbino; but they do not appear to be mentioned there. Baldi (1587), describing the Palace of Urbino, regrets that in the way of pictures he can record only the *Portraits of Famous Men* and a series of *Muses* (now Corsini, Florence); this is an indication that the *Liberal Arts* (?) were not at Urbino in Baldi's time.[9]

The Montefeltros had several palaces; after Urbino, the next in importance was at Gubbio, and there is some evidence that the *Liberal Arts* (?) came from there.

There was a studio at Gubbio comparable with the more famous one at Urbino. It was a little, high room; panelling (now in the Metropolitan Museum, New York) covered the lower part of the walls, but there seems to be no record of what decoration (if any) there was above. It is, however, probable that there was some. Not only is there the analogy of the room at Urbino; the following inscription runs along the top of the panelling:

ASPICIS AETERNOS VENERANDAE MATRIS ALVMNOS
DOCTRINA EXCELSOS INGENIOQVE VIROS
VT NVDA CERVICE CADANT ANTE ......
.... GENV
IVSTITIAM PIETAS VINCIT REVERENDA NEC VLLVM
POENITET ALTRICI SVCCVBVISSE SVAE.[10]

Although this fragmentary inscription is not altogether clear, several points in it would apply well enough to the *Liberal Arts* (?), if they were hung immediately above. One of the less obvious ones is quite strong; the text would apologize for the Duke of Urbino's somewhat strange homage to an Allegory.

There would have been room in the studio of Gubbio for seven—or more—pictures such as Nos. 755, 756[11]; if they came from there, a little might be added about their date. The panelling from Gubbio contains Federico's name, his Garter and his Ermine[12]; also the name of Guidobaldo Duke. The studio may therefore have been begun by Federico, and perhaps completed after his death in 1482 by Guidobaldo.[13] Pictorial decoration for it is most likely to have been done either in the last years of Federico's reign, or the first of Guidobaldo's.

An examination of the existing pictures leads to some conclusions as to their arrangement amongst themselves.[14]

If the subject was really the *Seven Liberal Arts,* there would have been the *Trivium* (Grammar, Rhetoric and Dialectic), and the *Quadrivium* (Geometry, Arithmetic, Music and Astronomy); it is a fact that *Rhetoric* (?) and *Dialectic* (?) are pictorially distinct from *Music* and *Astronomy*.

Thus, in the first group, the light comes from the left; the arch of the thrones is ornamented at the outside edge with twin circles; the throne has a round back; the upper mouldings of the dado, continuing round the throne, are separated by dark marble; and the other division of the dado, which forms also the arms of the throne, has no lower moulding. A glance at the photographs shows that these points are different on *Music* and *Astronomy,*[15] which, however, correspond with each other.

It has already been deduced from the inscription that *Rhetoric* (?) was picture No. 2, *Dialectic* (?) No. 3; the perspective of the thrones confirms this arrangement; and an enclosing wall coming forward on the right-hand side of *Dialectic* (?) proves that the group is finished.

Something about the missing first panel (*Grammar* ?) can be deduced from the shadow of its throne on the left-hand side of No. 755.[16] The outlines of the arm are perfectly clear, and show that the throne was in this part similar to the one in *Dialectic* (?) ex-Berlin, and not of the simpler form seen in No. 755; the arm of the throne rested on twin-pillared supports of elaborate profile, and had a ball on top. The profile of the arm itself is exactly similar to those of *Rhetoric* (?) and *Dialectic* (?), and different from that of the other two known pictures.

It is clear that the throne on the missing picture cannot have been far removed from what is seen of its shadow on No. 755. It is thus clear that the pictures were arranged together, with at most a very narrow strip of framing between them. Indeed, there is insufficient evidence to prove that the three sections formed separate pictures; it is conceivable that *Grammar* (?), *Rhetoric* (?) and *Dialectic* (?) formed together a single picture.

Less precision is obtainable for the other two known pictures. *Astronomy* cannot have been last, as is usually stated, but on the contrary must have been the first of its group. The perspective of the throne and the position of the kneeling figure indicate a place to the left; and the enclosing wall coming forward on the left makes this certain.

The inscription on No. 756 gives it a comparatively late place, but it is impossible to say how late. Obviously, it was either a centre-piece, or formed with a pendant a composite centre-piece. A peculiarity about it is that the panelling of the back-wall comes to an end on the right[17]; it is a fair deduction that a structural or decorative object separated it from the next of the series. It might have been placed immediately after the *Astronomy,* or have been separated from it by a missing panel; so long as the total number of pictures involved is uncertain, it is impossible to be more precise.

The attribution of the *Liberal Arts* (?) has been the subject of dispute. Although not exactly datable, they are obviously near in style to the pictures of 1476 or thereabouts listed in the biography above; it is there explained why the name of Joos, and not Berruguete's, has been chosen.

The style of Nos. 755, 756 is, however, of interest as being more Italianate than that of the other pictures called in this catalogue Joos, including even the two from the same series ex-Berlin. An Italian author for the pictures is unlikely in the extreme; collaboration between an Italian and Joos is, as Friedländer has excellently shown, almost impossible to conceive[18]; but it is licit (though not necessary) to suppose that Joos received some indications from an Italian. This hypothetical adviser need not have been a painter; thus, the semi-Ferrarese character of the thrones might have been introduced by any craftsman. Attempts to localize the Italian influences more or less discernible in the pictures are clearly useless; the execution by Joos (as is claimed here) must have seriously altered the character of any Italian models he may have had, and damage and restoration have continued the process. In any case, artists from several parts of Italy were working at Urbino or Gubbio.

Apart from what is left of the style in general, two points about Nos. 755, 756 are particularly Italian: (1) the incised architectural lines on both panels—these are normal in Italy, but probably unusual in the Netherlands; (2) the style of the drawings on the backs (whoever their author may be); these again seem common in Italy, but probably are not common on Netherlandish panels, which, being of oak, would be inapt for such scribbles. Neither of these points is proof, or even argument against the authorship of Joos; they merely imply that the studio where the pictures were produced was well up in Italian practice.

A picture that seems to show some connection with Nos. 755, 756, but is more Italian in style, is a *S. Sebastian* at Urbino, wrongly associated with the manner of Giovanni Santi.[19]

Lavalleye notes that the form of the organ on No. 756, with a top of mitred shape, is unusual; a similar organ occurs in a series of *Muses* already mentioned as having been painted for Urbino, so it is possible that an original of this form was in the Palace.[20]

PROVENANCE: In Casa Conti, Florence. Passed into the collection of William Spence, of Florence, between 1856 and 1859[21]; No. 756 was exhibited by him at the British Institution, 1863 (No. 28); both purchased from him, 1866. Exhibited at Ghent, *Juste de Gand, Berruguete et la Cour d'Urbino,* 1957 (Nos. 21, 22).

REPRODUCTIONS: *Illustrations, Italian Schools,* 1937, p. 227. *Plates, Early Netherlandish School,* 1947, Plates, 49, 50. The principal drawings on the reverses are reproduced in *Paintings and Drawings on the Backs of National Gallery Pictures,* 1946, Plates 20–23.

REFERENCES: **(1)** Cf. Gino Fogolari in *Dedalo,* May, 1932, p. 360. Similar drawings in this Gallery on Italian pictures are reproduced in *Paintings and Drawings on the Backs of National Gallery Pictures,* 1946. **(2)** Letter from B. J. Rendle of the Forest Products Research Laboratory in the Gallery archives. **(3)** It is likely that No. 755 was always a separate picture. The possibility that it once formed a single item with two similar pieces is mentioned later on in the text; in that case, the slightness of the cuts mentioned above would refer to gaps between the sides of No. 755 and the two pieces once joined on. **(4)** Berlin Gallery, 1931 Catalogue, Nos. 54, 54A (destroyed); both were in bad condition. The *Astronomy* is recorded in two states with variations in the background; the earlier restoration is shown in Schmarsow, *Melozzo*, 1886, Plate V, the more recent in the Berlin Illustrations, 1930, etc. (**5**) Cf. Lavalleye, *Juste de Gand*, 1936, pp. 156 ff., who, however, is justifiably reserved about the portraiture. (**6**) See Voll in the *Repertorium für Kunstwissenschaft*, 1901, pp. 55/8; he there reproduces all the inscriptions given by L. Schraderus, *Monumentorum Italiae, etc.*, 1592, f. 283 ff. The text is manifestly the one in the studio, given by L. Serra, *Il Palazzo Ducale*, etc., 1930, p. 97; there are only verbal variations. (**7**) Federico's identification led Schmarsow (*op. cit.*, 1886, and elsewhere) to name the other kneeling figures, and the allegorical ladies, both on the existing and on the missing panels (!). The only name even to be mentioned here is that of Costanzo Sforza, Lord of Pesaro and Federico's brother-in-law, born *ca.* 1447; comparison with his medal of 1474 by Enzola, first suggested by Julius Friedländer, shows a profile rather like that on No. 756, but not certainly the same. The medal is reproduced by Hill, *Corpus*, 1930, Plate 46. As Costanzo joined Federico's enemies in 1478, this date has been given as a *terminus ante quem* for the picture; cf. Crowe and Cavalcaselle, *Painting in Italy*, ed. Douglas and Borenius, Vol. V, 1914, p. 45. The argument, based on a doubtful identification, is itself doubtful; even if Costanzo's political moves would have affected a pictorial scheme (which is uncertain), he was not leagued against the Montefeltros for long. (**8**) For the subject, see D'Ancona in *L'Arte*, 1902, pp. 137 ff., 211 ff., 269 ff., 370 ff., and Künstle, *Ikonographie der christlichen Kunst*, Vol. I, pp. 145/56. The allegorical females are sometimes associated with a 'famous man' as a second figure; a conveniently accessible example, with the *Liberal Arts* and the *Virtues*, is in the S. H. Kress Collection at Birmingham, Alabama (see Fern Rusk Shapley, *Paintings from the Samuel H. Kress Collection, Italian Schools XIII–XV Century*, 1966, pp. 110/11 and fig. 302, as Pesellino and Studio). The Berlin/London panels are, however, remarkable in that the male figures are doing homage to the Allegories. So far as the female figures are concerned, it seems very possible that the arrangement was influenced by that of the *Virtues* of the Mercanzia, by Piero del Pollaiuolo and Botticelli, of *ca.* 1470 (in the Uffizi). (**9**) See Bernardino Baldi, *Memorie concernenti la città d'Urbino*, 1724 (preface dated 1587). P. Rotondi, *Il Palazzo Ducale di Urbino*, Vol. I, 1950, p. 384, says that the pictures are nowhere mentioned in old descriptions of the Palace. (**10**) Cf. Preston Remington in the *Bulletin of the Metropolitan Museum*, January 1941, pp. 3 ff.; or R. Papini, *Francesco di Giorgio Architetto*, 1946, Vol. II, Figs. 122/6. For a tentative reconstruction of the words missing from the inscription, see Hans Nachod, *The Inscription in Federigo da Montefeltro's Studio in the Metropolitan Museum: Distichs by his Librarian Federigo Veterano*, in *Medievalia et Humanistica*, No. 2, 1944, pp. 98 ff. (**11**) Theodore Rousseau kindly sent the information that there was approximately 10 feet between the top of the panelling and the ceiling, if the height of the room is correctly recorded as 19 feet in J. Dennistoun, *Memoirs of the Dukes of Urbino*, 1851, Vol. I, p. 163; and that the lengths of the walls are 13′ 4½″, 12′ 10½″, 9′ 0¾″, 6′ 7¼″. Provenance from the Gubbio studio is accepted by Cecil H. Clough in *Apollo*, October 1967, pp. 278 ff.; he suggests that the picture in the Royal Collection, mentioned in the biography above, may also come from there. (**12**) These are clearly Federico's orders; Guidobaldo received his Garter in 1504, but seems never to have belonged to the Order of the Ermine. (**13**) For the dates of various works at Gubbio, see Papini, *op. cit.*, Vol. I, pp. 137/8 and 250. (**14**) Schmarsow, *op. cit.*, pp. 92/3, supposes an arrangement demonstrably wrong. (**15**) The top of the throne in the *Astronomy* was a new addition. (**16**) Infra-red plate of this shadow in the compiler's *The National Gallery* (*Les Primitifs Flamands, Corpus*), Vol. II, 1954, Plate CCCLIII. (**17**) Some changes in the panelling in this area have already been briefly recorded; cf. the compiler's publication (as in previous note), pp. 143, 145, Plate CCCLIV (X-ray photograph). No complete explanation of the alterations has yet been made, but it is claimed that the back wall was always intended to come to an end here. (**18**) Friedländer, Vol. III, pp. 100 ff. (**19**) Serra, *Il Palazzo Ducale*, etc., 1930, p. 89. Reproduced by Briganti in *Critica d'Arte*, June, 1938, Tav. 71, Fig. 16. Rotondi, *Il Palazzo Ducale di*

Urbino, Vol. I, 1950, p. 466, note 223, claims that it is of 1474–82, because it includes the letters F D (for *Federicus Dux*). See further Lavalleye, *Le Palais Ducal d'Urbin*, 1964, p. 94 and Plate CLXXXI. The compiler had already noted some connection with Nos. 755, 756 before Briganti published it as certainly by the same hand (which he calls Berruguete). (**20**) Lavalleye, *op. cit.*, (1936) p. 167; see reproduction by Venturi, *Storia*, Vol. VII, Part II, Fig. 154. Further, the organ shown in the marquetry of the studio at Urbino has a mitred top (visible in Plate CLXXXVI of the Urbino Corpus volume, 1964). This organ was presumably made by 'Juliani Castellano', the name inscribed on it; he is thought to have been the same as the Maestro Castellano, an organ by whom belonged to Lorenzo the Magnificent (see C. de Fabriczy in *L'Arte*, 1888, p. 187). The organ shown in the marquetry of the Gubbio studio is of a different shape (see R. Papini, *Francesco di Giorgio Architetto*, 1946, Vol. II, Plate 124). Similar organs do occur elsewhere, e.g. in Boccati's *Madonna dell'Orchestra* at Perugia; reproduced by Venturi, *Storia*, Vol. VII, Part I, Fig. 292. A somewhat similar example is in this gallery (No. 169, Mazzolino). (**21**) This is deduced from references in Eastlake's MS. note-books. No. 756 is engraved in Litta's *Famiglie Celebri d'Italia* (*ca.* 1850 (?); as a portrait of Guidobaldo), at which time both pictures were in the Conti Collection.

Pieter KOECKE *See* Pieter COECKE

Lenaert KROES

Sixteenth century

Van Mander says that he was a teacher of Gillis van Coninxloo, apparently active at Antwerp.

See the MASTER of the PRODIGAL SON

Lucas van LEYDEN *See* LUCAS van Leyden

Lambert LOMBARD

ca. 1506–1566

Born and active at Liège. He is said to have been a pupil of a Jean Demeuse and stated by Lampsonius (1565) to have been a pupil of Gossaert and of Aerdt (a son of Jan) de Beer. He visited Italy in 1537/8. He had an antiquarian interest in early painting; but in his own works he seems to have been a leading 'Romanist,' and he was the teacher of F. Floris, W. Key and H. Goltzius. Some drawings of his are known; pictures at Liège and elsewhere are attributed by more or less trustworthy tradition. See A. Goldschmidt in the Prussian *Jahrbuch*, 1919, pp. 206 ff., Friedländer, Vol. XIII, pp. 46 ff., and Jean Yernaux in the *Bulletin de l'Institut Archéologique Liégeois*, Vol. LXXII (1957–8), pp. 267 ff.

See Ascribed to the Studio of the MASTER of the PRODIGAL SON

LUCAS VAN LEYDEN

active 1508, died 1533

Engraver: also painter and designer for stained glass. Active at Leyden. According to van Mander (1604), pupil of his father Huygh (or Hugo) Jacobsz., a painter of whom no works are known; later, again according to van Mander, pupil of Cornelis Engebrechtsz., of whom some fairly well documented pictures are at Leyden and elsewhere. He met Dürer at Antwerp in 1521; perhaps the 'Lucas de Hollandere, scildere,' Master at Antwerp, 1522. According to van Mander, he made a journey with Gossaert *ca.* 1527. The date of death is van Mander's; confirmation is given by a document of 1534 referring to his widow.

His signature, on engravings, drawings and pictures, is an L, often followed by a date. His earliest dated engraving is the *Mahomet* of 1508; others undated are often supposed to be earlier. Many woodcuts are by general consent attributed to him; the earliest appeared in a *Breviarium Trajectense* published at Leyden in 1508.

A reputation of being an infant prodigy has clung to Lucas. It is van Mander who has preserved this tradition; he says that Lucas was born in 1494. For the doubt concerning this, students should consult first D. Koning, *Het Geboortejaar, de Moeder en de Woning van Lucas van Leyden*, in the *Leids Jaarboekje*, 1959, pp. 82 ff.

The pictures by Lucas van Leyden are harder to study than his engravings. A *Self-Portrait* at Brunswick is traditionally supposed to be of 1509; if the date is correct, other pictures attributed to about this time are doubtful. A *S. Anthony* at Brussels is signed and dated 1511. It is not until *ca.* 1520 that there is any clarity. Pictures at Munich, signed and dated 1522, and at Nuremberg, signed and dated 1527. A *Last Judgment* at Leyden was commissioned in 1526; a signed altarpiece at Leningrad is said by van Mander to have been dated 1531.

It is difficult to say anything about the origins of Lucas, because the School of Leyden, from which he sprang, is particularly obscure. Dürer was an important influence, especially on his engravings. In his developed paintings, Lucas follows a manneristic style of 'Romanism'; there may be some connection with Gossaert or Scorel or the Master of the Death of the Virgin. The engravings of Marcantonio should perhaps also be mentioned.

3604 A MAN AGED 38

In his hand, a paper inscribed 38.

Oak, painted surface, $18\frac{3}{4} \times 16$ (0·465 × 0·405).

Cleaned in 1959. Painted up to the edge all round; the picture may well have been cut especially along the bottom.

Condition very good; damages particularly in the dress. Several *pentimenti* in the hat and the hand and paper.

The number 38, it seems clear, indicates the sitter's age.[1]

First attributed by Friedländer.[2] No very similar painting exists, but it is recognizably by Lucas. The nearest works for comparison are some portrait drawings, especially one at Leyden.[3] Several are signed and dated 1521; probably the picture is of much the same time. It is possible but not certain that these works in a large style were done under the influence of Dürer, whom Lucas met in 1521.

PROVENANCE: In the collection of Lewis Fry, Bristol; said to have been acquired *ca.* 1850.[4] Exhibited R.A. 1902 (No. 157).[5] Presented in his memory by his children, through the N.A.-C.F., 1921. Exhibited at the National Gallery, N.A.-C.F. Exhibition, 1945/6 (No. 10).

REPRODUCTION: *Illustrations, Continental Schools*, 1937, p. 191. *Plates, Early Netherlandish School*, 1947, Plate 52.

REFERENCES: **(1)** A Dutch portrait of a lady includes a paper (with a number) lying on a parapet in front of her, and the number is believed to indicate her age; see Hoogewerff, *De Noord-Nederlandsche Schilderkunst*, Vol. II, 1937, fig. 199 and p. 410. A portrait of a man in the Louvre ascribed to Scorel shows him holding a paper giving the date of the portrait and (explicitly) the sitter's age; see E. Michel, *Catalogue Raisonné des Peintures* (Louvre), *Peintures Flamandes du XVe et du XVIe Siècle*, 1953, pp. 254/5 and fig. 150. Memlinc's *Adoration of the Kings* of 1479 in St. John's Hospital at Bruges shows the number 36 on a wall near to the head of the donor Jan Floreins, and this number is interpreted as his age; see the reproduction on p. 144 of the Exhibition catalogue *Flanders in the Fifteenth Century*, Detroit, 1960; cf. Weale, *Hans Memlinc*, 1901, p. 33. A triptych showing *The Crucifixion*, assigned to the Master of the Death of the Virgin, at Naples, shows the donors each kneeling at a prie-dieu marked with a mark and a number. The numbers are interpreted as the ages; see L. Baldass, *Joos van Cleve*, 1925, No. 19 and fig. 16. One may also mention the double portrait of 1496 by the Master of Frankfort, where at the base of the frame on each side of the date, are the numbers 36 and 27, clearly the ages of the sitters; well seen in the Frontispiece to the Exhibition catalogue *Le Portrait dans les Anciens Pays-Bas*, Bruges, 1953. **(2)** Friedländer in the *Repertorium für Kunstwissenschaft*, 1902, p. 146; also his Vol. X, No. 138. **(3)** Reproduced in *The Burlington Magazine*, Vol. XL (1922), p. 178. **(4)** See Gleadowe in *The Burlington Magazine*, Vol. XL (1922), p. 179. **(5)** As Holbein.

Style of LUCAS VAN LEYDEN

3459 LOT'S DAUGHTERS MAKE THEIR FATHER DRINK WINE

In the background, right, Lot's wife as a pillar of salt; left, the flames of Sodom.

Oak, painted surface, $12\frac{3}{4} \times 9$ ($0{\cdot}325 \times 0{\cdot}23$).

Good condition.

The scene is described in Genesis, ch. xix.

The picture was ascribed by Beets[1] to Lucas van Leyden; it would be his earliest work, before 1508. This attribution is dubitatively accepted by Friedländer.[2]

An engraving by Lucas of the subject exists[3]; it is of 1530 and has no connection. Three versions of a painting of the subject are known, generally admitted to be by or after Lucas; the date would have to be very early. The version in the Louvre is perhaps the best[4]; Lot is wearing much the same hat as in our picture, but otherwise there is no connection.

There is some general resemblance in the style of No. 3459 to the earlier engravings of Lucas van Leyden; but the difference of technique affects the validity of such comparisons.

There would seem, therefore, to be three possibilities. (1) No. 3459 is apprentice work by the young Lucas. (2) It is a specimen of the Leyden School, which would be supposed to have been a formative influence on Lucas. (3) It is the nearly contemporary pastiche of a man who had seen engravings by Lucas, perhaps even a lost drawing by him. The pictures of the young Lucas are a misty, those of the Leyden School a murky subject, so neither (1) nor (2) can be excluded; but a glance at the picture makes (3) seem likely. The costume of Lot's daughters is likely to be nearer 1520 than 1510.[5]

Popham[6] has withdrawn a former suggestion of his, that the picture is by the same hand as a drawing in the British Museum.

PROVENANCE: Anon. sale, Christie's, 20 December, 1902 (lot 92),[7] bt. T. Blake Wirgman, from whom purchased, 1919.[8]

REPRODUCTION: *Illustrations, Continental Schools*, 1937, p. 97. *Plates, Early Netherlandish School*, 1947, Plate 53.

REFERENCES: (1) N. Beets in *Oud-Holland*, 1934, pp. 57 ff.; he seems not absolutely to exclude Lucas' father, Hugo Jacobsz. (of whom no works are known). or even Engebrechtsz. The latter name is unacceptable. (2) Friedländer, Vol. XIV, p. 122. (3) Reproduced by Friedländer, *Lucas van Leyden* (Meister der Graphik, Vol. xiii), 1924, Plate LXXIII. (4) Friedländer, Vol. X, Plate LXIX. (5) The exact dating of the costume in this picture is tricky; notes on it by Mrs. Newton in the Gallery archives. (6) A. E. Popham, *Catalogue of Dutch and Flemish Drawings in the British Museum*, V, 1932, p. 82. (7) As Early Flemish School. (8) In the 1929 Catalogue as Dutch School. The seller has an entry in Thieme-Becker.

LUCIDEL *See* NICOLAS DE NEUFCHÂTEL

MABUSE *See* JAN GOSSAERT

JAN MANDIJN

ca. 1500–not earlier than 1560

From Haarlem; active at Antwerp, where mentioned from 1530. A *Temptation of S. Anthony* at Haarlem is signed (genuinely ?); from this, from van Mander's statements and from pictures therefrom ascribed, he is considered to have painted rather like Peter Huys. A *Way to Calvary*, much nearer to Bosch, carries a monogram believed to be that of Jan Mandijn; see the catalogue *Le Siècle de Bruegel*, Brussels, 1963 (No. 151). He has been identified, but apparently unjustifiably, with the

MASTER of the PRODIGAL SON, q.v.

MARINUS VAN REYMERSWAELE

active 1509(?), died after 1567(?)

The signatures sometimes contain some spelling of Reymerswaele in conjunction with the name Marinus; Reymerswaele or Roymerswaele was a place in Zealand. The author of the signed works is generally identified with the following:

(1) A *Moryn Claessone, Zeelander*, pupil of a glass-painter at Antwerp in 1509. His father, which is relevant to the next mention, is supposed to have been the painter admitted as Master at Antwerp in 1475, *Claes van Ziericsee*: Zierikzee is a place near Middleburg. (2) A *Marino di Sirissea* (i.e. Zierikzee) mentioned among painters already dead by Guicciardini, the preface to whose *Descrittione dei Paesi Bassi* is dated 1566. Guicciardini's Sirissea became still further corrupted in Vasari and other Italian texts. (3) A *Marin Claeszoon von Romerswaele* (the spelling is from Wurzbach's *Niederländisches Künstler-Lexikon*) banished from Middleburg in 1567: the identification conflicts with the earlier death of Guicciardini's statement. (4) A *Marinus de Seeu, Schilder van Romerswaelen* (i.e. the Zealander, painter of Reymerswaele) mentioned by van Mander (1604). It is to be noted, against what is sometimes said, that Marinus is not a Latin form of Seeu (Zeeuw).

For signatures by Marinus, see F. de Mély in the *Gazette des Beaux-Arts*, 1908, ii, pp. 215 ff. According to the list in Friedländer's Vol. XII, the dates run from 1521 (No. 162) to 1547 (No. 162a). The date of 1521 on No. 162 is sometimes rejected as false (see below): in any case the signature is not *Marinus* but *Mdad* (?) (cf. also the Prado Catalogue, 1933, p. 365). The next earliest sure date on a signed picture is 1538 (Friedländer, Vol. XII, No. 170). There are dates later than 1547 on pictures in the style of Marinus but not admitted as autograph by Friedländer.

Marinus seems most often to have confined himself to a few types of picture, which he repeated (*S. Jerome*, *Two Tax-Gatherers* (?), *The Banker and his Wife* (?)). The third goes back to a Massys of 1514 in the Louvre: the second is sometimes said, on inadequate evidence, perhaps to be derived from a lost van Eyck (cf. Friedländer, Vol. I, pp. 114 f.). The first has some connection with a Dürer of 1521 at Lisbon: the rejection of the date 1521 on the version by or ascribed to Marinus may be due to a desire to give Dürer the priority. The caricatural types in these pictures are presumably derived (through Massys) from Leonardo.

Many pictures in the style of Marinus are by other hands, not all of them later copies. Two are said to bear signatures of Cornelis van der Capella 1533/4 and Corneille de la Chapelle. It is unreasonable to reject these signatures out of hand: equally unreasonable to attribute them to the French portrait painter we know as Corneille de Lyon. See L. Cust in *The Burlington Magazine*, Vol. XX (1911/12), pp. 252 ff., and Vol. XXIII (1913), pp. 59/60; and the large catalogue of the R.A. Exhibition, 1927, *sub* No. 245.

944 ‘TWO TAX-GATHERERS’

The principal man, on the left, appears to be a borough or city treasurer, responsible for the letting out or the accounting of various imposts put out to farm. The entries on the page of the book where he is writing have been deciphered as follows:

Dits den ontfanck vander stede (municipal revenues) *dair tseghen*
Item den wijn excijs is waerdich tot augus(tus)
toe die seven manden LXX lb. IX s.
Item den byer excys is waerdich tot. . . .
toe die seven maenden . . . XI lb
Item die visbrugge is waerdich tot. . . .
die seven maenden IIII lb. . . .
Item die waghe is waerdich
die seven maenden IIII lb
Item die tolle is waerdi. . . .
die seven manden
Item de veren sijn waer. . . .
die seven maenden
Item die brieffgelt is w. . . .
de seven maenden
Item den ommeslach
. . . . seven manden
. . . . . is
. . . . . molerye is w
maenden
Item d. . . .

Another page is also partly visible, headed *Rantsoene* (i.e. emoluments from the farming of municipal revenues), followed by . . . *Voxen Cornelis-zoon*. . . . The document immediately above the second man’s head has been deciphered as follows:

. . . . *Cornelis Danielsz. Schepenen in Rey*(merswae)*le*
. . . . *ghecoren voocht ende verlyde dat zij. . . .*
. . . . *brieff doersteken ende bezegelt es*
. . . . *Recht ende al dat hij inhout ende beg. . . .*
. . . . *met . . . eygen ende properen goe. . . .*
. . . . *ende al betaelt te syne den eersten pen. . . .*
. . . . *eenig manier off . . . quame dien. . . .*
. . . . *jaer des Heeren duysent* V^c *ende XV*
. . . . (shoof) *fs van Utrecht*

Next this paper are some seals that have not been identified; other inscriptions on various papers have not been read. Several of the gold coins in the right hand lower corner are identified as écus d’or au soleil of François Ier; two of the large silver coins as Joachimsthalers of Schlick.

Oak, painted surface, $36\frac{1}{4} \times 29\frac{1}{4}$ ($0{\cdot}925 \times 0{\cdot}745$).

In very good condition; some of the inscriptions slightly rubbed.

The picture is one of a large and loose group, showing variations in design and apparently in subject too.[1] It is possible to deduce the status of the principal man in No. 944 from the entries of the book in which he is writing; he is composing an account of the municipal revenues from imposts on wine, beer, fish, etc., let out to farm. In some of the variant pictures, the principal figure may receive an identification on the same grounds; but it is uncertain if the painter in each case intended a precise deduction to be made. It is more certain (though it has been disputed) that a satirical intention runs through these pictures, the point of the attack perhaps varying from covetousness in general to usury or extortion. It seems beyond dispute that, in most cases at least, these pictures are not portraits of actual officials. In No. 944, and in some of the variants, the figures appear to be in fancifully archaistic costume, though this may be based upon some uniform.[2]

In the inscriptions of No. 944, there is mention of the town of Reymerswaele; the Cornelis Danielsz. may be identical with a man of this name from Reymerswaele, recorded in 1524.[3] The date on the paper is 1515 'according to the style of the Court of Utrecht,' i.e. with the year beginning at Christmas; it is not necessary to suppose that this is the date of No. 944—indeed, the Joachimsthalers of Schlick would exclude a date earlier than 1526. Van Werveke[4] points out that Reymerswaele was one of the few towns where there was a 'visbrugge,' i.e. a fish market on a bridge.

The purpose of pictures such as No. 944 is at present not very clear; an analysis of all the evidence in all the variants might throw some light, but possibly not much.

No. 944 was formerly ascribed to Massys, who may have painted pictures of this kind[5]; the attribution to Marinus is due apparently to Sir Frederick Burton.[6] The composition differs considerably from those of most other pictures in the group. Friedländer[7] says that No. 944 is probably the only original Marinus among the pictures he refers to. Fokker[8] claims that the complicated and in some respects illogical design of this version indicates that it is a late development of the subject; for instance, the pot for sand is on a shelf in this version instead of on the table, where it is needed for drying the writing.

VERSIONS: See Friedländer. A fairly exact version was in an Anon. sale, Petit, 17 May, 1920 (lot 6).

PROVENANCE: Similar pictures are so frequent that the provenance cannot be established. According to the Leeds Catalogue, it was from the van Ravenstein Collection. Coll. Wynn Ellis; exhibited at Leeds, 1868 (No. 558)[9]; Wynn Ellis Bequest, 1876. Exhibited at Brussels, *Le Siècle de Bruegel*, 1963 (No. 210).

REPRODUCTION: *Illustrations, Continental Schools*, 1937, p. 206. *Plates, Early Netherlandish School*, 1947, Plate 54.

REFERENCES: *General:* Friedländer, Vol. XI, No. 168. See also the biography above.

In text: **(1)** This entry has been much corrected and expanded from the 1st edition. There are good recent publications on the group by H. van Werveke in *Gentse Bijdragen*, XII, 1949/50, pp. 43 ff., and by Georges Marlier in his *Erasme et la Peinture Flamande*, 1954, pp. 251 ff. The compiler is also greatly indebted to R. C. Jarvis of H.M. Customs for a memorandum on the subject of the picture; to Roger Ellis of the Public Record Office and H. Hardenberg of the Algemeen Rijksarchief at The Hague, for transcriptions of and comments on the inscriptions: and to R. H. Dolley of the British Museum, Mlle. Lallemand and Dr. Peter Berghaus, for identification of the coins. (2) One might think of something like what is seen for the man at a table (perhaps a money-changer) in the left hand bottom corner of the print of *Temperance* after Bruegel, No. 138 and Plate 138 of René van Bastelaer, *Les Estampes de Peter Bruegel l'Ancien*, 1908, though this differs and is much simpler. (3) H. Hardenberg kindly gave the reference to W. S. Unger, *Bronnen tot de geschiedenis van Middelburg*, III, 1931, p. 322; he suggested also a connection between the Voxen Corneliszoon of No. 944 and an Anthonis Cornelis Jansz. Voxen or Voxem, mentioned at Reymerswaele in 1519. (4) Van Werveke, *loc. cit.*, p. 48. (5) See Marlier, *loc. cit.* (6) Burton in the *Chronique des Arts*, 1879, p. 295. (7) Friedländer, Vol. XII, p. 74 and *sub* No. 167. (8) Fokker in the *Bollettino d'Arte*, 1928/9, pp. 122 ff. (9) As by Massys.

SIMON MARMION

active 1449, died 1489

Miniaturist and painter. Mentioned at Amiens from June, 1449, to June, 1454; from 1458, Valenciennes. 1468, Tournai Guild.

There are no documented pictures or miniatures; but the S. Bertin panels, of which Nos. 1302, 1303 below are fragments, are generally accepted without any proof as key works of Marmion. This identification is rejected by Hénault, who calls the painter the *Master of S. Bertin*. See Mgr. Dehaisnes, *Recherches sur le Retable de Saint-Bertin et sur Simon Marmion*, 1892, pp. 51/4, pp. 129 ff.; Maurice Hénault, in the *Revue Archéologique*, 1907, I, pp. 119, 282, 410, II, p. 108; E. Durand-Gréville in the *Chronique des Arts*, 1908, p. 388 and p. 395; L. de Fourcaud in the *Bulletin de l'Art ancien et moderne*, 1907, pp. 311, 319, 326, with Hénault's reply, *ib.*, 1908, p. 39.

Durrieu ascribed the panels to Jean Hennecart, a shadowy figure of whom some documented miniatures are known (*Bulletin de la Société Nationale des Antiquaires de France*, 1909, pp. 263/4); he seems inclined to be doubtful in *La Miniature Flamande*, 2nd edition, 1927, p. 60.

For attributions of pictures and miniatures to Marmion, see especially Winkler, e.g. in the Prussian *Jahrbuch*, 1913, pp. 251 ff. Also G. Ring, *A Century of French Painting*, 1949.

'SIMON MARMION'

1302 THE SOUL OF S. BERTIN CARRIED UP TO GOD (FRAGMENT)

Below, the tiled roof of a church (continued in the scene of S. Bertin's death, Berlin Gallery (Dahlem), No. 1645A).

Reverse: Grisaille, a spire-like construction in the Gothic style.

1303 A CHOIR OF ANGELS (FRAGMENT)

Below, the terminal of the gable to a building (Berlin Gallery (Dahlem), No. 1645) in which the Donor, Guillaume Fillastre, kneels.

Reverse: Identical with the reverse of No. 1302.

Each, oak, painted surface (obverse and reverse), $22\frac{3}{4} \times 8\frac{1}{8}$ (0·575 × 0·205) (with very small variations).

The panels extend beyond the painted surface all round; but along the bottoms the edges of the paint are recognizably different from the other (original) edges. The panels now at Berlin were separated from Nos. 1302/3 in the nineteenth-century. Examination shows convincingly that the paint continued without interruption.[1]

In very good condition except for small local damages. Cleaned in 1967.

The two panels are fragments of the shutters to a retable of precious metals, once on the High Altar of the Abbey Church of Saint-Bertin, Saint-Omer. When the shutters were closed, Nos. 1302, 1303 fitted over the top part of a tall central compartment, a *Crucifixion*. The retable has presumably been destroyed. The main parts of the shutters are at Berlin, Nos. 1645 and 1645A.

For the unproved attribution, see the biography above; the known facts are best dealt with by Hénault.[2] According to an inscription quoted by Dom de Witte,[3] the retable was dedicated in 1459 by Guillaume Fillastre, abbot 1450–1473; payments extend from 1455/6 to 1459. The shutters were almost certainly painted at the same time; Bernhard Klemm[4] dates them *ca.* 1480/90.

PROVENANCE: The shutters are mentioned in 1695 by d'Hailly.[5] The retable remained *in situ* until 1783; in that year Dom Joscio Dallennes placed it in the Ambulatory. Still there on 12 July, 1791,[6] the retable may be assumed to have been destroyed soon afterwards. Henri de Laplane[7] says (no need to doubt that he is referring to these shutters): 'lors de la dévastation de l'abbaye' (1792) 'ces belles peintures furent recueillies par un boulanger de Saint-Omer. C'est là qu'un amateur du pays les ayant découvertes les acquit.' Imported into England 1822 by Francia, an artist, and shown at 27, Leicester Square, as Memlinc[8]; this was Louis Francia, born at Calais 1772, died 1839, and he may have been the 'amateur du pays' of Laplane. Said to have been sold in England[9]; not (as sometimes stated) Anon. sale at the Hôtel Bullion, Paris, 1823 (lot 97).[10] Sold by a private owner in Paris in 1824 to C.-J. Nieuwenhuys.[11] Hédouin[12] says that it was Nieuwenhuys who separated Nos. 1302, 1303 from the rest (now at Berlin). Edmond Beaucousin acquired Nos. 1302, 1303 from the Nieuwenhuys family in 1847 or shortly before.[13] Purchased[14] with the rest of the Edmond Beaucousin Collection, Paris, 1860.

REPRODUCTIONS: *Illustrations, Continental Schools*, 1937, p. 206 (obverses). *Plates, Early Netherlandish School*, 1947, Plate 55 (obverses). One of the reverses is reproduced in *Paintings and Drawings on the Backs of National Gallery Pictures*, 1946, Plate 26.

REFERENCES: *General:* see the biography above.

In text: (1)The compiler is much indebted to Prof. Dr. Robert Oertel, Dr. Ernst Brochhagen and Herr Böhm for their kind help at Berlin. (2) M. Hénault in the *Revue Archéologique*, 1907. Perhaps the first writer to suggest the name of Marmion was Alfred Michiels, *Histoire de la Peinture Flamande*, 2nd edition, Vol. III, 1866, pp. 379, 396 ff. (3) See Dehaisnes, *Recherches*, etc., 1892, pp. 32,

35/6. (**4**) Klemm, *Der Bertin-Altar*, 1914, p. 112. (**5**) As Dürer; see the *Annales du Comité Flamand de France*, Vol. XXIV, 1898, p. 461, or the *Société des Antiquaires de la Morinie, Bulletin historique trimestriel*, No. 191, Vol. X (for 1897–1901), 1902, pp. 385/6. Also mentioned (without attribution) by Edmond Martène and Ursin Durand, *Voyage Littéraire de deux Religieux Bénédictins*, 1717, Part II, pp. 183/4; they published a tradition that Rubens coveted them. J.-B. Descamps, *Voyage pittoresque de la Flandre et du Brabant*, 1769, p. 327, noted an attribution to Memlinc. (**6**) O. Bled in *Société des Antiquaires de la Morinie, Bulletin historique trimestriel*, No. 196, Vol. X (for 1897–1901), 1902, pp. 613 ff. Consult also Dehaisnes, *op. cit.* pp. 28/9. (**7**) Laplane, *Mémoires de la Société des Antiquaires de la Morinie*, VII, 1844, pp. 54/5, note 2. (**8**) *Kunst-Blatt*, 1822, p. 120; cf. also Whitley, *Art in England*, 1821–37, 1930, p. 34. (**9**) Emmanuel Wallet, *Description de l'ancienne Abbaye de Saint-Bertin*, 1834, p. 23, note 37. (**10**) Cf. the *Gazette des Beaux-Arts*, 1931, ii, p. 346. (**11**) See Laplane, *loc. cit.*; also C. J. Nieuwenhuys, *Description de la Collection de Tableaux . . . . de S.A.R. Mgr. le Prince d'Orange*, 1837, p. 10. (**12**) P. Hédouin in the *Annales Archéologiques*, Vol. VI, 1847, pp. 272/3. See also Crowe and Cavalcaselle, *Early Flemish Painters*, 1857, p. 267. The main part belonged to the Prince of Orange in 1824; see E. Firmenich-Richartz, *Die Brüder Boisserée*, Vol. I, 1916, pp. 506, 529. (**13**) Hédouin; see also Crowe and Cavalcaselle, as in previous note. (**14**) As Memlinc.

Style of 'MARMION'

1939 THE VIRGIN AND CHILD, WITH SAINTS AND DONOR

The Child is handling a rosary. The donor, wearing a collar of the Golden Fleece, kneels at the entrance to a château, above the window of which is the *Flint and Steel.* Behind, SS. Francis, Lazarus, John the Evangelist, Catherine, Barbara, and S. Margaret (?) with a Cross. S. Michael drives Satan down across the sky.

Oak, painted surface, $10\frac{3}{4} \times 8$ ($0{\cdot}27 \times 0{\cdot}20$).

Painted up to the edges except on the left. There is at the left a clear trace of the beginning of an arched top to the picture. The picture would have been cut 1 cm. at the right, if the crown over the Virgin's head was intended to be central; a substantial amount seems to have been cut away at the top. Some change above the donor's head might doubtfully indicate that he was once shown wearing a hat (at present, a hat is on the parapet by him).

Condition probably good on the whole; but some retouches on the flesh. The picture suffers somewhat both from over- and from undercleaning.

Popham[1] points out that the design above the window is a device of the Dukes of Burgundy (it is also proper to the Order of the Golden Fleece),[2] and thinks that the donor may be Charles the Bold (1433–1477).

The picture, however, is probably of *ca.* 1490/95 (from the costume of the donor; note by Mrs. Newton). Popham reasonably considers that an explanation of its unevennesses would be that it is the work of a miniaturist, and brings forward the name of Philippe de Mazerolles (d. 1479/80)[3]; as the technique of miniatures makes them hardly comparable with a picture, it seems best to indicate in the attribution a vague connection with 'Marmion' (cf. Nos. 1302/3 above).[4] Winkler[5] points out that the design of the Virgin and Child occurs several times (with variations); he thinks it may go back to a lost Rogier.

Formerly catalogued as French School.

PROVENANCE: Seen by Passavant in 1831 in the collection of Karl Aders, a German merchant living in London.[6] Aders Exhibition, No. 36[7]; Aders Sale, 1 August, 1835 (lot 73), bt. Longdile.[8] Anon. (H. C. Robinson, or rather Aders Trust) Sale, London, 26 April, 1839 (lot 49), bt. Rodd. Perhaps Coll. Lord Northwick, Cheltenham.[9] Anon. Sale, London, 7 May, 1904 (lot 122),[10] bt. Agnew; purchased at cost price from Agnew's, Lewis Fund, 1904.

REPRODUCTION: *Illustrations, Continental Schools,* 1937, p. 129. *Plates, Early Netherlandish School,* 1947, Plate 56.

REFERENCES: (1) Popham in the *Annuaire des Musées Royaux de Belgique,* 1938, pp. 9 ff. (2) So the donor of No. 1939 is not necessarily of the House of Burgundy. (3) Popham, *loc. cit.* The drawing of *The Virgin and Child with a Donor,* which he reproduces as by a follower of Mazerolles, seems to be quite like No. 1939 in style. (4) Charles Sterling, *Les Peintres du Moyen Age,* 1942, p. 63, No. 31, doubts if No. 1939 is French. G. Ring, *A Century of French Painting,* 1949, p. 222, No. 191, says that it is French, probably from the North of France, and that it has no connection with the style of Marmion. (5) Winkler, *Der Meister von Flémalle,* 1913, pp. 76/7. See also Friedländer, *A Drawing by Roger van der Weyden,* in *Old Master Drawings,* Vol. I, 1926, pp. 29 ff. E. Panofsky, *Early Netherlandish Painting,* 1953, Vol. I, pp. 266 and 464, claims that the lost Rogier may be his Carmelite Madonna of 1446. (6) Passavant, *Kunstreise,* 1833, p. 96, as Antonello, apparently in a frame with an arched top (size given as $9\frac{3}{4}'' \times 6\frac{3}{4}''$). (7) For this exhibition, see Style of Aelbrecht Bouts, No. 1083, note 5. (8) In the catalogue said to come from the Duke de Feltre's Collection. Not identifiable in the Feltre sale catalogue of 1819 (Lugt, No. 9553). (9) Waagen, *Treasures,* 1854, iii, p. 205, as School of van Eyck. Apparently not in the Northwick Catalogue, 1858, or Sale, 1859. (10) As Early Dutch School.

2669 S. CLEMENT AND A DONOR (LEFT WING OF A TRIPTYCH)

On S. Clement's cope, SS. Peter, John the Evangelist and James the Great (?) are identifiable. Inscribed on the frame: ·*Credendo sēciā' q°d pnob dep̄ceris*·, i.e. credendo sentiamus quod pro nobis depreceris.

Oak, painted surface, $19\frac{3}{4} \times 14\frac{1}{2}$ (0·50 × 0·37).

Considerably softened by repairs; this is particularly apparent on the lower part of the Donor's face, the landscape and the sky. S. Clement is in fair state; the gold of his gloriole is new.

Left wing of a Triptych; the other two panels (*The Virgin and Child,* and a *Donatrix with S. Elizabeth*) are in the Thyssen-Bornemisza (Schloss Rohoncz) Collection at Lugano.[1] Reproductions of those pictures in the Seligmann Sale, Paris, 11 March, 1914 (lots 367, 368) show an inscription, in lettering corresponding to the one on No. 2669, on the then frame of the Donatrix. The frame of No. 2669 is not attached to the picture, but it is probably the original frame.

There is some, possibly indirect, connection with the S. Bertin shutters (Nos. 1302, 1303 above), but Friedländer's ascription to 'Marmion' himself is unacceptable.[2] The classification here is for convenience.

The picture (before its attribution to 'Marmion') was dated by Friedländer[3] *ca.* 1490. Dated by Hulin[4] *ca.* 1475; by Bouchot[5] *ca.* 1460/80. The 1480's seem the most likely date for the costume (note by Mrs. Newton).

PROVENANCE: Lent by L. de Somzée to the Exposition Universelle at Paris, Pavillon de la Belgique, 1900 (No. 4).[6] Exhibited at Bruges, 1902 (No. 148), lent by C. & G. de Somzée, Brussels.[7] Acquired by Agnew's with several other Somzée pictures, 1902.[8] Exhibited by Salting at the R.A. 1904 (No. 3)[9]; at the Primitifs Français, Paris, 1904 (No. 75).[10] On loan to the N.G. from 1907; George Salting Bequest, 1910. Lent to the Thyssen Bornemisza Collection at Lugano, and shown with the other parts of the triptych there, during the Summers of 1962–5.

REPRODUCTION: *Illustrations, Continental Schools*, 1937, p. 130. *Plates, Early Netherlandish School*, 1947, Plate 57.

REFERENCES: **(1)** Schloss Rohoncz Exhibition, Munich, 1930, Nos. 210, 211, Plates 113, 114. The two pictures were lent to the National Gallery and shown with No. 2669, November, 1963—Easter 1964. **(2)** The Schloss Rohoncz pictures have a Friedländer certificate as 'Marmion.' No. 2669 was formerly catalogued as French School; Charles Sterling, *Les Peintres du Moyen Age*, 1942, p. 49, No. 115, suggested the School of Amiens. G. Ring, *A Century of French Painting*, 1949, p. 221, No. 182, accepted it as Marmion. **(3)** Friedländer in the *Repertorium für Kunstwissenschaft*, 1903, p. 174. **(4)** Hulin, *Catalogue Critique*, 1902, pp. 37/8. **(5)** Bouchot, *Les Primitifs Français* (large volumes), II, Plate LVIII. **(6)** As van der Goes. **(7)** As Unknown. **(8)** Geoffrey Agnew, *Agnew's, 1817–1967*, 1967, p. 42, for the purchase in 1902 of a group of Somzée pictures; No. 2669 is assumed to have been in the group. **(9)** As Unknown, supposed to be the Master of Jehan Perréal. This appellation is stated to have been given with humorous intent by Salting himself (note by Sir Claude Phillips, in his copy of the 1915 National Gallery catalogue, in the Gallery Library). **(10)** As School of Burgundy, *ca.* 1460.

QUINTEN MASSYS

1465/6–1530

Also Quentin Matsys, Metsys. Born at Louvain, but active at Antwerp, where in the guild, 1491 (see Friedländer, Vol. VII).

Two documented altarpieces are at Brussels (1507/9: signed) and Antwerp (*ca.* 1508–1511): several other pictures are dated or datable from 1509 onwards, some of them being signed.

The style of pictures reasonably ascribed as early works shows some influence of Memlinc (Bruges); later he was in contact with the landscape painter Patenier at Antwerp. He was influenced by Leonardo da Vinci and perhaps by the Venetian School. An elaborate attempt to work out his stylistic development is made by Baldass in the Vienna *Jahrbuch*, 1933, pp. 137 ff.

Massys was the leading painter of his time at Antwerp.

3664 THE VIRGIN AND CHILD WITH SS. BARBARA AND CATHERINE

S. Catherine (her wheel behind) receives a ring from the Child; S. Barbara receives a chaplet (?) from the Virgin, her tower behind.

Tempera on linen or canvas (?), $36\frac{1}{2} \times 43\frac{1}{4}$ (0·93 × 1·10).

Gravely damaged, in places down to the ground. Fairly free from repaint, though there is some here and there, especially on the faces of the Virgin and S. Barbara: the toes of the Child seem to have been re-outlined.

The technique is usually described as tempera, sometimes as water-colour, on linen: another example is Bouts, No. 664.

S. Barbara's tower is clear in the copy recorded below.

Friedländer says that though there is no work really comparable with it, it is probably late.[1] First published by Borenius with an earlier dating.[2]

COPY: Friedländer mentions a small copy on the Paris market, 1926.[3]

PROVENANCE: Coll. John Linnell (died 1882): sale, Christie's, 15 March, 1918 (lot 60),[4] bt. Carfax. Via Buttery and Agnew to Coll. Charles Bridger Orme Clarke: lent by him to the Burlington Fine Arts Club, 1919 (No. 2): presented by him, 1922.

REPRODUCTION: *Illustrations, Continental Schools*, 1937, p. 209. *Plates, Early Netherlandish School*, 1947, Plate 58.

REFERENCES: *General:* Friedländer, Vol. VII, No. 28.

In text: **(1)** Friedländer, Vol. VII, pp. 59/60. **(2)** Borenius in *The Burlington Magazine*, Vol. XXXIII (1918), p. 3. **(3)** Photograph in the Friedländer archives in the Rijksbureau voor Kunsthistorische Documentatie at The Hague. **(4)** As after Massys.

6282 THE VIRGIN AND CHILD ENTHRONED, WITH FOUR ANGELS

Oak, painted surface, $24\frac{1}{2} \times 17$ (0·62 × 0·43); rounded top.

The flying Angel on the left is largely modern except for the head and arm; but the remainder of the picture seems in good condition.

This picture is reasonably accepted as an early work of Massys[1]; it clearly depends a good deal on Jan van Eyck.

PROVENANCE: Sale of the Sneyd Heirlooms from Keele Hall, 27 June, 1924 (lot 69), bought by Buttery. Passed to C. W. Dyson Perrins, who lent it to the Royal Academy, 1927 (No. 171) and 1953/4 (No. 95), to Bruges, 1956 (No. 31), to Manchester, 1957 (No. 26). Bequeathed by C. W. Dyson Perrins, 1958.

REPRODUCTION: Friedländer, *Die Altniederländische Malerei*, Vol. VII, Plate XXVI.

REFERENCE: **(1)** See Friedländer in *Cicerone*, 1927, pp. 6/7 and in his *Die Altniederländische Malerei*, Vol. VII, pp. 31/3 and No. 25.

Studio of QUINTEN MASSYS

715 THE CRUCIFIXION

The cross is inscribed .I̅.N̅.R̅.I̅. Present, the Virgin, S. John, the Magdalen and two Holy Women: Joseph of Arimathaea and Nicodemus in the background left. A skull (to indicate Golgotha) in the foreground.

Oak, irregular top, painted surface, $35\frac{1}{2} \times 23$ (0·90 × 0·585).

The picture is sometimes said to be in bad condition, but this is not so.

It suffers from undercleaning, which in places forms a spotty texture certainly not intended. There is a little obvious local damage in the sky and a few comparatively small areas elsewhere, some of them obvious. *Pentimenti* in Christ's right arm and hand; the round tower furthest back to the left was once taller.

It may be that damage has been assumed to explain the weaknesses of the execution, but these are largely original. The picture is certainly near in style to Massys, but hardly by his own hand.[1] Of the existing *Crucifixions* in the manner of Massys, the small picture acquired in 1954 by Ottawa from the Liechtenstein Gallery [2] is the nearest to Massys himself and to the present version.

Friedländer [3] thinks that the landscape is perhaps by Patenier; but it is not really like Patenier's surest works, and it is quite in the style of Massys.[4]

VERSIONS: The Liechtenstein-Ottawa variant is referred to above; a copy of this at Munich [5] bears or bore the false date of 1505.[6] There are other variants in the Musée Mayer van den Bergh, Antwerp; the Harrach Gallery, Vienna; and in Brussels.[7]

PROVENANCE: Inscribed on the back. *Diss. bild ist vmb fünffhundert gulden aestimiert / von mir aber nachmals vmb.* 105 *fl. bezahlt worden / Anno* 1688. 21. 8*brl.* Acquired in June, 1815, from Gallery Inspector Hüber, Munich, by Prince Ludwig Kraft Ernst von Œttingen-Wallerstein.[8] At Schloss Wallerstein.[9] Exhibited at Kensington Palace (for sale), 1848 (No. 77), bought with the rest of the collection by the Prince Consort. At Kensington Palace.[10] Exhibited at Manchester, 1857 (Provisional Catalogue, No. 540; Definitive Catalogue, No. 497), lent by Prince Albert. Presented by Queen Victoria at the Prince Consort's wish, 1863.

REPRODUCTION: *Illustrations, Continental Schools,* 1937, p. 208. *Plates, Early Netherlandish School,* 1947, Plate 61.

REFERENCES: **(1)** Friedländer, Vol. VII, No. 13, as Massys, damaged but autograph, *ca.* 1520. Baldass (MS. note of 1949 in the National Gallery) inclines to consider No. 715 autograph. **(2)** Friedländer, Vol. VII, No. 12 and Plate XVII. Ottawa, *Catalogue of Paintings and Sculptures,* Vol. I, *Older Schools,* 1957, p. 63, with repr. It seems unquestionable that the Ottawa picture is superior. **(3)** Friedländer, Vol. VII, No. 13. **(4)** The Massys-like quality of the landscape is pointed out by Durand-Gréville in the *Gazette des Beaux-Arts,* 1908, i, p. 64, and by Baldass in the Vienna *Jahrbuch,* 1933, pp. 155/6. This is approved by Robert A. Koch, *Joachim Patinir,* 1968, p. 55. **(5)** Friedländer, Vol. VII, No. 12a. **(6)** Cf. the Munich Catalogue, 1900, No. 140, under Patinir; later number, H.G. 761. **(7)** Friedländer, Vol. VII, Nos. 56, 57, 58, as studio pieces. **(8)** Details concerning the formation of the Œttingen-Wallerstein Collection were given orally to H. I. Kay. Georg Grupp in the *Jahrbuch des Historischen Vereins für Nördlingen und Umgebung,* 1917, p. 97, mentions a Patenier from Huber. **(9)** See *Kunst-Blatt,* 1824, p. 318, as Patenier; No. 30, as Patenier, of Wallerstein Catalogues of *ca.* 1826 and 1827 (originals at Munich; photostats in the National Gallery). The two catalogues say that the picture carries Patenier's famous monogram; maybe the reference is to an alleged form of signature, which is noted in this catalogue in the last paragraph of Patenier's biography, but which the compiler has not discovered on No. 715. The Wallerstein Collection was moved from Schloss Wallerstein after a time. **(10)** Waagen's *Catalogue,* 1854 (No. 60); cf. Waagen, *Treasures,* IV, 1857, p. 229.

After QUINTEN MASSYS

295 CHRIST: THE VIRGIN

Oak, rounded tops, original painted surfaces, each, 23 × 13 (0·585 × 0·33).

In good condition, except for the new gold backgrounds.

In the transparent (glass ?) globe in the panel showing Christ is seen a view of a town reflected; Christ's thumb and part of His hand, not reflected, show through from behind.

There are many versions. Friedländer [1] calls the present pair studio of Massys, but it is perhaps better to list them as copies. Friedländer says the versions at Antwerp [2] are original. There the Christ is of similar design, though cut: the Virgin faces the other way, is crowned and shows other differences. Baldass [3] says that the National Gallery pictures are derivations, not from the Antwerp pictures, but from an earlier and different design. The form is presumably derived, at several removes, from the Ghent altarpiece.

VERSIONS: See the list in Friedländer, Vol. VII, No. 5.

PROVENANCE: Brought to the Netherlands from Madrid in 1816. Coll. Prince of Orange, later King William II, at Brussels, then from *ca.* 1841 at The Hague [4]; Sale, Amsterdam, August 12, etc., 1850 (lots 23, 24), bt. De Vries (bt. in). Purchased from the Royal Collection at The Hague, 1857.

REPRODUCTIONS: *Illustrations, Continental Schools*, 1937, p. 207. *Plates, Early Netherlandish School*, 1947, Plates 59, 60.

REFERENCES: **(1)** Friedländer, Vol. VII, No. 5a. **(2)** Reproduced by Fierens-Gevaert, *Les Primitifs Flamands*, III, Plates CXXXIX–CXL. **(3)** Baldass, in the Vienna *Jahrbuch*, 1933, p. 166. Cf. also a picture in the Louvre, referred to by Baldass, *Joos van Cleve*, 1925, note 48, Plate 14. **(4)** Catalogue by Nieuwenhuys, 1843, Nos. 21, 22. Not in Nieuwenhuys' catalogue of the collection of the Prince of Orange, 1837; presumably the pictures noted by Boisserée in 1824, apparently called van Eyck (E. Firmenrich-Richartz, *Die Brüder Boisserée*, Vol. I, 1916, p. 505, No. 21).

After QUINTEN MASSYS (?)

5769 A GROTESQUE OLD WOMAN

Wood, original painted surface, $25\frac{1}{4} \times 17\frac{7}{8}$ (0·64 × 0·455). This excludes an addition on the left, $1\frac{1}{2}''$ (0·035) wide; an addition at the bottom, showing in some reproductions, was removed after the picture entered the Gallery. The paint continues all round to the edge of the original wood.

Very good condition.

This picture is certainly connected with a Leonardesque drawing at Windsor.[1] Picture and drawing might depend on some common source or on related sources [2]; or else the drawing might be derived from the picture; or else the picture might be derived from the drawing. On grounds of costume,[3] the third alternative is the most probable.

The headdress could be as early as *ca.* 1450, but it continued to be worn at the beginning of the sixteenth century; the dress with low neckline is unlikely to be earlier than the late 1480's. A theory that picture and drawing are derived from earlier sources, although not excluded, would be complicated and is unnecessary.

It is further probable that the picture is derived from the drawing rather than the drawing from the picture. The dress with low neckline and front lacing seems to be Italian, and it is rare in Teutonic countries for the neck and bosom to be exposed as in No. 5769. It is true that the headdress seems not to be Italian, being probably from Austria, Switzerland or South Germany rather than from further north. With this type of headdress, it is very rare for the hair to be shown as in No. 5769; one comparable example, from the Salzburg province, has been found.[4]

On this theory, the drawing could have been made from an Austrian (?) sitter at Milan *ca.* 1490. The picture, claimed to be derived from the drawing, shows a number of details not in the drawing; these are painted consistently, as if the painter were familiar with the costume. Among the details added in the picture, it may be noted that the goffered edge to the veil is likely to be Netherlandish, and that the frill inside the dress is unlikely before *ca.* 1510.

It may be claimed with some probability that the sitter was someone actually seen by Leonardo.[5] The lack of jewellery at the neck makes it unlikely that she was of the highest society. It has been suggested that she suffered from an oxycephalic syndrome.[6] She has been identified without good grounds as Margaret, Duchess of Carinthia and Countess of Tyrol (died 1369),[7] and as the Queen of Tunis (undefined).[8] The title here given is adapted from the first known record of No. 5769.[9]

Panofsky[10] claims that No. 5769 is not a portrait, but a study in the grotesque or piece of social satire; he claims that the Leonardesque drawing would not have been chosen as the subject of a large, independent painting, if Erasmus in his *Praise of Folly* (published 1512) had not supplied an iconographic 'theme,' viz. foolish old women who still wish to 'play the goat.' It should be noted that Hollar's connected engraving (see in *Versions and Engravings* below) associates a figure similar to No. 5769 with a man in profile. This man resembles somewhat a portrait by Massys in the Musée André at Paris[11]; but Dr. Reis-Santos has discovered a painting much nearer to Hollar's figure, that would seem to have been associated originally with No. 5769 or a version of it.[12] Liefrinck's engraving associates a figure similar to No. 5769 with another woman; see further in *Versions and Engravings* below. It appears very probable that Leonardo's intention was to record an ugly woman; the intention of the paintings remains obscure.

No. 5769 has been ascribed to Quinten Massys by Waagen,[13] Friedländer,[14] Baldass[15] and others. It seems justifiable to associate it with Massys, from the style generally considered, from the subject,[16] and because of the connection with Leonardo; but the execution appears too pedestrian to be by Massys, and suggests a rather later date. The picture is provisionally classed as a copy; the presumed original might have been of *ca.* 1510/20.

VERSIONS AND ENGRAVINGS: A version was at the Château d'Eu; it is unlikely that it could be identical with No. 5769, but no record of its present whereabouts appears to have been published.[17] A copy of the Eu portrait by Rioult (1790–

1855) is at Versailles.[18] Several French engravings are perhaps derived from an engraving by Demarteau.[19]

A connected Leonardesque drawing at Windsor has already been mentioned.[20]

An engraving by Hollar (1607–1677) associates a figure similar to No. 5769 with a man in profile.[21]

An engraving by Liefrinck associates a figure similar to No. 5769 or the Windsor drawing with another woman[22]; it may be a pendant to a Liefrinck engraving of two men.[23]

It is probable that the figure inspired Tenniel for his illustrations of the Duchess in *Alice in Wonderland*, first published in 1865.[24]

PROVENANCE: Inherited by Henry Danby Seymour, and in his collection by 1854.[25] He died unmarried in 1877 and the picture passed to his brother Alfred (1824–1888), and then to the daughter of Alfred Seymour. Miss Seymour Sale, 23 January, 1920 (lot 92), bt. Williams for Hugh Blaker. He lent it to the *Daily Telegraph* Exhibition at Olympia, 1928 (No. X31), and died in 1936. Bequeathed by Miss Jenny Louisa Roberta Blaker, 1947. Exhibited at Brussels, *Le Siècle de Bruegel*, 1963 (No. 166).

REPRODUCTION: E. Panofsky, *Early Netherlandish Painting*, 1953, Vol. II, Plate 332 (after cleaning).

REFERENCES: **(1)** K. Clark, *Catalogue of the Drawings of Leonardo da Vinci at Windsor Castle*, 1935, Vol. I, No. 12492, reproduced in Vol. II. **(2)** It is probable that both picture and drawing are copies. The phrase 'picture and drawing' in the text above means 'the original version of the picture, whether that is No. 5769 or not, and the original version of the drawing, whether that is the Windsor drawing or not.' **(3)** Detailed notes on the costume, by Mrs. Newton, are in the Gallery archives. **(4)** O. Pächt, *Österreichische Tafelmalerei der Gotik*, 1929, Plate 38, at Tamsweg. More generally, the most similar costume so far found is that worn by an old woman in *The Temptation of S. Anthony* by Massys and Patenier at Madrid (Friedländer, Vol. VII, Plate XXX); but the costume there may be a reminiscence of the costume here. **(5)** A fragmentary drawing by Leonardo at Windsor might even represent the same woman; K. Clark, *op. cit.*, Vol. I, No. 12447, reproduced in Vol. II. **(6)** Félix Regnault, *Les Dessins de Léonard de Vinci*, in the *Bulletin de la Société Française d'Histoire de la Médecine*, Vol. XIII, 1914, pp. 484 ff. The author claims that Demarteau's engraving, which may be taken from No. 5769 or a version of it (see *Versions and Engravings*), is medically more convincing than the Windsor drawing, which he judges from some engravings of it. **(7)** Cf. for instance W. A. Baillie-Grohman in *The Burlington Magazine*, Vol. XXXVIII, 1921, pp. 172 ff. This appears to be a French tradition, going back to the late eighteenth century and possibly to the seventeenth century (see notes 17 and 19). In Austria, the tradition of the features of this lady appears to bear no relation to No. 5769; see M. Henningus, *Tirolensium Principum Comitum . . . Genuinae Eicones, 1599*, or (same design) *Tirolensium Principum Comitum, Der Gefursten Grafen zu Tyrol von Anno 1229 biss Anno 1623 Eigentliche Contrafacturen . . .*, Augsburg, Wolfgang Kilian, 1623. **(8)** In Hollar's print; see in *Versions and Engravings* and note 21. **(9)** Waagen, *Treasures*, 1854, ii p. 243. In the 1920 Sale, the sitter was called the Duchess of Carinthia and Tyrol. **(10)** E. Panofsky, *Early Netherlandish Painting*, 1953, Vol. I, pp. 355/6 and notes. See also the remarks by Georges Marlier, *Erasme et la Peinture Flamande*, 1954, pp. 223/4. **(11)** Friedländer, Vol. VII, Plate XLVIII; Panofsky, *op. cit.*, Vol. II, Plate 331. There are entries for it in the Exhibition catalogues *Le Siècle de Bruegel*, Brussels, 1963 (No. 165) and *Le Seizième Siècle Européen*, Paris, 1965/6 (No. 202). **(12)** Oral communication from Dr. Reis-Santos, who is preparing the publication of this picture; he considers that the picture in the Musée André is no more than a reduced copy of it. **(13)** Waagen, *Treasures*, ii, p. 243. **(14)** M. J. Friedländer, *Neues zu Quentin Massys*, in *Cicerone*, 1927, I, pp. 1 ff., and *Die Altniederländische Malerei*, Vol. VII, p. 122, No. 52.

(**15**) L. Baldass, *Gotik und Renaissance im Werke des Quinten Metsys*, in the Vienna *Jahrbuch*, 1933, pp. 148 ff. (**16**) There are various old records of pictures of a similar type by Massys, e.g. one once in the Austrian collections (cf. Baldass, *loc. cit.*, p. 149). (**17**) As Margaret Countess of Tyrol in the *Catalogue Historique et Descriptif des Tableaux appartenans à S.A.S. Mgr. le Duc d'Orléans*, Vol. I, 1823, No. 17, size given as 34 × 46 pouces; and in the *Indicateur de la Galerie des Portraits, tableaux et bustes qui composent la collection du Roi* (i.e. Louis-Philippe) *au château d'Eu*, 1836, pp. 10–11, No. 10. Its identity is established from the copy at Versailles (see the next note). In the first reference, the portrait is marked as being from the Montpensier Collection (as representing the Countess of Tyrol?). In the preface to a book on the *Château d'Eu* in the Victoria and Albert Museum library (Imprimerie de Pihan Delaforest (Morinval), n.d.), pp. 2 ff., it is stated that Mlle. de Montpensier bought Eu in 1662. It passed in 1681 to the Duc du Maine; then to his sons, the Prince de Dombes (Duc du Maine in 1736, died 1755) and the Comte d'Eu (died 1775); then in 1776 to their first cousin, Louis-Jean-Marie de Bourbon, Duc de Penthièvre (son of the Comte de Toulouse). He died in 1793, and Eu passed to his daughter, the Duchesse d'Orléans; it was sequestrated during the Revolution, and she did not regain it until 1818. She died in 1821, when it passed to her son, the Duc d'Orléans, later Louis-Philippe. It is further stated that Louis-Philippe at once set about reacquiring the Montpensier collection of portraits, which had been scattered during the Revolution. (**18**) Inscribed as representing the Countess of Tyrol. Soulié's catalogue, 3rd part, 1861, No. 4003, size 21 × 18 cm.; engraved by Conquy in the *Galeries Historiques de Versailles*, Series X, Section II, pp. 76/7, No. 1719. Letter about it from M. Jallut, 19 March, 1954, in the Gallery archives. (**19**) Marcel Roux, *Bibliothèque Nationale, Inventaire du Fonds Français, Graveurs de XVIIIe Siècle*, Vol. VI, 1949, p. 492, No. 69, as by Gilles-Antoine Demarteau le jeune. The print is inscribed *G Paris del. 1777, Demarteau sculp.* 1787. This print, and others perhaps derived from it, identify the sitter as the Countess of Tyrol; Champfleury in the *Gazette des Beaux-Arts*, 1879, I, pp. 197 ff., gives some account of them and protests against the identification. (**20**) K. Clark, *Catalogue of the Drawings of Leonardo da Vinci at Windsor Castle*, 1935, Vol. I, No. 12492, reproduced in Vol. II. (**21**) Parthey, No. 1603; reproduced by Friedländer in *Cicerone*, 1927, I, p. 2. It is inscribed *Rex et Regina de Tunis, Leonardo da Vinci inu. W Hollar fecit.* It contains many details present in No. 5769 but absent from the Windsor drawing; although associated with Leonardo, it cannot be based on the Windsor drawing alone. Baldass, *loc. cit.*, p. 149, comments on this point. As for the title, E. Tietze-Conrat, *Dwarfs and Jesters in Art*, 1957, p. 19, claims without much supporting evidence that names such as the Queen of Tunis were applied to dwarfs. One may wonder, rather, if Hollar had not, though confusedly, in mind Tunis itself; students may consider a woodcut believed to be derived from Vermeyen, not earlier than 1535, showing a man with the inscription *Rex Thvnissae* (reproduced in the *Marburger Jahrbuch für Kunstwissenschaft*, Vol. VI, 1931, p. 100, fig. 15; see further J. S. Held's article on works by Rubens deriving from Vermeyen in *The Art Quarterly*, 1940, pp. 173 ff.). (**22**) Paris, Bibliothèque Nationale, Cabinet des Estampes, *Recueil de pièces facétieuses et bouffonnes*, Vol. I (Marolles, No. 222), Tf 1 Rés., p. 89. The Liefrinck who made the print seems to be Hans Liefrinck I, died 1573. Inscribed: *Sordida deformis sic est coniuncta marito / Foemina, quo quaerat quisque sibi similem.* (**23**) On the same page as the other print in the Recueil Marolles. (**24**) It is uncertain if this is due to Tenniel or to Lewis Carroll himself. There is nothing relevant in an earlier form of the book, with illustrations by Lewis Carroll (*Alice's Adventures under Ground*, published in 1886). The exact source of Tenniel's illustrations seems not to have been established. The French engravings mentioned above could have been seen by him, so could an engraving of the Windsor drawing in John Chamberlaine's publication (engr. H. Pastorini, 1806); he might have had access to the Windsor drawing itself or some or all of the painted versions. (**25**) Waagen, *Treasures*, 1854, ii, p. 243. He was the son of Henry Seymour, who died in 1849; cf. Burke's *Peerage*, s.v. Duke of Somerset.

Follower of QUINTEN MASSYS

1081 A DONOR

Oak, painted surface, 27 × 13 (0·685 × 0·33). Painted up to the edge and perhaps cut all round.

A little damaged, especially in the shadows, by rubbing and with some spots of repaint here and there, especially in the hands. He seems at one time to have been wearing a flat cap, and his hair appears to have come down further on his right shoulder.

Left wing of a triptych.

Published as by Massys by C. H. Collins Baker,[1] but in Friedländer[2] among the dubious and workshop pieces. The figure is near in style to Massys, but not by him. The landscape is perhaps by a different hand, somewhat in the style associated with Patenier (but not by him).

A Donatrix, said to be part of the same altarpiece, was in 1935 in a German collection.[3]

PROVENANCE: A label with *King* (?)/*158* on the back.[4] Coll. Karl Aders, a German merchant living in London, 1831[5]; Aders Exhibition, No. 6[6]; Sale, 1 August, 1835 (lot 109).[7] Coll. J. H. Green, Hadley.[8] Exhibited at Manchester, 1857 (Provisional Catalogue, No. 519: Definitive Catalogue, No. 431). Bequeathed by Mrs. Joseph H. Green, 1880.

REPRODUCTION: *Illustrations, Continental Schools*, 1937, p. 208. *Plates, Early Netherlandish School*, 1947, Plate 62.

REFERENCES: (1) C. H. Collins Baker in *The Burlington Magazine*, Vol. XLVII (1925), p. 76. (2) Friedländer, Vol. VII, No. 75. (3) Photograph in the Gallery archives. (4) Cf. David, Nos. 1078, 1079. (5) Passavant, *Kunstreise*, 1833, p. 94, as Memlinc. (6) For this exhibition, see Style of Aelbrecht Bouts, No. 1083, note 5. (7) As Memlinc. (8) Waagen, *Treasures*, 1854, ii, p. 460, as Mabuse.

3901 A FEMALE FIGURE STANDING IN A NICHE (WING OF AN ALTARPIECE)

Oak, painted surface, $45\frac{1}{8} \times 13\frac{3}{4}$ (1·145 × 0·35).

May have been very slightly cut along the bottom.

Good condition. *Pentimenti* in the outlines of nose and hands.

Probably the outside of the right shutter to an altarpiece; No. 3902 below could have been the inside. Outsides were not always painted in grisaille; cf. No. 2606, ascribed to the Studio of Coecke.

To judge from the costume, the figure might represent the Virgin; called in the 1929 Catalogue, *A Holy Woman.*

PROVENANCE: See No. 3902 below.

REPRODUCTION: *Illustrations, Continental Schools*, 1937, p. 209. *Plates, Early Netherlandish School*, 1947, Plate 63.

3902 S. LUKE PAINTING THE VIRGIN AND CHILD (WING OF AN ALTARPIECE)

Oak, painted surface, $44\frac{3}{4} \times 13\frac{3}{4}$ (1·135 × 0.35).

Good condition; has suffered a little from flaking here and there. *Pentimento* in the outline of the face.

Probably the inside of the right shutter to an altarpiece; No. 3901 above could have been the outside. Probably No. 3902 is dirtier than No. 3901; there is no need to postulate a difference of hand, or at any rate of studio control, between the two panels.

In the picture on the easel the Virgin stands holding the Child, in front of a tent; the design apparently does not recur.

The pictures are by a follower of Massys. A note in the 1929 Catalogue connecting them with the Master of the Morrison Triptych was based on a letter from Friedländer, 1924[1]; Friedländer has not confirmed the suggestion he then made. Winkler[2] thinks that it is based on a design by van der Goes; the connection, if any, is very loose.

No. 3902 is of interest as representing a painter's studio in the early sixteenth century. It is discussed from this point of view by G. L. Stout.[3]

PROVENANCE: Nos. 3901, 3902 were in the collection of Lord Cowley, formed[4] when the first Lord Cowley was Minister at Madrid (1810–22). Sale, Christie's, 18 July, 1885 (lot 34),[5] bt. Wagner. Presented by Henry Wagner, 1924. No. 3902 was exhibited at Hampstead, *The Artist at Work*, 1966, Exhibit 8.

REPRODUCTION: *Illustrations, Continental Schools* 1937, p. 209. *Plates, Early Netherlandisch School,* Plate 63.

REFERENCES: (1) Letter from Max J. Friedländer in the Gallery archives. (2) F. Winkler, *Das Werk des Hugo van der Goes*, 1964, p. 221. (3) G. L. Stout in *Technical Studies*, April, 1933, pp. 191 ff. (4) According to Christie's Catalogue. (5) As by Dürer.

MASTER OF 1500 (BRUGES) *See* MASTER OF THE BRUGES PASSION SCENES

MASTER OF 1518

active early sixteenth century

The name was given by Friedländer (Prussian *Jahrbuch*, Vol. XXXVI, and his Vol. XI) to a painter to whom he attributes many works of the Antwerp School of the earlier part of the sixteenth century. The date 1518 is on an altarpiece in S. Mary's, Lübeck (Friedländer, Vol. XI, No. 70).

In the Brussels Catalogue, 1922, he is re-baptized *Master of the Abbey of Dilighem*, after a picture once there (Friedländer, Vol. XI, No. 72). This picture is dated 1537/8 by A.-J. Wauters in his Brussels *Catalogue*, 2nd edition, 1906, p. 46, on the ground of a possible or probable identification of the donor. The style would be old-fashioned for so late a date; but Friedländer, Vol. XI, p. 47, is perhaps overbold in saying it would be impossible. On the date, see further Robert A. Koch in the *Gazette des Beaux-Arts*, November 1965, pp. 276 and 282.

Friedländer, Vol. XI, No. 103, and Vol. XII, p. 65, remarks that some compositions of his group are repeated in pictures associated with the name of Pieter Coecke van Aelst (q.v.). This has led G. Marlier to suggest that the Master of 1518 should be identified with Jan van Dornicke,

Pieter Coecke's father-in-law (see especially his *Pierre Coeck d'Alost*, 1966, pp. 109 ff.).

Some of the pictures grouped by Friedländer seem to form a coherent whole, but not all; Friedländer (Vol. XI, pp. 51/2) remarks on the difficulty of attempting to separate into groups the existing pictures of the Antwerp School. As with many other sixteenth-century pictures, it is proper to apply the prefix 'Studio' to all attributions, though in this case a standard of autograph quality may eventually be defined.

Studio of the MASTER OF 1518

718 THE CRUCIFIXION

The Magdalen embraces the foot of the Cross. To the left stand the Virgin and S. John: to the right Longinus and another soldier. A skull and a bone in the foreground (to indicate Golgotha). On the Cross is inscribed .Ī.N̄.R̄.Ī.

Oak, upper angles cut, painted surface, $37\frac{1}{4} \times 26\frac{1}{2}$ (0·945 × 0·67). Painted up to the edge of the panel, and probably cut all round.

Condition fair though it suffers from local damages (especially along the vertical joins and the faces of Virgin and S. John), cracking and patches of undercleaning. There is a painted-out bone in the foreground.

The attribution is due to Friedländer[1]; it is very near indeed in style to Nos. 1082/4.

PROVENANCE: Claimed to have been bought in 1814 from Johann Georg Günther, Augsburg, by Prince Ludwig Kraft Ernst von Œttingen-Wallerstein.[2] At Schloss Wallerstein.[3] Exhibited at Kensington Palace (for sale) 1848 (No. 71),[4] bought with the rest of the collection by the Prince Consort. At Kensington Palace.[5] Exhibited at Manchester, 1857 (Provisional Catalogue, No. 511; Definitive Catalogue, No. 504), lent by Prince Albert. Presented by Queen Victoria at the Prince Consort's wish, 1863.

REPRODUCTION: *Illustrations, Continental Schools*, 1937, p. 7. *Plates, Early Netherlandish School*, 1947, Plate 64.

REFERENCES: **(1)** Friedländer, Vol. XI, No. 93. **(2)** Details concerning the formation of the Œttingen-Wallerstein Collection were given orally to H. I. Kay. Georg Grupp in the *Jahrbuch des Historischen Vereins für Nördlingen und Umgebung*, 1917, p. 96, says that the Prince had acquired before 1818 a Mabuse from J. G. Günther. Mabuse was the ascription of No. 718 in the Wallerstein Collection. The compiler inclines to believe, but cannot aver, that the statement of Grupp (and of H. I. Kay's informant) should be applied to No. 718; Grupp gives the subject as *Christ Carrying the Cross*, adding that a pendant, a *Deposition*, was offered to the Prince, and refused, by Johann Georg Deuringer of Augsburg in 1818. Günther has an entry in Thieme-Becker. **(3)** No. 44, as Mabuse, of Wallerstein catalogues of *ca.* 1826 and 1827 (originals at Munich; photostats in the National Gallery). The collection was moved from Schloss Wallerstein after a time. **(4)** As Mabuse. **(5)** Waagen's *Catalogue*, 1854 (No. 68), as Herry de Bles; cf. Waagen, *Treasures*, IV, 1857, p. 230.

1082 THE VISITATION OF THE VIRGIN TO S. ELIZABETH (PANEL FROM AN ALTARPIECE)

In the background, S. Zacharias (?) or S. Joseph (?).

See No. 1084 below.

1084 THE FLIGHT INTO EGYPT (PANEL FROM AN ALTARPIECE)

In the background, the miracles of the statue and the corn (cf. the Index to Religious Subjects), and the Massacre of the Innocents.

Each, oak, painted surface, $31\frac{1}{2} \times 27\frac{1}{2}$ (0·80 × 0·695).

Two panels from one altarpiece. Both are in very good condition, though there is a little damage on No. 1084, round the head of the ass and S. Joseph's gourd. There is a *pentimento* in the left hand of the Virgin in No. 1082.

The attribution is Friedländer's [1]; he thinks two further panels from the same altarpiece are (a) formerly in the Henry Goldman collection, New York, now at Honolulu, and (b) in the Musée Mayer van den Bergh, Antwerp, No. 357. They would be early works, *ca.* 1515. See also No. 718 above, which is very near in style.

PROVENANCE: On the back of each is a seal with the monogram V.G. below a coronet. Stated to have been in Noble sale, Christie's, 7 April, 1796 (lots 53, 52).[2] Coll. Karl Aders, a German merchant living in London, by 1817.[3] Aders Exhibition, Nos. 18 and 5[4]; Sale, 1 August, 1835 (lots 79, 80), bought by Green.[5] Coll. J. H. Green, Hadley [6]; bequeathed by Mrs. Joseph H. Green, 1880.

REPRODUCTIONS: *Illustrations, Continental Schools,* 1937, pp. 265, 266. *Plates, Early Netherlandish School,* 1947, Plates 65, 66.

REFERENCES: (1) Friedländer, Vol. XI, No. 71. In the 1929 catalogue of the Gallery (wrongly) as School of Patenier. (2) As J. v. Eyck. The identification is from Weale and Brockwell, *The Van Eycks and their Art,* 1912, p. 243, where it is stated that the owner was Noble, and that the pictures were bought in. In Christie's copy of the catalogue, the purchaser is indeed recorded as Noble; 'The flight into Egypt,' 'The visitation, companion to the above,' without further description. The pictures are not identifiable in the William Noble sale of 1805 (Lugt, No. 6956). (3) In London, as van Eyck; see E. Firmenich-Richartz, *Die Brüder Boisserée,* Vol. I, 1916, p. 509. The pictures were also seen by Passavant, *Kunstreise,* 1833, p. 97, as H. met de Bles. (4) For this Exhibition, see Style of Aelbrecht Bouts, No. 1083, note 5. (5) As Bles. (6) Waagen, *Treasures,* 1854, II, p. 461.

See also NETHERLANDISH SCHOOL, Nos. 264, 719, 4573

MASTER OF THE BRUGES PASSION SCENES

active early sixteenth century

This name replaces Friedländer's 'Bruges Master of 1500.' The change has been made with reluctance; but, (1) Friedländer's name would be out of order in an alphabetical catalogue; (2) the date 1500 is a false date.

The name is given from an altarpiece with *Scenes from the Passion* in S. Sauveur, Bruges; this was traditionally ascribed to Gerard van der Meire (died 1512), a painter of whom no works are known. A photograph exists in the Gallery archives, with the date 1500 and Gerard van der

Meeren on the frame; the falsity leaps to the eye, but see also Crowe and Cavalcaselle, *Les Anciens Peintres Flamands*, 1862/3, I, pp. 123/4. These inscriptions are now (1954) no longer on the frame. One figure on this altarpiece is stolen from Dürer's engravings, the horse being from *The Four Horsemen* (1498), the rider from the large *Way to Calvary* (probably 1511). There are also reminiscences of Memlinc, and of an altarpiece ascribed to 'Campin,' which may have been in Bruges.

Friedländer ascribes to the same hand No. 1087 below and a *Miracle of S. Anthony* in the Prado. See Friedländer in the *Repertorium für Kunstwissenschaft*, 1903, p. 80, or *Meisterwerke*, 1903, p. 20, or his Vol. IX, Nos. 184–6, Plates LXXX, LXXXI.

1087 CHRIST PRESENTED TO THE PEOPLE (LEFT WING OF AN ALTARPIECE)

Pilate stands behind Christ holding a reed. The dresses of the men in the right foreground, and centre (behind the raised hand), and the cap of a man further back carry marks partly in the form of letters; these seem to be mere decoration. In the background, the Flagellation and Christ Mocked (the Crowning with Thorns). Of the statues under canopies, Moses is identifiable to the left. One of the medallions above is marked CE/ZAR; the other has unmeaning forms of letters on the collar. The subject of the frieze higher up is not identified.

Oak, painted surface, $36\frac{3}{4} \times 16\frac{1}{4}$ (0·93 × 0·41).

Condition excellent. A few small *pentimenti.*

The figures of Christ and of Pilate standing behind Him are taken from an engraving by Schongauer (died 1491).[1] The *Flagellation* and *Christ Mocked* correspond, except for slight variations, with these scenes in Memlinc's picture at Turin.[2]

The attribution is Friedländer's, under his name of the Bruges Master of 1500.[3] The date may be *ca.* 1510 or a little earlier.[4] The picture was once known as Schongauer,[5] later as German School.[6]

PROVENANCE: In the collection of Karl Aders, a German merchant living in London, 1831.[7] Aders Exhibition, No. 32[8]; Sale, 1 August, 1835 (lot 104), bought by Charles. Anon. (H. C. Robinson, or rather Aders Trust) sale, 26 April, 1839 (lot 58), bt. Green. Coll. J. H. Green, Hadley.[9] Exhibited at Manchester, 1857 (Provisional Catalogue, No. 442; Definitive Catalogue, No. 421). Bequeathed by Mrs. Joseph H. Green, 1880.

REPRODUCTION: *Illustrations, Continental Schools*, 1937, p. 120. *Plates, Early Netherlandish School*, 1947, Plate 67.

REFERENCES: **(1)** Schongauer's engraving is reproduced by Lehrs, *Martin Schongauer*, 1914, Plate xiv. See also Lehrs, *Geschichte und Kritscher Katalog des Kupferstichs*, etc., Vol. V, dealing with Schongauer, 1925, p. 146, where the borrowings in No. 1087 are recorded. **(2)** C. Aru and Et. de Geradon, *La Galerie Sabauda de Turin* (*Les Primitifs Flamands, Corpus*), 1952, Plates XXIX and XXX. **(3)** See Friedländer, Vol. IX, No. 185. **(4)** L. Baldass thinks 1510 rather too late. **(5)** As Schongauer in Passavant, *Kunstreise*, 1833, pp. 97/8. **(6)** E.g., 1913 catalogue of this Gallery. **(7)** See Passavant, *Kunstreise*, 1833, pp. 97/8. **(8)** For this exhibition, see Style of Aelbrecht Bouts, No. 1083, note 5. **(9)** Waagen, *Treasures*, 1854, ii, p. 459.

MASTER OF THE DEATH OF THE VIRGIN

active 1507–1537

Author of a large group of works, named after two altarpieces representing the *Death of the Virgin* at Cologne and Munich. Several of his altarpieces were painted for Cologne and Genoa.

An *Adam and Eve* in the Louvre is dated 1507: a portrait, No. 78 of Friedländer's list, Vol. IX, is dated 1537: several other pictures are also dated.

He often repeated himself and often borrowed motives from other painters: the strongest influences on him seem to have been, first Memlinc and David (Bruges), then Massys and Patenier (Antwerp), then Leonardo da Vinci. Friedländer supposes that he was trained by Jan Joest, and points out that he exercised a very strong influence on the elder Bruyn of Cologne.

He is usually identified with Joos van Cleve (q.v. for biography).

2603 THE HOLY FAMILY

Oak, painted surface, $19\frac{3}{4} \times 14\frac{3}{8}$ (0·49 × 0·365).

Condition fair; somewhat rubbed and repainted.

One of many versions, none known exactly corresponding to this, many of them copies.

Part of the damage to the picture is due to the artist's *pentimenti*. Except for the lily, which seems always to have been as now, the composition originally corresponded very precisely with Baldass, Plate 34.[1] The Child was sitting on the Virgin's right knee, His legs across the white drapery, the folds of which have been modified where still visible, and the Virgin's left cuff came farther forward, with the fingers (apparently) as in Baldass Plate 34; the lemon was once smaller.

A variation of this original design, where the Virgin's left hand rests on the parapet, is in the George Blumenthal Bequest to New York[2]; a derivation from this with further variations, especially in the flower-pot and S. Joseph, is at Chicago.[3]

When in the National Gallery picture the painter put the Child to stand on the parapet, he left practically unaltered the position of His head (except for the direction of the eyes), and of the Virgin's right hand (except for minor variations in the fingers); this distinguishes the present version from others with a standing Child, e.g. in the Cook Collection.[4]

The Cook version and some others have a landscape behind S. Joseph, and thus connect with a different group of Madonnas, of which the best-known example was in the Holford Collection, now at Manchester, New Hampshire.[5]

The Virgin's head in No. 2603 reappears frequently in a single figure with the hands in prayer, of which Baldass reproduces two versions,

Plates 32 and 76; this composition is apparently derived from a Massys, of which No. 295 of this catalogue is a version.

Simplified examples of the Virgin and Child alone are reproduced by Baldass on Plates 9 and 10; these forms have a long Netherlandish tradition ('Campin,' David).

Baldass and Friedländer agree in calling No. 2603 early, Baldass dating it *ca.* 1515/20. The *pentimenti* do not make it certain that it is the earliest version with a standing Child.

Although Leonardesque influence is chiefly discernible in the later works of the Master of the Death, it is possible that the Virgin's extended left hand, whether in the original form (Baldass, Plate 34) or as now, is derived from Leonardo (*passim*).

The Child standing on the parapet is also perhaps an imported motive; it is common in the Florentine and Venetian Schools (Verrocchio, Bellini, etc.), and appears at Milan.[6] The motive appears in the Netherlandish School in a picture by Lucas van Leyden, probably of slightly later date than No. 2603, at Oslo,[7] etc.

The figure of S. Joseph in a straw hat, in many of the versions (as here) with spectacles, seems to be an original caprice. The straw hat may be taken from some *Flight into Egypt*, where it is more proper; compare No. 1084, Studio of the Master of 1518. It reappears in Bruegel's *Adoration of the Kings*, No. 3556.

The presence of a cut lemon in this and other versions is said to indicate that the true subject is the weaning of Christ.[8]

VERSIONS: Some are mentioned above; see the lists in Baldass and Friedländer.

PROVENANCE: Bought by George Salting, 1890.[9] Exhibited at the Burlington Fine Arts Club, 1892 (No. 48); on loan to the Gallery from 1895. George Salting Bequest, 1910.

REPRODUCTION: *Illustrations, Continental Schools*, 1937, p. 211. *Plates, Early Netherlandish School*, 1947, Plate 68.

REFERENCES: *General*: Baldass, *Joos van Cleve*, 1925, No. 32. Friedländer, Vol. IX, No. 66.

In text: (1) Baldass Plate 34 is Friedländer, Vol. IX, No. 66r. (2) The Blumental picture is Friedländer, No. 66m. (3) The Chicago picture is Friedländer, No. 66l. (4) Cook Coll., No. 465, reproduced in the large catalogue. Others are Friedländer, Nos. 66h, i, q, etc. A version in the Vienna Academy has been published since cleaning by Ludwig Münz, *Katalog des Wiederöffneten Teiles der Gemäldegalerie* (Vienna Academy), 1948, No. 21, where Baldass' latest views on the dating may be found. (5) The Holford picture is Friedländer, Vol. IX, No. 64. (6) Cf. the Luinesque picture, No. 3090 of this Gallery. (7) Friedländer, Vol. X, Plate LXXIV. (8) See Wurzbach, *Niederländisches Künstler-Lexikon*, II, p. 609, where all the versions are described as old fakes. (9) Salting MSS.

After the MASTER OF THE DEATH OF THE VIRGIN

2155 THE ADORATION OF THE KINGS (CENTRAL PANEL OF A TRIPTYCH)

On the dagger of the kneeling King is a mark like ƎB, apparently mere ornament (see below). S. Joseph behind to the left. The figures in the right background are presumably the following of the Kings: the young man on the left of the group is pointing towards the star (which appears in the originals of this picture).

Oak, painted surface, $26\frac{1}{4} \times 21\frac{3}{4}$ (0·665 × 0·55).

Probably cut top and left. A great deal of repaint all over the picture.

A copy of the sixteenth century, but not necessarily done in the studio.

An original with variations in the landscape, etc., is at Naples.[1] Friedländer appears to prefer another version formerly in the van Gelder Collection.[2] The van Gelder picture is supposed to carry the initials J B, in the place where No. 2155 has the decorative device 'ꟼ B'; J.B. is supposed to be a signature (see the biography of Joos van Cleve). Friedländer mentions yet another version under his No. 10b. Another is in the Monasterio de las Descalzas Reales at Madrid.[3] These are all triptychs, with one King on the central panel (as in No. 2155), the other two on the wings, which are missing from the present version. A further related picture is in the Fitzwilliam Museum at Cambridge.[4]

VERSIONS: See above.

PROVENANCE: Coll. Krüger, Minden.[5] Purchased with most of the rest of the Krüger Collection, 1854. From 1857 for many years on loan to Dublin.[6]

REPRODUCTION: *Illustrations, Continental Schools*, 1937, p. 211. *Plates, Early Netherlandish School*, 1947, Plate 69.

REFERENCES: (1) The Naples picture is Baldass, *Joos van Cleve*, 1925, Plate 56, and Friedländer, Vol. IX, No. 10a. (2) The van Gelder picture is Friedländer, Vol. IX, No. 10. It is now at Detroit (Whitcomb Catalogue, 1954, p. 55). E. P. Richardson kindly sent photographs of it, including a detail of the supposed signature. The mark at Detroit is rather more like J.B. than is the mark on No. 2155, but it appears very doubtful if letters are intended. The elements of the mark somewhat resemble the Duke of Burgundy's 'flint and steel,' shown sideways. (3) P. Junquera and T. Ruiz Alcón, *Monasterio-Convento de las Descalzas Reales*, Madrid, 1961, p. 41 and Plate X. (4) *Catalogue of Paintings*, Vol. I, *Dutch and Flemish Schools*, 1960, pp. 21–2, No. 1784, Plate 21, as School of Joos van Cleve. (5) Krüger Catalogue, 1848, ii, No. 20, as Schwarz (*sic*). For biographical facts concerning Carl Wilhelm August Krüger (1797–1868), living at Aachen from 1830(?) until 1835, when he moved to Minden, see Wilhelm Karl Schmidt in *Mindener Heimatblätter*, June–August 1953, pp. 62 ff. (6) As Bruyn.

5470 THE HOLY FAMILY

Through a mistake in identification on the part of the executors, this picture was presented to the Gallery as part of a bequest and appeared in the *Plates, Early Netherlandish School*, 1947, p. 70. It was later withdrawn when the mistake was discovered.

Follower of the MASTER OF THE DEATH OF THE VIRGIN

1088 THE CRUCIFIXION, A TRIPTYCH

Christ on the cross marked $\overline{\text{INRI}}$ between the Virgin and S. John. On the ground a skull and some bones (to indicate Golgotha).

Left wing, the Donor. On the prie-dieu, a coat of arms, *argent, an engrailed cross sable*; this cross appears also on a helmet painted above, and on the ring he wears. Above the arms, the letters WB. At the foot of the prie-dieu, the remains of a monstrance (?) surmounted by a cross; a plant has been painted over this to cover it. In the background, the Way to Calvary.

Right wing, the Donatrix. The arms have been rubbed out—probably three eagles displayed gules, ground uncertain. Monstrance (?) and cross as above. In the background, the Resurrection.

Wood, much reduced in thickness and mounted on canvas. Central part, $28\frac{1}{2} \times 19\frac{3}{4}$ (0·725 × 0·50); wings, each, $29\frac{3}{4} \times 8\frac{1}{2}$ (0·755 × 0·215). The central part and perhaps the wings have been slightly cut: compare the outsides of the wings, No. 1088A.

In very bad condition—much rubbed and repainted.

1088a THE ANNUNCIATION (IN GRISAILLE)

Two panels of oak: each, painted surface, $30 \times 8\frac{1}{2}$ (0·76 × 0·215).

The sawn-off outsides of the wings of No. 1088. Perhaps very slightly cut. Much damaged and repainted, but Gabriel is in less bad condition than the rest of the altarpiece.

The donors are on a different scale to the other figures, but could be by the same hand.

The costume indicates a date of *ca.* 1525/30 or a little later; the style of painting of the Christ is more likely a little after 1530. Angels in a hole in the sky appear at about that time.[1]

The picture appears to be by a remote follower of the Master of the Death[2]; no exact original designs are known.[3]

VERSION: A *Crucifixion* on the same design, slightly larger and probably nearer to the Master of the Death, was owned by Counts A. and V. Bloudoff, Leningrad.[4] The donors there are different, but some of the accessories are the same; to judge from the reproduction, these donors might be by a different hand from the central panel.

PROVENANCE: In the collection of Karl Aders, a German merchant living in London; Aders Exhibition, No. 14 (no mention of No. 1088a)[5]; Sale 1 August, 1835 (lot 53),[6] bt. J. H. Green. Coll. J. H. Green, Hadley[7]; bequeathed by Mrs. Joseph H. Green, 1880.

REPRODUCTIONS: *Illustrations, Continental Schools*, 1937, pp. 8, 9. *Plates, Early Netherlandish School*, 1947, Plates 71, 72.

REFERENCES: (1) Cf. the cherubs in the *Crucifixion* attributed to Pieter Coecke van Aelst, reproduced by Friedländer, Vol. XII, Plate XXII. (2) Ascribed to the last period of the Master of the Death by Lippmann in *The Burlington Magazine*, Vol. XII (1907/8), p. 108; to his following by Durand-Gréville in the *Gazette des Beaux-Arts*, 1908, i, p. 72. Ascribed to Sotte Cleef by A.-J. Wauters in his Brussels *Catalogue*, 2nd edition, 1906, p. 42. At one time catalogued as German School. (3) An *Annunciation* and a *Crucifixion* vaguely similar in design are reproduced by Baldass, *Joos van Cleve*, 1925, Plates 51, 52. (4) Reproduced in *Trésors d'Art en Russie*, Vol. V, 1905, Plates 50, 51. See a summary in French on the Bloudoff family on pp. 59 f. The triptych appeared in the Bloudoff Sale, Amsterdam, 25th November, 1924; the *Crucifixion* (identifiable from the description) being lot 108, Ecole Néerlandaise, *ca.* 1560; the wings (partly reproduced) being lot 116, as Marten van Heemskerck. (5) For this Exhibition, see Style of Aelbrecht Bouts, No. 1083, note 5. (6) As Mabuse; no mention of No. 1088A, which presumably still formed the back of the wings. (7) Waagen, *Treasures*, 1854, ii, p. 460, as Mabuse.

MASTER OF DELFT

active early sixteenth century

The name was given by Friedländer. According to a rather complicated argument from a composite altarpiece (Friedländer, Vol. X, Plates XXXVII–XXXVIII), he was working in Delft *ca.* 1510. His principal picture is No. 2922 below, which, as is noted in the entry for it, also has a connection with Delft. Friedländer sees some connections with the Master of the Virgo inter Virgines, who was probably active at Delft towards the end of the fifteenth century; both of these Masters may have been employed on woodcuts for book illustrations.

2922 SCENES FROM THE PASSION (A TRIPTYCH)

Left Wing: Christ presented to the People

Christ is being made to descend some steps towards the Cross, at which is busy a man with a belt marked ANE. A Holy Woman (?) in the foreground. Pilate (?) with a reed to the extreme left—unless he is the figure seated at a window. In the background, the two thieves have already set out on the Way to Calvary.

Central Panel: The Crucifixion

Christ is on the Cross marked Ī.N̄.R̄.Ī., between the two thieves. The Magdalen is at the foot of the Cross. Left foreground, the Virgin, S. John and two Holy Women. The white horse to the right has on the harness E/LANT(?)/M/AR; the rider with a reed is the same as the Pilate (?) of the left wing. Longinus (?) holding a lance behind. In the background (left) the Procession to Calvary with Pilate (?), (centre) Judas hanging from a withered tree, and in another scene, the Virgin swooning with S. John and three Holy Women, (right) the Agony and preparations for the Capture. In the foreground at the extreme left, the donor in a white habit.

Right Wing: The Deposition

Foreground, the Virgin, S. John, the Magdalen (?) and two Holy Women. In the middleground, Joseph of Arimathaea and Nicodemus let down Christ's body from the Cross.

Left Wing, Reverse: in grisaille, the Virgin and Child and S. Augustine, in a niche with a flattened arch.

Right Wing, Reverse: in grisaille, S. Peter and the Magdalen, in a similar niche.

Oak, painted surfaces, centre panel, $38\frac{1}{2} \times 41\frac{1}{2}$ (0·98 × 1·055); wings (obverse and reverse), $40\frac{1}{4} \times 19\frac{1}{2}$ (1·025 × 0·495).

The picture has not been cut. Condition very good; the central panel excellent. Several *pentimenti*, e.g. on the harness of the white horse to the right on the central panel, and (right wing, reverse) on S. Peter's right hand and the line of the Magdalen's cheek.

There are many actors, some not clearly identifiable. If Pilate is correctly identified in the three scenes, the painter was presumably following S. John, who says that Pilate was present at the Crucifixion (xix, 19). The various letters or forms of letters are decoration. On the nearly contemporary and perhaps comparable Oultremont Triptych at Brussels, two men have the letters A.S., P.P. and E.V. The first two pairs are supposed to stand for *Anna Sacerdos* and *Pontius Pilatus*[1]; the last is supposed by Hulin to be a signature.[2] But it is difficult to doubt that lettering was often used merely as a decoration.[3]

The attribution is Friedländer's.[4] The Triptych from which the painter takes his name may well have been painted for the Charterhouse, called S. Bartholomew in Jerusalem, near Delft. Hoogewerff[5] thinks the donor of No. 2922 may also have belonged to this House, though it seems that the white habit might perhaps alternatively be that of a Premonstratensian.

The tower seen in the background at the left of the central panel is recognizably that of the New Church at Delft.[6] It was completed in 1496; its top was altered from what is seen here following on a fire in 1536. The two horsemen on the right recur fairly similar in a picture at Warsaw attributed to the Master of the S. Catherine Legend.[7]

PROVENANCE: Possibly Coll. Lord Northwick, Thirlestaine House: 1846 Catalogue, No. CCCCXXXVI (?)[8]; 1858 Catalogue (No. 474); sale, 26 July, 1859 (lot 83), bt. J. Scott. Purchased by Lord Brownlow in London *ca.* 1860.[9] Exhibited, R.A. 1893 (No. 170). Presented by Earl Brownlow, 1913.

REPRODUCTION: *Illustrations, Continental Schools*, 1937, p. 212 (obverse). *Plates, Early Netherlandish School*, 1947, Plates 73, 74 (obverse). The reverses of the wings are reproduced in *Paintings and Drawings on the Backs of National Gallery Pictures*, 1946, Plates, 32, 33.

REFERENCES: **(1)** See the Brussels *Catalogue* by A.-J. Wauters, 2nd edition, 1906, p. 37. **(2)** See the biography of Mostaert in this catalogue. **(3)** Cf. the Master of the Bruges Passion Scenes, No. 1087 of this catalogue. **(4)** Friedländer, Vol. X, No. 60. **(5)** Hoogewerff, *De Noord-Nederlandsche Schilderkunst*, II, 1937, p. 395. **(6)** This was pointed out in the catalogue of the Exhibition *Middeleeuwse Kunst der Noordelijke Nederlanden*, Amsterdam, 1958, p. 71; the compiler is much indebted to Dr. S. J. Gudlaugsson and Miss H. A. J. Hos of the Rijksbureau voor kunsthistorische Documentatie at The Hague for help in connection. The slight representation of the tower in No. 2922 is possibly the most authentic record of it as it was before 1536. Other records of it in this state are as follows. (a) a painting, size 192 × 30 cm., in the Town Hall at Delft (photo in the Gallery archives), apparently dated 1620 on the frame, which also carries an inscription concerning the tower; if this painting is of the XVII century, presumably it derives from reliable records. What is clearly this painting is recorded by D. van Bleyswijck, *Beschryvinge der Stadt Delft*, 1667 and later, p. 128 (inscription but not 1620, given). (b), an engraving of the tower in Bleyswijck's book by A. de Blois, 1679, seems clearly taken from (a), with variations especially of proportions, frame not included; photo in the Gallery archives. (c), the tower in this state is seen in an engraved view of Delft in Braun-Hogenberg, *Civitates Orbis Terrarum* (the first edition is of 1572); photo in the Gallery archives. (d), the tower is seen similarly in a view of Delft illustrating Guicciardini's *Descrittione di tutti i paesi bassi*, first in the first Plantin edition of 1581; although the matter has been questioned, it seems that the illustration in Guicciardini is taken from that in Braun-Hogenberg. For bibliographical comments on Guicciardini's book, see

P. A. M. Boele van Hensbroek, 'Lodovico Guicciardini, Descrittione di tutti i paesi bassi', in *Bijdragen en Mededeelingen van het Historisch Genootschap gevestigd te Utrecht*, I, 1877, and J. Denucé, *Oud-Nederlandsche Kaartmakers in betrekking met Plantijn*, Vol. I, 1912, pp. 140 ff. **(7)** See in the *Corpus* series, *Pologne*, 1966, p. 9 and Plate VII, XVIII. **(8)** As Schongauer here and subsequently. **(9)** N. G. Annual Report, 1913.

MASTER OF THE ABBEY OF DILIGHEM

See MASTER OF 1518

MASTER OF THE EXHUMATION OF S. HUBERT

See Follower of ROGIER VAN DER WEYDEN, No. 783

MASTER OF 'FLÉMALLE' *See* ROBERT CAMPIN

MASTER OF SAINT GILES

active *ca.* 1500

A painter clearly of Netherlandish training who worked at Paris about the turn of the century: named from the pictures in this Gallery. No dates are on his works; Friedländer's latest list of pictures attributable to him is in the *Gazette des Beaux-Arts*, 1937, i, pp. 221 ff. He seems to have been slightly influenced by the styles of Hugo van der Goes and Gerard David. Several of his pictures include views in or near Paris (see below).

1419 S. GILES AND THE HIND

S. Giles is seated to the right, the King of France (?) and a bishop (?) kneel left centre. The town shown in the background is most probably Pontoise (see below).

Reverse, in grisaille, a bishop in a niche. It has been suggested that he is S. Loup (see below).

Oak, painted surface (obverse and reverse), $24\frac{1}{4} \times 18\frac{1}{4}$ (0·615 × 0·465).

Clearly from the same series as No. 4681 (q.v.) and seemingly connected with two other pictures discussed below.

There is a little damage on the face of the kneeling cleric, but on the whole the picture is in excellent state. There is a *pentimento* in the church tower in the background to the left; the large tree is painted on top of the landscape; some alterations to S. Giles' head.

Weale[1] suggests that the cleric kneeling left centre is the donor, but this personage has a place in the story. S. Giles (Ægidius) retired into the desert in Provence, where a hind was his only companion; the Royal Hunt tried several times to capture the hind, until at last one of the huntsmen shot an arrow blindly among the brambles where it had taken refuge.

The arrow struck S. Giles; the King of France or, according to some, Flavius Wamba, King of the West Goths, and a bishop (Aregius ?) came later to ask pardon.[2]

The town in the background is most probably Pontoise, only fairly accurately recorded. Canon Nicholas, however, thinks the town is Saint-Gilles-du-Gard, near Arles, and even says that he used this picture to work out the exact sites of its former seven parishes.[3]

The picture is datable from the costume *ca.* 1500.

Besides No. 4681 below, there exist two other pictures by, or possibly in part from the studio[4] of the Master of S. Giles, very nearly of the same size, now at Washington; one represents *S. Loup* (*Leu*) *curing the Children*, the other is claimed to represent *S. Denis baptizing Lisbius*. The *Baptism* scene is shown as taking place in the lower chapel of the Sainte-Chapelle, Paris (freely varied in part); the setting of the other is the square in front of Notre-Dame.[5] These two and Nos. 1419 and 4681 of this Gallery have been published by Friedländer[6] as the two wings of a large Triptych; the *Saint Giles and the Hind*, he says, was placed above the *Mass of S. Giles*, the scene in front of Notre-Dame above the *Baptism of Clovis*. Consideration of the reverses shows that this order is most unlikely. The niche (containing a figure of S. Giles) formerly on the back of the scene before Notre-Dame has an arched top, the niche on the back of No. 1419, supposed to correspond, has a flat top; such asymmetry would be very peculiar.[7]

So far as the two National Gallery pictures are concerned, the bishop on the back of No. 1419 is in a frontal attitude rather than facing to the right; but the S. Peter on the back of No. 4681 certainly faces to the right. It was suggested in the 1955 edition of this catalogue that No. 1419 might have been the central panel of a small triptych, No. 4681 the (fixed) right wing.[8] In this case, the Washington pictures would be parts of a distinct altarpiece.[9] Hinkle[10] modified this, suggesting that the *Baptism* at Washington could have been the fixed left wing of a triptych with Nos. 1419 and 4681, the other Washington picture being separate. Hinkle properly comments on the difficulty of the arrangement; it is true that in Italian art double-sided altarpieces are met with, a back that can be considered as fairly well comparable with what is suggested for the Master of S. Giles pictures being on an altarpiece by Antonio Vivarini and Giovanni d'Alemagna in S. Zaccaria, Venice,[11] but the compiler is unable to cite an example even approximately comparable in Northern art. It seems best to have reserves about all the suggestions so far put forward.

Hinkle[12] thinks that the bishop on the back of No. 1419 is S. Loup. He claims that all four panels were painted for the Church of St.Leu-St. Gilles at Paris.[13]

PROVENANCE: Thomas Emmerson Sale, London, 27 May, 1854 (lot 63),[14] bt. Webb, who sold it to Thomas Baring, 1854. Exhibited R.A. 1872 (No. 224).[15] Mr. Baring died in 1873 and bequeathed his collection of pictures to his nephew, the 1st Earl of Northbrook. Northbrook catalogue, 1889 (No. 2); exhibited Burlington Fine Arts Club, 1892 (No. 35)[16]; R.A. 1894 (No. 181).[17] Bought with several other pictures from the Northbrook Collection, 1894.

REPRODUCTION: *Illustrations, Continental Schools*, 1937, p. 222 (obverse), p. 220 (reverse). *Plates, Early Netherlandish School*, 1947, Plate 75 (obverse).

REFERENCES: **(1)** *Northbrook Catalogue*, 1889, No. 2. **(2)** There is a version of the story with some variations in the Garnier edition of the *Golden Legend*, I, pp. 406/7. The legends are very much confused: S. Giles was probably living *ca.* A.D. 700, at which time there were no Gothic kings in the region of Arles. The Latin form of Giles is Ægidius; according to some, the whole story of the hind has been invented from this name—*αἴξ* being a goat, the form *αἰγίδιον*, kid, also occurring. **(3)** Canon Nicholas, *Une Nouvelle Histoire de Saint-Gilles*, 1912, p. 137. The suggestion of Pontoise is recorded to have been made by the Comte de Montesquiou (*Bulletin de la Société Nationale des Antiquaires de France*, 1939/40, p. 92). This was elaborated by W. M. Hinkle in *The Journal of the Warburg and Courtauld Institutes*, Vol. XXVIII, 1965, pp. 124 ff., to which students are referred. **(4)** The suggestion has been made that a French assistant collaborated with the Master of S. Giles in the two Washington panels; see Charles Sterling, *Les Peintres du Moyen Age*, 1942, p. 51 of the catalogue section, and comments by Hinkle, *op. cit.*, p. 140. **(5)** Students are referred to Hinkle, pp. 110 ff. The convincing identification of S. Loup is given on pp. 130 ff.; the claim for S. Denis on pp. 114 ff.; comments about the representation of the Sainte-Chapelle on pp. 121 ff. Much remains unknown about No. 1419, No. 4681 below and the two Washington pictures; various suggestions by Hinkle have not been taken up in the present entries. The two Washington pictures had previously been discussed by Champeaux in the *Chronique des Arts*, 1883, pp. 186/7, by Held in the Prussian *Jahrbuch*, 1932, pp. 3 ff. and by Michèle Hébert in the *Mémoires de la Fédération des Sociétés Historiques et Archéologiques de Paris et de l'Ile de France*, Vol. I, 1949 (1952), pp. 213 ff. Before Hinkle's article, the subjects were wrongly claimed to be scenes with S. Remi. **(6)** Friedländer, in the *Gazette des Beaux-Arts*, 1937, i, pp. 223/4. **(7)** See the reproductions in Hinkle, *op. cit.*, figs. 20, 21. **(8)** I.e. an altarpiece such as the *Johannesaltar* by Rogier van der Weyden at Berlin. Friedländer's reconstruction, of course, implies that Nos. 1419 and 4681 together formed a *folding* wing; in which case, the left, not the right wing. **(9)** The *S. Loup* seems, even more clearly than No. 1419, to have been a centre-piece. There is no proof that the four panels are parts of one altarpiece, Friedländer's argument being indecisive. **(10)** Hinkle, *op. cit.*, pp. 139 ff. **(11)** R. Pallucchini, *I Vivarini*, n.d., pl. 32. **(12)** Hinkle, *op. cit.*, p. 135. The possibility of his being S. Remi, mentioned in the previous edition of this catalogue, was suggested from the wrong identification of the subjects of the Washington pictures. **(13)** Hinkle, *op. cit.*, pp. 137 ff. **(14)** As by van Eyck. **(15)** As by Lucas van Leyden. **(16)** As Early Netherlandish. **(17)** As Netherlands School.

4681 THE MASS OF S. GILES

The Saint elevates the Host; the orphrey of his chasuble is formed of a series of squares, each showing an angel holding a Cross, on which hangs the Crown of Thorns. Charles Martel (?) kneels at the left. An angel flies downwards towards the altar, carrying a paper inscribed: *Egidi me / rito re / missa sunt / peccata / karolo.*

The miracle depicted has been set by the painter before the high altar of the Abbey of Saint-Denis, near Paris. Many of the objects represented can be proved to have existed in the Church: in particular, the retable, the Cross above and the monument to Saint Louis behind. The monument to Dagobert on the right still exists in a somewhat altered form. A full account is given below. There are three inscriptions: on the retable, SANCTV / S / DEVS / DOMINV / SABAOTH /; on the reliquary at the foot of the Cross, *de crv / ce dnī*; on the monument to Saint Louis, IVS (*sic* for (SANC)TVS) LVDOVICVS. REX. Elucidation of these inscriptions is given below.

Reverse, in grisaille, S. Peter in a niche; at the right-hand bottom corner, a monogram or mark, the central part of which appears to be a P.

Oak, painted surface (obverse and reverse), 24¼ × 18 (0·615 × 0·455).

Clearly from the same series as No. 1419 above, and seemingly connected with two other pictures discussed in the entry for No. 1419.

In good condition, but it suffers a trifle from overcleaning here and there (e.g. the letters on the paper the angel carries), and a little from undercleaning. There is a *pentimento* in the outline of one arm of the Cross: also in one of the lines of division of the bas-reliefs on the monument to Dagobert. One of the curtains enclosing the altar originally passed over a part of this monument, on the extreme right of the picture. Some other alterations, apparently of little importance.

The miracle depicted is described in the Golden Legend.[1] Charles Martel had committed a sin, which he dared not confess. He asked S. Giles to pray for him: on the following Sunday, while S. Giles was celebrating Mass and praying for the King, an angel placed a paper on the altar. On the paper was written the King's sin and that it was pardoned, thanks to S. Giles' prayers, if the King repented, confessed and did not commit it again. This incident is said to have taken place at Orléans in 719. In some forms of the legend, Charlemagne takes the place of Charles Martel.[2]

As stated above, the scene of the miracle has been laid by the painter before the high altar of the Abbey Church of Saint-Denis, near Paris; this picture is the only extant representation of the church as it existed about the year 1500. Much of what is visible in the picture can be identified in old inventories and descriptions[3]; a little, in part falsely restored, still exists. Just as in the Washington panels referred to under No. 1419, the accuracy of archaeological detail is most unusual in a painter of about 1500; but the perspective is somewhat confused, and the painter has simplified the scene by reducing both the number of objects in the church and the richness of their ornamentation.

Above the altar, the retable of gold studded with gems (much simplified in the picture) was almost certainly the gift of Charles the Bald (823–77); it is mentioned in an inventory of 1505[4] and remained in existence until the Revolution. It had been used at first as an altar-frontal. For a description of the original, see Doublet.[5] In the picture, God sits enthroned under two cherubim in the central compartment; inscription (as noted above), SANCTV / S / DEVS / DOMINV / SABAOTH. The cusped form of the mandorla is found in some other early works.[6] The two side panels were similar to each other, but only very little of the one to the right is visible in the picture: at the top a hand holds a ring from which descend three chains supporting a crown, an angel on each side; below, three saints, each holding a book.

The Cross above was attributed to and was very probably by S. Eloy, Bishop of Noyon (*ca.* 588–658/9); Doublet[7] says that it was given to the church by Dagobert. It is mentioned in an inventory of 1739.[8] It was of the height of a man, but the painter has made it look much smaller. A cameo seen in the centre is mentioned by Doublet. The reliquary at the foot, inscribed on the picture *de crv / ce dnī*, contained a fragment of the True Cross.

The angels of copper, holding candlesticks and standing on pillars of brass that support the curtains round the altar, are mentioned in the 1505 inventory.[9]

The structure of gilded brass behind,[10] with six arches on four columns, formed the platform that supported the coffin of S. Louis; inscription (as noted above), IVS (*sic* for (SANC)TVS) LVDOVICVS. REX. According to an obscure passage in an inventory of 1634, it seems to have been constructed by Pierre Rozette in 1398 at the gift of Charles VI. At least part of this monument (the columns and the angels holding candlesticks), and presumably the rest, was destroyed in 1610.

Behind is seen the entrance to the crypt, with a wooden screen above shutting off the apse. Suger's Cross, attributed to the workshop of Godefroy de Claire, and datable *ca.* 1140/7, was wrongly claimed in the 1955 edition of this catalogue to be probably the structure hardly visible between the angel's body and the monument to S. Louis, the upper part mostly hidden by the angel's left wing.[11]

As background to the picture, part of the south aisle of the choir and the apse; the main arches round the apse are decorated with hangings.

On the right of the picture, half cut off at the edge, is the monument to Dagobert I (died 639). This monument is still *in situ* in the church; it dates apparently from the middle of the thirteenth century, but was heavily restored in the nineteenth.[12] Dagobert is lying on his side, right; the standing figure left is his second wife, Nanthilde. In the archivolt above, three angels with censers. The bas-reliefs in the tympanum of the arch (only half visible) tell of the vision of a hermit Jean, after the death of Dagobert.[13] (1) In the lowest row, S. Denis adjures the hermit to pray for Dagobert who had died that very day; the torment of Dagobert's soul continues the story to the right, but is outside the field of the picture. (2) SS. Denis, Maurice and Martin save Dagobert's soul from the boat where devils had been tormenting it; left, an angel with holy water. (3) Of the topmost scene of the triumph of Dagobert's soul, only an angel and one of the saints are visible. The scenes in bas-relief are somewhat compressed in the picture. It is to be noted that these sculptures are without colour on the picture although they are supposed to have been coloured originally.

The textiles seem to be all of the fifteenth century, and are not particularly important.

The crown worn by the King in the picture may be one of the Royal Insignia, used for the Coronations at Rheims, but at other times preserved at Saint-Denis. It may be the Sainte Couronne, also called the Crown of Charles the Bald, said to have been used to crown every King of France from Charles the Bald until Henri IV, and destroyed by the Ligue during the reign of the latter.[14]

PROVENANCE: Duc de Tallard Collection by 1752; Sale, Paris, 22 March, etc., 1756 (lot 132).[15] Richard Cosway catalogue (for private sale ?), London, June (?), 1791, Breakfast Room, p. 48, No. 46.[16] Seen in the collection of the Earl of Dudley, 1831, by Passavant.[17] Lord Dudley died in 1833: his heir was his second cousin, the 10th Lord Ward, who died in 1835. In the collection of his son William, 11th Lord Ward,[18] created Earl of Dudley (of the second creation) 1860. Exhibited at Manchester, 1857 (Provisional Catalogue, No. 473; Definitive Catalogue, No. 381)[19]; R.A. 1871 (No. 326) and 1892 (No. 173).[20] Dudley sale, London, 25 June, 1892 (lot 29),[21] bt. Vokins. Lent by Edward Steinkopff to the Burlington Fine Arts Club, 1892 (No. 24)[22]; R.A., 1902 (No. 9). Passed to Mr. Steinkopff's daughter, who married Mr. Stewart-Mackenzie, created Lord Seaforth in 1921. Exhibited at the Society of Antiquaries, London, 4 February, 1915. R.A. 1927 (No. 70). Purchased from the trustees of the late Lady Seaforth, and presented by the National Art-Collections Fund, 1933. Exhibited at the National Gallery, N.A.–C.F. Exhibition, 1945/6 (No. 26).

REPRODUCTION: *Illustrations, Continental Schools*, 1937, p. 221 (obverse), p. 220 (reverse). *Plates, Early Netherlandish School*, 1947, Plate 76 (obverse).

REFERENCES: **(1)** *La Légende Dorée*, Garnier edition, I, p. 407. **(2)** Cf. E. Mâle, *L'Art Religieux du XIIIe Siècle en France*, 5th ed., 1923, pp. 353 ff. W. M. Hinkle, in an article several times referred to the entry for No. 1419 above, in the *Journal of the Warburg and Courtauld Institutes*, Vol. XXVIII, 1965, pp. 112 f., explains that one version of the story does place the miracle in Saint-Denis. Charlemagne would, of course, not suit the time when S. Giles is supposed to have lived (late seventh to early eighth centuries), any more than the Gothic Wamba for No. 1419. **(3)** See especially Dom Doublet, *Histoire de l'Abbaye de Saint-Denis*, 1625. An elaborate but not final account of the furnishings of the Abbey with many references to No. 4681 is given by Conway in *Archaeologia*, 1915, Vol. LXVI. Much of the information given in the text is derived from Conway; see especially pp. 108 ff., 125 ff., 134 ff., 147 ff. **(4)** 1505 Inventory, No. 188. **(5)** Doublet, *op. cit.*, pp. 330 ff. The student may also consult S. McK. Crosby, *The Abbey of St.-Denis*, Vol. I, 1942, pp. 84/5 and E. Panofsky, *Abbot Suger on the Abbey Church of Saint-Denis*, 1946, p. 179. **(6)** For a discussion of this form of mandorla, see Walter W. S. Cook, *The Earliest Painted Panels of Catalonia* (II), in *The Art Bulletin*, Vol. VI (1923/4), pp. 10 ff. of the offprint. His Figs. 38, 39, 41 (all of later date) are closely comparable with the present example. **(7)** Doublet, *op. cit.*, pp. 333 and 1197. **(8)** 1739 Inventory, No. 100; also in the 1505 Inventory, No. 189. A surviving fragment of it was identified in the Cabinet des Médailles in the Bibliothèque Nationale, Paris, by B. de Montesquiou-Fézensac (*Une Epave du Trésor de Saint-Denis* in the *Mélanges Martroye*, 1940, pp. 289 ff.). **(9)** 1505 Inventory, No. 191. **(10)** 1505 Inventory, No. 192. **(11)** Evidence about Suger's Cross is unfortunately scanty, but it seems clear that it was misused by the compiler previously. For what is known, see particularly Rosalie B. Green in *De Artibus Opuscula XL* (*Essays in Honor of Erwin Panofsky*), 1961, pp. 163 ff. **(12)** A reproduction of the monument in its present state is given by Vitry and Brière, *L'Eglise Abbatiale de Saint-Denis*, 2nd ed., 1925, p. 101. **(13)** A brief version of the story is in the Garnier edition of the Golden Legend, II, p. 199. See also Montfaucon, *Monuments de la Monarchie Française*, I, 1729, pp. 164 f., and Vitry and Brière, *op. cit.*, pp. 129 ff. **(14)** See Doublet, *op. cit.*, p. 367. This crown is No. 205 of the 1505 Inventory. The identification was suggested but left uncertain by Conway, *loc. cit.*, **(15)** In the sale as by Albert Dürer. It was noted by Mariette, *Abecedario*, ii, p. 161: he wrongly read the inscription as the Latin for *Seigneur conservez Charles*. The details given leave little or no doubt of the identity. The earlier date is from Dezallier D'Argenville, *Voyage Pittoresque de Paris*, 2nd edition, 1752, p. 213: 'Un Roi qui entend la Messe, Albert Durer.' **(16)** The description corresponds with that of an unidentified cutting formerly on the frame (according to the catalogue of the R.A. exhibition of 1892, No. 173): *S. Thomas Aquinas performing Mass in the Abbey of S. Denis to Louis IX King of*

France, with an ascription to Mabuse. **(17)** Passavant, *Kunstreise*, 1833, p. 104, as Jan van Eyck or School. Waagen saw the picture in August, 1835, and ascribed it to Jan Joest: *Kunstwerke*, 1837, ii, p. 205. **(18)** Among the pictures of Lord Ward on view for some years at the Egyptian Hall; see *The Athenaeum*, 1851, p. 723. Waagen, *Treasures*, 1854, ii, p. 237, as Dutch School. **(19)** Cf. W. Burger, *Trésors d'Art*, 1857, p. 153. **(20)** In these three exhibitions as by Jan van Eyck. **(21)** As Early Netherlandish School. **(22)** As Early Netherlandish, possibly G. v. d. Meire.

MASTER OF THE VIEW OF SAINTE GUDULE

active later fifteenth century

Named after a picture in the Louvre of enigmatic subject, in the background of which is a view of the façade of Sainte Gudule, Brussels (Friedländer, Vol. IV, Plate LV). The name was first given by Friedländer in *Belgische Kunstdenkmäler*, 1923, I, pp. 317 ff.: expanded lists of attributions, in part due to Hulin, are in Friedländer, Vol. IV, Nos. 70 sqq., and Vol. XIV, pp. 94/5. See also Friedländer in the *Annuaire des Musées Royaux des Beaux-Arts de Belgique*, II, 1939, pp. 23 ff.

No dates are on his pictures, but the costume makes it probable that he was active *ca.* 1470/90. The North tower of Sainte Gudule, Brussels, is shown as unfinished in his Louvre picture; this would accord with a date shortly before 1490 (cf. Maere in *La Revue d'Art*, 1925, II, pp. 150 ff.).

Besides this view of Sainte Gudule, the portal of Notre Dame du Sablon, Brussels, appears in No. 2612 below and in another picture grouped as his (Friedländer, Vol. IV, Plate LIX); it is therefore likely that he worked at Brussels. He carried on a debased imitation of Rogier van der Weyden (died 1464), and is thus typical of Brussels painting before the advent of Bernaert van Orley.

2612 PORTRAIT OF A YOUNG MAN

He holds a heart-shaped prayer(?)-book; an inkpot on the ledge in front of him. Behind, the south transept of Notre Dame des Victoires au Sablon, Brussels.

Oak, rounded top, painted surface, $8\frac{7}{8} \times 5\frac{5}{8}$ (0·227 × 0·144).

Excellent condition. *Pentimenti* in the outlines of the cap; outlines of some extra figures in the background are seen in an infra-red photograph.

It is possible, but not very likely, that it was the right wing of a diptych.

In the background are seen the portal and rose window of the south transept of Notre Dame du Sablon, Brussels.[1] The same portal seen from a nearer viewpoint recurs in *The Marriage of the Virgin*, also grouped as by the Master of S. Gudule.[2] The chief difference is that there there is a statue on the trumeau between the two doors, but this variation may be due to the painter's fancy. The avenue to the right in the present picture is also repeated there with slight variations.

Formerly catalogued, though doubtfully, as a portrait of King Louis XI of France (1423–1483). The identification goes back to the Strawberry

Hill catalogue, 1784 (see note 10); it is probably wrong. Several authentic portraits of Louis XI are known[3]; they afford little or no confirmation.

Further, the view of Notre Dame du Sablon in the background would be difficult to explain unless the picture was done at Brussels. Louis was in Flanders between 1456 and 1461; but this picture is almost certainly *ca.* 1480 (from the costume).[4]

A related portrait was in the Duke of Anhalt's collection at Wörlitz, later Dessau, now in the Metropolitan Museum at New York.[5] The sitter is not known to have been called Louis XI, and is in any case different; the authorship may be the same. In that picture a young man in very similar costume, in much the same pose, holds a very similar heart-shaped book; the background is quite different.

No. 2612 is somewhat strangely conceived; the painter is presumably within a room and is looking through a window at the man standing (or kneeling ?) out of doors. It is presumably an imitation of some such picture as Friedländer, Vol. VI, No. 16B, Plate XIX (Memlinc), where there would seem to be some justification for the conceit. The arrangement occurs sometimes in pictures of the Virgin and Child, for Whom it is more proper.[6]

Baron Henri de Rothschild owned a heart-shaped book of songs (French and Italian) of the latter part of the fifteenth century (now in the Bibliothèque Nationale at Paris).[7] The object on the ledge in the picture is the normal form of inkpot and pen(?)-case at the time; compare Netherlandish School, No. 622 of this catalogue. It is not clear why they should have been put in.[8]

The attribution is due to Friedländer[9]; it may be accepted with the mild reserve that pictures of this class tend towards anonymity. It was formerly catalogued as Burgundian, then French School.

VERSION: The ex-Wörlitz picture referred to above is hardly a version, but is related.

PROVENANCE: In Horace Walpole's Collection at Strawberry Hill, in the Holbein Chamber, 1784 catalogue, p. 47[10]; Strawberry Hill sale, XX Day, 17 May, 1842 (lot 71).[11] Hollingworth Magniac sale, London, 2 July, 1892 (lot 35), bt. Mainwaring. Massey-Mainwaring sale, London, 16 March, 1907 (lot 18), bt. Agnew. George Salting Bequest, 1910.

REPRODUCTION: *Illustrations, Continental Schools*, 1937, p. 129. *Plates, Early Netherlandish School*, 1947, Plate 77.

REFERENCES: (1) This was pointed out by René van Bastelaer in the *Académie Royale de Belgique, Bulletin de la Classe des Beaux-Arts*, 1924, pp. 16–25. The portal and rose window in their present state are reproduced by Maere in *De Kunst der Nederlanden*, 1930/1, p. 206. For further comments on the topography, see the compiler's *The National Gallery* (*Les Primitifs Flamands, Corpus*), Vol. II, 1954, pp. 203/4. (2) Friedländer, Vol. IV, Plate LIX; now at Haarlem, Bisschoppelijk Museum. (3) Most are reproduced by Bouchot in the *Gazette des Beaux-Arts*, 1903, I, pp. 213 ff. (4) Notes on the costume, by Mrs. Newton, are in the Gallery archives. (5) It is reproduced side by side with No. 2612 in *Belgische Kunstdenkmäler*, 1923, I, p. 320. Also reproduced in *The Burlington Magazine*, I, 1903, p. 209. Exhibited at Brussels, 1935 (No. 59). According to an inscription on the back, it was acquired from an aged painter at Lille by L(eopold) F(riedrich) Franz (of Anhalt: 1740–1817). (6) E.g. Memlinc; Friedländer, Vol. VI, Plate

XXX. (**7**) Letter from J. Porcher in the Gallery archives. Published by J. Porcher and E. Droz in *Trésors des Bibliothèques de France*, Fasc. XVIII, 1933. See further the Bibliothèque Nationale catalogues, *La Bibliothèque Henri de Rothschild*, 1949, p. 13 and pl. IV (Chansonnier de Jean de Montchenu, *ca.* 1470), and *Les Manuscrits à Peintures en France du XIIIe au XVIe Siècle*, 1955/6, No. 297, as between 1460 and 1476. (**8**) It has been claimed that the sitter was secretary or treasurer of the Guild of Archers at Brussels; for this, and another even more unlikely proposal, see the compiler's comments in *The National Gallery* (*Les Primitifs Flamands, Corpus*), Vol. II, 1954, pp. 205/6. It would be more reasonable to consider the sitter to be the writer, probably the scribe, of the book he is holding; this would receive some confirmation from the turned back cuff of his sleeve, which seems to be associated with manual labour at the period. (**9**) It is Friedländer, Vol. IV, No. 76. (**10**) 1784 catalogue as Louis XI, painter not given. (**11**) 1842 sale as Louis XI, by Massys; the same attribution recurs for the 1892 and 1907 sales.

MASTER OF THE FEMALE HALF-LENGTHS

active second quarter of the sixteenth century

Author, or rather production overseer, of a large group of works; named after a picture of a concert of three female figures (at more than half length) in the Harrach collection, Vienna (Friedländer, Vol. XII, No. 106). This studio was perhaps active at Antwerp, Koch (*Joachim Patinir*, 1968, p. ix) reasonably claiming close connections with Patenier, though the style is related to that of Benson (Bruges) and to some extent that of 'Ysenbrandt' (Bruges). None of the pictures are dated. As with many sixteenth-century groupings, no standard of autograph quality has been set. Perhaps in this particular case something may eventually be achieved; meanwhile, all the pictures ascribed should bear the prefix 'Studio.' M. Rostworowski in *Biuletyn Historii Sztuki*, 22, 1960, pp. 371 ff., thinks that more than one painter is responsible for the pictures grouped.

Wickhoff tried to identify the Master of the Female Half-Lengths with Jean Clouet, Wurzbach with Lucas de Heere; the curious may consult Friedländer's Vol. XII, and Wurzbach's *Niederländisches Künstler-Lexikon*. Recently, a name proposed (on very inadequate evidence) is that of Hans Vereycke; see Benesch in the *Gazette des Beaux-Arts*, May, 1943, pp. 269 ff.

Studio of the MASTER OF THE FEMALE HALF-LENGTHS

717 S. JOHN ON PATMOS

An eagle holds his inkpot: a devil hard by. In the sky, the apocalyptic vision of the Woman and Child, and the seven-headed dragon.

Oak, original painted surface, $14\frac{1}{4} \times 9\frac{1}{2}$ (0·36 × 0·24).

The sea has been badly rubbed.

The devil is presumably trying to prevent S. John from making his *Revelation*. The Apocalyptic visions are very roughly indicated.

The figure is characteristic of the Half-Length Master, and the landscape is not unlike that of No. 720. Koch[1] unreservedly accepts this classification for both figure and landscape. The picture is of the type associated with Patenier, among whose following it was formerly catalogued. At one time Friedländer [2] supposed the figure to be by the Master of the Female Half-Lengths, the landscape by Patenier; he now rightly rejects this hypothesis.[3] Durand-Gréville [4] says the figure is from the studio of Joos van Cleve; the style of the picture is not his, but the general conception of the subject may have come from him rather than from Patenier.[5]

PROVENANCE: Stated to be from the Coll. Count Joseph von Rechberg, Mindelheim, and bought in 1815 by Prince Ludwig Kraft Ernst von Œttingen-Wallerstein[6]. At Schloss Wallerstein.[7] Exhibited at Kensington Palace (for sale), 1848 (No. 75),[8] bought with the rest of the collection by the Prince Consort. At Kensington Palace.[9] Exhibited at Manchester, 1857 (Provisional Catalogue, No. 539; Definitive Catalogue, No. 477), lent by Prince Albert. Presented by Queen Victoria at the Prince Consort's wish, 1863. Exhibited at Manchester, *European Old Masters*, 1957 (No. 30).

REPRODUCTION: *Illustrations, Continental Schools*, 1937, p. 264. *Plates, Early Netherlandish School*, 1947, Plate 78.

REFERENCES: **(1)** Robert A. Koch, *Joachim Patinir*, 1968, p. 88, No. 10 of his catalogue of the Master of the Half-Lengths. **(2)** Friedländer, *Von Eyck bis Bruegel*, 2nd edition, 1921, p. 108. **(3)** Friedländer, Vol. IX, p. 121, and Vol. XII, No. 80. **(4)** Durand-Gréville in the *Gazette des Beaux-Arts*, 1908, i, p. 66. **(5)** Cf. the picture reproduced by Baldass, *Joos van Cleve*, 1925, Plate 55; No. 50 of his list as *ca.* 1525. **(6)** Cf. *Kunst-Blatt*, 1824, p. 353. Details concerning the formation of the Œttingen-Wallerstein Collection were given orally to H. I. Kay. **(7)** No. 47, as Patenier School or Style, of Wallerstein catalogues of *ca.* 1826 and 1827 (originals at Munich; photostats in the National Gallery). The collection was moved from Schloss Wallerstein after a time. **(8)** As Patenier. **(9)** Waagen's *Catalogue*, 1854 (No. 59); cf. Waagen, *Treasures*, IV, 1857, p. 229.

720 THE REST ON THE FLIGHT INTO EGYPT

In the background is the miracle of the corn (cf. the Index to Religious Subjects).

Oak, irregular top, original painted surface, 32¼ × 24½ (0·82 × 0·625).

Good condition.

One of the principal works of the group.[1] A rather similar composition (inverted) is in the J. G. Johnson collection, Philadelphia, No. 389.[2]

The fountain is of the type of the *Manneken Pis* at Brussels.

PROVENANCE: Claimed to have been in the Coll. Count Joseph von Rechberg, Mindelheim, and bought in 1815 by Prince Ludwig Kraft Ernst von Œttingen-Wallerstein.[3] Exhibited at Kensington Palace (for sale), 1848 (No. 74),[4] bought with the rest of the collection by the Prince Consort. At Kensington Palace.[5] Exhibited at Manchester, 1857 (not in Provisional Catalogue; Definitive Catalogue, No. 498), lent by Prince Albert. Presented by Queen Victoria at the Prince Consort's wish, 1863.

REPRODUCTION: *Illustrations, Continental Schools*, 1937, p. 212. *Plates, Early Netherlandish School*, 1947, Plate 79.

REFERENCES: **(1)** Friedländer, Vol. XII, No. 74. Durand-Gréville in the *Gazette des Beaux-Arts*, 1908, i, p. 68, wrongly ascribes the landscape to Patenier. **(2)** Reproduced in the second volume of the large catalogue. **(3)** Cf. *Kunst-Blatt*, 1824, p. 353. Details concerning the formation of the Œttingen-Wallerstein collection were given orally to H. I. Kay. The provenance from Rechberg appears doubtful, since the compiler has been unable to identify the picture in Wallerstein catalogues of *ca.* 1826 and 1827 (originals at Munich; photostats in the National Gallery). No. 721 below is another picture that has not been identified in these catalogues; the compiler feels no doubt about the identification of all the other Œttingen-Wallerstein pictures in the present catalogue with entries in the catalogues of 1826/7 (except slightly for No. 708, Follower of Dieric Bouts; and that chiefly because the size in 1826/7 is given as 8 × 9 pouces, which almost certainly contains some error). The only pictures listed in these catalogues of 1826/7 that were acquired by the Prince Consort *ca.* 1848 appear to be among those numbered 1–85; but it seems certain that some of the pictures 1–85 were not acquired by the Prince Consort, and highly probable that the Prince Consort acquired some Œttingen-Wallerstein pictures that are not in the 1826/7 catalogues at all. No. 720 was perhaps acquired for the Wallerstein Collection after 1827. **(4)** As Scorel. **(5)** Waagen's *Catalogue*, 1854 (No. 54), as Bernaert van Orley; cf. Waagen, *Treasures*, IV, 1857, p. 229.

Ascribed to the Studio of the MASTER OF THE FEMALE HALF-LENGTHS

721 A FEMALE HEAD (FRAGMENT)

Oak, painted surface, $10\frac{1}{4} \times 7\frac{3}{8}$ (0·26 × 0·188).

Cleaned in 1957. Fair condition.

Perhaps the head of a female Saint (the Magdalen ?).

Not certainly of the group, though apparently near in style.[1]

PROVENANCE: Claimed to have been in the Coll. Count Joseph von Rechberg, Mindelheim, and bought in 1815 by Prince Ludwig Kraft Ernst von Œttingen-Wallerstein.[2] Exhibited at Kensington Palace (for sale), 1848 (No. 70),[3] bought with the rest of the collection by the Prince Consort. At Kensington Palace.[4] Exhibited at Manchester, 1857 (Provisional Catalogue, No. 528; Definitive Catalogue, No. 453), lent by Prince Albert. Presented by Queen Victoria at the Prince Consort's wish, 1863.[5]

REPRODUCTION: *Illustrations, Continental Schools*, 1937, p. 213. *Plates, Early Netherlandish School*, 1947, Plate 80.

REFERENCES: **(1)** Admitted by Durand-Gréville in the *Gazette des Beaux-Arts*, 1908, i, p. 68, and by Friedländer, Vol. XII, No. 107. Georges Marlier, *Ambrosius Benson*, 1957, p. 200, seems to place the picture between the Master of the Half-Lengths and Benson. **(2)** Cf. *Kunst-Blatt*, 1824, p. 353. Details concerning the formation of the Œttingen-Wallerstein Collection were given orally to H. I. Kay. Nevertheless, No. 721, like No. 720 above, has not been identified by the compiler in Wallerstein catalogues of *ca.* 1826 and 1827 (originals at Munich; photostats in the National Gallery). It may have been acquired for the Wallerstein Collection after 1827. See note 3 to No. 720 above. **(3)** As Bernaert van Orley. **(4)** Waagen's *Catalogue*, 1854 (No. 55); cf. Waagen, *Treasures*, IV, 1857, p. 229. **(5)** As Scorel.

Style of the MASTER OF THE FEMALE HALF-LENGTHS

716 S. CHRISTOPHER CARRYING THE INFANT CHRIST

The hermit of the legend is on the right.[1]

Reverse: on the back is the lay-in of another landscape, the sky being a greeny-blue wash, the rest a brown wash, over very thin priming. Some figures have been roughly drawn in with the brush—three standing together on the right, the principal one pointing left; and one seated on the left. No other details of the landscape have been put in, and the figures may be disconnected jottings.

Oak, painted surface, 9¾ × 21½ (0·25 × 0·545). The lay-in on the back is probably of much the same size; paper an inch or more wide is stuck round the edges and prevents an exact measurement. The height of the figures is about 4½ in. (11 cm.).

Good state.

The figures of S. Christopher and the Child on the front, the 'subject' of the picture, appear to be rather different from the rest, including the hermit: perhaps by a follower of Massys.[2] The rest seems to be rather in the style of the Master of the Female Half-Lengths than from the following of Patenier, among which it was previously classed.

PROVENANCE: Stated to be from the Coll. Count Joseph von Rechberg, Mindelheim, and bought in 1815 by Prince Ludwig Kraft Ernst von Œttingen-Wallerstein.[3] At Schloss Wallerstein.[4] Exhibited at Kensington Palace (for sale), 1848 (No. 76),[5] bought with the rest of the collection by the Prince Consort. At Kensington Palace.[6] Exhibited at Manchester, 1857 (Provisional Catalogue, No. 538: Definitive Catalogue, No. 476), lent by Prince Albert. Presented by Queen Victoria at the Prince Consort's wish, 1863. Exhibited at Manchester, *European Old Masters*, 1957 (No. 27).

REPRODUCTIONS: *Illustrations, Continental Schools*, 1937, p. 263 (obverse). *Plates, Early Netherlandish School*, 1947, Plate 80 (obverse). The figures on the back are reproduced in *Paintings and Drawings on the Backs of National Gallery Pictures*, 1946, Plates 17, 18.

REFERENCES: **(1)** Cf. *La Légende Dorée*, Garnier edition, I, pp. 195/6. **(2)** Massys painted this subject in a picture at Antwerp; it is not very similar (Friedländer, Vol. VII, Plate XXXI). The design of the figure was probably traditional; it appears in the Bouts region and perhaps goes back to van Eyck. **(3)** Cf. *Kunst-Blatt*, 1824, p. 353. Details concerning the formation of the Œttingen-Wallerstein Collection were given orally to H. I. Kay. **(4)** No. 32, as Patenier or style, of Wallerstein catalogues of *ca.* 1826 and 1827 (originals at Munich; photostats in the National Gallery). The collection was moved from Schloss Wallerstein after a time. **(5)** As Patenier. **(6)** Waagen's *Catalogue*, 1854 (No. 58); cf. Waagen, *Treasures*, IV, 1857, p. 229.

MASTER OF THE MAGDALEN LEGEND

active late fifteenth to early sixteenth century

The name is from a large, dispersed triptych (see Friedländer, Vol. XII, No. 10, Plates I–III); Friedländer estimates a date of *ca.* 1515/20. The style, without being strongly marked, would seem to be recognizable. Round this altarpiece, a very large number of pictures has at one time or another been grouped; they are the work of one or more factories. Friedländer in his twelfth volume (with references to previous volumes) may be consulted; also J. Tombu, in the *Gazette des Beaux-Arts*, 1929, ii, pp. 258 ff., and 1930, i, pp. 190 ff., where many of Hulin's ideas are brought forward; and the *Catalogue* of the Brussels Exhibition, 1935, pp. 43 ff.

Briefly, the Master of the Magdalen Legend is supposed to have been active at Brussels, partly as a court portrait painter. The earliest date in Friedländer's lists of attributions is 1483, the latest 1527 (Vol. XIV, p. 127). He is said to have started as a retarded follower of Rogier van der Weyden, and later to have suffered some influence from van Orley, the Master of the Death of the Virgin and others.

Friedländer and Hulin incline to apply different historical names to the Master. On inadequate evidence, Friedländer calls him Pieter van Coninxloo (q.v.); Hulin, Bernaert van der Stockt (q.v.).

Studio of the MASTER OF THE MAGDALEN LEGEND

2614 THE MAGDALEN

Oak, total painted surface, 14¾ × 10¾ (0·37 × 0·27). Rather more than an inch has been added all round at some recent period; the paint has been made up to the edges. The original painted area of the picture cannot be measured exactly; it is *ca.* 12 × 8 (*ca.* 0·30 × 0·20).

The original paint is rather heavily cracked; a few local mends.

Formerly catalogued as 'A Lady as S. Mary Magdalene.' But on the one hand the features are of an anonymous cast, not having the air of a portrait; on the other, the picture is repeated many times, which in the case of portraits is most likely to happen for prominent and so identifiable sitters. Friedländer [1] is therefore probably right in calling it simply *The Magdalen*: she is in contemporary fancy dress.

The date cannot be exactly determined, but *ca.* 1520 should be approximately right.

The picture is ascribed by Friedländer[1] to the Master of the Magdalen Legend: this seems to be correct as a general indication. The word 'Studio' here added does not assert that it is by a different hand from that of the Magdalen series, but merely stresses the anonymity of the performance. The other versions follow the same design, but many differ somewhat in execution; in some cases there is a halo.

VERSIONS: A list of eleven, perhaps not all different, has been published by the compiler.[2]

PROVENANCE: On the back, 'Holbeen 1530.' Exhibited at the Burlington Fine Arts Club, 1892 (No. 6), lent by William Spread[3]; bought by George Salting, 1893,[4] and lent to the National Gallery from 1895. Salting Bequest, 1910.

REPRODUCTION: *Illustrations, Continental Schools*, 1937, p. 130. *Plates, Early Netherlandish School*, 1947, Plate 81.

REFERENCES: (1) Friedländer, Vol. XII, No. 24. A version at Chantilly (Marcel Aubert, *La Collection de Poncins-Biencourt*, Fondation Piot, Monuments et Mémoires, Vol. XLII, 1947, p. 21, No. 588 and Plate XIX) has a later inscription that it represents Mary of Burgundy. Colin Eisler thinks that this claim for the various versions need not be completely disregarded (*New England Museums*,

Corpus series, 1961, pp. 99 f.). (2) *The National Gallery* (*Les Primitifs Flamands, Corpus*), Vol. II, 1954, p. 209. Yet others are known. (3) As Early French School—an attribution formerly maintained by the Gallery. MS. note of the identity in the National Gallery copy of the exhibition catalogue. (4) Salting note-books.

See also NETHERLANDISH SCHOOL, No. 2613

MASTER OF THE MANSI MAGDALEN

active early sixteenth century

A follower of Quinten Massys, named by Friedländer. The Mansi *Magdalen* is a picture at Berlin; Friedländer attributes a rather miscellaneous group to the same hand. He notes several borrowings from Dürer's engravings, one as late as 1511 (see Friedländer, Vol. VII, pp. 87 ff.). As Friedländer, Vol. XIV, p. 109, points out, a somewhat later date than this may reasonably be claimed for the picture at Berlin, because the design on the Magdalen's pot there corresponds with the main design on a goblet etched by Altdorfer (reproduced by E. Waldmann, *Albrecht Altdorfer*, 1923, Plate 94).

4891 JUDITH AND THE INFANT HERCULES

Nude except for slight drapery. Hercules grasps a serpent in each hand; Judith holds the head of Holofernes and a sword. They seem to be standing on a flowery hill against a night (?) sky.

Oak, painted surface, $35\frac{1}{4} \times 20\frac{3}{4}$ (0·895 × 0·525).

Painted up to the edge all round. Fair state in general; the shadows rubbed.

The subject is obscure. The identification of Hercules seems sure. The female figure can be accepted as Judith; it seems strange that she should be represented naked, but various examples could be cited. The reason for the association is not clear.[1]

The attribution is Friedländer's[2] and seems quite likely.

PROVENANCE: From the collection of Charles Ricketts (died 1931) and Charles Shannon; on loan to the National Gallery from 1933. Bequeathed by Charles Haslewood Shannon, 1937. *Cleaned Pictures* Exhibition at the National Gallery, 1947 (No. 34).

REPRODUCTION: *Plates, Early Netherlandish School*, 1947, Plate 82. Not in the *Illustrations, Continental Schools*, 1937.

REFERENCES: (1) W. Krönig suggests that the two are associated as Victors (*Der italienische Einfluss in der flämischen Malerei*, 1936, p. 11). See also Georges Marlier, *Ambrosius Benson*, 1957, pp. 217 ff. (2) Friedländer, Vol. VII, No. 102.

MASTER OF MERODE *See* ROBERT CAMPIN

MASTER OF THE MORRISON TRIPTYCH

active *ca.* 1500?

Named* from a triptych once in the Morrison Collection at Fonthill and now at Toledo, U.S.A. (Friedländer, Vol. VII, Plates LVI, LVII). Friedländer's attributions in Vol. VII, pp. 80 ff., and Vol. XIV, p. 109, are few, hesitating and (it would seem) in need of confirmation.

The Morrison triptych is a difficult point of departure; it is copied without great variations in style or design from a standard type of Memlinc, and is apparently dated by Friedländer soon after 1500. Friedländer professes to see the influence of Massys in the variations; this point is the more obscure in that there are no certain works by Massys of so early a date. An angel with a lute on the central panel, not known to be copied from Memlinc, is said to be on the same design as an angel holding a paper in an altarpiece by the Master of the Death of the Virgin. This picture, which is in the Ince Blundell Collection, is of later style; it is reproduced by Baldass, *Joos van Cleve*, 1925, Plate 36. It is true that both angels are kneeling on one knee, both seen from the front; but the ordinary reader may well share the doubts of Baldass, *op. cit.*, note 61.

Friedländer's first attribution to the hand of the Morrison Triptych is No. 1085, here catalogued under the Netherlandish School. There is little in this picture reminiscent of Memlinc or Massys; the influence of the pictures associated with Geertgen tot Sint Jans, though perhaps not precise, is apparent; and the more van Eyckish style of a version in the Escorial is a further bewilderment. It is not denied that the Morrison Triptych and No. 1085 might be by the same painter; but the pictures are so strikingly different that it would seem confusing to associate them until the identity of hand has been very clearly shown. This might be achieved if other pictures were published, combining characteristics of the Morrison Triptych and No. 1085, and thus linking them stylistically.

Friedländer's other attributions in Vol. VII are all put forward with reserves, except his Plate LIX, an *Adoration of the Kings* in the J. G. Johnson collection, Philadelphia, No. 369. It has a view of Antwerp in the background. The unfinished state of the cathedral tower there probably indicates a date within a few years of 1510; cf. J. Duverger in *Annuaire des Musées Royaux des Beaux-Arts de Belgique*, 1938, p. 26, and the completed tower on a picture dated 1517, reproduced in *The Burlington Magazine*, December, 1936, p. 268 (E). Some panels in Valladolid, doubtfully ascribed to the Morrison Master by Friedländer, are apparently not later than 1504 (see the exhibition catalogue *L'Art Flamand dans les Collections Espagnoles*, Bruges, 1958, Nos. 24–27).

The early history of the Antwerp school is almost unknown. Perhaps the Johnson picture and No. 1085 are tardy representatives of a tradition

* Valentiner in the *Gazette des Beaux-Arts*, January 1955, pp. 5 ff., suggests that the Morrison Master should be identified with Simon van Herlam (recorded at Antwerp, apparently from 1502 until 1524); the reasons given appear weak.

distinct from 'Antwerp Mannerism' and to a large extent independent of Massys.

The sum of this discussion is that the Master of the Morrison Triptych seems (at present) an obscure and unfortunate term. Therefore No. 1085, previously attributed to him, is catalogued here under Netherlandish School.

MASTER OF THE PEARL OF BRABANT

See DIERIC BOUTS

MASTER OF THE PRODIGAL SON

active 1535(?)- *ca.* 1560(?)

In German, *Meister des Verlorenen Sohnes.* Named after a picture at Vienna. He has been thought of as the overseer of a factory producing many replicas; connections have been noted with several Netherlandish painters active at Antwerp. There are also some connections with Italian art. He was at one time identified with Jan Mandijn, but this seems to be excluded. For one of the pictures associated with him, a date 1535 and a monogram of L and K have been claimed; from this, identification with an obscure painter Lenaert Kroes has been proposed, but the authenticity of the monogram and date have been questioned. Some of the pictures ascribed to him seem to be from after the middle of the sixteenth century. See Georges Marlier in *Koninklijk Museum voor Schone Kunsten*, Antwerp, *Jaarboek*, 1961, pp. 75 ff.

Ascribed to the Studio of the MASTER OF THE PRODIGAL SON

266 PIETÀ

The body of Christ is supported by the Virgin and S. John; the Holy Ghost above.

Oak, irregular top, painted surface, $42\frac{1}{2} \times 27$ ($1{\cdot}08 \times 0{\cdot}685$) approx. The frame (with rounded top) covers some of the surface. The original paint was left in a slightly irregular and unfinished state along the edges: partly made up.

Excellent state.

Presumably derived from Venetian tradition (Bellini, etc.); but no exact prototype has been found.

Perhaps *ca.* 1550. One of a group of works of feebly characterized style, some known in several repetitions; they bear a traditional ascription to Lambert Lombard. Goldschmidt[1] says that these may have come from his studio, though there is no certainty that they are connected. A *Deposition*, perhaps wrongly placed in this group [2] bears a signature with date 1556; but Goldschmidt suspects it. Marlier,[3] with better justification, associates No. 266 with the studio of the Master of the Prodigal Son.

VERSIONS: Fairly frequent.[4]

PROVENANCE: Coll. Krüger, Aix-la-Chapelle, by 1833 [5]; later Minden [6]; purchased with most of the rest of the collection, 1854.

REPRODUCTION: *Illustrations, Continental Schools*, 1937, p. 195. *Plates, Early Netherlandish School*, 1947, Plate 51.

REFERENCES: (**1**) A. Goldschmidt in the Prussian *Jahrbuch*, 1919, p. 237 (and p. 225). (**2**) Reproduced by Fierens-Gevaert, *Les Primitifs Flamands*, IV, Plate CCXIX. (**3**) See G. Marlier in Koninklijk Museum voor Schone Kunsten, Antwerp, *Jaarboek*, 1961, pp. 98 ff. No. 266 (under the title *Ecce Homo*) is perhaps the picture associated with the Master of the Prodigal Son by Winkler, *Die Altniederländische Malerei*, 1924, p. 300. (**4**) One was exhibited at Bruges, *L'Art Flamand dans les Collections Espagnoles*, 1958, No. 72, repr. (**5**) Passavant, *Kunstreise*, 1833, p. 399. (**6**) Krüger Catalogue, 1848, II, No. 12. For biographical facts concerning Carl Wilhelm August Krüger (1797–1868), living at Aachen from 1830(?) until 1835, when he moved to Minden, see Wilhelm Karl Schmidt in *Mindener Heimatblätter*, June-August 1953, pp. 62 ff.

QUINTEN MATSYS *See* QUINTEN MASSYS

HANS MEMLINC

active 1465, died 1494

Usually called Memling; formerly falsely Hemling, Hemmelinck, etc. Born at Seligenstadt near Frankfort on the Main (R. A. Parmentier, *Indices op de Brugsche Poorterboeken*, 1938, Vol. I, p. xxxvi and Vol. II, Plate II; cf. *The Burlington Magazine*, Vol. LXXV (1939), p. 124). Active at Bruges. Several sure works exist; for the nature of the present inscription on *The Marriage of S. Catherine* in S. John's Hospital at Bruges, see the *Bulletin de l'Institut Royal du Patrimoine Artistique*, Vol. II, 1959, pp. 91, 95. Many works are datable. Although his origin is German, his style seems to have been formed in the Netherlands: the influences of Rogier and Bouts are discernible. His use of swags and *putti* as decorations betrays some Italian influence, presumably Squarcionesque (cf. the National Gallery picture No. 904, ascribed to Giorgio Schiavone).

His style seems to have changed little, so that it is difficult to give a dating to undated pictures, especially as a varying amount of many of them may be assigned to assistants. Early dates for pictures associated with him: portrait at Williamstown (1472), the *Last Judgment* at Gdańsk (not later than 1473), Ottawa ex-Liechtenstein (1472?), Melbourne (1475?).

747 SS. JOHN THE BAPTIST AND LAWRENCE (WINGS OF AN ALTARPIECE)

On the *reverse* (studio execution) cranes and a fox (?); and on one a coat of arms, *gules two chevrons argent between three pairs of compasses or shears*, and a crest, an arm holding a pair of compasses or shears.

Oak, each, painted surface, $22\frac{1}{2} \times 6\frac{3}{4}$ (0·57 × 0·17); *reverse*, each, painted surface, $22\frac{1}{2} \times 7$ (0·57 × 0·175).

Cleaned in 1956. The reverses are a good deal restored. The obverses are in very good condition though there are some local repairs.

Wings of a small altarpiece, of which the central panel is missing.

The arms on the back have not been identified; the crest is described in detail by Weale.[1]

PROVENANCE: Purchased from Emmanuel Sano,[2] Paris, 1865.

REPRODUCTIONS: *Illustrations, Continental Schools*, 1937, p. 227 (obverses). *Plates, Early Netherlandish School*, 1947, Plate 83 (obverses). The reverses are reproduced in *Paintings and Drawings on the Backs of National Gallery Pictures*, 1946, Plate 19.

REFERENCES: *General:* Friedländer, Vol. VI, No. 19 (as *ca.* 1485).

In text: (1) Weale, *Memlinc*, 1901, p. 63. (2) Emmanuel Sano (presumably the same) was one of the supporters of Jongkind; see E. Moreau-Nélaton, *Jongkind Raconté par lui-même*, 1918, index.

2594 A YOUNG MAN AT PRAYER (LEFT WING OF A TRIPTYCH?)

Oak, painted surface, $15\frac{1}{4} \times 10$ (0·39 × 0·255). The frame (regilt) may be original, although the picture has the appearance of having been cut a little; overall size, $19 \times 13\frac{1}{2}$ (0·48 × 0·345).

Cleaned in 1959. The flesh parts are in good state. The background is now clearly seen to be green. A few small *pentimenti*. An infra-red photograph shows incoherent underdrawing, very similar in character to what is found in the *Pietà* at Melbourne.

Formerly catalogued as the *Duke of Cleves*[1]; this name seems to have been invented since the Bruges Exhibition of 1902.

Friedländer dates the picture *ca.* 1475.[2] There are some similarities in the architecture and general style to the Benedetto Portinari (?) of 1487 in the Uffizi.[3]

PROVENANCE: Coll. Eugen Felix; exhibited by his son, Hans Felix, at Leipzig, 1889 (No. 143) and 1897 (No. 1111). Purchased by Agnew's from H. H. Felix, 1900; in the same year acquired by George Salting.[4] Exhibited: R.A., 1902 (No. 2); Bruges, 1902 (No. 77). On loan at the National Gallery from 1903. George Salting Bequest, 1910.

REPRODUCTION: *Illustrations, Continental Schools*, 1937, p. 227. *Plates, Early Netherlandish School*, 1947, Plate 84.

REFERENCES: *General:* Friedländer, Vol. VI, No. 78.

In text: (1) Presumably John II, Duke of Cleves (1458–1521). (2) Friedländer, Vol. VI, No. 78. (3) Friedländer, Vol. VI, No. 23B. (4) Geoffrey Agnew, *Agnew's, 1817–1967*, 1967, p. 43 and lettering of the plate of No. 2594.

6275 TRIPTYCH: THE VIRGIN AND CHILD WITH SAINTS AND DONORS

Centre panel: the Virgin is seated with the Child in her lap. He blesses Sir John Donne, who kneels on the left under the protection of S. Catherine. On the right, under the protection of S. Barbara, kneels Sir John Donne's wife Elizabeth; a child who is clearly one of their daughters (Anne ?) kneels behind. Two angels. Sir John and Lady Donne wear the Yorkist collar of roses and suns, with King Edward IV's pendant, the Lion of March.

Wings: left, S. John the Baptist, and behind him a figure claimed (from the manner in which he appears in the picture) to be the portrait of the painter; right, S. John the Evangelist. The architectural setting of the wings continues that of the central panel.

Wings, reverses (in grisaille): S. Christopher carrying the Child, and S. Anthony Abbot.

Oak, painted surfaces: central part, $27\frac{7}{8} \times 27\frac{3}{4}$ (0·707 × 0·705); wings (in all four cases), 28 × 12 (0·71 × 0·305).

Very good condition; the most important loss on the front is on the Virgin's face, right centre. There are more losses from the reverses, especially the one showing S. Christopher, but even here the condition is to be called good.

The identification of the sitters is to be considered certain from the coats of arms appearing on two of the capitals shown in the central panel, and in the glass on the right wing. The main coat (although rather roughly represented) is safely interpreted as *azure a wolf salient argent*, in one case (on the capital right centre) *langued gules*, for Donne.[1] The lady's arms, impaled with Donne on one capital, are *argent a maunch sable*, for Hastings; Sir John Donne's wife Elizabeth was a sister of William, Lord Hastings.[2]

The sitters were thus identified by J. G. Nichols,[3] who accepted an incorrect record that Sir John Donne was slain at the Battle of Edgecote in 1469. In fact, the Sir John Donne of the picture,[4] knighted at Tewkesbury in 1471, died in 1503.[5] His wife died in 1507/8. There is reason to believe that they married in 1465; the marriage was not later; if it was earlier, it was not earlier than 1462.

Sir John Donne's death in 1469 had until recently for some decades been accepted by writers on the picture, and its date had regularly been claimed to be of the later 1460's; but this need not stand. The attribution to Memlinc is now accepted,[6] so it is probable that the picture was painted in Bruges. It is not known how often Sir John Donne was in Bruges; but he was there in 1468 for the marriage of Margaret of York to Charles the Bold,[7] and he was again in Flanders on a mission in 1477.[8] He is further recorded at several dates in Calais, where he seems to have lived a good deal. The picture seems characteristic of Memlinc's developed style; if the choice for the commission were thought to lie between the two known dates of Donne's visits to Flanders, the later one is to be preferred on stylistic grounds. But journeys to Bruges from Calais could have taken place. The picture need not have been painted immediately upon its commission.

The historical evidence available is not in disaccord with a date for the picture as late as the late 1470's, but nothing absolutely precise has been found. Sir John Donne is indeed known to have had two sons and two daughters, and since one daughter is shown, it would seem that she alone was alive at the time of the painting. In the present state of knowledge, it seems reasonable to believe that the daughter in question is Anne, who could have been born soon after her parent's marriage, but has been considered unlikely to have been born much earlier than 1470 and may even have been born a few years later. She apparently predeceased her mother, not being mentioned like the other three children in Lady Donne's will.[9]

It has often been supposed that the small figure appearing on the left wing of No. 6275 is the painter himself. Figures in several of Memlinc's works have been supposed to be self-portraits. Special mention should be made of one in the middle ground towards the right of the central panel of *The Marriage of S. Catherine* in S. John's Hospital at Bruges[10]; there is perhaps some similarity in the faces there and here, but not enough to show that the same man is represented. The figure at Bruges is considered to have a markedly pink complexion, with hair dark brown or black and eyes brown (?). The complexion of the figure in No. 6275 is certainly reddish; the hair is very dark grey or black, the eyes grey. It seems impossible that both of these figures can be self-portraits of Memlinc; it does not seem improbable that neither is. Weale[11] states that the figure at Bruges represents a Brother of the Hospital, which might seem reasonable. The costume of the figure in No. 6275 seems purely secular. The man at Bruges may appear younger than the man in No. 6275, and it is to be mentioned that the picture at Bruges bears the date 1479; it would be a pity to make a deduction for the date of No. 6275 from this.

ENGRAVING: A print of the heads of Sir John and Lady Donne, as representing George Talbot, 4th Earl of Shrewsbury and Anne his first wife, with a date 1478, was published in 1793 by J. Thane, 'From an ancient Picture on Board in the Possession of John Thane'.[12]

VERSION: See the preceding section.

PROVENANCE: Records of the picture earlier than the eighteenth century have not been found, but a direct genealogical line may be recorded, down which the picture could have passed by inheritance to the Dukes of Devonshire. Sir Griffith Donne was a son (though clearly not the eldest son) of Sir John Donne.[13] His sole daughter and heiress Elizabeth (d. 1590) married Thomas Hughes.[14] Their daughter Grisold (d. 1613) married secondly Francis Clifford, 4th Earl of Cumberland.[15] He died in 1641 and was succeeded as 5th Earl by his son Henry, on whose death in 1643 the Earldom of Cumberland became extinct. The heiress to the Clifford fortune was the 5th Earl's daughter Elizabeth (d. 1691),[16] who in 1664 married Richard Boyle, created Earl of Burlington (d. 1698). No. 6275 (with the sitters supposed to be Lord Clifford and his Lady) is recorded in the 3rd Earl of Burlington's villa at Chiswick *ca.* 1744.[17] This Earl of Burlington died in 1753. His daughter Charlotte Elizabeth had married William, Marquess of

Hartington; she died in 1754, and he succeeded in 1755 as the 4th Duke of Devonshire. The picture is often recorded in the Chiswick villa, which had passed to the Duke of Devonshire [18]; moved in December 1892 to Chatsworth.[19] Exhibited: National Portraits, 1866 (revised catalogue, No. 18); R.A. 1876 (No. 172); Brighton, 1884 (No. 141); B.F.A.C., 1892 (No. 20); Bruges, 1902 (No. 56)[20]; Guildhall, 1906 (No. 21); B.F.A.C., 1909 (No. 22); R.A., 1927 (No. 47); Agnew, 1948 (No. 33); National Gallery, 1948–1952; R.A., 1953/4 (No. 27). Acquired under the terms of the Finance Act, 1956, from the Duke of Devonshire's Collection, 1957.

REPRODUCTIONS: The three parts of the front, after cleaning at the National Gallery, in the National Gallery Catalogue *Acquisitions 1953–62*. All parts of the picture have often previously been reproduced, e.g. by Friedländer, *Die Altniederländische Malerei*, Vol. VI, Plates XI–XIII.

REFERENCES: **(1)** T. W. Newton Dunn, *The Genealogies of the Dwnns of South Wales*, 1953, No. 39, records from the Visitations (late sixteenth and early seventeenth centuries) of Lewis Dwnn 'a field azure and a silver wolf armed red as to the teeth and tongue' as the arms of Sir John Donne's father. Donne, and some other names to be mentioned, are recorded with variations of spelling. **(2)** For the relationship, see N. H. Nicolas, *Testamenta Vetusta*, 1826, Vol. I, p. 372. The Lord Hastings in question is recorded in Burke's *Peerage*, 1956, under *Huntingdon*. Mr. K. B. McFarlane has most generously made available his extensive research on the genealogies and on the picture. **(3)** *The Gentleman's Magazine*, 1840, ii, pp. 489 ff. The identification was also made by Weale in *Notes and Queries*, 3 December, 1864, pp. 451/2. **(4)** There existed a different Sir John Donne at this period; cf. Ormerod, *History of Cheshire*, 1882, Vol. II, p. 248. **(5)** T. W. Newton Dunn, *op. cit.*, No. 45, gives information about him; he is often mentioned in documents of the time. His will and the wills of his wife and of his two sons Edward and Griffith are at Somerset House; photostats in the National Gallery. **(6)** It seems first to have been made, though tentatively, by Waagen, *Kunstwerke*, 1837, i, pp. 264 ff. The picture is usually treated of at some length in books on Memlinc. **(7)** *Mémoires d'Olivier de La Marche*, ed. H. Beaune and J. d'Arbaumont, III, 1885, p. 111. The editors give the name as 'Jehan Don' (reading kindly confirmed by Mlle. Sonkes); they record that in Buchon's edition 'Jehanston' is given. **(8)** Rymer, *Foedera*, XII, 1711, pp. 42/3; Cora L. Scofield, *The Life and Reign of Edward IV*, 1923, II, p. 186, records this. The mission was to Ghent (cf. Scofield, p. 185), which is near Bruges; indeed, Bruges may fairly be considered to be on the way to Ghent from England. **(9)** K. B. McFarlane has weighed a mass of evidence to establish probabilities for the dates of birth of the children; he considers that Anne's brothers Edward and Griffith and her sister Margaret were probably a good deal younger than she was. Dr. R. R. Davies has also kindly enquired further into this matter. **(10)** Reproduced as a presumed self-portrait in the catalogue *Flanders in the Fifteenth Century*, Detroit, October/December 1960, p. 140. Notes on the colouring were kindly sent by Mlle. Sonkes (letter of 4 July, 1967). **(11)** Weale, *Hans Memlinc*, 1901, p. 37. **(12)** Cf. G. Scharf in *Archaeologia*, Vol. XL, 1866, p. 473. This Lady Shrewsbury was indeed a Hastings, being a daughter of William, Lord Hastings, and thus a niece of Lady Donne. The arms seen on the capitals and in the glass of No. 6275 are (more or less accurately) added on the print of the two heads. Maybe the Donne arms were supposed to show a talbot (dog); talbots are certainly associated with the Shrewsburys as the supporters of their arms. Further, the 1st Earl of Shrewsbury, when still Baron Talbot and Furnival, used two talbots on his seal, 1406; and the 4th Earl had one on his standard in 1513 (see A. Colin Cole in *Country Life*, 25 February, 1965, p. 425). But it seems excluded that at any time a talbot formed their coat of arms. Even if this were so, the animal shown on No. 6275 is not reasonably identified as a talbot. This identification of the sitters might nevertheless appear to be attractive, since Margaret, one of the daughters, and perhaps the eldest daughter, of this Earl and Countess of Shrewsbury, was the first wife of Henry, 1st Earl of Cumberland, and this would link up with the ownership for No. 6275 suggested under *Provenance.* It cannot be excluded at present that the descent for the picture via Lady Donne's niece is right; indeed it should be added that the 4th Earl of Shrewsbury was overseer of Lady Donne's will, and was sufficiently interested in her welfare in 1503 to write on her behalf to Sir Reginald Bray. But (apart from the heraldic objections) this identification of the sitters is impossible from the dates. The 4th Earl of Shrewsbury was born in 1468; at Memlinc's death in 1494 he was 26. Further, he was made a Knight of the Garter in 1488, and one might well be puzzled if thereafter he were depicted without any indication of it. But it is not credible that the donor in No. 6275 is under 20, or even under 26. The print referred to is from a (partial ?) version or copy of No. 6275; presumably it was the picture without attribution, lot 65 of the Thane Sale, 2 March, 1820, 'George Talbot, Earl of Shrewsbury, and his first Couness, 1618' (*sic*)—the date on the print could carelessly be read as 1418. John Thane (d. 1818) is recorded in the D.N.B. and elsewhere. **(13)** He died in 1543/4; his brother Sir Edward Donne died in 1552. **(14)** Monumental inscription in North Mimms Church, given by Robert Clutterbuck, *History . . . of Hertfordshire,* Vol. I, 1815, p. 463. **(15)** Monumental inscription in Londesborough Church, given by T. D. Whitaker, *The History and Antiquities of the Deanery of Craven,* 3rd edition, 1878, p. 359. Cf. also the record on the Clifford family picture (Whitaker, pp. 346/7). Another way in which the picture could have passed to the Cliffords is mentioned in note 12; it seems less likely. **(16)** Her will is at Somerset House. **(17)** Vertue, published by the Walpole Society, Vol. V, pp. 30/1. The attribution was to Jan van Eyck, 'his name burnt in on the back'. No. 6275 has indeed on the back IOHANES VAN EYCK, apparently in black pigment (Scharf in *Archaeologia,* Vol. XL, 1866 p. 472, says black ink). **(18)** E.g., *London and its Environs Described,* Vol. II, 1761, p. 122. Here a date 1444 is added to the attribution to Jan van Eyck. The back of No. 6275 is now partly obscured by wax, but it seems clear that no date is now written there (Scharf, *loc. cit.* in previous note, records none); to the right of the name, nevertheless, the panel had been buttoned for conservation, and a date might previously have been legible in that place. Among later records of the picture at Chiswick, see Walpole, *Anecdotes,* Vol. I, 1762, p. 26 (Dallaway's edition, 1826, Vol. I, pp. 50/1); J. J. Volkmann, *Neueste Reisen durch England,* II, 1782, p. 440; Neale's *Views of Seats,* 2nd Series, Vol. V, 1829. Louis Simond, *Voyage en Angleterre,* 2nd edition consulted, 1817, II, p. 161 (April 1811), or in English, 1815, II, p. 119, is less explicit, but is surely recording the same. **(19)** Illustrated Catalogue of the B.F.A.C. Exhibition, *Early Netherlandish Pictures,* 1892, p. XV. The home of the Memlinc in the Devonshire Collection until then appears constantly to have been Chiswick, although indeed the pictures there were off the walls for a time for James Wyatt's additions to the house of 1788 (see Lysons, *Environs of London,* Vol. II, 1795, p. 195; passage modified in the second edition, Vol. II, Part I, 1811, p. 125). Some confusion was caused by Passavant, *Kunstreise,* 1833, p. 72, who identified the picture mentioned by Walpole (see previous note), not with No. 6275, but wrongly with another picture in the Devonshire Collection, now associated with Pieter Pourbus. This picture, seen at Devonshire House, London, by Passavant, appears to have been in that house already in 1743 (Vertue, published by The Walpole Society, Vol. V, p. 23, 'a Quire. of priest & religion'); it is reproduced by S. Arthur Strong, *The Masterpieces in the Duke of Devonshire's Collection of Pictures,* 1901, Plate 17. **(20)** *Meisterwerke,* No. 27.

Studio of MEMLINC

686 THE VIRGIN AND CHILD WITH AN ANGEL, S. GEORGE AND DONOR

A Crucifix hangs from the chain round S. George's neck. S. Joseph (?) in the background.

Oak, painted surface, $21\frac{1}{4} \times 14\frac{3}{4}$ (0·54 × 0·375).

A good deal damaged, especially in the flesh, by overcleaning, and repainted; the landscape is both overcleaned and undercleaned. Several changes of composition, some of them only first outlines; the most important are in the position of the Child, Whose left leg was at one time stretched out further.

A small altarpiece probably for private devotion; at best executed in the studio by an assistant and touched up by Memlinc himself. Several little altarpieces comparable with this are known by Memlinc or his studio or in his style: the standard of autograph quality is set by the altarpiece at Vienna.

The Virgin and Child is on a design that appears often with slight variations in Memlinc's works, but the action of the Child is here not well explained: contrast the Chatsworth triptych (No. 6275 above) or the *Vierge de Jacques Floreins* in the Louvre (originals). The asymmetry of the present composition is most marked.

VERSION: A version, apparently of dubious status, is or was at Sigmaringen.[1]

PROVENANCE: On the back IF in chalk and scratched on the wood, and a seal with a three-masted sailing vessel. From the collection of Christian Geerling at Cologne.[2] It belonged to the dealer Lafontaine in 1842; it was he, apparently, who sold it, by 1847, to Johann Peter Weyer of Cologne. Weyer Sale, Cologne, 25 August, etc., 1862 (lot 234), bt. Mündler for the National Gallery.

REPRODUCTION: *Illustrations, Continental Schools*, 1937, p. 226. *Plates, Early Netherlandish School*, 1947, Plate 86.

REFERENCES: *General:* Weale, *Memlinc*, 1901, pp. 59/60 (Memlinc, *ca.* 1475). Friedländer, Vol. VI, No. 63 (Memlinc).

In text: (1) Sigmaringen Catalogue, 1883, No. 194. Cf. A. J. Wauters, *Sept Etudes pour servir à l'Histoire de Hans Memling*, 1893, pp. 48, 108 and L. Kaemmerer, *Memling*, 1899, p. 134. (2) For a discussion of the provenance, see the compiler's *The National Gallery* (*Les Primitifs Flamands, Corpus*), Vol. II, 1954, pp. 159/60. Cf. especially Weale in the *Messager des Sciences Historiques*, 1862, pp. 464/6; E. Förster in *Kunst-Blatt*, 1843, p. 269; and E. Firmenich-Richartz, *Die Brüder Boisserée*, Vol. I, 1916, p. 522.

709 THE VIRGIN AND CHILD (CENTRAL PANEL OF A TRIPTYCH?)

Oak, painted surface, $14\frac{3}{4} \times 11$ (0·375 × 0·28). Small additions to the panel top and bottom were removed in 1954.

This picture was cleaned in 1954 and much slight, but misleading, restoration was removed. Good condition; worn in places, especially the lower part of the Virgin's hair on the right. The fingers of the Virgin's left hand were drawn in further across the Child's body; her neck-line was once rounded.

Reserve about the attribution was expressed in the first edition of this catalogue. It seems clear now that No. 709 is a studio piece, that is, on Memlinc's design, and perhaps with some contribution by Memlinc to the execution.[1]

PROVENANCE: Probably bought in 1815 from Count Joseph von Rechberg[2] by Prince Ludwig Kraft Ernst von Œttingen-Wallerstein. At Schloss Wallerstein. Exhibited at Kensington Palace (for sale) 1848 (No. 53), bought with the rest of the collection by the Prince Consort. At Kensington Palace.[3] Exhibited at Manchester, 1857 (Provisional Catalogue, No. 488; Definitive Catalogue, No. 402), lent by Prince Albert. Presented by Queen Victoria at the Prince Consort's wish, 1863.

REPRODUCTION: *Illustrations, Continental Schools*, 1937, p. 226. *Plates, Early Netherlandish School*, 1947, Plate 85.

REFERENCES: *General:* Friedländer, Vol. VI, No. 47 (as *ca.* 1475).

In text: **(1)** It is admitted by Friedländer, but not mentioned in Weale's *Memlinc*, 1901. **(2)** In the first edition of this catalogue, it was stated to have been bought in 1817 from Graf Vichy, Munich; but the Vichy picture is probably not No. 709, and the provenance from Rechberg is probable. See the discussion of this point by the compiler in *The National Gallery* (*Les Primitifs Flamands, Corpus*), Vol. II, 1954, pp. 165/6. No. 709 is mentioned in *Kunst-Blatt*, 1824, p. 318, as van Eyck. Œttingen-Wallerstein catalogues of *ca.* 1826 and 1827 (No. 38) (originals at Munich; photostats in the National Gallery); the one of 1827 has an old annotation in the margin, 'von Vichy.' **(3)** Waagen's *Catalogue*, 1854 (No. 32), as Memlinc; cf. Waagen, *Treasures*, IV, 1857, p. 225.

QUINTEN METSYS *See* QUINTEN MASSYS

MONOGRAMMIST OF BRUNSWICK
See JAN VAN AMSTEL

ANTHONIS MOR VAN DASHORST

active 1544, died 1576/7

The name is often given in the Spanish form, Antonio Moro; he is said to have been knighted by Mary I of England. Van Mander and Buchelius are our only authorities for the date of birth; they are confused, but their indications seem to put it between 1517 and 1521.

Mor was from Utrecht: he was a pupil of Jan van Scorel of Utrecht; his earliest signed work is a double portrait of two Utrecht canons, 1544. In 1547 he was admitted Master at Antwerp.

His career was that of a court portraitist. By 1549 he was working in the service of Bishop (later Cardinal) Granvella and for the Spanish Court at Brussels. Within the next few years he was painting Royalty at Lisbon and Madrid: he also visited Rome, but the documents are confused about the exact date. In 1554 he painted the English Queen Mary. The picture, which is in the Prado, may have been done in London, on the occasion of her alliance with King Philip of Spain; but no documents have been discovered concerning Mor's work in this country. Thenceforward, he seems to have lived mostly in the Netherlands, at first chiefly at Utrecht, from 1568 chiefly at Antwerp.

There is a sufficient number of his signed works to distinguish him from his Netherlandish contemporaries, who, however, are not easily separable from each other.

His double portrait of 1544 is in the style of Scorel, who combined a strong 'Romanizing' tendency with Netherlandish technique. Mor's first characteristic work, his portrait of Granvella of 1549, reflects an influence that was to be lasting, that of Titian: Titian's portrait of the same sitter being of the previous year.

Mor's Titianesque portraits are important in the history of Spanish art; Sánchez Coello, Pantoja, and to some extent even the young Velázquez followed his tradition. His influence in England was negligible; the style here being dominated first by Holbein, then by Flemings and Germans contemporary with Mor.

The most careful biography is by Georges Marlier, 1933.

Some curious documents published by Henri Hymans, *Antonio Moro*, 1910, pp. 35 ff., establish two points: (1) that already by 1550 Mor had several assistants and a pupil; (2) that one of these assistants and the pupil moved to Antwerp when Mor quitted the Netherlands and painted Edward VI in the British Embassy there, obviously after a portrait by another hand.

1231 A MAN

Falsely signed: *A. Morro f.*

Oak, original painted surface, 19½ × 16 (0·495 × 0·405).

In bad condition: much rubbed and made up. Damaged in part by cracking.

In spite of its condition, recognizably an original.[1] Portraits at less than half length are rare in Mor's work, but it is not a fragment. It seems to be of the painter's later time; Hymans[2] dates it *ca.* 1575, but such precision is unjustified.

PROVENANCE: Coll. James Whatman, Maidstone. Exhibited at the British Institution, 1856 (No. 84); Leeds, 1868 (No. 896). Purchased, Walker Fund, lot 37 of the Whatman sale, 2 July, 1887.[3]

REPRODUCTION: *Illustrations, Continental Schools,* 1937, p. 236. *Plates, Early Netherlandish School,* 1947, Plate 87.

REFERENCES: (1) Listed by Friedländer, Vol. XIII, No. 385. (2) Henri Hymans, *Antonio Moro,* 1910, p. 154. (3) In the sale (but not in the exhibitions) as a Self-Portrait.

JAN MOSTAERT

ca. 1472/3–1555/6

In Latin, *Sinapius.* Working from 1498 in Haarlem (see the Exhibition catalogue *Le Siècle de Bruegel,* Brussels, 1963, p. 137; the information, as that for the date of birth, is based on a biographical article by Thierry de Bye Dolleman in the *Jaarboek XVII* (1963) *van het Centraal Bureau voor Genealogie,* kindly sent by Mlle. Ninane). From 1519 in the service of

Margaret of Austria (L. van Puyvelde, *La Peinture Flamande au Siècle de Bosch et Brueghel*, 1962, p. 305). Later, again at Haarlem; 1549, Hoorn. The documentary mentions are to be supplemented by the statements of van Mander (1604), who had fairly reliable sources in this case. Van Mander says that he was a Haarlem painter, for eighteen years in the service of Margaret of Austria (i.e. at Brussels and Malines); his is also the authority for the date of death given above. He describes a good many of his pictures.

The attribution of a group of paintings to Mostaert is due originally to Glück in the *Zeitschrift für bildende Kunst*, 1896, pp. 265 ff.; the group was known at first as by the Glück'sche Mostaert, to distinguish him from the Waagen'sche Mostaert (mostly='Ysenbrandt'), but as later discoveries have confirmed rather than weakened the hypothesis, he is here referred to simply as 'Mostaert.'

The author of this group had stylistic relations with Geertgen, i.e. connections with Haarlem, and painted several sitters of Haarlem and elsewhere in Holland. Comparisons of existing pictures with van Mander's fairly detailed descriptions are tantalizing in showing partial but not full agreement. The most persuasive, on account of the rarity of the subject, is with van Mander's 'West Indian Landscape': a picture of this kind (see the catalogue *Le Siècle de Bruegel*, Brussels, 1963, No. 177), now at Haarlem, is considered to form part of the group. These and other arguments are set forth in Friedländer, Vol. X. (See also Vol. XIV, p. 120). For a *Holy Family with S. John* in Palazzo Venezia, Rome, showing the letters IM on the Virgin's dress, also apparently A, see *Oud-Holland*, 1959, pp. 247 f.

Hulin (*Catalogue Critique*, 1902, under No. 270) separated some pictures, including No. 3900 below, from the group: he ascribed these to the Master of Oultremont, so called from a triptych now at Brussels formerly belonging to the Oultremont family. Hulin's chief reason for not ascribing them to Mostaert is the existence of the letters EV on a page's wallet in the Oultremont triptych: these are perhaps comparable to the letters AW on Gerard David, No. 1079 (q.v.), and in any case the triptych seems stylistically inseparable from the other pictures of the group.

Of datable works, Hoogewerff, *De Noord-Nederlandsche Schilderkunst*, II, 1937, pp. 449 ff., thinks the Oultremont triptych not long after 1500, a triptych at Bonn soon after 1510, and a portrait in the Louvre *ca.* 1516/23.

S. Pierron (*Les Mostaert*, 1912, p. 117) points out that there were traces of a Mostaert signature on a picture by 'Ysenbrandt' (the Waagen'sche Mostaert) in Palazzo Doria, Rome, but presumably the signature was false (nothing about it in Sestieri's Catalogue, 1942, No. 523).

'Jan MOSTAERT'

1080 THE HEAD OF S. JOHN THE BAPTIST, WITH MOURNING ANGELS AND *PUTTI*

On the medallions, left, the Baptism of Christ; right, Salome receiving the Baptist's head. The dresses of several of the angels and *putti* are ornamented with a white cross, recalling the Maltese cross of the Order of S. John of Jerusalem; one angel has a dark cross, one *putto* a dark T. The scenes below are hard to decipher. The centre and left seems to show S. John preaching, apparently according to John, i, 35–41, with that account of the calling of S. Andrew; on the right, perhaps S. John again, with two figures (one a donor ?).

Oak, painted surface, $10\frac{1}{4} \times 6\frac{3}{4}$ (0·26 × 0·17).

Rubbed and a good deal retouched. Two of the *putti* now draped appear to have been naked originally.

The subject of the Head of S. John the Baptist on a Charger may be taken from the School of Milan, e.g. No. 1438 of the National Gallery, or the Solari of 1507 in the Louvre. It is possible that its vogue was due in the first place to Gentile Bellini.[1]

In spite of its condition, the picture is still recognizably by 'Mostaert'; first ascribed by Friedländer.[2] At one time catalogued as from the School of the Lower Rhine; this was no doubt the effect of a dubious ascription to the Master of S. Bartholomew by Firmenich-Richartz, who corrected himself later.[3] The little *putti* are, in fact, not dissimilar to those of the Bartholomew Master, but are also in the 'Dutch' tradition.[4]

VERSION: Friedländer[5] mentions a variant at Dijon (on copper) as an old copy.

PROVENANCE: Coll. Karl Aders, a German merchant living in London, 1831.[6] Aders Exhibition, No. 22[7]; Sale, London, 1 August, 1835 (lot 106), bt. Willis.[8] Anon. (H. C. Robinson, or rather Aders Trust) sale, 26 April, 1839 (lot 16),[9] bt Green. Coll. J. H. Green, Hadley[10]; bequeathed by Mrs. Joseph H. Green, 1880. Exhibited at Amsterdam, *Middeleeuwse Kunst der Noordelijke Nederlanden*, 1958 (No. 81).

REPRODUCTION: *Illustrations, Continental Schools,* 1937, p. 120. *Plates, Early Netherlandish School,* 1947, Plate 88.

REFERENCES: **(1)** Cf. the story, of which the details are suspicious, related by Ridolfi, *Le Maraviglie dell'Arte*, 1648, I, pp. 40/1. **(2)** Friedländer in *Werk über die Renaissance Ausstellung*, Berlin, 1898, p. 23. See also his Vol. X, No. 21. K. G. Boon kindly wrote to the compiler in 1947 about various problems connected with the picture. **(3)** Firmenich-Richartz in the *Zeitschrift für christliche Kunst*, 1900, col. 16/7, note 11. **(4)** Some indications on this subject are given by Grete Ring in *Oud-Holland*, 1939, pp. 26 ff. **(5)** Friedländer, Vol. X, sub No. 21. It is reproduced in J. Magnin's Dijon Catalogue, 1918, p. 153; and in Hoogewerff, *De Noord-Nederlandsche Schilderkunst*, II, 1937, p. 459 (as Master of S. Bartholomew). **(6)** Passavant, *Kunstreise*, 1833, p. 97, as School of van Eyck. **(7)** For this Exhibition, see Style of Aelbrecht Bouts, No. 1083, note 5. **(8)** As by H. van Eyck. **(9)** As by H. van Eyck. **(10)** Waagen, *Treasures*, 1854, ii, p. 461, as Unknown, *ca.* 1480.

Style of 'MOSTAERT'

3900 CHRIST CROWNED WITH THORNS

Oak, painted surface, $12 \times 8\frac{1}{4}$ (0·305 × 0·205).

Many small local damages; it suffers somewhat from undercleaning. *Pentimenti* in the dress, right.

One of several variants, all connected with and perhaps derived from the figure on the left wing of the Oultremont Triptych at Brussels.[1] Some of these versions are merely copies; it is impossible to tell which of the rest are by 'Mostaert's' own hand, which from the studio. No. 3900 could be a later copy; an X-ray photograph gives an appearance radically different from an X-ray photograph of No. 1080 above.

The Oultremont Triptych is not exactly datable, but is perhaps from *ca.* 1510[2]; there is good reason for supposing that a variant of the present picture, of which there is an example at Verona, was in existence by 1523.[3]

VERSIONS: See Friedländer.[4] A fairly exact version was in the 1st Exhibition of Antwerp Collections, 1935 (No. 260), reproduced in the Catalogue. A variant, now at Brighton, was in the same collection as No. 3900 (Willett); 1964 Catalogue, p. 34.

PROVENANCE: Coll. Henry Willett, Brighton; exhibited at the Burlington Fine Arts Club, 1892 (No. 22),[5] and Bruges, 1902 (No. 338)[6]; probably exhibited at the Brighton Gallery, 1903 (No. 41). Sale after death, 10 April, 1905 (lot 88), bt. Wagner. Presented by Henry Wagner, 1924.

REPRODUCTION: *Illustrations, Continental Schools,* 1937, p. 237. *Plates, Early Netherlandish School,* 1947, Plate 89.

REFERENCES: (1) Friedländer, Vol. X, Plate II. (2) Cf. Hoogewerff, *De Noord-Nederlandsche Schilderkunst,* II, 1937, pp. 476 ff., for a dating a little earlier than Friedländer's *ca.* 1520 (Vol. X, No. 1). (3) Hoogewerff, *op. cit.*, pp. 452/3. (4) Friedländer, Vol. X, Nos. 16, 17 (the present picture), 18; see also the *Repertorium für Kunstwissenschaft,* Vol. XXVIII, 1905, p. 518. Friedländer, No. 17a, at Burgos, not much varied from No. 3900, is reproduced in the Burgos catalogue, 1935, Plate LIII. (5) As School of Tournai. (6) As Unknown; in Hulin's *Catalogue Critique,* 1902, as Master of Oultremont (see Mostaert's biography above).

See also NETHERLANDISH SCHOOL, No. 1298

NETHERLANDISH SCHOOL

264 S. AMBROSE WITH AMBROSIUS VAN ENGELEN(?) (RIGHT WING OF A TRIPTYCH)

On the mitre, Christ on the Cross (marked III R II for I.N.R.I.) between Mary and John; on the crozier, Cain killing Abel. On S. Ambrose's morse, Moses.

Reverse: on a black background, a crozier with a scroll inscribed, NE QVID NIMIS.

Oak, painted surface (obverse and reverse), $28\frac{1}{2} \times 9$ ($0{\cdot}725 \times 0{\cdot}23$).

The scourge S. Ambrose holds is painted on top of his cope, which shows through. There are a few *pentimenti*, e.g. in the line of S. Ambrose's cheek.

The flesh parts are very much restored, especially the donor's face and his hands, which have been re-outlined; the effect of these parts is thus considerably changed. The rest of the picture, including S. Ambrose's gloves, is in good condition. The reverse has suffered a good deal from flaking and cracking.

The donor is probably a Premonstratensian. Destrée, using the facts given by J. E. Jansen,[1] thinks that the picture was painted for the Premonstratensian Abbey of Le Parc, near Louvain, and suggests for the donor[2] Ambrosius van Engelen, born 1481, abbot 1515, died 1543. The device *ne quid nimis* was adopted by this abbey, and was used by Ambrosius van Engelen.[3] Further, there was in the seventeenth century in the Abbey a triptych of 1520, representing *The Virgin and Child, SS. Ambrose and Augustine, and Abbot Ambrose.*[4] No. 264 may be the right wing of that work; the date of 1520 would be suitable. Ambrosius van Engelen appears in miniatures of 1521 and 1539[5]; the features are unlike, but the portraiture on such rather commonplace miniatures has little claim to be considered exact or even taken from the life. Further, the condition of No. 264 makes it not altogether reliable as a portrait.

Attribution is rendered very uncertain by the condition of the flesh parts. It has been compared in style with the Dilighem Altarpiece at Brussels.[6] That is ascribed by Friedländer to the Master of 1518 (q.v.); the date of 1537/8 for it is disputed. The donor of that altarpiece is indeed fairly closely comparable with the donor here.

PROVENANCE: Coll. Krüger, Minden.[7] Purchased with most of the rest of the Krüger Collection, 1854.

REPRODUCTION: *Illustrations, Continental Schools,* 1937, p. 122 (obverse). *Plates, Early Netherlandish School,* 1947, Plate 90 (obverse). The reverse is reproduced in *Paintings and Drawings on the Backs of National Gallery Pictures,* 1946, Plate 1.

REFERENCES: **(1)** Joseph Destrée in the *Revue Belge d'Archéologie et d'Histoire de l'Art,* 1931, pp. 289 ff. The factual statements in the text are according to J. E. Jansen, *L'Abbaye Norbertine du Parc-le-Duc,* 1929, pp. 208 and 228. **(2)** The donor was traditionally called a Count of Hainault. **(3)** Jansen, *op. cit.*, pp. 116 and 228; Destrée, *loc. cit.*, p. 294. **(4)** This is in a note by Libert de Paepe added to J. Masius' chronicle of the abbey (information from P. Lenaerts, O. Praem.). **(5)** The miniature of 1521 is in a missal at Wadham College, Oxford, exhibited at the R.A., 1953/4 (No. 618), photo of the portrait in the Gallery archives. The miniature of 1539, at Brussels, is reproduced by Jansen, *op. cit.*, p. 115. It may be mentioned that the Wadham missal nowhere includes the motto *ne quid nimis*. The Psalter of Ambrosius van Engelen of 1527 (Brussels MS. 11556) appears to contain nothing relevant to No. 264. **(6)** By A.-J. Wauters in his Brussels *Catalogue*, 2nd edition, 1906, p. 44, where the Dilighem Altarpiece appears under the name of Cornelis van Coninxloo. The connection was pursued by Destrée, *loc. cit.* The 1929 Catalogue makes an obscure reference to the School of Valenciennes and wrongly says it is under the influence of van der Goes. **(7)** 1848 Catalogue, II, No. 11, as Gerard van der Meire. For biographical facts concerning Carl Wilhelm August Krüger (1797–1868), living at Aachen from 1830(?) until 1835, when he moved to Minden, see Wilhelm Karl Schmidt in *Mindener Heimatblätter,* June-August 1953, pp. 62 ff.

265 THE VIRGIN AND CHILD

The first letter on the book she holds is D.

Oak, painted surface, $27\frac{1}{2} \times 20\frac{1}{4}$ (0·70 × 0·15).

Gold new. The picture is perhaps in fair state at bottom, but it has been a good deal retouched, and is dirty. As it stands, it seems best to leave it without attribution.[1]

The Child has just blown a soap bubble. This motive is no doubt in some way connected with the saying πομφόλυξ ὁ ἄνθρωπος (man's a bubble), which had a certain fortune; thus, a label *Homo Bulla* is very properly found on the wall of a cell where S. Jerome meditates on immortality.[2] But it is doubtful if the painter of the present picture had any allegorical intention.[3]

PROVENANCE: Bought from a private collection, Münster,[4] by Krüger, in whose Collection at Minden.[5] Purchased with most of the rest of the Krüger Collection, 1854.

REPRODUCTION: *Illustrations, Continental Schools*, 1937, p. 116. *Plates, Early Netherlandish School*, 1947, Plate 91.

REFERENCES: (1) Friedländer has orally suggested an attribution to Bellegambe, but the picture does not appear in his list, Vol. XII; there may well be stylistic connection with Bellegambe's work, nevertheless. The 1929 Catalogue seems to associate it with the Master of the Death of the Virgin. (2) Friedländer, Vol. IX, Plate XXVIII. (3) A note on *Homo Bulla* by W. Stechow appeared in *The Art Bulletin*, 1938, pp. 227/8; it follows an article in the same journal, 1937, pp. 423 ff. by Janson, who reproduces on Fig. 21 an engraving by Goltzius of a *putto* blowing bubbles (see also Janson's note 91). (4) As Mabuse; see *Kunst-Blatt*, 1847, p. 23. (5) Catalogue, 1848, I, No. 37, as Ludger tom Ring. For biographical facts concerning Carl Wilhelm August Krüger (1797–1868), living at Aachen from 1830(?) until 1835, when he moved to Minden, see Wilhelm Karl Schmidt in *Mindener Heimatblätter*, June-August 1953, pp. 62 ff.

622 A GIRL WRITING

Oak, original painted surface, $10\frac{3}{4} \times 9\frac{1}{4}$ (0·27 × 0·235).

Good condition; cleaned in 1959.

The subject, *A Girl*, sometimes called *The Magdalen, Writing*, occurs frequently among the works of the Master of the Female Half-Lengths.[1] The lightening of the background round the head of No. 622 is apparently not meant to be a halo. She follows a peculiar system of writing, part of the paper being off the table and held in her left hand.

The costume is from *ca.* 1530. It recurs very exactly in two pictures of *A Girl Weighing Gold* and *A Girl Playing a Spinet* at Berlin and Worcester (U.S.A.),[2] which are sometimes classed as by Jan de Hemessen.

The present picture has some stylistic similarity to No. 1860, of *ca.* 1550, doubtfully ascribed to Katharina de Hemessen; it appears not attributable, but may well have been painted at Antwerp.

PROVENANCE: In the collection of Prince Ludwig Kraft Ernst von Œttingen-Wallerstein, at Schloss Wallerstein.[3] Exhibited at Kensington Palace (for sale), 1848 (No. 101),[4] bought with the rest of the collection by the Prince Consort. At Kensington Palace.[5] Exhibited at Manchester, 1857 (Provisional Catalogue, No. 515; Definitive Catalogue, No. 454), lent by Prince Albert. Presumably among the pictures presented by Queen Victoria at the Prince Consort's wish, 1863, although no official record seems to exist of its inclusion in the gift.

REPRODUCTION: *Illustrations, Continental Schools*, 1937, p. 123. *Plates, Early Netherlandish School*, 1947, Plate 92.

REFERENCES: (1) Friedländler, Vol. XII, Nos. 91 sqq. One is reproduced by Fierens-Gevaert, *Les Primitifs Flamands*, III, Plate CLXXI. (2) Reproduced, Berlin Illustrations, *Die Deutschen und Niederländischen Meister*, 1929, p. 201 and Worcester Catalogue, 1922, p. 46. (3) No. 46, as Unknown, of Wallerstein Catalogues of *ca.* 1826 and 1827 (originals at Munich; photostats in the National

Gallery). The collection was moved from Schloss Wallerstein after a time. (4) As Unknown. (5) Waagen's *Catalogue*, 1854 (No. 64), as Mabuse. See also Waagen, *Treasures*, IV, 1857, p. 230.

719 THE MAGDALEN

The two figures on the pot may be Cain and Abel.

Oak, painted surface, 20¾ × 13¾ (0·525 × 0·35).

The flesh is damaged, especially the face, which is much retouched.

The rocks in the background recognizably represent La Sainte-Baume in Provence, where the Magdalen is said to have spent many years in penitence.[1]

The picture in its present state, it seems, is not exactly attributable. Friedländer[2] ascribes it to the Master of 1518, but it is unlikely to be of the same group as Nos. 718 and 1082/4 of this catalogue. A *Magdalen*, No. 721 of the Liechtenstein Gallery (formerly Vienna), there ascribed to Bruyn, has some points of general resemblance.[3]

PROVENANCE: Stated to have been bought in 1815 from Count Joseph von Rechberg, Mindelheim, by Prince Ludwig Kraft von Œttingen-Wallerstein.[4] At Schloss Wallerstein.[5] Exhibited at Kensington Palace (for sale) 1848 (No. 72),[6] bought with the rest of the collection by the Prince Consort. At Kensington Palace.[7] Exhibited at Manchester, 1857 (Provisional Catalogue, No. 537; Definitive Catalogue, No. 487), lent by Prince Albert. Presented by Queen Victoria at the Prince Consort's wish, 1863.

REPRODUCTION: *Illustrations, Continental Schools*, 1937, p. 8. *Plates, Early Netherlandish School*, 1947, Plate 92.

REFERENCES: (1) This was pointed out by Robert A. Koch in the *Gazette des Beaux-Arts*, November 1965, pp. 273 ff., where several examples in XVI Century Netherlandish (mostly or even all Antwerp) pictures are brought forward; not all the pictures show the Magdalen, though presumably whatever picture may have made the first use of this site did. (2) Friedländer, Vol. XI, No. 83. (3) Photo in the Gallery Archives. (4) Cf. *Kunst-Blatt*, 1824, p. 353. Details concerning the formation of the Œttingen-Wallerstein Collection were given orally to H. I. Kay. (5) No. 56, as Mabuse, *Artemisia*, of Wallerstein Catalogues of *ca.* 1826 and 1827 (originals at Munich; photostats in the National Gallery). The collection was moved from Schloss Wallerstein after a time. (6) As Mabuse. (7) Waagen's *Catalogue*, 1854 (No. 57), as Patenier; cf. Waagen, *Treasures*, IV, 1857, p. 229.

1036 A MAN WITH A PANSY AND A SKULL

Oak, painted surface, 10¾ × 8½ (0·275 × 0·215).

Condition very good; the face better than the hands.

Formerly supposed to represent Thomas Linacre, physician (*ca.* 1460–1524); there is no authentic record of his features. As in No. 195, Style of Neufchâtel (q.v.), the skull probably suggested the medical profession; but a skull in sixteenth-century portraits may, it seems often, be only a *memento mori*.

No satisfactory attribution has been suggested for this picture.[1] Perhaps *ca.* 1535 (from the costume, which seems to be fairly precisely datable, and seems further to be Dutch).[2]

PROVENANCE: Bought from Farrer, 1849, by W. Fuller Maitland.[3] Exhibited[4]:

British Institution, 1852 (No. 118); Leeds, 1868 (No. 553); R.A., 1872 (No. 214). Purchased, Lewis Fund, from W. Fuller Maitland, 1878. .

REPRODUCTION: *Illustrations, Continental Schools*, 1937, p. 119. *Plates, Early Netherlandish School*, 1947, Plate 93.

REFERENCES: (1) According to the 1911 Catalogue, Sir Walter Armstrong thought it an early work of Amberger, and Count Cavens suggested the Master of Oultremont (='Mostaert'). Lippmann, in *The Burlington Magazine*, Vol. XII (1907/8), p. 108, said the middle period of the Master of the Death of the Virgin. Winkler, *Die Alt-Niederländische Malerei*, 1924, p. 283, seems to call it Scorel, but this is probably a slip. (2) Notes on the costume by Mrs. Newton in the Gallery archives. (3) According to a copy of the Stansted Hall Catalogue, 1872, communicated to H. I. Kay. (4) As Holbein.

1063 A YOUNG MAN PRAYING (LEFT WING OF A TRIPTYCH?)

Oak, painted surface, $9\frac{1}{2} \times 7\frac{1}{4}$ (0·24 × 0·185). Painted up to the edge top and bottom.

The line of the hair went originally higher and further to the left. The fingers also seem to have met rather higher and a little to the left.

Flesh condition good, except for a slight wearing in some of the shadows. The hands are in a peculiar, loose style, quite different from the face; an X-ray photograph stresses the dissimilarity.

The picture has been connected with the style of 'Ysenbrandt,'[1] but the connection, if it exists, seems remote. The costume would accord with a date in the later 1520's.[2]

PROVENANCE: Bought by J. H. Anderdon in Bath 'at the period of Mr. Beckford's Sale' in 1845.[3] Purchased at the Anderdon Sale, 30 May, 1879 (lot 47).

REPRODUCTION: *Illustrations, Continental Schools*, 1937, p. 119. *Plates, Early Netherlandish School*, 1947, Plate 94.

REFERENCES: (1) Bodenhausen, *Gerard David*, 1905, No. 125, as connected with David and 'Ysenbrandt.' Lippmann in *The Burlington Magazine*, Vol. XII (1907/8), p. 108, as by 'Ysenbrandt.' (2) Note on the costume, by Mrs. Newton, in the Gallery archives. (3) Label on the back. Mr. Anderdon found it or baptized it as *Luther* by Holbein.

1085 THE VIRGIN AND CHILD WITH SAINTS AND ANGELS IN A GARDEN

S. Catherine kneels on the left, holding a ring towards the Child. The edifice in the background, brightly illuminated within, may well stand for the gateway into Heaven; the statue against its window is doubtfully claimed to be S. Michael.

Left wing, S. John the Baptist kneeling, SS. Agnes and Agatha in the background.

Right wing, S. John the Evangelist.

Oak: painted surfaces, centre panel, $26\frac{3}{8} \times 17\frac{1}{8}$ (0·67 × 0·435); left panel, $26\frac{3}{4} \times 6\frac{7}{8}$ (0·678 × 0·175); right panel, $26\frac{3}{4} \times 7$ (0·678 × 0·178).

The central panel has been cut at the top, the wings both at the top and the bottom. Small areas of unpainted wood, at the top of the central panel both left and right, and at the top of S. John the Evangelist's panel on the left, suggest that the tops of the panels originally had arched forms of some kind. The level of the horizon on the three panels suggests that the cut from the bottom of the wings was of about half an inch; if this is so, the arched tops of the wings would seem to have sprung from slightly higher up than the arched top of the central panel.

Although the background continues across the picture, it was always of triptych form: the reverse of the wings (but not of the central panel) have a simple marbled coating of pigment.

Condition very good. There is a little damage here and there, partly due to wear or cracking, and there are a few small *pentimenti*. Wrongly stated in some National Gallery Catalogues to be unfinished. X-rays reveal no contrast between the different colours; the technique is more direct than is normal with Netherlandish primitives.

The subject of the central panel is a mystic treatment of the *Marriage of S. Catherine*, related to the type of picture known as the *Virgo inter Virgines*. The mystic fountain recurs in No. 2606, ascribed to the Studio of Coecke, and fairly frequently.

With regard to the building brightly illuminated within, and the interpretation suggested above, one comparable case may be thought sufficient; in Memlinc's triptych at Danzig (Gdańsk), on the left wing showing the entry of the elect into paradise, the building into which they are passing is shown against clouds but the open doors show for its interior gold.[1]

The execution seems to date from *ca.* 1500, or perhaps even later. The picture is an attributional puzzle. There are perhaps faint traces of the influence of van Eyck, Memlinc and Massys: more apparent is a connection with the style associated with Geertgen tot Sint Jans (Haarlem).[2] It would, however, be unwise to press the comparison; it is not by the same hand as the pictures called Geertgen or others grouped on whatever evidence as of the Haarlem School.

Friedländer[3] ascribes it to the Master of the Morrison Triptych, in whose biography (q.v.) the attribution is claimed to have little meaning. An *Adoration of the Kings* on Friedländer's list,[4] in the J. G. Johnson Collection, Philadelphia, No. 369, might be by the same hand as the present picture: in particular, some of the dressses there seem to have no clamps, and it was this peculiarity on No. 1085 that caused it to be considered unfinished. There is a view of Antwerp in the background of the Johnson picture, which probably indicates a date *ca.* 1510 (cf. a note in the biography of the Morrison Master). The setting of No. 1085, however, suggests the South of Europe rather than Antwerp.

VERSION: A triptych with different wings is in the Escorial. The central panel shows the figures of all three panels of No. 1085, with several variations. The top part of the edifice in the background is there included; the peculiar lighting within it is the same as here. It is doubtful if it is by the same hand as No. 1085.[5]

PROVENANCE: Inscribed on the back: *Ex Coll: Henrici Hamal Leod:* followed apparently by 1812,[6] i.e. Henri Hamal of Liège, probably 1744–1820, probably the canon at Liège drawings and engravings belonging to whom were sold by auction in Paris in 1805. The picture was seen in the collection of Karl Aders, a German merchant living in London, in 1828 in his villa at Godesberg,[7] and was soon afterwards transferred by him to London.[8] Aders Exhibition, No. 10[9]; Sale, 1 August, 1835 (lot 108), bt. Dr. Willis. Anon. (H. C. Robinson, or rather Aders Trust) Sale, 26 April, 1839 (lot 59), bt. Green. Coll. J. H. Green, Hadley[10]; exhibited at Manchester, 1857 (Provisional Catalogue, No. 502; Definitive Catalogue, No. 416). Bequeathed by Mrs. Joseph H. Green, 1880.[11]

REPRODUCTION: *Illustrations, Continental Schools*, 1937, p. 134. *Plates, Early Netherlandish School*, 1947, Plates 95, 96.

REFERENCES: **(1)** See J. Bialostocki, *Les Musées de Pologne* (*Les Primitifs Flamands, Corpus*), 1966, p. 66 and Plates CXXXIV, CXLI, CXLVIII. **(2)** Sir Claude Phillips ascribed it to Geertgen tot Sint Jans in *The Burlington Magazine*, Vol. VI (1904/5), pp. 6 ff. It is incorrect that a cushion under the Child is in a tradition peculiar to Geertgen; there are examples by Memlinc, etc. **(3)** Friedländer, Vol. VII, No. 83. The compiler saw No. 1085 and the Morrison Triptych side by side in 1946, and remained doubtful if they could be by the same hand. **(4)** Friedländer, Vol. VII, Plate LIX. **(5)** Reproduced in the compiler's *The National Gallery* (*Les Primitifs Flamands, Corpus*), Vol. I, 1953, Plate II. It may be mentioned that the Escorial picture is most probably later than 1500, one reason for this being the shape of the tops of the three panels; but this does not prove that No. 1085 is later than 1500. **(6)** Other inscriptions apparently in the same writing indicate that the picture is the combined work of Hubrecht, Jan and Margriete van Eyck. The writing might be the same as for No. 1231 of Lugt's *Marques de Collections*, Vol. I, 1921. See the photographic reproductions of the backs of No. 1085, Plates XXI–XXII of the National Gallery *Corpus* volumes, Volume I, 1953. **(7)** See Johanna Schopenhauer, *Ausflug an den Niederrhein und nach Belgien im Jahre 1828*, 1831, Vol. I, pp. 116 ff., as by Margriete van Eyck. **(8)** Passavant, *Kunstreise*, 1833, p. 93, as Margriete van Eyck. **(9)** For this Exhibition, see Style of Aelbrecht Bouts, No. 1083, note 5. **(10)** Waagen, *Treasures*, 1854, ii, p. 460, with an attribution to Massys. **(11)** As School of the Lower Rhine.

1089 THE VIRGIN AND CHILD WITH S. ANNE

Oak, painted surface, $15\frac{3}{4} \times 12$ (0·40 × 0·305).

The flesh very much damaged, the draperies and landscape somewhat.

The female figure Christ is touching was formerly called S. Elizabeth; it need not be doubted that it is S. Anne.

The picture is a feeble work, possibly of the School of Bruges. The date may be *ca.* 1525; the soldier in the background left seems to be in developed sixteenth-century costume.

It was wrongly grouped by Durand-Gréville[1] with several other pictures, including No. 1151 of this catalogue, Style of 'Ysenbrandt.' The existence of three versions (recorded below), two in a slightly different and one in a very different style, suggests that a cartoon of this picture passed into different hands; this may have been by a painter of a style different from that of any of the four versions.

VERSIONS: A variant, in a fairly similar style, is at Vienna; the figures recur with only slight changes, and the house in the background on the right of No. 1089 is also at Vienna without much alteration.[2] Another variant is at Strasbourg; the figures are repeated without great variations in the design, but the Strasbourg picture is in the style of 'Antwerp Mannerism.'[3] Another variant, with two extra figures, belonged in 1938 to Douwes at Amsterdam (as Ysenbrandt).[4]

PROVENANCE: A label on the back, *a.m.rijns* (?). In the collection of Karl Aders, a German merchant living in London; Aders Exhibition, No. 12[5]; Sale, 1 August, 1835 (lot 107), bt. Longmore[6]; Anon. (H. C. Robinson, or rather Aders Trust)

Sale, 26 April, 1839 (lot 51), bt. Green. Bequeathed by Mrs. Joseph H. Green, 1880.

REPRODUCTION: *Illustrations, Continental Schools*, 1937, p. 121. *Plates, Early Netherlandish School*, 1947, Plate 97.

REFERENCES: (1) E. Durand-Gréville in the *Gazette des Beaux-Arts*, 1908, i, p. 70. (2) Vienna, 1938 *Katalog*, No. 679, as Goosen van der Weyden; photograph in the Gallery archives. (3) Strasbourg, 1938 *Catalogue*, No. 81, as Antwerp School; Friedländer, Vol. XI, No. 51, as *Meister der Antwerpener Anbetung*; photograph in the Gallery archives. (4) Photograph in the Witt Library. (5) The identity can be established as for the entry in the Sale catalogue; see the next note. For the Exhibition, see Style of Aelbrecht Bouts, No. 1083, note 5. (6) No description, but size given, as H. van Eyck. The identity may be accepted, since many Aders pictures reappeared in the Robinson Sale of 1839, where lot 51 (as noted in the text) was bt. Green. Title and attribution of lot 107 of the 1835 sale and lot 51 of the 1839 sale correspond.

1094 A MAN

Oak, painted surface, $23\frac{5}{8} \times 19\frac{1}{2}$ (0·60 × 0·495). Painted up to the edge all round.

There is apparently a worn sixteenth-century picture here, but the surface is at present almost entirely covered with fairly old repaint.

Now unattributable. Formerly classed as Mor,[1] then F. Pourbus I.[2]

PROVENANCE: On the back, a label: *Anthony More | Painter given | Dr. Gifford 1758.*[3] Presented by the Trustees of the British Museum, 1880.

REPRODUCTION: *Illustrations, Continental Schools*, 1937, p. 271. *Plates, Early Netherlandish School*, 1947, Plate 97.

REFERENCES: (1) Doubtfully admitted as Mor by H. Hymans, *Antonio Moro*, 1910, p. 170. (2) According to the 1913 Catalogue, the ascription to Pourbus was Friedländer's. (3) No doubt one of the unspecified pictures given to the British Museum by Dr. Andrew Gifford in December 1758; information from A. E. Popham.

1298 LANDSCAPE: A RIVER AMONG MOUNTAINS (FRAGMENT?)

Oak, painted surface, 20 × 27 (0·51 × 0·685).

Probably a fragment of a larger work; there is no 'subject' to the picture as it is except a man drawing, and the paint is continued up to each edge of the panel. It is much rubbed and a good deal repainted.

The picture was catalogued in 1929 as of the School of Patenier. There are some stylistic connections, but the name of Patenier is misleading; the colour is reminiscent of Massys. It is probably of the Antwerp School, but is not exactly attributable. There is no sure means of dating it, but it may perhaps be more nearly of 1525 than 1550.

The most certain thing about it is that it is in some way connected with an engraving. According to the inscription on it, this engraving appears to have been executed by Hoefnagel after a design made by Pieter Bruegel the Elder in Rome in 1553.[1] A mythological subject is indicated by the presence of two small figures of Mercury and Psyche in the sky of the engraving (no trace of such figures found in No. 1298).[2] The rest of

Bruegel's design offers many similarities to the picture: two artists are sketching under a tree; there is a winding river with a raft and a masted boat; there is a rock with twin openings and a castle on a rock; even the reflections of the rocks in the water are treated in much the same way as in the picture. This engraving fairly obviously does not represent an Italian scene; the inscription, indeed, makes no such claim. It is uncertain whether it is derived from the picture or both from a common source; it is certain, if certainty of undocumented attribution exists, that No. 1298 is not by Bruegel.[3]

The picture has been the subject of the ingenuity of many critics. It was traditionally called a *View of Lake Maggiore, near Arona*, by Luini[4]; it may be remarked in passing that it is not by the mysterious Bernazzano, traditionally supposed to have painted the Patenierish background to a large *Baptism* by Cesare da Sesto.[5] Hulin suggested a connection with a predella ascribed to J.v.d. Elburcht; Conway denies it.[6] Winkler[7] ascribed it to 'Mostaert'; it has no connection with normal 'Mostaerts,' and if his landscape style is truly illustrated by the '*West Indian Landscape*' referred to in his biography,[8] Winkler's attribution is wrong. Wescher[9] called it Jan de Cock; Friedländer's[10] reconstruction of that shadowy figure excludes this picture. On comparison with some drawings, Baldass[11] ascribed it to Matthys Cock (son of Jan); the attribution of drawings to Matthys can with some difficulty be made,[12] but no pictures are satisfactorily associated with his name, it seems. Boon went further, considering that the Errera album of drawings at Brussels is M. Cock's early work, and claiming that the drawing on p. 106 of the album should be considered a study for No. 1298 (it shows no precise connection).[13]

PROVENANCE: The (damaged) seal on the back does not, as the 1929 Catalogue says, contain SC in monogram. Acquired by Conte Teodoro Lechi of Milan, then Brescia, at Milan before 1814.[14] Bought from Stefano Bardini, Florence, 1889.[15]

REPRODUCTION: *Illustrations, Continental Schools*, 1937, p. 264. *Plates, Early Netherlandish School*, 1947, Plate 98.

REFERENCES: (1) The engraving after Bruegel is reproduced with a pendant in René van Bastelaer and Georges H. de Loo, *P. Bruegel*, 1907, opp. p. 55. Bastelaer discusses it on p. 55, note 1; pp. 205 ff.; and p. 220: he wrongly calls it probably a view of the Tiber. For the subject, see further Guy de Tervarent, *Les Enigmes de l'Art*, III, *L'Héritage Antique*, 1947, pp. 37/8. Baldass, in the Vienna *Jahrbuch*, Vol. XXXIV, pp. 148/50, admits some connection between the engraving and the picture. (2) It has been claimed that the two figures were not included originally in the engraving, e.g. by K. Arndt in *Pantheon*, March–April 1967, pp. 102 ff., who published as an original a drawing without these figures, but otherwise closely corresponding with the print, at Besançon. (3) The ascription to Bruegel referred to in the 1929 Catalogue is apparently a suggestion of Roger Fry's, quoted by Conway, *The Van Eycks*, 1921, p. 500. It is surprising that Glück, *loc. cit.*, pp. 169 ff., ascribes it to Bruegel. He says that he knows of no example of a landscape with an artist sketching earlier than the engraving and No. 1298. (4) See the Lechi Catalogues, 1814 (No. 16), 1837 (No. 45) and 1852 (No. 30). (5) Cesare's *Baptism* (in the Gallarati Scotti Collection) is reproduced by Suida, *Leonardo und sein Kreis*, 1929, Plate 282. On pp. 217 ff. Suida discusses Bernazzano's part in the picture, and makes some further attributions to him. (6) Hulin, *Catalogue Critique*, 1902 (No. 201). Conway, *The Van Eycks*, 1921, pp. 354/5. (7) Winkler in *Monatshefte*, vi, 1913, p. 216. The attribution to 'Mostaert' was for a time accepted by Baldass; see the Vienna *Jahrbuch*, Vol. XXXIV, p. 132. It is dubiously accepted by Hoogewerff, *De Noord-Nederlandsche Schilderkunst*, II, 1937, p. 496. (**8**) See the biography of 'Mostaert' in this Catalogue. (**9**) Wescher, in the *Zeitschrift für bildende Kunst*, 1924/5, p. 100, and 1925/6, p. 153. For 'Jan de Cock,' see further in *The Burlington Magazine*, August, 1950, p. 239. (**10**) Friedländer, Vol. XI, pp. 59 ff. (**11**) Baldass, in the *Zeitschrift für bildende Kunst*, 1927/8, p. 90. (**12**) For drawings ascribed to M. Cock, see Popham's *Catalogue of Dutch and Flemish Drawings in the British Museum*, 1932, p. 8; and W. Stechow, in the Prussian *Jahrbuch*, 1935, pp. 74 ff., and in *Old Master Drawings*, xi, p. 40. (**13**) K. G. Boon in the *Bulletin des Musées Royaux des Beaux-Arts*, Brussels (*Miscellanea Erwin Panofsky*), 1955, pp. 215 ff., esp. pp. 224 f. A photograph of the drawing was kindly sent by the Centre National de Recherches 'Primitifs Flamands', Brussels. (**14**) 1814 Catalogue (No. 16), also (see note 4), in later Lechi catalogues. Still in the Lechi Collection in 1855 (Mündler's Diary, MS. in the National Gallery). (**15**) As Venetian School, possibly Basaiti.

1652 MEVR. VAN DER GOES, NÉE VAN SPANGEN

Dated 1543. A coat of arms is referred to below.

Oak, painted surface, 18¼ × 16¼ (0·46 × 0·41).

Painted up to the edges except at the top.

Condition good, though some of the features and shadows are softened by repairs.

The sitter is Anna van Spangen, who married Adriaen van der Goes, Lord Advocate of Holland (1505–1560); she died in 1548. The arms, according to Rietstap [1] are as follows: Goes, *de sa. à trois têtes de bouc d'arg., accornées d'or*; Spangen, *d'or à la fasce d'azur, acc. de trois têtes de lion de gu. arm. et lamp. d'azur.* These arms are somewhat cursorily reproduced on the picture, with an additional quartering to van Spangen, three red-billed birds on a field argent (?). This presumably indicates some alliance of the van Spangen family, probably at Delft.

An engraving of her husband exists, which may (if it is inverted) record the pendant to this picture. The text is: *Mr. Adriaan van der Goes. | Advokaat van Holland, in't jaar* 1543, *oud* 38 *jaaren. | Door J. M. Quinkhard geschild, naar een Origineel by den Heer en Mr Cs. van der Goes, Burgermr. te Delft. Door J. Houbraken gesn.*

Another pair of these sitters is still with the van der Goes family.[2] The lady is recognizably the same.

PROVENANCE: A branch of the van der Goes family descending from the sitter's son Christiaen died out about 1800, and the property was sold by auction at The Hague in 1820 (Lugt, No. 9816); but this picture is not identifiable in the sale catalogue. Bequeathed by Miss Martha Brown,[3] 1897.

REPRODUCTION: *Illustrations, Continental Schools*, 1937, p. 96. *Plates, Early Netherlandish School*, 1947, Plate 99.

REFERENCES: (**1**) J. B. Rietstap, *Armorial Général*, 1884. (**2**) Photos in the Gallery archives. The identification of the sitter and the information concerning her were given in letters by W. del Court, 1909. Moes, *Iconographia Batava*, I, 1897, p. 338, seems to identify this portrait of Adriaen with the engraving mentioned above; but they are different. (**3**) As Katherine Parr.

1864 THE VIRGIN AND CHILD IN A LANDSCAPE (TONDO)

In the background left, S. John (or S. Joseph?), carrying a lantern and preceded by the *Agnus Dei*.

Oak, oval (meant for circular), painted surface, 32 × 31½ (0·81 × 0·80). Painted up to the edge all round.

Several *pentimenti* on the horizon. The two principal figures are very much damaged, especially in the flesh; the landscape is in better condition, though it suffers somewhat in parts both from under- and from over-cleaning.

Circular pictures are not very common in the early Netherlandish School.

The figures have been supposed to be in the style of 'Ysenbrandt';[1] this might seem to be on the right lines, but the bad condition makes it unwise to attribute them to any one. Friedländer[2] said that the landscape might possibly be by Patenier: it is at least less unlike those of Nos. 3115, 4826 (ascribed to Patenier) than that of No. 2585 ('Ysenbrandt'). Nevertheless, the main towers of the town in the background are (in their slight execution) strongly suggestive of those of Bruges, from right to left Notre-Dame, the Belfry and the Poortersloge.[3] So, contrary to what was said in the previous edition of this catalogue, the picture may be rather from Bruges than from Antwerp.

There is a rather remote compositional connection with the design ascribed to 'Campin,' often known as *The Madonna in the Apse* (see No. 2608 of this catalogue).

PROVENANCE: On the back, *Gregorio Alberti* and a number in old writing. Coll. Prince Ludwig Kraft Ernst von Œttingen-Wallerstein, at Schloss Wallerstein.[4] Exhibited at Kensington Palace (for sale), 1848 (No. 60),[5] bought with the rest of the collection by the Prince Consort. At Kensington Palace.[6] Exhibited at Manchester, 1857 (Provisional Catalogue, no entry; Definitive Catalogue, No. 413), lent by Prince Albert. Presented by Queen Victoria at the Prince Consort's wish, 1863.

REPRODUCTION: *Illustrations, Continental Schools*, 1937, p. 415. *Plates, Early Netherlandish School*, 1947, Plate 100.

REFERENCES: (1) The picture was in the 1929 Catalogue as 'Ysenbrandt.' Friedländer, Vol. XI, No. 176, as 'Ysenbrandt.' (2) Friedländer, oral communication. (3) This was kindly pointed out by Dr. H. Pauwels, in a letter of 13 July, 1967 (in the Gallery archives). For the Belfry, which from 1501 had a spire, see for instance Ad. Duclos, *Bruges, Histoire et Souvenirs*, 1910, p. 439 and reproductions on pp. 41, 114/15; for the Poortersloge, Duclos, reprs. on pp. 33, 44, and *Belgische Kunstdenkmäler*, ed. P. Clemen, Vol. I, 1923, rep. of part of M. Gheeraerts' plan of Bruges, 1562, on p. 92 (left, towards the top of this reproduction); for the tower of Notre-Dame, see Duclos, repr. on p. 273, etc. (4) No. 65, as Hugo van der Goes, of Wallerstein Catalogues of *ca.* 1826 and 1827 (originals at Munich; photostats in the National Gallery). The Collection was moved from Schloss Wallerstein after a time. (5) As Unknown. (6) Waagen's *Catalogue*, 1854, No. 65, as Mabuse; cf. Waagen, *Treasures*, IV, 1857, p. 230.

2209 EDZARD THE GREAT, COUNT OF EAST FRIESLAND (1462–1528)

In his hat, a brooch with an eagle (?); on his sword a perhaps modern inscription, *victor est qvi in | nomen domini pvgnavit.*

Oak, painted surface, 19¼ × 14¼ (0·49 × 0·36).

Painted up to the edge all round.

Extensively made up, especially in the shadows; many small repairs.

A bust copy in armour, may be even as late as the eighteenth century, from a portrait in robes and with hands, of which the original is supposed to be the version at Oldenburg.[1]

The Oldenburg version has been ascribed to Jacob Cornelisz. van Oostsanen, but it is not accepted as such by Friedländer,[2] etc.

The identification of the sitter, who visited the Netherlands in 1516/7, is due to a tradition attached to the Oldenburg exemplar. On the back of No. 2209 is inscribed, in fairly modern pigment not certainly more recent than the picture: *Ulricus Sircsena | comes Frisiae Orientalis | Primus.* Ulrich Cirksena I was born *ca.* 1410, died in 1466; Edzard was his second son.

The present picture seems to make no useful contribution to the iconography, the design or the authorship of the original.[3]

VERSIONS: Oldenburg, with a formal design as background; the same figure before a niche at Belvoir[4]; another with a landscape background at Dijon[5]; another was in the F. Baars *et. al.* Sale, Cologne, 14 May, 1900 (lot 2), repr.

PROVENANCE: Bought by C. L. Eastlake in London[6]; presented by Mrs. C. L. Eastlake in memory of her husband, Keeper of the National Gallery, 1907.

REPRODUCTION: *Illustrations, Continental Schools*, 1937, p. 72. *Plates, Early Netherlandish School*, 1947, Plate 101.

REFERENCES: (1) The Oldenburg example was exhibited at the R.A., 1929 (No. 8); *Commemorative Catalogue*, p. 3. See further H. W. Keiser, *Gemäldegalerie Oldenburg*, 1967, p. 33. (2) See the R.A. Catalogue, 1929. (3) The original is therefore not discussed in this entry. (4) Exhibited at the Guildhall, 1892 (No. 44). Reproduced in the Album, p. 6. (5) Dijon Catalogue, 1918, by J. Magnin, pp. 183/4, reproduced. Repr. better in the Exhibition catalogue, *Le Portrait dans les Anciens Pays-Bas*, Bruges, 1953, No. 33, Plate 36. (6) According to the National Gallery Catalogue, 1915.

2295 PORTRAIT OF A BEARDED MAN

Walnut,[1] painted surface, 16½ × 12 (0·415 × 0·305). Painted up to the edges all round.

A good deal repaired, and pitted with varnish coagulations.

The dress and the background have been left unfinished. If it is not simply an unfinished portrait, it might be a study for one sitter in a group. Formerly called a *Spanish General*, then a *Military Commander*; the small piece of dress visible was supposed to be armour. From the costume, the date is probably *ca.* 1570/80; until 1929, the picture was ascribed to F. Pourbus II, whose activity was later.

PROVENANCE: Lent by George Fielder to an Exhibition at Guildford, 1884 (No. 17); George Fielder Bequest, 1908.[2]

REPRODUCTION: *Illustrations, Continental Schools*, 1937, p. 272. *Plates, Early Netherlandish School*, 1947, Plate 101.

REFERENCES: (1) Letter from B. J. Rendle of the Forest Products Research Laboratory in the Gallery archives. (2) The bequest was made in a will of 1878 by Mr. Fielder, a life interest being reserved to the testator's widow.

2602 A YOUNG MAN HOLDING A RING

Background, a repeating design of rain falling from clouds, under which in each case *har . las . uber . gan* (Lord, let (them) pass over). The letters *i d* are perhaps inscribed on the ring.

Oak, painted surface, $7 \times 4\frac{7}{8}$ (0·18 × 0·12).

Excellent state; small local damages. Small *pentimenti*.

Perhaps *ca.* 1450/60.[1] The dialect of the inscription is perhaps from the frontiers of Holland and Germany.[2] Not particularly Eyckian in style,[3] the picture shows some connection with the *Raising of Lazarus* ascribed to 'Ouwater' at Berlin, though certainly not by the same hand; perhaps therefore it is one of the few remaining examples of the 'Early Dutch' School.[4]

An emblem, apparently of rain falling from clouds, appears on a huntsman's sleeve in the Boar and Bear Hunt, in the series of sporting tapestries formerly in the Devonshire Collection and now at the Victoria and Albert Museum.[5]

VERSIONS: Winkler[6] published as a copy a drawing at Berlin almost line for line following the picture, though the features (redone ?) do not altogether correspond. A painted replica is said to have been on the Frankfort market.[7]

PROVENANCE: Old ascription to Cranach, also 'GM' on the back. Anon. (Salter ?) Sale, Christie's, 25 February, 1905 (lot 15),[8] bt. Fairfax Murray. George Salting Bequest, 1910.

REPRODUCTION: *Illustrations, Continental Schools*, 1937, p. 55. *Plates, Early Netherlandish School*, 1947, Plate 102.

REFERENCES: (1) The indications of date from the costume are not very precise; notes on the costume and the emblem of rain falling from clouds by Mrs. Newton in the Gallery archives. (2) Letter from Dr. Schmidt-Degener in the Gallery archives. (3) The picture was wrongly ascribed to Christus in the 1925/9 Catalogues. It was wrongly associated with No. 696, Follower of Jan van Eyck, by Hulin de Loo, *Un Portraitiste de Style Eyckesque vers 1440*, in *Apollo* (Belgium), December 1941, pp. 8 ff. (4) Cf. Martin Davies in *The Burlington Magazine*, Vol. LXX (1937), p. 143. (5) Cf. Betty Kurth in the Vienna *Jahrbuch*, XXXIV, p. 65, note 6; reproduced, Tafel V. Other examples of what appear to be similar emblems are known; e.g. in *The Marriage of the Virgin* in the Bisschoppelijk Museum at Haarlem, assigned to the Master of S. Gudule (Friedländer, Vol. IV, Plate LIX). (6) Winkler in *The Burlington Magazine*, Vol. XXIV (1913/4), p. 231. No. 4502 of Bock and Rosenberg's Berlin Drawings Catalogue, I, *Niederländer* (After van Eyck), Weale, *Hubert and John van Eyck*, 1908, Plate opp. p. 64, calls the sitter a Goldsmith. (7) Bock and Rosenberg, *op. cit.* (8) As Cranach.

2613 PHILIP THE FAIR AND HIS SISTER MARGARET OF AUSTRIA (*ca.* 1493/5?)

He wears the collar of the Golden Fleece; behind his head, *Phs̄ dei grā archi* | *dux austrie* | *dux* (   )(u ?)*rg'zī* (i.e. Burgundiae ?). Behind her head, *Margareta filia* | *Regis* | *Romanorū*. The backgrounds are studded with coats of arms. At the centre top, on his panel, his arms, with a collar of the Golden Fleece, and a coronet above; on her panel, on one side the same arms, the other side blank (showing an unmarried woman). The other coats are each inscribed with a name. On his panel, (Aus)*tria*, *Stiri* (a), | (Carn)*iole* (i.e. Krain), *Carintie*, *Tirole*, *Cili* (i.e. Cilli, Celje), | *Habsbu*(r)*g*, *Schelcklīgen* (wrong, see below), *Alsatie*, | *Slauonice* (i.e. Slavonia), *Burgou* (i.e. Burgau, near Günzburg), | *Kiburg* (i.e. Kyburg), *Phirt* (i.e. Pfirt, Ferrette), | *Terraentia* (i.e. Country on the Enns, Upper Austria; wrong, see below), *Port' Nauonis* (i.e. Pordenone), | *Nellēburg*, *Ortēburg*. On her panel, *B*(o)*urgūdia* (i.e. the Duchy), *Lotheringia* (i.e. Lorraine), | *Brabātia*, *Limburgia*, *Luxēburgia*, *Gheldres* (i.e. Gelderland), | *Flandria*, *Bourgūdia* (i.e. the County Palatine), *Artesium* (i.e. Artois), | *Hānonia* (i.e. Hainault), *Namureū*, | *Hollādia*, *Zeelādia*, | *Zutphania* (i.e. Zutphen), *Frisia*, | *Salins*, *Malins* (i.e. Malines).

Oak, rounded tops; painted surfaces, each $9\frac{1}{4} \times 6\frac{1}{8}$ (0·235 × 0·155).

Local damages; the flesh in fairly good condition. The outlines of the noses have been slightly changed by the painter.

Philip the Fair, born 22 July, 1478, died 1506, became Philip I of Spain. Margaret of Austria,[1] born 10 January, 1480, died 1530, lost her expectations of being at one time Queen of France, then Queen of Spain; she later refused an offer from Henry VII to become Queen of England, being at that time widow of the Duke of Savoy. She had, as Regent of the Netherlands, a good deal of political and cultural influence, and is still remembered, thanks perhaps in part to some verses by Matthew Arnold, for having built the Church of Brou.

The titles with coats of arms covering the backgrounds belonged to the House of Austria; but it is extremely doubtful if they here form two sets, one to be applied to Philip, one to Margaret. It is to be remarked that Philip is explicitly called Duke of Burgundy (if the reading is correct), but the arms of this Duchy are on Margaret's panel; so the position of the arms probably does not signify a division of the titles.

Dr. Loehr[2] has pointed out some confusions in the inscriptions. The arms labelled Schelklingen are really those of Upper Austria ('Terraentia'). The arms labelled Terraentia are like but are not those of Schelklingen (bends black); they are those of another Suabian title, Ehingen (bends red).

The picture is thus not quite clear or correct in its facts; this should be remembered throughout the following arguments for establishing the date.

Maximilian, the father of Philip and Margaret, is referred to on the picture as King of the Romans; he was elected in February, crowned in April, 1486.[3] He became in effect Emperor in 1493 on his father's death, but as he was not crowned until 1508, he was in the interval more properly referred to by the lesser title.[4]

A brief history of Margaret's youth must now be given; some of the details will indicate more exactly the date of the picture.

Margaret was betrothed, one might almost say married, at the age of three to the French Dauphin, to become within a few months King Charles VIII. She entered Paris on 2 June 1483, and lived at Amboise for eight or nine years, where she was treated as Queen of France. In 1491, Charles VIII jilted her, marrying Anne, Duchess of Brittany, in December. As Anne was the betrothed of Maximilian, a war was needed to straighten out the tangle. Margaret was sent to Melun, almost as a hostage, until the Peace of Senlis (23 May, 1493); only then did she travel back to Flanders.

Soon after, Maximilian planned a double Spanish marriage for his children; this was finally settled on 5 November, 1495. Philip married Joan the Mad, second daughter of Ferdinand and Isabella, in 1496: Margaret in 1497 set off for Spain, where she married John, Prince of Asturias, heir to the Spanish throne. Prince John died after a few months, but Margaret did not return to Flanders until early in 1499. In 1501 she married Philibert II (the Fair), Duke of Savoy.[5]

In the light of these historical facts, the following points may be raised. Philip is apparently described on the picture as Duke of Burgundy; but it seems, whatever the argument may be worth, that this Duchy was part of Margaret's dowry to Charles VIII, and that Maximilian did not get it back until the Peace of Senlis in 1493.[6]

Further, Margaret is shown as an unmarried woman: it is unlikely that she would have been so described except between 1493 and 1495 (or perhaps 1497).

Confirmation of a date 1493/5 is given by the existence of a diptych of the same sitters at Vienna[7]; their ages are written on the frame there as sixteen and fourteen, so that date is *ca.* 1494. The Vienna picture is in such bad condition that a comparison is awkward; but there are similarities of costume, and the list of titles on the frame corresponds exactly, except that Margaret there has *Saint Empire* (Antwerp) instead of Zutphen.

The dating of the picture has been arrived at without reference to the sitters' apparent ages; arguments based on such evidence are often misleading.

As for the occasion of No. 2613 and the picture at Vienna, it is to be remarked that in both Philip and Margaret are associated very closely together, and that great stress is laid on their possessions. As Glück[8] supposed, there would seem to be some connection with the double Spanish marriage.

There is no need to postulate that either picture was done from life.

No. 2613, formerly catalogued under the meaningless term 'Burgundian School,' is obviously Netherlandish (Brussels ?). The Vienna picture is too much damaged for comparison. A diptych of Philip's children exists, similar in lettering and treatment: it is fairly exactly datable *ca.* 1508.[9] A triptych of three of Philip's children, 1502, at Vienna, is another rather similar example of official iconography.[10] These works are hardly to be considered as pictures; they are comparable with the contemporary coats of arms of the Knights of the Golden Fleece.[11]

To attribute to an individual hand a picture such as No. 2613 seems, indeed, merely a waste of time. Some[12] (but not Friedländer) have connected it with the Master of the Magdalen Legend (q.v.). This name is at best a vague and elastic term, covering perhaps several factories; one of the restrictions to be put on the anonymity of the present picture is that it is not like the Magdalen series.[13]

PROVENANCE: It is not likely to be either No. 134 or No. 247 of Margaret's inventory at Antwerp, 1524.[14] From the Chigi Collection, Rome. Lent by Agnew's to the *Exposition des Primitifs Français*, Paris, 1904 (No. 143). Coll. George Salting; Bruges, *Toison d'Or* Exhibition, 1907 (No. 44); George Salting Bequest, 1910. Exhibited, *Marguerite d'Autriche, Fondatrice de Brou*, Bourg, June–July 1958 (No. 4), and *Margareta van Oostenrijk en haar Hof*, Malines, July–September 1958 (No. 98).

REPRODUCTIONS: *Illustrations, Continental Schools*, 1937, p. 41. *Plates, Early Netherlandish School*, 1947, Plates, 103, 104.

REFERENCES: (1) As the sitter is identified by a genuine inscription on the picture, it is worth a passing mention that Louise Roblot-Delondre calls her Philip's wife, Joan the Mad; she commits the same error with regard to a diptych of Philip and Margaret at Vienna, referred to below. See *Portraits d'Infantes*, 1913, pp. 8 ff. and 153. (2) Letters from Dr. Loehr in the Gallery archives. For the coats of arms and inscriptions on No. 2613, compare especially the Chapelle de Bourgogne at Antwerp, the Généalogie de Charles-Quint (MS. 14569 at Brussels), a triptych by J. van Battele at Malines and a diptych at Vienna (referred to in note 7). Some details about these works may be found in the compiler's *The National Gallery* (*Les Primitifs Flamands, Corpus*), Vol. I, 1953, pp. 12 f. (3) Philip was granted his collar of the Golden Fleece, which he is wearing, in 1481; this collar is therefore irrelevant to the dating. (4) Thus a portrait of Maximilian by Ambrogio Preda at Vienna, dated 1502, is inscribed MAX. RO. REX. (5) Most of the historical facts are taken from Eleanor E. Tremayne, *The first Governess of the Netherlands—Margaret of Austria*, 1908. See also Max Bruchet, *Marguerite d'Autriche*, 1927. (6) Tremayne, *op. cit.*, pp. 3 and 11. Perhaps, however, the point is invalid, the use of titles being very difficult to understand. Thus, a seal of 1485 shows both Maximilian and Philip, and assigns a list of titles (rather similar to the one on No. 2613) to both; including the Duchy of Burgundy and other titles, which Mrs. Tremayne says were Margaret's dowry to the King of France. This seal is described in the Catalogue of the *Exposition de la Toison d'Or*, Bruges, 1907, p. 224. (7) The Vienna picture is reproduced with its frame by Tremayne, *op. cit.*, opp. p. 12. For Mme Roblot-Delondre's mistaken identification of Joan the Mad instead of Margaret, see note 1. In its present state, it has no coats of arms. A third double portrait of Philip and Margaret is irrelevant, being dated 1483; it is divided between Versailles and the Johnson Collection, Philadelphia. The two pictures were first recognized as belonging together by A.-J. Wauters in the *Bulletin des Musées royaux du Cinquantenaire*, 1914; see also Winkler in the Prussian *Jahrbuch*, 1932, pp. 129 ff. (8) Glück in the Vienna *Jahrbuch*, 1905, pp. 233 ff. (9) It was in the Fétis Sale, 1909; exhibited at Paris, *De Van Eyck à Bruegel*, 1935 (No. 58), lent by Mme. F. Franchomme. The female half of this diptych is reproduced by Louise Roblot-Delondre, *Portraits d'Infantes*, 1913, Plate 7. (10) Reproduced by Tremayne, *op. cit.*, opp. p. 69. (11) See the *Toison d'Or* Exhibition of 1907, Memorial Volume, the section entitled *Blasons* by A. van Zuylen van Nyevelt, pp. 217 ff., with plates. (12) See Jeanne Tombu in the *Gazette des Beaux-Arts*, 1929, ii, p. 284, with her correction, *ib.* 1930, i, p. 193. She apparently says that No. 2613 is from the Studio of the Master of the Magdalen Legend and a replica of the picture at Vienna, which she says is not by the Master of the Magdalen Legend. (In the same journal, 1930, ii, p. 261, she ascribes the Vienna picture to the Master of the Guild of S. George, unjustifiably.) It may be remarked that No. 2613 is no replica of the picture at Vienna. See also P. Wescher in *Pantheon*, December, 1941, p. 276 (Master of the Magdalen

Legend). (**13**) Friedländer, Vol. XII, Plates I–III. (**14**) This inventory is given by Tremayne, *op. cit.*, pp. 305 ff. Winkler, Prussian *Jahrbuch*, 1932, p. 132, applies No. 134 to the Johnson-Versailles Diptych. No. 247 must be considered together with No. 248; they contained four or more children of the King of the Romans. If Maximilian's are meant, they would be his bastards; he had no legitimate children except Philip and Margaret. Glück seems to think that these entries are additions *ca.* 1530 to the inventory of 1524, and supposes that the children of Ferdinand are referred to; see the Vienna *Jahrbuch*, 1933, p. 195. Glück's correction in the Vienna *Jahrbuch*, 1934, p. 179, does not refer to the identity of the sitters.

2615 THE MAGDALEN (?)

She holds a pot. Her necklace is, it seems, ornamented with scourges; bracelets on each arm have a suggestion of manacles.

Oak, rounded top (painted surface), $16\frac{1}{4} \times 12\frac{3}{4}$ (0·41 × 0·32).

Condition very good. In places the paint is slightly worn, and therefore the shadowed parts of the face, especially on the forehead and right eye, have been stippled. The hatching lines on the preparation show a good deal in the flesh parts.

The pot replaces a book with clasp and tooled binding. The position of the hands does not seem to have been altered; there are only a few very small *pentimenti* in the outlines. The painting of the pot is old, and seems to be by the original painter. Some corrections in the contours of the hair.

The pot clearly indicates the Magdalen; the original picture, with book alone, would hardly have done so. In any case, it may well be a portrait. It is certain that portraits were made at the time in the guise of saints.[1] This picture has the air of being one; it has at least a better claim than two other pictures in this Gallery of about the same time, whose pretensions to represent anything but *The Magdalen* are in this Catalogue disputed.[2] The claim of the present picture would be greatly strengthened if the necklace could be proved to be that of some unofficial 'Order'; the compiler does not at present exclude that it may be only a fancy.

As for the identity of the sitter, comparison of such weakly marked features with portraits on other designs and by other hands is a trap; all the same, there are three claimants.

A tradition, not proved to be as much as one hundred years old, calls her 'Mary Tudor, Queen of France.'[3] Mary, 1496 (?)–1533, was the third daughter of Henry VII; she was betrothed in 1508 to the Archduke Charles (later the Emperor Charles V) but married (1) in 1514, Louis XII, who died almost at once; (2) in 1515, Charles Brandon, Duke of Suffolk. Only the slightest confirmation of this tradition is given by a small picture in the Musée des Arts Décoratifs, Paris,[4] also supposed to represent *Mary Tudor as the Magdalen*; the dressing of the hair (perhaps merely a girl's) is similar, the features less so. The best portrait of Mary seems to be the one with her second husband in the Duke of Bedford's Collection at Woburn[5]; it is not dated but would seem to be from not very long after the marriage in 1515. The appearance should therefore resemble that of No. 2615; one may believe it if one wishes. A portrait of her at Sudeley is recorded to have borne on the original frame the name of the sitter, the date 1532 and the name of the painter Johannes Corvus[6]; the likeness is not great.

Louis Dimier[7] identified the sitter as Eleanor of Austria. She was the eldest daughter of Philip the Fair and Joan the Mad, born 1498, died 1558; she married (1) in 1519 King Manuel of Portugal (who died in 1521); (2) in 1529, François Ier. An authentic portrait of her is known in many repetitions[8]; after making due allowance for some difference of age, one may incline to follow Mme Roblot-Delondre[9] in rejecting this identification.

Sánchez Cantón,[10] thinking the jewellery Portuguese, suggested another Queen of Portugal, Eleanor's younger sister Catherine. She was born in 1507, died in 1578; her husband, whom she married in 1525, became King Juan III. A supposed portrait of her in youth under the guise of S. Catherine, bearing a signature Carvalho, is in the Prado, No. 1320[11]; Sánchez Cantón compares this picture with No. 2615, but it is difficult to see any correspondence in the features.

No very exact dating can be given to the present picture; it may be *ca.* 1520.

The attribution is very doubtful. It is here classed under the School of the Netherlands, where was the central place of production for pictures of this technique and type; but the style does not seem to be purely Netherlandish. It might be Spanish or (preferably) Portuguese; the dress and hair-style are rather in favour of this. A former attribution to the French School might conceivably be correct; it would be by a painter later than the Master of Moulins (the Moulins Triptych is of *ca.* 1498), and earlier than Jean Clouet (first mentioned in 1516), of whom many 'presumed' works are known.

PROVENANCE: In the Collection of Hollingworth Magniac, Colworth, by 1862[12]; Sale, London, 2 July, 1892 (lot 83),[13] bt. Durlacher, Coll. Wickham Flower; exhibited at the New Gallery, 1900 (No. 30)[13]; Sale, London, 17 December, 1904 (lot 45),[13] bt. Agnew. Coll. George Salting; exhibited at the Burlington Fine Arts Club, Early English Portraiture, 1909 (No. 69).[14] Salting Bequest, 1910.

REPRODUCTION: *Illustrations, Continental Schools*, 1937, p. 131. *Plates, Early Netherlandish School*, 1947, Plate 105.

REFERENCES: **(1)** See Glück in the Vienna *Jahrbuch*, 1933, p. 192. **(2)** Follower of Gossaert, No. 2163, and Studio of the Master of the Magdalen Legend, No. 2614. On the whole subject, see the remarks by Georges Marlier, *Ambrosius Benson*, 1957, pp. 189 ff. **(3)** The identification is recorded on a label on the back in a nineteenth-century hand, probably Hollingworth Magniac's. **(4)** Paris, Musée des Arts Décoratifs, *Guide*, 1934, p. 39. Letter from Paul Alfassa and photograph in the Gallery Archives; reproduced in the *Gazette des Beaux-Arts*, May, 1948, p. 271. In 1954 this picture was labelled at the Arts Décoratifs as representing *Madeleine de France reine d'Ecosse*, i.e. the daughter of François Ier and wife of James V of Scotland. A photograph of a variant of it (Coll. Prince de Ligne, Beloeil) is in the Witt Library. **(5)** Reproduced in the *Biographical Catalogue, Woburn Abbey*, Vol. I**, p. 425. **(6)** Exhibited at the Burlington Fine Arts Club, Early English Portraiture, 1909 (No. 28); Plate VII of the Illustrated Catalogue. **(7)** Louis Dimier, *Portraits des Rois et Reines de France*, 1910, pp. 69/70. **(8)** Friedländer, Vol. IX, No. 108, Plate LII. Some other versions are reproduced by Louise Roblot-Delondre, *Portraits d'Infantes*, 1913, Plates 10–12; drawing, Plate 13. The ringless portrait in Friedländer, Vol. VIII, No. 74, Plate LIII, can hardly be Eleanor and in any case does not resemble No. 2615. **(9)** Louise Roblot-Delondre, *Portraits d'Infantes*, 1913, p. 24, note 3. **(10)** Letter from Sánchez Cantón in the Gallery archives. **(11)** The picture is recorded on p. 839 of the Prado Catalogue, 1933; it is reproduced by Allende Salazar and Sánchez Cantón, *Retratos del Museo del Prado*, 1919, Plate II. Catherine's authentic portrait by Mor in the Prado is of 1552, and therefore not comparable. **(12)** Sir Charles Robinson's *Catalogue*, 1862 (No. 218). **(13)** In the two sales and the exhibition as Early Flemish. **(14)** Ascribed to Jean Perréal. The attribution was made because Perréal was sent to London in 1514 to adjust Mary Tudor's trousseau, and apparently to paint her portrait, on her betrothal to Louis XII (cf. the *Gazette des Beaux-Arts*, 1948, I, pp. 267/8). Jean Perréal has often been identified (without proof) as the Master of Moulins, who did not paint the present picture.

3045 THE VIRGIN AND CHILD ENTHRONED

Oak, rounded top, painted surface, $9 \times 5\frac{3}{4}$ (0·23 × 0·145).

The beginning of a semi-circular form of the step on the lower edge might suggest that the picture had been cut; but the (regilded) frame, fixed to the picture, seems to be original. Overall size, $11\frac{3}{8} \times 8\frac{1}{2}$ (0·29 × 0·215).

The two square pedestals on the front of the throne are additions by the original painter. At first, the Virgin's drapery spread out further to each side; a piece is still visible behind the right-hand pedestal. The present red drapery was put in on top of the pedestals; a piece of her blue drapery has been extended over the step. There are also a few *pentimenti* in the canopy.

Good condition. There are small gashes on the Virgin's right hand and over the Child—especially across His forehead.

A similar kind of picture was exhibited at the R.A., 1927[1]; in the large catalogue, Hulin associates it with Cornelis van Coninxloo.[2] The architecture in that picture and in No. 3045 is less Gothic than in Cornelis' signed picture[3] and tends rather towards that of the Dilighem Triptych.[4] The present picture may date from *ca.* 1520 and may be from Brussels or Antwerp.

PROVENANCE: Before 1885, owned by the Rev. H. E. Richards, Claygate; bought from his widow in 1891 by Sir Charles Archer Cook,[5] and presented, 1916.

REPRODUCTION: *Illustrations, Continental Schools*, 1937, p. 124. *Plates, Early Netherlandish School*, 1947, Plate 106.

REFERENCES: **(1)** R.A., 1927 (No. 164); Plate LXX of the large catalogue. **(2)** Some information about Cornelis van Coninixloo is given in the commentary to No. 2606, ascribed to the Studio of Coecke. It appears that Hulin did ascribe also No. 3045 to Cornelis van Coninxloo; this attribution (with others to the same painter) is approved by J. Maquet-Tombu in the volume of essays by various hands entitled *Bernard van Orley*, 1943, pp. 162/3. **(3)** At Brussels; reproduced by Fierens-Gevaert, *Les Primitifs Flamands*, III, Plate CLXXXV. **(4)** Friedländer, Vol. XI, Plate XXXVII. The date has been supposed to be 1537/8, but see the biography of the Master of 1518 in this Catalogue. **(5)** Information given to C. H. Collins Baker.

3116 THE MAGDALEN WEEPING

Top left: No. 511.

Oak, painted surface, 20½ × 15 (0·52 × 0·38). Painted up to the edge top and bottom.

Much repainted, but the general character has not been affected. The headdress originally went further to the left.

Perhaps *ca.* 1520. By an undistinguished hand; perhaps a late and vague reminiscence of Rogier van der Weyden's large figures (e.g. the Prado *Deposition* from the Escorial). Friedländer suggested for the authorship the region of the Magdalen Master or Colijn de Coter.[1]

PROVENANCE: Bought by Sir Austen Henry Layard in Madrid in the autumn of 1871[2]; in his Collection at Venice, 1881.[3] Layard Bequest, 1916.

REPRODUCTION: *Illustrations, Continental Schools,* 1937, p. 123. *Plates, Early Netherlandish School,* 1947, Plate 107.

REFERENCES: **(1)** Friedländer, oral communication, made with reserves. **(2)** Letter from Layard to Morelli, 21 December, 1871; cf. also 26 October, 1872 (British Museum, Layard Papers, Vol. XXXVI, Add. MS. 38966). Further, letter to Sir W. H. Gregory, 1 November, 1871 (Add. MS. 38949, ff. 101/2). Cf. also the Layard MSS. in the National Gallery. **(3)** Layard Valuation, 1881. From the Layard papers at the British Museum, it may be deduced that the transfer to Venice took place in 1875/6.

3379 THE VIRGIN AND CHILD WITH TWO ANGELS

Oak, painted surface, 18½ × 13½ (0·47 × 0·345).

Fair state.

It is doubtful if an acceptable attribution for this picture can be made[1]; it may eventually be possible to establish the region from which the picture comes.

PROVENANCE: Murray Marks Sale, 5 July, 1918 (lot 32), bt. Brown and Phillips, from whom purchased, Lewis Fund, 1918.

REPRODUCTION: *Illustrations, Continental Schools,* 1937, p. 222. *Plates, Early Netherlandish School,* 1947, Plate 107.

REFERENCE: **(1)** Formerly A. Bouts, Daret, the Ursula Master. The possibility of its being a fake, left open in the first edition of this catalogue, can be excluded.

3650 THE BIRTH OF THE VIRGIN(?)

On the left, Noah with the dove in the Ark, with inscription. *Gen̄.* 8°. On the right the Parable of Balaam, with a carelessly written abbreviation for *Numeri.* 2 (?) 4°.

Oak, painted surface, 28 × 17¾ (0·71 × 0·45).

Painted up to the edge all round.

Fair condition.

Probably one panel of a series.

Noah and the Dove are referred to in Genesis, viii, 7–8. In the other scene, Balaam and Balak with an attendant (?) are pointing to the Star: *Numbers*, xxiv, 17, *there shall come a Star out of Jacob.* The tents presumably recall v. 5 of the same chapter, *How goodly are thy tents, O Jacob.*

These two 'allegories' would settle the identification of the main subject (which has also been called *The Birth of S. John*), if the painter's source could be discovered. *The Birth of the Virgin* is probably correct. In the *Speculum Humanae Salvationis*, Balaam's star is a symbol of the birth of the Virgin; the ark is only a general allegory of redemption, but as such it appears in the chapter of the *Speculum* immediately preceding.[1]

May date from *ca.* 1520. Formerly catalogued as 'Dutch' School, which is obviously wrong; it was probably painted at Brussels. The style is perhaps in the same tradition as that of the wings of an altarpiece at Forest, published by Jeanne Maquet-Tombu[2] with an attribution to Jan van Coninxloo, *ca.* 1540.

PROVENANCE: Ralph Bernal Sale, London, 8th Day, 13 March, 1855 (lot 965).[3] Lot 77 of some sale at Christie's.[4] G. P. Boyce Sale, 3rd Day, 3 July, 1897 (lot 287), bt. Murray. Coll. Sir Henry Howorth; exhibited at the Burlington Fine Arts Club, Winter 1912 (No. 37); presented in memory of Lady Howorth, through the N.A.-C.F., 1922. Exhibited at the National Gallery, N.A.-C.F. Exhibition, 1945/6 (No. 8).

REPRODUCTION: *Illustrations, Continental Schools*, 1937, p. 97. *Plates, Early Netherlandish School*, 1947, Plate 108.

REFERENCES: (1) See the edition of the *Speculum Humanae Salvationis*, by J. Lutz and P. Perdrizet, 1907/9, Vol. I, pp. 123/4. (2) J. Maquet-Tombu in the *Gazette des Beaux-Arts*, 1931, ii, pp. 148 ff. Cornelis van Coninxloo received in 1511/2 a payment that might seem connected; see A.-J. Wauters in the *Biographie Nationale . . . de Belgique*, Vol. XXI, Col. 697 (s.v. Schernier). But the identification is rejected by J. Maquet-Tombu in *Apollo* (Brussels), June-July 1943, pp. 16 ff. (3) As Early German here and subsequently. (4) Fragment of a label on the back.

4573 ACTS OF CHARITY(?)

The person in bed is of uncertain sex. The actors seem to be poorly dressed—all the feet visible are bare; but the boy, who is dressed only in a shirt, is holding a pair of shoes. The man to the right and the woman hold shirts; the woman also a basket of unidentifiable red things. The man to the left is probably holding nothing.

Oak, painted surface, 10 × 16¾ (0·255 × 0·425). The paint goes up to the edges of the panel, so it may have been cut all round; but the carpentry of the panel is against its being a fragment. The picture consists of a thin central panel, with a thicker strip joined along each of the four sides; the join is marked on the surface along the bottom, where there has been a split, but it is clear that these strips are not additions but an original reinforcement to the panel.

In bad condition.

The picture is presumably one piece of a larger ensemble, perhaps part of a predella (?). The subject is unclear. As several figures are holding shirts and shoes, Dr. Betty Kurth[1] thinks it may be the *Clothing of the Naked*; this suggestion seems very possible, but it is not clear which figure is to receive the clothes. Dr. Kurth further thinks that one or two other Acts of Charity may be included in the scene—*Comforting the Dying* to the right, perhaps *Feeding the Hungry* to the left; in that case, the rest of the series of the *Acts of Charity* would have occupied one or two similar panels.

Friedländer [2] ascribes it to the Master of 1518 (q.v.). A boy's head not dissimilar to the one here appears in a picture reproduced by Friedländer,[3] but there seems to be little other connection with 'Antwerp Mannerism.' The picture is too much damaged for attribution beyond the general term of Netherlandish School, which is very probable.

PROVENANCE: Probably Anon. Sale, Foster's, 6 December, 1911 (lot 209), bt. Carfax. Bought by Sir Michael Sadler *ca.* 1910/1 from the Carfax Gallery, London; presented by him [4] in memory of Lady Sadler, through the N.A.-C.F., 1931. Exhibited at the National Gallery, N.A.-C.F. Exhibition, 1945/6 (No. 23).

REPRODUCTION: *Illustrations, Continental Schools,* 1937, p. 136. *Plates, Early Netherlandish School,* 1947, Plate 108.

REFERENCES: **(1)** Letters from Dr. F. Saxl and Dr. Betty Kurth in the Gallery archives. **(2)** Friedländer, Vol. XI, No. 86. **(3)** Friedländer, Vol. XI, Plate XLIII. **(4)** As German (?); letter from the donor in the Gallery Archives.

6161 A LITTLE GIRL WITH A BASKET OF CHERRIES

Canvas, $31\frac{1}{4} \times 20\frac{1}{2}$ (0·795 × 0·52).

Fair state. Corrections in the collar, and in the sitter's left shoulder.

Datable in the 1570's from the costume. It entered the Gallery as by Martin de Vos; it is fairly like his *Family Group* of 1577 at Brussels, but does not seem to be by the same hand.

PROVENANCE: Bequeathed by Mrs. Elizabeth Carstairs, 1952.[1]

REPRODUCTION: A negative exists, prints obtainable from the National Gallery.

REFERENCE: **(1)** Will dated 1947.

NICOLAS DE NEUFCHÂTEL

active 1561–1567

Little is known for certain of this portrait painter, save that he worked in Nuremberg. He is recorded there, e.g. in 1567, but it is the literary sources, Sandrart and Doppelmayr, that tell us nearly all we know about him. Sandrart's *Teutsche Akademie*, 1675, may be consulted in Peltzer's reprint, 1925; Sandrart says his facts are taken from notes by Nicolaus Juvenel I, a portrait painter at Nuremberg who may have been Neufchâtel's pupil. The passage in J. G. Doppelmayr, *Historische Nachricht von den Nürnbergischen Mathematicis und Künstler*, 1730, is reproduced by W. Schmidt in Zahn's *Jahrbücher*, V, 1873, p. 144.

Sandrart calls the painter Nicolaus Neufschattel (in his Latin edition, Neufchastel) and says that he was known as Lucitell or (p. 318 of Peltzer's edition) Lucidel. Doppelmayr says that Nutzschidell and Lucidell were simply corruptions of Neufchâtel. That the last form is right is shown for instance by the (renewed) inscription on the frame of a portrait at Munich, representing the Nuremberg mathematician Neudörfer with his son, 1561: *autor Nicolaus de Novo Castello.*

This Munich picture is the only sure work of the painter.

His origins are, apparently, Netherlandish. He is generally identified with the *Colyn van Nieucasteel*, pupil of Pieter Coecke van Aelst at Antwerp, 1539. Sandrart says he was born in the 'Grafschaft Bergen' in Hainault (i.e the district of Mons) and that he learnt to paint at Mons, *ca.* 1540. It is indeed claimed that he was born *ca.* 1527, the son of Antoine de Neufchâtel of Mons (H. Delanney, 1927, pp. 5 f.); this appears probable. Peltzer, in the Munich *Jahrbuch*, 1926, p. 190, quotes a reference to Neufchâtel of 1566 as from Friesland.

The statement in the 1929 Catalogue that he worked in Prague is apparently derived from a record of his having painted the Emperor and his daughter, and from Otto Mündler. Mündler saw a lot of portraits in Prague, many of them under the name of Juvenel, ascribed them all to Neufchâtel and deduced that he lived at Prague for some time. See Schmidt in Zahn's *Jahrbücher*, V, 1873, p. 146.

Neufchâtel is supposed to have died towards the end of the sixteenth century.

Literature: Peltzer in the Munich *Jahrbuch*, 1926, pp. 187 ff., and Henry Delanney, *Nicolas de Neufchâtel*, 1927.

184 PORTRAIT OF A YOUNG LADY

Inscribed top right, in poor but old lettering: ÆTAT[I]S SVÆ · I(?)(·)/ ANNO DOM. 15(61?).

Canvas, painted surface, $31\frac{3}{4} \times 25\frac{3}{4}$ (0·805 × 0·655). These measurements give the size on the stretcher until 1968. At both top and bottom, about 2″ (0·05) of painted canvas had been folded over that stretcher; at each side about $\frac{3}{4}$″ (0·02) had been folded. This makes a total area of about $35\frac{3}{4} \times 27\frac{1}{4}$ (0·905 × 0·695): canvas and paint being missing, owing to the folding, at the four corners. As the paint, so far as the damaged condition of the canvas at the edges allows one to judge, continues up to each of these edges, the measurements given may be less than the original size of the picture.

Being cleaned in 1968. The former bituminous varnish had in places eaten slightly into the paint, and there is some wearing, in the background especially; but the condition on the whole was found to be good.

Two coats of arms, recorded from an X-ray photograph in the previous edition of this catalogue, are now seen on the cleaned background. At the time of writing, they are still being freed from overpaint. They are certainly somewhat damaged, and are likely to be difficult to see with the requisite precision, and then to identify. All that can be said pending research is that one of them may correspond somewhat with the arms of the Böckhli family of Augsburg, as given by Rietstap.

A typical example of Neufchâtel's Nuremberg portraiture. Three-quarter lengths of women in embroidered dresses and with folded hands occur frequently, with only slight variations; e.g. at Budapest, Marseilles (Musée Labadié-Grobet), Prague (Nostitz), Duc de Leuchtenberg Sale (Amsterdam, 19 November, 1929). The faces differ; these pictures are relevant to the present one only in showing that Neufchâtel had a stock pose.

PROVENANCE: Beckford Collection, Fonthill, by 1812[1]; Sale, 15 October, 1822 (lot 38)[2]; Sale, 11 October, 1823 (lot 160).[3] Col. Hugh Baillie Sale, London, 15 May, 1858 (lot 12), bt. Nieuwenhuys. Purchased from Nieuwenhuys, 1858.

REPRODUCTION: *Illustrations, Continental Schools*, 1937, p. 196. *Plates, Early Netherlandish School*, 1947, Plate 109.

REFERENCES: *General:* Peltzer in the Munich *Jahrbuch*, 1926, p. 227, No. 18.
In text: **(1)** James Storer, *A Description of Fonthill Abbey*, 1812, p. 19; reprinted by Lewis Melville, *The Life and Letters of William Beckford*, 1910, p. 364. In this catalogue and the subsequent sales, it was called *Jeanne d'Archel of the House of Egmont*, by Mor; the identification of the sitter is dismissed by E. W. Moes, *Iconographia Batava*, 1897, I, No. 192. The compiler does not know who is intended by this name. The two coats of arms on No. 184 are not those of Egmond or Arkel. **(2)** This sale did not take place; catalogued for the 7th Day, 15 (misprinted 16) October. Fonthill was sold privately to John Farquhar. **(3)** Apparently bought at this sale by Col. Baillie; cf. Redford's *Art Sales*.

Style of NEUFCHÂTEL

195 A MAN WITH A SKULL

In the left-hand top corner, a coat of arms quartered: (1) and (4), or a saltire gules, centre top a star sable; (2) and (3) gules, three mallets (?) of uncertain colour.

Oak, painted surface, $38\frac{1}{4} \times 29\frac{3}{4}$ (0·965 × 0·755).

Apparently in fairly good condition; but the background (including the coat of arms) is perhaps rather suspicious. A *pentimento* in the hat.

Formerly called a *Medical Professor*; but a skull in sixteenth-century portraits seems not necessarily to signify a doctor but often to be merely a *memento mori.*[1]

The costume, without being exactly datable, would be likely about the middle of the sixteenth century.

The picture was purchased as by Holbein and then labelled German School. Friedländer[2] says he thinks it Netherlandish. An attribution to Neufchâtel was long ago suggested by 'several eminent connoisseurs'[3]; among others, Waagen.[4] This suggestion was repeated independently by A. B. de Vries.[5] Presumably, Neufchâtel before he went to Nuremberg is intended; there are no dated portraits of this period among the pictures attributed to Neufchâtel.[6]

The attribution of the picture is not altogether convincing. So little is known about the quality of early nineteenth-century fakes that the possibility that this is one is not at present entirely excluded.

PROVENANCE: Imported from Paris by S. J. Rochard,[7] from whom purchased, 1845.

REPRODUCTION: *Illustrations, Continental Schools*, 1937, p. 135. *Plates, Early Netherlandish School*, 1947, Plate 110.

REFERENCES: (1) For one particularly clear example of a skull thus used, see H. Westhoff-Krummacher, *Barthel Bruyn der Ältere als Bildnismaler*, 1965, No. 20, repr. on p. 113. Cf. National Gallery, Netherlandish School, No. 1036 of this catalogue. In the first edition of this catalogue, it was recorded (from an old note in the National Gallery) that a similar coat of arms is said to occur on a tomb in S. Jacques, Antwerp. The arms are in fact on a picture there, the portrait of Madeleine Hockaert (wife of Jan Doncker), by A. de Rijckere. They are in part similar to the arms on No. 195, but are not the same. (2) Friedländer, oral communication. (3) See the Wornum-Eastlake *Descriptive and Historical Catalogue of the National Gallery*, 1854. (4) Waagen, *Treasures*, 1854, I, p. 349. (5) Letter from A. B. de Vries in the Gallery Archives. (6) A pair in the Doria Gallery at Rome, sometimes ascribed to Neufchâtel, is dated 1545, but the date has been changed from 1575; see Ettore Sestieri's Doria Catalogue, 1942, Nos. 170, 178. The woman is reproduced in the *Städel-Jahrbuch*, 1930, p. 92, Plate XXIa. (7) He has an entry in Thieme-Becker. The picture is said to have belonged to Nieuwenhuys for some time; see *The Art-Union*, Vol. VII, 1845, p. 321.

BERNAERT VAN ORLEY

active 1515, died 1541

School of Brussels. For his dates and family, see especially O. le Maire in *Bernard van Orley*, publ. Charles Dessart, 1943, pp. 167 ff.; it is claimed that he was born probably *ca.* 1488. For his date of death, see also Pl. Lefèvre in *Pictura*, 1945, p. 40. Already in 1515 he was working for Margaret of Austria, Regent of the Netherlands; in 1518 he was appointed her painter, and he continued in the post under her successor, Mary of Hungary. Apart from court portraits, he also painted many altarpieces; towards the end of his life, he was much occupied with designs for tapestries and stained glass.

Many signed or documented works exist: the principal are the altarpieces of *S. Thomas and S. Matthias* (Vienna and Brussels; signed); of the *Trials of Job* (Brussels; signed, 1521); of the *Last Judgment* (Antwerp; documented, finished 1525). A portrait of Georges de Zelle at Brussels is signed and dated 1519.

Studio execution seems to enter a good deal into his extensive work.

Orley became (with Gossaert) one of the principal 'Romanists' in the Netherlands; the chief Italian influence is that of Raphael. He is said to have visited Italy twice; however that may be, he could have seen Raphael's cartoons in Brussels, where they were sent *ca.* 1515/9 for tapestries to be made from them. He met Dürer in 1520.

Style of ORLEY

714 THE VIRGIN AND CHILD IN A LANDSCAPE

Oak, $13\frac{5}{8} \times 10\frac{1}{2}$ (0·345 × 0·265).

Painted up to the edge top and bottom.

Several *pentimenti* in the outlines of the Child.

Fairly good condition, but stippling on the flesh affects the character. In parts it suffers from undercleaning.

The picture was ascribed by Friedländer[1] to Bernaert van Orley. There is some stylistic relation, but it seems not by Orley, nor from his studio. Removal of the repaint might make it look less or more like Orley; meanwhile a vague association with his name is justifiable. The landscape is somewhat in the style associated with Patenier, but there is no need to suppose that it was done at Antwerp.

PROVENANCE: Stated to be from the collection of Count Joseph von Rechberg, Mindelheim, and bought in 1815 by Prince Ludwig Kraft Ernst von Œttingen-Wallerstein.[2] At Schloss Wallerstein.[3] Exhibited at Kensington Palace (for sale) 1848 (No. 66),[4] bought with the rest of the collection by the Prince Consort. At Kensington Palace.[5] Exhibited at Manchester, 1857 (Provisional Catalogue, No. 516; Definitive Catalogue, No. 432), lent by Prince Albert.[6] Presented by Queen Victoria at the Prince Consort's wish, 1863.

REPRODUCTION: *Illustrations, Continental Schools*, 1937, p. 255. *Plates, Early Netherlandish School*, 1947, Plate 111.

REFERENCES: **(1)** Friedländer in the Prussian *Jahrbuch*, 1909, p. 29, as *ca.* 1515/20; also in Vol. VIII, No. 130, without a dating. **(2)** Cf. *Kunst-Blatt*, 1824, p. 353. Details about the formation of the Œttingen-Wallerstein Collection were given orally to H. I. Kay. **(3)** Identifiable, as Engebrechtz., in a mention in *Kunst-Blatt*, 1824, p. 318; No. 31, as Engebrechtz., of Wallerstein Catalogues of *ca.* 1826 and 1827 (originals at Munich; photostats in the National Gallery). The Collection was moved from Schloss Wallerstein after a time. **(4)** As Engebrechtz. **(5)** Waagen's *Catalogue*, 1854 (No. 39), as by a Master related to the earlier time of Mabuse. See also Waagen, *Treasures*, IV, 1857, p. 227. **(6)** As Mabuse.

JOACHIM PATENIER

active 1515, died not later than 1524

Also Patinir, Patinier. Most of the signatures contain a D between Joachim and some spelling of Patenier. The meaning of this D is obscure; it probably does not stand for de. E. Gérard, *Dinant et la Meuse dans l'Histoire du Paysage*, 1960, pp. 23, 71, thinks it stands for Dinant; Patenier was a landscape painter from Bouvignes or Dinant. 1515, Master at Antwerp, where active. For the date of death, see Rombouts and van Lerius, *De Liggeren . . .*, I, p. 83. He was confused by van Mander with Herry de Patenir (Herri met de Bles ?).

Friedländer (Vol. IX) mentions signatures on three pictures in Vienna, Antwerp and Carlsruhe: in his *Von Eyck bis Bruegel*, 2nd edition, 1921, he says that a *Rest on the Flight* on the London market is seemingly signed and dated 1520: two of the four important pictures in Madrid bear signatures (see the Prado *Catalogue*, 1933, pp. 417/8). Gérard, *op. cit.*, records various further pictures assigned. Some comments on this matter that could not be further studied for the present publication are given by Robert A. Koch, *Joachim Patinir*, 1968.

His signed works seem notably uneven in quality: the Prado pictures afford the best means for attempting to establish his *œuvre*. As he died apparently both young and popular, it is likely that the imitations far outnumber the originals: but No. 4826 below may be by his own hand.

Patenier specialized in landscape, and is mentioned as a landscape painter by Dürer: but his pictures generally have some principal figures, which serve for the subject. Sometimes these figures are by another hand: thus, in the *Temptation of S. Anthony* in the Prado, the figures are recorded to be by Massys in an inventory of 1574. Sometimes the figures may be by Patenier himself.

He may have been original in the form of his landscapes, without very large figures: but elements of his style are found in the backgrounds of earlier Netherlandish altarpieces. Baldass sees some influence of Gerard David, later of Bosch (Vienna *Jahrbuch*, xxxiv, pp. 111 ff.).

It may be well to ignore the statement of the garrulous van Mander (*Schilder-Boeck*, 1604, f. 219 a) that there is an incident depicted on Patenier's genuine works as constantly as the owl on those of Bles.

Literature: Robert A. Koch, *Joachim Patinir*, 1968.

Ascribed to PATENIER

4826 S. JEROME IN A ROCKY LANDSCAPE

Foreground, S. Jerome with the lion. Centre middleground, before a monastery, the Abbot, two kneeling merchants, two camels and an ass; they are the actors in a story given below.

Oak, painted surface, $14\frac{1}{4} \times 13\frac{1}{2}$ (0·365 × 0·34).

Good condition.

The legend indicated by the small figures in the middleground is as follows.[1] S. Jerome's lion had the task of looking after an ass belonging to the monastery. The lion one day was asleep; some merchants passing with camels took the ass. Later on, these merchants with their camels and the ass came again into the neighbourhood. The lion recognized the ass and carried him off with the camels to the monastery; the merchants followed and knelt to ask pardon of the Abbot.

The picture is the left part of a Patenierish composition, known in several complete versions; the best of these, in the Prado, shows considerable variations.[2] The present picture has not been cut. In style it is indistinguishable from the signed picture at Vienna; though inferior in quality to the Prado version and the three other pictures by Patenier there, it is considerably better than the two signed works at Antwerp and Carlsruhe. It seems reasonable, therefore, to catalogue it as Patenier, but provisionally with the qualification 'ascribed to.' The preceding sentences have been left unchanged from the previous edition; Koch's studies, only in part available for the present edition, may make modifications desirable.[3]

VERSIONS: See above.

PROVENANCE: Coll. Rodolphe Kann, Paris (buying from *ca.* 1880 onwards); sold *en bloc* to Duveen.[4] Acquired by Mrs. Henry Oppenheimer, a niece of Rodolphe Kann, by 1916.[5] Exhibited at the Burlington Fine Arts Club, Winter 1912 (No. 29); R.A., 1927 (No. 107). Bequeathed by Mrs. Henry Oppenheimer, 1936.

REPRODUCTION: *Illustrations, Continental Schools*, 1937, p. 263. *Plates, Early Netherlandish School*, 1947, Plate 112.

REFERENCES: (1) See the Garnier Edition of *La Légende Dorée*, II, pp. 168/70. (2) The Prado variant is reproduced by Friedländer, Vol. IX, No. 240, Plate XCVII. For the others, see Robert A. Koch, *Joachim Patinir*, 1968, p. 76, No. 12a of his Patenier catalogue and p. 88, No. 9 of his Master of the Half-Lengths catalogue (Zürich, Ruzicka Stiftung, ascribed by Koch to the Master of the Half-Lengths): p. 76, No. 12b, Wuppertal-Elberfeld, Von der Heydt Museum (called by Koch a weak copy): p. 76, No. 12c, Palermo, Prince di Trabia Collection, recorded by Koch as a triptych probably produced in Patenier's studio, the S. Jerome composition being incorporated in the left wing and central panel. A somewhat varied version, with an attribution to Herri met de Bles going back (in Rome) into the seventeenth century, is in the Borghese Gallery; Paola Della Pergola, *Galleria Borghese, I Dipinti*, Vol. II, 1959, No. 257 and fig. 259. (3) Koch, *op. cit.*, p. 33, thinks that Patenier painted an original variant of the Prado composition, and himself copied the left part of this, his own copy being No. 4826. See also p. 76, No. 12 of his Patenier catalogue. He thinks (p. 88, No. 9 of his Master of the Half-Lengths catalogue) that the original variant was probably paired with a *Landscape with the Ecstasy of Mary Magdalene*. (4) Rodolphe Kann Catalogue, 1907, II, No. 107. (5) Letter of 20 November, 1916, from Lord Conway, in the National Gallery archives.

Studio of PATENIER

3115 LANDSCAPE WITH THE REST ON THE FLIGHT INTO EGYPT

In the background, on the left the miracle of the Corn and the massacre of the Innocents (cf. the Index to Religious Subjects), on the right S. Joseph (?).

Oak, painted surface, 13 × 21½ (0·33 × 0·495).

Painted up to the edges except on the right-hand side.

Good condition; local damages. *Pentimenti* in a line of the landscape above the Virgin's head; another goes through the ass.

Close in style to No. 4826, but rather inferior. In the previous edition of this catalogue, it was provisionally classed as ascribed to Patenier's own name; Koch's[1] researches make this association appear too precise, and his loosely defined classification of Studio of Patenier is here followed.

The design of the Virgin and Child occurs fairly frequently with variations, e.g. in a picture at Brussels by the Master of the Death of the Virgin.[2] The town with harbour on a bridged river recurs in a picture in the Comte de Vogüé Collection at Dijon and in one at Brussels; the buildings surrounding a temple, originating from the *Rest on the Flight* in the Prado, occur also in a *Rest on the Flight* that belonged to Mrs. George Kidston at Bristol.[3]

VERSION: A version was in the Museo Filangieri, Naples.[4] See also the commentary above.

PROVENANCE: Bought by Sir A. H. Layard in Madrid in the autumn of 1871;[5] in his collection at Venice, 1881.[6] Layard Bequest, 1916.

REPRODUCTION: *Illustrations, Continental Schools*, 1937, p. 265. *Plates, Early Netherlandish School*, 1947, Plate 111.

REFERENCES: (1) Robert A. Koch, *Joachim Patinir*, 1968, pp. 46 and 79/80, No. 23 of his catalogue of the Workshop of Patenier, inclines to class this and other pictures that include more than one (separate) Patenierish *motif* as from the studio. (**2**) Baldass, *Joos van Cleve*, 1925, Plate 11 (Friedländer, Vol. IX, No. 49, with note). See further E. P. Richardson in the *Journal of the Walters Art Gallery*, Baltimore, 1939, pp. 37 ff. Koch, *op. cit.*, p. 53, comments on this in connection with a relationship between the Master of the Death of the Virgin and Patenier. (**3**) Koch, *op. cit.*, p. 46, note 76 (see also pp. 79/80, No. 23 of his Patenier workshop catalogue) comments on this and on other Patenierish *motifs* incorporated in various pictures. (**4**) Recorded and reproduced in the 1961 Catalogue, p. 65 and Plate 87, and reproduced in the *Revue d'Art*, 1928, II, p. 134, Fig. 15. See also Koch, *op. cit.*, p. 80, No. 23a of his Patenier Workshop catalogue, as a copy. It was destroyed in 1943 (*Burlington Magazine*, 1944, p. 75, No. 1469). (**5**) Letter from Layard to Morelli, 21 December, 1871 (British Museum, Layard Papers, Vol. XXXVI, Add. MS. 38966); letter to Sir W. H. Gregory, 1 November, 1871 (Add. MS. 38949, f. 101). See also the Layard MS. Catalogue, No. 53. (**6**) Layard Valuation, 1881. From the Layard papers at the British Museum, it may be deduced that the transfer of the pictures to Venice took place in 1875/6.

Style of PATENIER

945 THE VIRGIN AND CHILD WITH A CISTERCIAN NUN (?)

Oak, painted surface, $13\frac{1}{8} \times 9\frac{1}{2}$ (0·335 × 0·245).
Painted up to the edges all round.
Excellent state. It suffers a little from undercleaning.

The kneeling figure is probably the donatrix; formerly called S. Catherine of Siena or S. Agnes.

First half of the sixteenth century, perhaps *ca.* 1525. Vaguely in the style of Patenier; 1929 Catalogue as Flemish.

PROVENANCE: Wynn Ellis Bequest, 1876.

REPRODUCTION: *Illustrations, Continental Schools*, 1937, p. 118. *Plates, Early Netherlandish School*, 1947, Plate 113.

For some other landscapes more or less in the style of Patenier, see
Studio of Quinten *Massys*, No. 715
Follower of Quinten *Massys*, No. 1081
Studio of the *Master* of the Female *Half-Lengths*, No. 717
Style of the *Master* of the Female *Half-Lengths*, No. 716
Netherlandish School, No. 1864

JAN PROVOOST

living 1491, died 1529

In French Prévost. From Mons. By 1491 he had married the widow of the painter Simon Marmion, who had died at Valenciennes in 1489: see M. Hénault, *Les Marmion*, in the *Revue Archéologique*, 1907, document No. 80. A *Jan Provoost* was Master at Antwerp, 1493: this may be the painter in question, though Thieme-Becker mentions two other painters named Jean Prévost living at or about this time. The present Provoost in any case settled in Bruges in 1494. For the date of death, see *La Flandre*, I, 1867, pp. 351/2: for the other facts about Provoost, see *Le Beffroi*, iv, pp. 205 ff.

A *Last Judgment* at Bruges (Friedländer, Vol. IX, Plate LXXIV) is a documented work of 1524–6, until 1956 partly repainted by P. Pourbus (see A. Janssens de Bisthoven, 'De Herstelling van het Laatste Oordeel van Jan Provoost', in *Gentse Bijdragen*, Vol. XVII, 1957–8, pp. 123 ff., or more recent publications). An altarpiece at Leningrad (Friedländer, Vol. IX, Plate LXXIX) seems to be identical with a documented work of 1524. The only other dates on the pictures in Friedländer's list are 1521 and 1522 on Nos. 160 and 126. These pictures show Provoost's late style. It is doubtful if he really painted all the works brought forward by Friedländer as early, and his origins are obscure.

Ascribed to PROVOOST

713 THE VIRGIN AND CHILD IN A LANDSCAPE

Oak, painted surface, $23\frac{3}{4} \times 19\frac{3}{4}$ (0·605 × 0·50).

Flesh parts in untrustworthy condition, especially the Child; the picture has apparently suffered both from neglect and from overcleaning, though probably the repairs are excessive.

The Child's eyes were originally more cast down, His right elbow was raised higher, and there is a *pentimento* in the Virgin's right thumb.

Although the style seems to fit easily with that of Provoost,[1] the condition of prominent parts of the picture makes a slight doubt of the attribution prudent. The distant landscape may be by a different hand.[2]

The object held by the Child is a toy that could be made to rise like a helicopter and then fall; several examples are known, one certainly earlier than No. 713.[3]

PROVENANCE: Stated to be from the Coll. Count Joseph von Rechberg, Mindelheim, and bought in 1815 by Prince Ludwig Kraft Ernst von Œttingen-Wallerstein.[4] At Schloss Wallerstein.[5] Exhibited at Kensington Palace (for sale), 1848 (No. 34),[6] bought with the rest of the collection by the Prince Consort. At Kensington Palace.[7] Exhibited at Manchester, 1857 (Provisional Catalogue, No. 527; Definitive Catalogue, No. 423),[8] lent by Prince Albert. Presented by Queen Victoria at the Prince Consort's wish, 1863.[9]

REPRODUCTION: *Illustrations, Continental Schools*, 1937, p. 281. *Plates, Early Netherlandish School*, 1947, Plate 114.

REFERENCES: (1) The attribution was first made by Hulin in *Kunst & Leven*, 1902/3, No. 5, p. 20 (as an early work). See also Weale in *The Burlington Magazine*, Vol. II, 1903, p. 332, and Friedländer, Vol. IX, No. 168. (2) Durand-Gréville in the *Gazette des Beaux-Arts*, 1908, i, p. 68, attributes the landscape to Patenier, which is most unlikely. (3) This was kindly pointed out by C. H. Gibbs-Smith, who published a note on other examples as an Appendix to Ivor B. Hart, *The World of Leonardo da Vinci*, 1961, pp. 356 f. (4) Cf. *Kunst-Blatt*, 1824, p. 353. Details of the origin of the Œttingen-Wallerstein Collection were given orally to H. I. Kay. (5) No. 66 of Wallerstein Catalogues of *ca.* 1826 and 1827 (originals at Munich; photostats in the National Gallery). The size is given as 1 French foot

7½ pouces × 1 French foot 2½ pouces; but the ascription is to Aldegrever, which recurs in the 1848 Catalogue, and there is no need to doubt the identity. The Collection was moved from Schloss Wallerstein after a time. (6) As Aldegrever. (7) Waagen's *Catalogue*, 1854 (No. 52); see also Waagen, *Treasures*, IV, 1857, p. 228 (as Unknown). (8) As Jan Swart. (9) As Mostaert.

Marinus van REYMERSWAELE

See MARINUS van Reymerswaele

ROGIER van der Weyden

See Rogier van der WEYDEN

Bernaert van der STOCKT

active 1489, died 1538 or later

Member of a family of painters at Brussels. The terms of his father's will in 1489 imply that he was already active: he made his own will in 1538. His works are not recorded. See Thieme-Becker, Vol. XXXII (1938), s.v. Stock. Hulin identified him with the Master of the Magdalen Legend for two reasons: (1) his daughter Katharina is represented on the wing of a triptych at Münster; (2) a tree stump or 'estoc' appearing in several pictures is to be considered a signature. Hulin's arguments are set forth by J. Tombu in the *Gazette des Beaux-Arts*, 1929, ii, pp. 288 ff.

See the MASTER OF THE MAGDALEN LEGEND

Meyken VERHULST *See* Jan van AMSTEL

Jan Cornelisz. VERMEYEN

1500–1559

In Latin Maius, in Spanish Juan de Barbalonga. Van Mander, whose information seems to be reliable, says that he was born in 1500 at Beverwijck, near Haarlem, and that he died in 1559. He was active at Malines and elsewhere in Europe, chiefly as a portraitist, for the Regents of the Netherlands, Margaret of Austria and Mary of Hungary, and for the Emperor Charles V; several documents were published by Pinchart in the *Revue Universelle des Arts*, 1856, III, pp. 135 ff., and by J. Houdoy in the *Gazette des Beaux-Arts*, 1872, i, pp. 516/8. He was employed from about 1525. Van Mander says that he accompanied the Emperor on the

Tunis Campaign of 1535; this is confirmed by his being granted a privilege to publish engravings of it in 1536. He also designed tapestries of the subject, the cartoons (at Vienna) being in hand in 1546; they are partly of studio execution. He was still working for the Emperor in 1555.

A considerable number of his engravings survive; see Popham in *Oud-Holland*, 1927, pp. 174 ff.

His pictorial style is somewhat obscure. A signed *Holy Family* is now at Haarlem. A *Tourney at Toledo*, signed and dated 1539, is in the Stopford-Sackville Collection at Drayton House; it is reproduced by Glück in the Vienna *Jahrbuch*, 1933, p. 200. A signed *gouache* of the *Pacification of Ghent*, 1540, is in the Library at Brussels; reproduced by Fierens-Gevaert, *Les Primitifs Flamands*, IV, Plate CCXXIX. The principal composition ascribed to him is a triptych at Brussels of the *Raising of Lazarus* with donors of the Michault family, 1551–1559. The attribution is due to A.-J. Wauters (following Camille Benoît) in his Brussels *Catalogue*, 2nd edition, 1906, pp. 195/6; it seems to depend on the possibility that some Roman ruins of Tunis may be in the background. The picture is reproduced by Fierens-Gevaert, *op. cit.*, IV, Plate CCXXX. A *S. Jerome* claimed to be monogrammed IC is in the Rijksmuseum at Amsterdam (see E. Pelinck in the *Bulletin*, 1960, pp. 135 ff.); this is objected to by B. Haak in the *Bulletin*, 1963, p. 18, who reads IG.

Vermeyen has recently been the subject of many attributions as a portrait painter. His portrait engraved by Johan Wierix in Lampsonius' publication of 1572 (reproduced in Hymans' *Van Mander*) is presumably after a self-portrait mentioned by van Mander; but the original is lost. His etching of the head of Erard de la Marck, Bishop of Liège, corresponds with a picture once in the Pannwitz Collection (now Rijksmuseum, Amsterdam; Friedländer, XII, No. 390). Vermeyen does not clearly say on his etching that it is after a picture of his, but he is recorded to have painted the sitter twice. The Pannwitz picture has therefore been ascribed to him; see particularly B. Haak in the *Bulletin van het Rijksmuseum*, 1963, pp. 11 ff., 87. A good many other portraits, some of which are probably by the same hand, have been grouped round. Some of these portraits, originals or copies, are of Habsburg sitters; this may be called confirmation of the ascriptions.

The style of the Pannwitz picture is near to that of Scorel, to whom it was formerly ascribed. Van Mander says that Vermeyen was a friend of Scorel's, but their association was apparently in connection with a land-drainage scheme, 1551. It has not been clearly established if it is by the same hand as the subject pieces by or attributed to Vermeyen.

Style of VERMEYEN

2607 A MAN HOLDING A COLOURED MEDAL

He seems to be pointing towards himself with his left hand. In his other hand he holds a coloured medal with a damaged inscription: MERCVRIVS. DE. GATTINARIA. CAR^LIS (   )M. CACELLAR̄.

Oak, painted surface, $16\frac{1}{2} \times 13\frac{1}{4}$ (0·42 × 0·335).

Painted up to the edge all round, perhaps original paint.

In untrustworthy condition. There are, no doubt, extensive remains of a worn old picture on the panel, but it is impossible to be sure how much of the modelling at present visible is genuine.

Several examples of the medal exist[1]; the true inscription is, MERCURIUS. DE. GATTINARIA. CAR. V. IMP. CANCELL.[2] Gattinaria (1465–1530) was a lawyer and politician; 1518, Chancellor to the Emperor Charles V. He became a Cardinal in 1529. The medal is not dated, but is supposed to be of *ca.* 1530; it may have been struck soon after Gattinaria's death as a memorial.

It might at first seem probable that the sitter made the medal; Simone Bergmans[3] makes a poor case for dismissing this idea.

It would, nevertheless, be in the taste of the time if the sitter were a *protégé* of Gattinaria. Glück[4] suggested that he might be Nicholas Perrenot de Granvella (father of the better-known Cardinal Antoine Perrenot de Granvella), 1486–1550; he owed his political fortune chiefly to Gattinaria. Simone Bergmans,[5] without acknowledgment to Glück, pursued this theory, reproducing a portrait at Besançon, usually accepted as by Titian *ca.* 1548; the identity is not impossible.

Meanwhile, Glück[6] had already rejected his suggestion of Granvella and on comparison with a medal[7] identified the sitter as Gattinaria's secretary, Alfonso de Valdés, who, he says, died at Vienna in 1532. The likeness would seem to be superficial.

All these theories imply that the date of the portrait is not likely to be very different from that of the medal, i.e. *ca.* 1530 or soon after. The costume, on the other hand, indicates *ca.* 1545/50 as likely.[8]

Even if much were known about Netherlandish portraiture of 1530 onwards, it would be difficult to give an accurate attribution to the picture; for the condition is untrustworthy. There seems to be fairly general agreement about an attribution to Vermeyen.[9] This means, the same hand as the Pannwitz picture, which is questionable; the association with Vermeyen is provisionally admitted here for convenience. Simone Bergmans[10] ascribes it to the same hand as well-known portraits of Pieter Bicker and his wife, 1529, usually admitted as by Martin van Heemskerck, which is extremely unlikely.

PROVENANCE: AD in monogram on the back. (Hon. Miss Canning) Sale, Christie's, 6 May, 1905 (lot 108), bt. Agnew[11]; George Salting Bequest, 1910. Exhibited at Brussels, *Le Siècle de Bruegel*, 1963 (No. 232).

REPRODUCTION: *Illustrations, Continental Schools*, 1937, p. 116. *Plates, Early Netherlandish School*, 1947, Plate 115.

REFERENCES: **(1)** Reproduced by Simone Bergmans in *The Burlington Magazine*, November, 1936, p. 215. **(2)** According to Georg Habich, *Die Deutschen Schaumünzen*, 1929, Vol. I, Part I, No. 395. **(3)** Simone Bergmans, *loc. cit.*, pp. 213/4. **(4)** Glück in the Vienna *Jahrbuch*, 1933, p. 197. **(5)** Simone Bergmans, *loc. cit.*, pp. 213 ff. According to the *Biographie Universelle*, XVII, 1857, p. 360, it is wrong to say that Granvella succeeded Gattinaria as Chancellor; the post was abolished. **(6)** Glück in the Vienna *Jahrbuch*, 1934, p. 80, and in the *Gazette des*

Beaux-Arts, 1936, ii, p. 199. (**7**) Georg Habich, *Die Deutschen Schaumünzen*, 1929, Vol. I, Part I, No. 397, Plate LII, 4. (**8**) Notes on the costume, by Mrs. Newton, in the Gallery archives. (**9**) Originally made (on Glück's suggestion) by Otto Benesch in the Munich *Jahrbuch*, 1929, p. 215. Approved of by Glück in the Vienna *Jahrbuch*, 1933, p. 197, and by Friedländer, Vol. XII, No. 400. (**10**) Simone Bergmans, *loc. cit.*, p. 217. Friedländer, Vol. XII, Nos. 384/5, hesitates between Scorel and Heemskerck for the Bicker portraits. (**11**) As Cranach.

WASSENHOVE *See* JOOS VAN WASSENHOVE

ROGIER VAN DER WEYDEN

ca. 1399–1464

The name in French is de le Pasture, in Latin de Pascuis. Born at Tournai. The date of birth is deduced from two documents given in Destrée, *Roger de la Pasture* etc., 1930, I, pp. 58/9 and 66/7. They are not exactly concordant; for in one he is said to be aged thirty-five on 21 October, 1435, in the other aged forty-three on 15 March, 1441 (1442 n.s.). He was active at Brussels during a large part of his life; first mentioned as being there, 1435. In 1450, he was probably in Rome, and just possibly in Ferrara (cf. Ernst Kantorowicz in the *Warburg and Courtauld Journal*, III, pp. 178 ff.).

He is identical with Roger of Louvain, referred to by Molanus (*ca.* 1575); most probably identical with Roger of Bruges, referred to in many old sources.

There is very weak documentary evidence that he was a pupil of Jan van Eyck. In 1426, the town of Tournai gave a present of wine to *maistre Rogier de le Pasture* (*sic*); in 1427, *Rogelet de le Pasture, natif de Tournay* (*sic*) began his apprenticeship with the painter Robert Campin at Tournai; *Maistre Rogier de le Pasture, natif de Tournay* (*sic*) was received into the guild there in 1432. Other documents brought forward to elucidate these three entries are secondary; it is legitimate (though not necessarily sensible) either to admit or to deny that any or all of these three refer to the well-known Rogier van der Weyden. So far as the second and third are concerned, the reader is referred to the biography of Robert Campin in this catalogue. See further E. Panofsky, *Early Netherlandish Painting*, 1953, Vol. I, pp. 154 ff. A useful study of the documents concerning Rogier, with comment on what was happening at Tournai, is given by Theodore H. Feder in *The Art Bulletin*, 1966, pp. 416 ff.

There are no signed works by Rogier, and a basis for attribution is hard to establish. The best point of departure is the *Deposition* until recently in the Escorial and now in the Prado, although the references to it as by Rogier are all later than 1550. After this, the two least badly documented pictures are the *Crucifixion* in the Escorial and the Miraflores Altarpiece at Berlin. The former is in an inventory of 1574 as by Rogier; the latter is apparently the picture given to the Charterhouse at Miraflores as by Rogier in 1445, but it is now very often called a replica, not by his own hand.

Although the basis is so vague, a group of pictures has been reasonably ascribed to Rogier. A group with many stylistic connections, generally labelled as by the Master of Flémalle, is referred to in this catalogue as by 'Campin' (q.v.).

Attribution to Rogier is rendered more difficult by the difficulty of dating. Four panels certainly of *ca.* 1434 are certainly by Jacques Daret, a pupil of Campin at the same time as 'Rogier de le Pasture'; these show some affinities with the pictures ascribed to our Rogier, and are the earliest dated works in his style. The Werl wings in the Prado, ascribed to 'Campin,' are dated 1438; these much more accurately show Rogier's style. A few pictures by Rogier himself, or at least from his studio, are probably of the 40's, although the exact year is not given. The dates in the 50's are less inadequate.

The position has been still further complicated by attempts to class the group Master of Flémalle ('Campin') as the work of Rogier's youth. This theory is not admitted in the present catalogue; it is to be stressed that an opinion on the point depends in the present state of knowledge upon stylistic criticism only.

The relation of Rogier van der Weyden to 'Campin' has been the subject of lengthy dispute. On opposing sides, Jules Destrée wrote *Roger de la Pasture van der Weyden*, 2 vols., 1930, and Emile Renders *La Solution du Problème van der Weyden Flémalle Campin*, 2 vols., 1931; neither of these is satisfactory, though both are useful for the publication (partly in facsimile) of many documents. For method of treatment, the 2nd Volume, 1924, of Friedländer's *Altniederländische Malerei* is far the best; this takes full account of the earlier studies of Tschudi, Firmenich-Richartz, Hulin, Winkler, but is partly out of date. Friedländer's recent views are dimly shadowed forth in his XIVth Volume, 1937, pp. 81 ff. See also Paul Rolland, *Les Primitifs Tournaisiens*, 1932, *La Peinture Murale à Tournai*, 1946, and in the *Revue Belge d'Archéologie et d'Histoire de l'Art*, 1949, pp. 145 ff.; Martin Davies in *The Burlington Magazine*, September, 1937, pp. 140 ff.; W. Schoene, *Dieric Bouts*, 1938, pp. 58 ff.; Hulin in the *Biographie Nationale . . . de Belgique*, XXVII (1938), Cols. 243/4; Charles de Tolnay, *Le Maître de Flémalle et les Frères van Eyck*, 1939, especially note 13, pp. 41/4; Winkler in *Pantheon*, 1941, pp. 145 ff. and in Thieme-Becker, Vols. XXXV (Weyden) and XXXVII (Flémalle); E. Panofsky, *Early Netherlandish Painting*, 1953. A summary of the views is given in the Editor's note in the second edition of Friedländer, *Early Netherlandish Painting*, Vol. II, *Rogier van der Weyden and the Master of Flémalle*, 1967, pp. 95 ff.

As for the style of the pictures ascribed to Rogier, it depends largely on that of 'Campin'; occasional traces of influence by Jan van Eyck can be found.

The origins of Netherlandish painting owe little to Rogier, if he is not the author of the pictures ascribed to 'Campin'; but his influence was dominant on painting in the second half of the century throughout Flanders and to some extent elsewhere in Northern Europe.

654 THE MAGDALEN READING (FRAGMENT OF AN ALTARPIECE)

Behind the Magdalen is a headless figure, holding prayer beads and supporting himself on a stick, identified as S. Joseph. At the left, some toes and the drapery of a figure of S. John the Evangelist.

Mahogany, painted surface, $24\frac{1}{4} \times 21\frac{1}{2}$ (0·615 × 0·545).

Painted up to the edges all round.

The mahogany is West Indian (species Swietenia)[1]; the picture has been transferred from another panel, but there is no record of when this was done.

Cleaned in 1955/6. By no means badly preserved.[2] Painted up to the edges all round. Possibly not much cut at the right or the bottom, though this cannot be proved. In the recent cleaning an almost uniform nineteenth (?) century background was removed.[3]

The head of the figure in No. 654 identified as S. Joseph (who is shown with prayer beads in a number of cases[4]) is preserved separately at the Calouste Gulbenkian Foundation, Lisbon, where also is the head of a female saint, perhaps S. Catherine, probably from the left of the altarpiece (specifically its central panel, if it had wings).[5] A drawing probably of the late fifteenth century, assigned to a man who seems to have liked drawing copies of works of art, the Master of the Coburg Roundels, is at Stockholm.[6] In the drawing is seen, not the Magdalen nor S. Joseph nor S. Catherine (?), but the complete figure of S. John the Evangelist, the small parts included in No. 654 closely corresponding; in the drawing, S. John is seen to be kneeling, and holding an inkwell and a book for the Child Christ to write on. The Child is shown on the lap of the Virgin, who is seated on a bench (one arm-rest of this is seen in No. 654, above S. John's drapery). The drawing further shows, to the left of the Virgin, a full-length standing figure, clearly of the Baptist. Still further to the left, another full-length standing figure, a Bishop or Abbot; it would seem that he was not on the central panel of the altarpiece.

The complete picture from which No. 654 comes was of considerable size.

Attention has often been called to a similarity of pose and type to the *S. Barbara* at Madrid (ascribed to 'Campin'), the pendant to which is dated 1438. There is also similarity in the position of the cupboard behind in the two pictures. The Magdalen is holding her book in a much less convincing way than S. Barbara hers; several different explanations are possible.

The attribution of No. 654 to Rogier is now generally accepted.[7] It was at one time considered a borderline picture between Rogier and 'Campin,'[8] but it fits in well with the pictures ascribed to Rogier, and it is obviously unlike the 'Flémalle' and Merode panels.

VERSIONS: Besides the S. Barbara at Madrid, more or less accurate repetitions of the figure occur on the right wing of Rogier's *Sacraments* Altarpiece at Antwerp (inverted); and—a later derivation—on the Maria-ter-Heide Altarpiece of 1513.[9] Winkler notes a drawing of 1519 or 1517 at Brunswick.[10]

PROVENANCE: In the Collection of the Demoiselles Hoofman, Haarlem (?).[11] Most of this collection, which is said to have been in the family for nearly two hundred years, was sold *en bloc* to Nieuwenhuys in 1846.[12] Purchased with the rest of the Edmond Beaucousin Collection, Paris, 1860.[13]

REPRODUCTION: *Illustrations, Continental Schools*, 1937, p. 401. *Plates, Early Netherlandish School*, 1947, Plate 116. For a reproduction after cleaning, see the National Gallery *Report*, January 1955–June 1956, fig. 7. No. 654 after and before cleaning and the two heads and the drawing referred to in notes 5 and 6 are conveniently reproduced in the second edition of Friedländer, *Early Netherlandish Painting*, Vol. II, *Rogier van der Weyden and the Master of Flémalle*, 1967, Plates 20, 21.

REFERENCES: *General:* An article by the compiler in the *Miscellanea Prof. Dr. D. Roggen*, 1957, pp. 77 ff. Friedländer, Vol. II, No. 12. See also the works referred to in the biographies of Rogier (above) and Campin.

In text: (**1**) Letter from B. J. Rendle of the Forest Research Laboratory in the Gallery archives. Two heads in the Calouste Gulbenkian Foundation at Lisbon, referred to presently, one of them the head of the headless figure in No. 654, are on oak. (**2**) There is a reproduction of it cleaned but not restored in the compiler's article (see *General References*), fig. 2 on p. 81. The condition before cleaning appeared considerably less good than it is, partly because of unnecessarily large overpaintings on the main figure. (**3**) Earlier reproductions are thus very misleading. (**4**) Among various examples that could be cited, it is sufficient to note the background figure, clearly S. Joseph, in the *Virgin and Child* accepted as by Petrus Christus, at Kansas City: Friedländer. *Early Netherlandish Painting*, Vol. I, 1967, Plate 109. (**5**) Friedländer, Vol. II, Plates XXXII, XXXIII. *Pinturas da Colecção da Fundação Calouste Gulbenkian*, Lisbon, 1961, Nos. 9, 10, repr. Mojmír S. Frinta, *The Genius of Robert Campin*, 1966, p. 78, thinks that the female head was not associated originally. (**6**) See the compiler's article, in *General References*, fig. 4 on p. 83. A drawing after No. 783 below is assigned to the same man; see the section *Copy* and note 20 of the entry for it. (**7**) E.g. (but before cleaning) by Winkler, *Der Meister von Flémalle*, 1913, pp. 100/1, as early; by Friedländer, Vol. II, No. 12, as *ca.* 1440; by Hulin in the *Biographie Nationale . . . de Belgique*, XXVII (1938), Col. 239, as perhaps before 1440. (**8**) See Tschudi in the Prussian *Jahrbuch*, 1898, p. 34. Frinta, *op. cit.* in note 5, pp. 77 ff., thinks No. 654 nearer to Campin than to Rogier, perhaps by a pupil of Campin, an open question whether this is Rogier or some other pupil. (**9**) Reproduced in the *Gazette des Beaux-Arts*, 1911, ii, p. 429; for a note about the Maria-ter-Heide Altarpiece, see Popham, *Catalogue of Dutch and Flemish Drawings in the British Museum*, V, 1932, pp. 80/1. (**10**) Winkler, *Der Meister von Flémalle*, 1913, p. 100, note 1. A photograph was kindly sent by Mlle. Sonkes of Brussels; a connection is not apparent. Pächt in *The Warburg Journal*, Vol. IV, 1940/1, p. 88, claims that a figure in the Hours of Isabel of Brittany is related to No. 654, but the connection appears slight. The manuscript was in the Clumber Library Sale, 21 June, 1937 (lot 1); photo of the miniature in the Courtauld Institute. For some further comment upon figures more or less related to the Magdalen here, see the compiler's *The National Gallery* (*Les Primitifs Flamands, Corpus*), Vol. II, 1954, p. 177. (**11**) According to the National Gallery MS. Catalogue (name spelt Hoffman). (**12**) Cf. the *Cabinet de l'Amateur*, 1845/6, p. 430. (**13**) As by Rogier van der Weyden the Younger.

1433 PORTRAIT OF A LADY

Reverse, Christ Crowned with Thorns, shown frontally.

Oak, original painted surface, $14\frac{1}{4} \times 10\frac{1}{2}$ (0·365 × 0·27). The reverse is of approximately the same size, but is not exactly measurable.

Cleaned in 1967. The condition of the front on the whole is extremely good, in particular for the face and the sitter's left hand; an area along the bottom, fortunately not including parts of major importance, is missing. Before the cleaning, the sitter's left sleeve from the shoulder had been widened.

Perhaps rather a simple portrait than the right wing of a diptych. The darker areas of the background, left and top, are presumably conceived of as suggesting shadows from the original frame; this, indeed, is found quite often, at least in the sixteenth century.

Formerly catalogued as Studio of Rogier; but the obverse is acceptable as from his own hand. On no theory of Rogier's *œuvre* can it be placed very early, but the evidence is insufficient for an exact dating. The head-dress is of a later type than No. 653B (ascribed to 'Campin'); almost certainly after 1440, probably *ca.* 1450/60. A portrait of a woman by Rogier, similar in design, but apparently rather different in treatment, is at Washington (ex-Wörlitz)[1]; that is not dated either.

No. 1433 was originally attributed to Rogier by Friedländer.[2] Attributed to 'Campin' by Hulin[3]; this ascription is rightly rejected by Winkler.[4] Recently, Hulin has accepted it as Rogier, *ca.* 1460.[5]

It has been unconvincingly suggested, on comparison with two drawings in the *Recueil d'Arras*, that the sitter is Beatrice of the Portuguese Royal Family, who married in 1452 Adolphe of Cleves, Lord of Ravenstein, and died young in 1461.[6]

The reverse, although the execution is poor, is important as a representation of the subject from the studio of Rogier (as distinct from Bouts; cf. No. 712 in this catalogue).

PROVENANCE: Sale of Mme. Bl. (i.e. Blanc, belle mère de Alf. Stevens), Paris, 3 May, 1876 (lot 15), bt. de Beurnonville.[7] Coll. Baron de Beurnonville; exhibited at Paris, Musée des Arts Décoratifs, August, 1878 (No. 178); Sale, Paris, 14/6 May, 1881 (lot 363).[8] Bequeathed by Mrs. Lyne Stephens,[9] Paris, 1895.

REPRODUCTION: *Illustrations, Continental Schools*, 1937, p. 402 (obverse and reverse). *Plates, Early Netherlandish School*, 1947, Plate 117 (obverse).

REFERENCES: *General:* Friedländer, Vol. II, No. 34, as *ca.* 1460.

In text: **(1)** Cf. C. J. Holmes in *The Burlington Magazine*, XLVIII, p. 122. **(2)** Friedländer, *Werk über die Renaissance Ausstellung*, Berlin, 1898, p. 7. **(3)** Hulin, *Catalogue Critique*, 1902, p. xxxvi. **(4)** Winkler, *Der Meister von Flémalle*, 1913, pp. 51 ff. **(5)** Hulin in the *Biographie Nationale . . . de Belgique*, XXVII (1938), Col. 241. **(6)** José Cortez in *Belas Artes*, Lisbon, 1955, No. 8, pp. 13 ff. **(7)** Not B(rooks) Sale, Paris, 16/8 April, 1877. **(8)** As Memlinc. **(9)** Mrs. Lyne Stephens had been a dancer, Yolande-Marie-Louise, known as Pauline, Duvernay; there is a short essay on her by C. W. Beaumont. *Three French Dancers of the 19th Century*, 1935. She is mentioned in *The Ingoldsby Legends*.

6265 PIETÀ

On the left, S. Jerome with a donor; on the right, S. Dominic (?).

Oak, painted surface, 14 × 17¾ (0·355 × 0·45).

Very good condition. An infra-red photograph shows underdrawing, especially in the Virgin's mantle, and some small *pentimenti*. The first rough drawing of the donor's features seems to be a little to the left of the present position, and the first drawing of the Virgin's left hand was higher than now. An X-radiograph shows that the first finger of the donor's right hand was once painted a little to the left of its present position.

Another picture of the *Pietà*, accepted as Rogier van der Weyden's and believed to be earlier than No. 6265, is at Granada. The figures there are compressed within an elaborately sculptured setting of architecture; here the landscape is more closely united with the figures, which are spread out to form a horizontal composition (the panel at Granada is vertical in shape). The National Gallery picture may reasonably be considered the best of several free variants of this, which are fairly closely related to each other; in the production of them Rogier's own participation is disputed in varying degrees. The attribution of No. 6265 to Rogier himself is accepted by Friedländer and others.[1] Although this seems fully satisfactory for its quality, some awkwardnesses of composition—to be compared from this point of view with its variants—may suggest that it is not Rogier's ur-original of the design.

VARIANTS: The Granada picture is referred to above.[2] Among the more closely connected variants may be mentioned the one at Brussels,[3] and those (closer to No. 6265 in the details of the main group) at Madrid[4] and Berlin.[5]

PROVENANCE: In the Collection of the Earl of Powis by 1895.[6] Exhibited at the Burlington Fine Arts Club, 1902 (No. 27),[7] at the Guildhall, 1906 (No. 9), at Agnew's 1925 (No. 33), at the Royal Academy, 1927 (No. 27) and 1953/4 (No. 17) and at Bruges, 1956 (No. 4). Acquired in 1956 from the Earl of Powis through Messrs. Thomas Agnew & Sons under the terms of the Finance Act, 1956.

REPRODUCTION: The National Gallery Catalogue *Acquisitions 1953–62* and M. J. Friedländer, *Early Netherlandish Painting*, Vol. II, *Rogier van der Weyden and the Master of Flémalle*, 1967, Plate 40 (both after cleaning at the Gallery).

REFERENCES: **(1)** Friedländer, *Die Altniederländische Malerei*, Vol. II, No. 20, as *ca.* 1450. Cf. further what Friedländer says in the *Repertorium für Kunstwissenschaft*, 1903, p. 70 and 1906, pp. 574/5. Hulin in the Memorial Catalogue of the Exhibition of *Flemish and Belgian Art* at the Royal Academy, 1927, notes to Nos. 27 and 31, dates No. 6265 *ca.* 1440, and comments on its relationship to other pictures recorded under *Variants*; cf. also a long discussion of these relationships by Otto Seeck in the *Zeitschrift für bildende Kunst*, 1907, pp. 197 ff. There are some not very definite comments on the picture by Weale in *The Burlington Magazine*, Vol. I, 1903, p. 205 and Vol. IX, 1906, p. 186. Panofsky, *Early Netherlandish Painting*, 1953, Vol. I, p. 462 (note 4 to p. 261) reserves judgement about it, not having seen it in the original. **(2)** See the Corpus volume *Grenade* by Roger van Schoute, 1963, No. 101, with reproductions. It is one panel of a triptych, of which there is a repetition (usually assigned to Rogier's Studio), The Miraflores Altarpiece at Berlin, reproduced in Corpus *Grenade*, Plate CLXXXVIII. **(3)** Reproduced in the Brussels *Catalogue de la Peinture Ancienne*, 1949, Plate VI; M. J. Friedländer, *Early Netherlandish Painting*, Vol. II, *Rogier van der Weyden and the Master of Flémalle*, 1967, Plate 41. **(4)** Reproduced in F. J. Sánchez Cantón, *The Prado Museum*, 1949, Plate CXC; Friedländer, *op. cit.*, in note 3, Plate 41. **(5)** Reproduced in the Berlin Illustrations; Friedländer, *op. cit.* in note 3, Plate 41. **(6)** This is deduced from the date given on a label, formerly on the back of the frame, now in the Gallery archives. **(7)** For confirming the identity, cf. *The Athenaeum*, 31 January, 1903, p. 154.

Follower of ROGIER VAN DER WEYDEN

783 THE EXHUMATION OF S. HUBERT

The scene is the choir of a Gothic church. The body of S. Hubert is in the centre; left, Louis le Débonnaire, King of France, and Walcandus, Bishop of Liège; right, perhaps Adelbald, Archbishop of Cologne. On the altar a reliquary with figures, among which S. Hubert is identifiable in the centre; behind, a painted retable with a female saint with a sword and crown (S. Catherine ?), S. Peter, Christ on the Cross between Mary and John, a male saint with a pike (S. Matthew ?) and S. Gudula; above, a statue of S. Peter in a tabernacle with painted wings. S. Peter reappears in the stained glass with S. Paul. The only other identified figures on the stained glass are the Virgin and Child, left. Ten Apostles above the capitals, SS. Peter and Paul in the places of honour; SS. Andrew, John the Evangelist and Bartholomew (?) also identifiable. Four angels bearing candlesticks are on columns round the altar. SS. John the Evangelist, Bartholomew (?) and two other saints on the Bishop's cope, left: God (?) on the morse of the prelate standing right.

Oak, painted surface, $34\frac{5}{8} \times 31\frac{3}{4}$ (0·88 × 0·805).

A companion panel, *The Dream of Pope Sergius*, passed from the Mortimer L. Schiff Sale, London, 24 June, 1938 (lot 84) into the von Pannwitz Collection.[1]

The original paint goes up to the edge of the panel on the left.

The picture has suffered losses from cracking and flaking, and is somewhat rubbed; but the most important parts are intact, or nearly so. It was cleaned in 1953/4, when a good deal of irresponsible retouching was removed, including the painting out of the left arm and hand of the figure standing on the right.

Several *pentimenti*, especially on the left side of the picture. The head of the man second from the left in the top (diagonal) row is painted over another head a little lower down; in the next row, the eyes of the woman were originally higher, and the man next her on the right is painted over a figure a little lower. There are other changes in this area. As for the rest of the picture, it may be mentioned that the priest to the right of Adelbald (?) was once intended to show his left hand.

S. Hubert was twice exhumed, in 743 and in 825[2]; the second occasion is here intended. Walcandus (or Walcaudus), Bishop of Liège, presided at the ceremony; Louis le Débonnaire, King of France and Emperor, and Adelbald, Archbishop of Cologne, were then present. The occasion was the translation of S. Hubert's body from S. Pierre, Liège, to the Abbey of Andagium or Andainum, ever since known as Saint-Hubert-des-Ardennes. This identification of the subject appears to be indisputable.[3]

The church in the picture thus stands for S. Pierre, Liège; this church was built in the first instance by S. Hubert, rebuilt *ca.* 1185 in the Romanesque style and destroyed in 1811. As the architecture on the picture is vaguely that of Brabant of the earlier fifteenth century, it cannot be copied from the actual church of S. Pierre, and it seems to have no particular interest.[4] The reliquary in the picture is somewhat in the style of the early fourteenth century.

The stoles of the two monks raising S. Hubert are ornamented with a form of swastika: this is not very rare in the fifteenth century. Other examples of rather different swastikas on stoles are to be seen on a drawing in the British Museum that has been ascribed to the same hand as this picture (see note 11); also on a picture at Louvain ascribed to 'Campin,' and on an *Annunciation* in the Prado, also ascribed to 'Campin.'[5] The pattern on the antependium before the altar reappears closely similar in the dress of the Holy Woman supporting the Virgin in Rogier's *Deposition* in the Prado (ex-Escorial), and in the strip of stuff on which the Virgin kneels in the *Annunciation* of the S. Columba altarpiece at Munich, also acceptable as Rogier's.[6]

The Church (i.e. S. Peter's, Rome) in the background of the companion picture reappears with variations in the *Presentation of the Virgin* in the Escorial by a follower of Rogier.[7]

There is little reason to doubt that this picture was painted for the chapel of S. Hubert in S. Gudule at Brussels, where it (clearly) is recorded, with its pendant, *ca.* 1623 or soon after by Dubuisson-Aubenay.[8] The two pictures formed then a diptych (No. 783 to the spectator's left), and from the centralized perspective of both it is probable that they were a diptych from the beginning, and were not shutters of a larger altarpiece. The chapel was founded in 1437, and it is reasonable to believe that the pictures were painted then or soon afterwards.[9]

Friedländer ascribes No. 783 to Rogier van der Weyden,[10] but this is difficult to accept. The compressed design, the inexpressive contours and the caricatural types (not much better since the cleaning) are arguments against the ascription. Possibly it is by an independent follower rather than a studio assistant.

The picture was catalogued in 1929 as of the Flemish School. It was at one time associated (as Master of the Exhumation of S. Hubert or the Edelheer Master[11]) with a *Marriage of the Virgin* in Antwerp Cathedral,[12] a female portrait by a different hand, formerly in the Heseltine Collection,[13] and the Edelheer altarpiece, apparently again different.[14] Curiously, the types in No. 783 bear some slight relation to those of the early *Marriage of the Virgin* in the Prado ('Campin'): perhaps this was what Hulin was thinking of when he said that it is under the double influence of Rogier and 'Campin,' especially the latter.[15] In his latest statement, Hulin calls it Rogier *ca.* 1435/43.[16] Winkler also, in his entry for Rogier van der Weyden in Thieme-Becker, has recently called it Rogier. The pendant, but not this picture, is from a photograph ascribed to 'Campin' by Tolnay.[17] Lippmann sees the influence of the Master of Oultremont and 'Ouwater'[18]: there is, in fact, some compositional similarity to the *Raising of Lazarus* ascribed to 'Ouwater' at Berlin.[19]

COPY: A drawing after the picture with colour notes in French and an old inscription *Quintyn Messis*, was formerly in the Weigel Collection, later Koenigs, Haarlem, now at Rotterdam.[20]

PROVENANCE: What are clearly this picture and its pendant are recorded *ca.*

1623 or soon after in S. Gudule at Brussels, in the chapel of Notre Dame de Fleurs, by which it is reasonable to understand the one dedicated to S. Hubert; it seems likely that the two pictures were painted for the chapel. They may have been removed *ca.* 1627.[21] The pictures are not known to be recorded together again, though at different dates both are mentioned in the Bessborough Collection. No. 783 was in the collection of the 2nd Earl of Bessborough (d. 1793) at Roehampton, probably by 1781,[22] certainly by 1792.[23] Earl of Bessborough Sale, London, 7 February, 1801 (lot 73), bt. Foxall (Foxhall) for William Beckford of Fonthill.[24] Sale, Fonthill, 15 October, 1822 (lot 80)[25]; Sale, Fonthill, 10 October, 1823 (lot 80), bt. Bentley. Edward Harman Sale, London, 28 May, 1847 (lot 397), bt. Smith. Coll. Sir Charles Eastlake, London, by 1847[26]; purchased from the Eastlake Collection, 1868.

REPRODUCTION: *Illustrations, Continental Schools*, 1937, p. 117. *Plates, Early Netherlandish School*, 1947, Plate 118 (both before cleaning). Friedländer, *Early Netherlandish Painting*, Vol. II, 1967, *Rogier van der Weyden and the Master of Flémalle*, Plate 38 (after cleaning).

REFERENCES: (**1**) For some account of these two pictures, see an article by Seymour de Ricci in *Mélanges Hulin*, 1931, pp. 283 ff., corrected in many particulars by Canon Joseph Coenen in *Fédération Archéologique et Historique de Belgique, Congrès de Liége*, 1932, pp. 208 ff. (**2**) Coenen, *loc. cit.* Douhet, *Dictionnaire des Légendes* (Vol. XIV of Migne's *Encyclopédie Théologique*), Cols. 596/7, argues for dates 744 and 817. The text follows Coenen in saying what the painter should have represented. (**3**) The only difficulty is in Dubuisson-Aubenay's text (see note 8), clearly referring to No. 783, and the earliest known reference to it. He confusedly writes of the exhumation and translation of the body of S. Lambert; for a discussion of this (which must be a mistake), see the compiler's *The National Gallery* (*Les Primitifs Flamands, Corpus*), Vol. II, 1954, p. 183. (**4**) Coenen, *loc. cit.* (**5**) Friedländer, Vol. II, Plates LXI and XLV. (**6**) This was pointed out by A.-M. Mariën-Dugardin in *Miscellanea Tornacensia* (Congrès de Tournai, 1949), 1951, Vol. II, pp. 650–1. (**7**) Friedländer, Vol. II, Plate LXVIII. (**8**) Published by Léon Halkin in the *Revue Belge d'Archéologie et d'Histoire de l'Art*, 1946, p. 60, and by the compiler, *op. cit.*, Vol. II, 1954, p. 188, discussion on p. 184, with an amended text kindly communicated by Mme. Maquet-Tombu. (**9**) In the first edition of this catalogue, the compiler tentatively suggested *ca.* 1440 from the costume. (**10**) Friedländer, Vol. II, No. 18, as *ca.* 1450. See the criticism by Conway in *The Burlington Magazine*, Vol. XLVIII (1926), p. 29. It should be mentioned that Dubuisson-Aubenay *ca.* 1623 (see note 8) records what must be No. 783 as ascribed to Rogier. (**11**) See Friedländer in the *Repertorium für Kunstwissenschaft*, 1903, p. 72, and Winkler, *Der Meister von Flémalle*, 1913, pp. 124/6, and *Die Altniederländische Malerei*, 1924, p. 370. A drawing of a Procession in the British Museum was included in this group: reproduced by Popham, *Drawings of the Early Flemish School*, 1926, Plates 16, 17. Cf. Popham's *Catalogue of Dutch and Flemish Drawings in the British Museum*, V, 1932, pp. 56/7. Vitzthum associates this drawing, No. 783, and its pendant with the miniatures of the Master of Girart de Roussillon: see the *Repertorium für Kunstwissenschaft*, 1927, p. 270 and Thieme-Becker, Vol. XXXVII, pp. 119 (and 97). (**12**) Destrée, *Rogier de la Pasture*, etc., 1930, Plate 119. The compiler inclines to believe that this picture is by the same hand as No. 783. (**13**) Friedländer, Vol. II, No. 127; reproduced in Aru and Geradon, *La Galerie Sabauda de Turin* (*Les Primitifs Flamands, Corpus*), 1952, Plate LIV, in association with two wings at Turin often ascribed to Rogier van der Weyden (Panofsky, *Early Netherlandish Painting*, 1953, Vol. I, pp. 300/1, justifiably objects to this association). (**14**) Destrée, *op. cit.*, Plate 64. (**15**) Hulin, *Catalogue Critique*, 1902, p. xxxvii. (**16**) Hulin in the *Biographie Nationale . . . de Belgique*, XXVII (1938), Col. 234. (**17**) Tolnay, *Le Maître de Flémalle, etc.*, 1939, p. 58, No. 14. (**18**) Lippmann in *The Burlington Magazine*, Vol. XII (1907/8), p. 108. (**19**) There need be no direct connection; cf. W. Schoene in the Prussian *Jahrbuch*, 1942, p. 12 (though

Panofsky, *op. cit.*, p. 494, note 4 to p. 321, objects to this). Compare also a miniature by 'Marmion,' reproduced in the Prussian *Jahrbuch*, 1913, p. 259. **(20)** Reproduced by the compiler, *op. cit.*, Vol. II, Plate CDXXX; also in the second edition of Friedländer, *Early Netherlandish Painting*, Vol. II, *Rogier van der Weyden and the Master of Flémalle*, 1967, Plate 37. This drawing is assigned by Winkler to the Meister der Gewandstudien (or Meister der Koburger Rundblätter) in the *Wallraf-Richartz-Jahrbuch*, 1930, p. 151; the activity of this master seems to cease *ca.* 1495. **(21)** The mention by Dubuisson-Aubenay *ca.* 1623 is quite clear (see note 8). When the pictures were removed is uncertain; for the little evidence that is known, see the compiler's publication, *cit.*, Vol. II, pp. 188 ff. **(22)** This is from R. E. Raspe, *A Critical Essay on Oil-Painting*, 1781, pp. 64/5. Raspe would not at first sight appear to be referring to No. 783, but he probably is; see the compiler's publication, *cit.*, Vol. II, pp. 190/1. **(23)** Daniel Lysons, *The Environs of London*, Vol. I, 1792, p. 433 (as van Eyck). **(24)** Cf. Lysons, *Supplement to the First Edition of the Environs of London*, 1811, p. 64. **(25)** This sale did not take place; catalogued for the 7th Day, 15 (misprinted for 16) October. Fonthill was sold privately to John Farquhar. **(26)** Smith's Day-Book, MS., for 1837–48, ff. 687–8, in the Victoria and Albert Museum Library.

1086 CHRIST APPEARING TO THE VIRGIN (RIGHT WING OF A TRIPTYCH?)

Through the windows (left) an angel and two sleeping soldiers by the Tomb, (right) three Holy Women on their way thither (Mark xvi, 1–5).

Transferred from panel to canvas, 49 × 28 (1·245 × 0·71).

The heads are damaged. The hands and feet are in fair state; the Virgin's left hand the best. The gold of Christ's aureole is new. The general surface is spotty from undercleaning, but the condition may be called not bad for a transferred picture.

The composition is a weak reminiscence of the picture by Rogier in the Metropolitan Museum, New York.[1] A design more nearly similar occurs in two other pictures.[2] The present picture may have been painted between 1450 and 1475.

It was in the 1929 Catalogue as School of 'Campin'; this attribution was perhaps due originally to a misconception.[3] As there is little evidence for a following of 'Campin' in the later fifteenth century, and plenty for a following of Rogier, the latter is clearly the more justifiable term; especially as No. 1086 is more nearly in Rogier's than in 'Campin's' style.[4]

PROVENANCE: In the collection of Karl Aders, a German merchant living in London; Aders Exhibition, No. 34[5]; Sale, 1 August, 1835 (lot 74), bt. Charles.[6] Probably Anon. (H. C. Robinson, or rather Aders Trust) Sale, 26 April, 1839 (lot 47), bt. Lemmé; probably L. Lemmé, a brother-in-law of J. H. Green of Hadley, in whose collection the picture certainly was.[7] Bequeathed by Mrs. Joseph H. Green, 1880.

REPRODUCTION: *Illustrations, Continental Schools*, 1937, p. 43. *Plates, Early Netherlandish School*, 1947, Plate 119.

REFERENCES: **(1)** Friedländer, Vol. II, Plate I. **(2)** Ascribed to Rogier, Friedländer, Vol. II, No. 41 (Washington Catalogue, 1941, p. 214, No. 45), and the Ursula Master, Friedländer, Vol. VI, Plate LII (New York Catalogue, *Early Flemish*, etc., 1947, pp. 76 f.). **(3)** A connection with 'Campin' was claimed by Hymans in the *Gazette des Beaux-Arts*, 1902, ii, p. 97; but Hymans' views on 'Campin' are peculiar. **(4)** Cf. Martin Davies in *The Burlington Magazine*, September, 1937, p. 145. **(5)** For this Exhibition, see Style of Aelbrecht Bouts, No. 1083, note 5. **(6)** As Scoorels. **(7)** Green MS. catalogue.

ADRIAEN YSENBRANDT

active 1510, died 1551

Also Isenbrandt. Master in Bruges, 1510, where active, though he was not born there.

Supposed to be the author of an extensive group of works, formerly known as by the Pseudo- or Waagen'sche Mostaert (cf. Friedländer, Vol. X, p. 15; a few of the attributions to this hand have been transferred to Benson, q.v.). Sometimes known as the *Master of Notre-Dame des Sept Douleurs*, after a picture referred to below.

The name of Ysenbrandt was proposed for this group by Hulin, *Catalogue Critique*, 1902, pp. LXIII ff. The only evidence adduced is that Ysenbrandt is said to have been a pupil of Gerard David, whose influence is discernible in the pictures; the authority for the statement is apparently Dionysius Harduinus (died 1605), reference to whom is given by Sanderus in his *Flandria Illustrata*, and by A. Buchelius, 1621 (see the edition by Hoogewerff and van Regteren Altena, 1928, pp. 53/4).

Of the pictures ascribed to this hand an altarpiece in S. Sauveur, Bruges, may have been painted before 1510, which might make the authorship of Ysenbrandt unlikely (cf. Friedländer, Vol. XI, pp. 87/8); Hulin rejects this dating. A portrait (Friedländer, Vol. XI, Plate LXXIX) is dated 1515; an altarpiece at Lübeck is dated 1518. The donor of the diptych of the *Seven Sorrows of the Virgin* (Bruges, Notre-Dame) died in 1528; but Hulin argues for a date between 1528 and 1535 for this picture.

Friedländer, Vol. XI, lists No. 2585 below as one of eight key-pieces; by the aid of these he attempts to introduce some order into the mass of his material, which he admits is neither homogeneous (Vol. XI, p. 128) nor certainly by Ysenbrandt (*ib.*, p. 80). The style of the painting derives chiefly from Gerard David (Bruges); there are also connections with Benson (Bruges), and less precisely with the Master of the Female Half-Lengths (Antwerp ?). 'Ysenbrandt' copied the triptych by Gossaert at Palermo (Friedländer, Vol. VIII, Nos. 2 c, d); he is claimed not merely to have copied works produced in other studios, but even to have adapted particular examples by overpainting parts of them (Friedländer, Vol. XI, p. 89 and Vol. XIV, p. 124). See further Georges Marlier, *Ambrosius Benson*, 1957, pp. 60 f.

There is no cogent reason for supposing that Ysenbrandt could not have painted some or all of these pictures, so his name is retained here, in inverted commas. Another candidate for authorship is Aelbrecht Cornelis (q.v. for biography); and see Marlier, *op. cit.*, pp. 52 f.

'YSENBRANDT'

2585 THE MAGDALEN IN A LANDSCAPE

An angel holds a Crucifix (Cross marked INRI) towards the kneeling

Magdalen. In the background, the Magdalen reading in a cave, with another Crucifix.

Oak, painted surface, $15\frac{3}{4} \times 12\frac{1}{4}$ (0·40 × 0·31).

Very fair condition. A few small *pentimenti*; it is not clear if some in the region of the Crucifix indicate a major alteration.

Friedländer[1] calls it one of the key-pieces for the understanding of the painter and says that it is early work.[2]

VERSIONS: Other Magdalens ascribed to 'Ysenbrandt' are partial repetitions.[3]

PROVENANCE: According to a label in English in a nineteenth-century hand on the back, for about two hundred years in the possession of the family of Count Livio Odescalchi at Rome (he died *ca.* 1720). Then Conte Guazzo, Padua, later Rome. C. J. Nieuwenhuys Sale, Brussels, 4 May, 1883 (lot 6).[4] Coll. Léon Somzée, Brussels. Exhibited at the Burlington Fine Arts Club, 1892 (No. 31).[5] Lent by L. de Somzée to the Exposition Universelle, Paris, Pavillon de la Belgique, 1900 (No. 9).[6] Exhibited at Bruges, 1902 (No. 182), lent by C. and G. de Somzée. Acquired by Agnew's with several other Somzée pictures, 1902.[7] George Salting Bequest, 1910.

REPRODUCTION: *Illustrations, Continental Schools,* 1937, p. 416. *Plates, Early Netherlandish School,* 1947, Plate 120.

REFERENCES: **(1)** Friedländer, Vol. XI, pp. 80/1 (No. 210); under the circumstances, it seems unnecessary to catalogue it as from the Studio, though 'Ysenbrandt' is a painter who might qualify for that prefix. **(2)** Friedländer, *Meisterwerke,* 1903, p. 19. **(3)** Cf. Friedländer, Vol. XI, Plates LIX, LXXVI. **(4)** As Hugo van der Goes. **(5)** As School of Mostaert, i.e. the Waagen'sche Mostaert = 'Ysenbrandt.' **(6)** As Mostaert. **(7)** Geoffrey Agnew, *Agnew's, 1817–1967,* 1967, p. 42, for the purchase in 1902 of a group of Somzée pictures; No. 2585 is assumed to have been in the group.

Style of 'YSENBRANDT'

1151 THE ENTOMBMENT

Present, the Virgin, S. John, Joseph of Arimathaea, Nicodemus, the Magdalen and two Holy Women. In the background, the Deposition.

Oak, painted surface, $6\frac{7}{8} \times 4\frac{3}{4}$ (0·17 × 0·12).

Much damaged.

This picture is very exactly copied from an engraving by Schongauer (died 1491).[1]

It was formerly catalogued as of the German School. What style there is to it is reminiscent of 'Ysenbrandt'; but a precise attribution would have little meaning. The connection with 'Ysenbrandt' was pointed out by Durand-Gréville[2] and Lippmann.[3]

VERSION: A copy from the Schongauer engraving, assigned to Koffermans, in the Prado,[4] is cited here.

PROVENANCE: On the back, a label with a triple device—the Virgin and Child, a lion crowned and a pelican. Purchased from G. Baslini, Milan, 1883.

REPRODUCTION: *Plates, Early Netherlandish School,* 1947, Plate 121. Not in the *Illustrations, Continental Schools,* 1937.

REFERENCES: **(1)** This is pointed out by Lehrs, *Geschichte und Kritischer Katalog des Kupferstichs*, etc., in volume V, dealing with Schongauer, 1925, p. 157. The engraving is reproduced by Lehrs, *Martin Schongauer*, 1914, Plate XVII; also by Wendland, *Martin Schongauer als Kupferstecher*, 1907, p. 36. **(2)** E. Durand-Gréville in the *Gazette des Beaux-Arts*, 1908, i, p. 70. What he actually says is that it is closely connected with several pictures (including Netherlandish School, No. 1089 of this catalogue, which is obviously wrong), of which the principal is No. 153 of the Munich 1904 Catalogue. The Munich picture was then called Mostaert, i.e. the Waagen'sche Mostaert = 'Ysenbrandt,' and is No. 153 of Friedländer's list, Vol. XI; but Durand-Gréville says his group is to be classed apart, as by a different pupil of Gerard David. **(3)** Lippmann in *The Burlington Magazine*, XII, p. 108 (by 'Ysenbrandt'). **(4)** J. Lavelleye, *Les Primitifs Flamands*, II, *Répertoire des Peintures . . ., Collections d'Espagne*, I, 1953, No. 19 and Plate XXII.

See also NETHERLANDISH SCHOOL, No. 1864

LIST OF CHANGED ATTRIBUTIONS

An alphabetical list of Attributions that have been changed from the 1929 *Catalogue*

Note: Mere changes of form are not here listed. Further, changes of the qualification of a name (as 'Style of A. Bouts' instead of 'A. Bouts') are not noted.

Anonymous works in the 1929 Catalogue were classed under the *Antwerp, Burgundian, Dutch, Flemish, French Schools*; anything from these sections still anonymous in the present catalogue will be found under *Netherlandish School.*

1929 *Catalogue*	*Present Catalogue*
ANTWERP SCHOOL, No. 718	Studio of the MASTER OF 1518, No. 718
ANTWERP SCHOOL, Nos. 1088, 1088A	Follower of the MASTER OF THE DEATH OF THE VIRGIN, Nos. 1088, 1088A
CALCAR, Jan Stephan, No. 2597	Ascribed to Dirck BARENDSZ., No. 2597
CAMPIN, School of Robert, No. 1086	Follower of Rogier van der WEYDEN, No. 1086
CHRISTUS, Petrus, No. 696	Follower of Jan van EYCK, No. 696
CHRISTUS, Ascribed to, No. 2602	NETHERLANDISH SCHOOL, No. 2602
CLAEISSINS, Ascribed to Antoine, No. 2159	After Hugo van der GOES (?), No. 2159
CORNELISZ., Jacob, No. 657	Follower of Gerard DAVID, No. 657
CORNELISZ., Ascribed to, No. 2209	NETHERLANDISH SCHOOL, No. 2209
DUTCH SCHOOL, No. 3459	Style of LUCAS van Leyden, No. 3459
FLEMISH SCHOOL, No. 708	Follower of Dieric BOUTS, No. 708
FLEMISH SCHOOL, No. 783	Follower of Rogier van der WEYDEN, No. 783
FLEMISH SCHOOL, No. 945	Style of Joachim PATENIER, No. 945
FLEMISH SCHOOL, No. 1080	'Jan MOSTAERT,' No. 1080
FLEMISH SCHOOL, No. 1087	MASTER OF THE BRUGES PASSION SCENES, No. 1087
FLEMISH SCHOOL, No. 2606	Ascribed to the Studio of Pieter COECKE, No. 2606
FLEMISH SCHOOL, No. 2607	Style of Jan Cornelisz. VERMEYEN, No. 2607
FLEMISH SCHOOL, No. 3066	Studio of Gerard DAVID, No. 3066
FRENCH SCHOOL, No. 1939	Style of 'Simon MARMION,' No. 1939
FRENCH SCHOOL, No. 2612	MASTER OF THE VIEW OF S. GUDULE, No. 2612
FRENCH SCHOOL, No. 2614	Studio of the MASTER OF THE MAGDALEN LEGEND, No. 2614
FRENCH SCHOOL, No. 2669	Style of 'Simon MARMION,' No. 2669
GEERTGEN tot Sint Jans, Follower of, No. 1085	NETHERLANDISH SCHOOL, No. 1085
GERMAN SCHOOL, No. 195	Style of Nicolas de NEUFCHÂTEL, No. 195
GERMAN SCHOOL, No. 1151	Style of 'Adriaen YSENBRANDT,' No. 1151

1929 Catalogue	*Present Catalogue*
GOES, Ascribed to Hugo van der, No. 658	Imitator of 'Robert CAMPIN,' No. 658
LOMBARD, Lambert, No. 266	Ascribed to the Studio of the MASTER OF THE PRODIGAL SON, No. 266
MASTER OF THE S. URSULA LEGEND, No. 3379	NETHERLANDISH SCHOOL, No. 3379
MELOZZO da Forlì, School of, Nos. 755/6	Joos van Wassenhove, Nos. 755/6
PATINIR, School of Joachim, No. 716	Style of the MASTER OF THE FEMALE HALF-LENGTHS, No. 716
PATINIR, School of Joachim, No. 717	Studio of the MASTER OF THE FEMALE HALF-LENGTHS, No. 717
PATINIR, School of Joachim, Nos. 1082, 1084	Studio of the MASTER OF 1518, Nos. 1082, 1084
PATINIR, School of Joachim, No. 1298	NETHERLANDISH SCHOOL, No. 1298
POURBUS, Frans, the Elder, No. 1094	NETHERLANDISH SCHOOL, No. 1094
POURBUS, Frans, the Younger, No. 2295	NETHERLANDISH SCHOOL, No. 2295
WEYDEN, School of Rogier van der, Nos. 711/2	Studio of Dieric BOUTS, Nos. 711/2
YSENBRANDT, Adriaen, No. 1864	NETHERLANDISH SCHOOL, No. 1864

INDEX TO RELIGIOUS SUBJECTS

Order: 1. God. 2. The Virgin and Child. 3. Period of the Old Testament and the Apocrypha. 4. Life of Christ, from the Annunciation to the Ascension. 5. Other scenes and figures of the New Testament period. 6. Saints since the times of the New Testament.

1. GOD

This section contains single figures, whether of God or of Christ, including devotional effigies such as 'The Man of Sorrows.' One or other of the figures of the Trinity appears normally in certain scenes, e.g. the Holy Ghost (as a Dove) in the Annunciation, etc.; none of these has been indexed. For the scenes in which Christ took part on Earth, see Section 4, *LIFE OF CHRIST*.

2. THE VIRGIN AND CHILD

The Virgin with the infant Jesus is the commonest devotional subject of mediaeval times. Very often there is a symbolical meaning in the attitudes, costumes or actions portrayed, or in some particularity of the surroundings. As this symbolism is too complicated to be treated of here, the reader is referred for elementary indications to Mrs. Jameson's *Legends of the Madonna*, 6th edition, 1879, especially pp. xliv ff.

Other figures are frequently added. If S. Joseph is prominent, the subject is known as the *Holy Family*. Very often there is an Infant John the Baptist; sometimes his mother, S. Elizabeth, or the Virgin's mother, S. Anne. Sometimes, especially in the German school, many more figures of supposed kindred were added (*die heilige Sippe*). Another tendency was to put the Virgin and Child in the centre of an altarpiece, adding angels, saints and donors as required. All these variations are indexed under *The Virgin and Child*; but scenes, such as the *Adoration of the Kings*, in which the two figures appear, occur under the appropriate heading in Section 4, *LIFE OF CHRIST*.

* An asterisk denotes that the figure or scene is not a principal part of the picture.

3. PERIOD OF THE OLD TESTAMENT AND THE APOCRYPHA

4. LIFE OF CHRIST

For purely devotional representations of Christ as God, see Section 1, *GOD*.

* An asterisk denotes that the figure or scene is not a principal part of the picture.

ANNOUNCEMENT TO THE SHEPHERDS (Luke ii. 8 sqq.)

According to some traditions the angel was S. Michael.

ANNUNCIATION (Luke i. 26 sqq.)

There is no gospel authority for the lily, which is usually present (but not in this reference); the lily is, of course, one of the most widespread emblems of the Virgin.

BAPTISM OF CHRIST BY S. JOHN (Matthew iii. 13, etc.)

BETRAYAL AND CAPTURE

May include S. Peter cutting off the ear of Malchus (John xviii. 10). The Agony in the Garden often includes in the background Judas and his followers coming from Jerusalem to effect the Capture.

CHRIST APPEARING TO HIS MOTHER

There is no Gospel authority for this subject which appears, however, in the Coptic Resurrection of Christ by Bartholomew the Apostle, etc. See James D. Breckenridge, 'Et Prima Vidit' in *The Art Bulletin*, 1957, pp. 9 ff.

CHRIST BEFORE PILATE

Pilate is often seen washing his hands (Matthew xxvii. 24).

CHRIST CARRYING THE CROSS (THE WAY TO CALVARY)

According to the Synoptic Gospels, the Cross was carried by Simon the Cyrenian; but in the vast majority of cases, painters follow John xix. 17.

CHRIST IN HELL

A descent of Christ into Hell or Limbo before the Resurrection has been received by the Church from early times: it is mentioned in the Creed, and a long account appears in the *Gospel of Nicodemus* (*Acts of Pilate*). The purpose was to bring up to Heaven the saints of the Old Testament; painters often limited themselves to Adam and Eve. Compare Dante, *Inferno*, iv. 46–63.

CHRIST MOCKED

The scene most often represented is the Crowning with Thorns. It is classified here under the more general title in order to distinguish it clearly from the devotional subject of Christ crowned with Thorns (The Man of Sorrows), for which see Section 1.

* An asterisk denotes that the figure or scene is not a principal part of the picture.

CHRIST NAILED TO THE CROSS

The Gospels say nothing of the manner of Christ's Crucifixion; representations vary, but most often Christ is being nailed to the Cross on the ground.

DAVID, Gerard . . . . No. 3067

CHRIST PRESENTED TO THE PEOPLE

Usually, from John xix. 5, called the *Ecce Homo*, a term so often misapplied that it has been omitted altogether from this catalogue.

MASTER OF THE BRUGES PASSION SCENES . . . . . . No. 1087
MASTER OF DELFT . . . . ,, 2922

CROWNING WITH THORNS See CHRIST MOCKED

CRUCIFIXION

The representations vary from Christ on the Cross between the Virgin and S. John to a complete rendering according to the Gospel texts, the legends, and any additions (as of a donor) that may have been wanted. The Magdalen often embraces the foot of the Cross; there is often in the foreground a skull, marking the spot as Golgotha. There was a widespread belief that the skull was the skull of Adam; cf. for instance J. J. M. Timmers, *Symboliek en Iconographie der Christelijke Kunst*, 1947, pp. 270 f., §§ 553/4. The most widely received name for the good thief is S. Dismas, for the bad thief Gestas. According to John xix. 19, Pilate was present. Painters often add angels.

*EYCK, Jan van . . . . No. 186
MASSYS, Studio of Quinten . . . . ,, 715
MASTER OF 1518, Studio of . . . . ,, 718
MASTER OF THE DEATH OF THE VIRGIN . . . . . . ,, 1088
MASTER OF DELFT . . . . ,, 2922
*NETHERLANDISH SCHOOL . . . . ,, 264
*WEYDEN, Follower of Rogier van der . . . . ,, 783

DEPOSITION: ENTOMBMENT: PIETÀ

Representations of the Deposition and the Entombment tend to merge. According to the Gospels, it was S. Joseph of Arimathaea who obtained Pilate's leave to bury Christ; John xix. 39, says that he was assisted by S. Nicodemus. In pictures there are generally also present the Virgin, S. John, the Magdalen, and several of the Holy Women. Sometimes the subject is treated devotionally rather than historically: Christ is seen in the Tomb, usually supported by angels or by the Virgin and S. John. This is usually known as a *Pietà*.

BOUTS, Dieric . . . . No. 664
DAVID, Gerard . . . . ,, 1078
*EYCK, Jan van . . . . ,, 186
MASTER OF DELFT . . . . ,, 2922
MASTER OF THE PRODIGAL SON, Studio of . . . . . . ,, 266
WEYDEN, Rogier van der . . . . ,, 6265
'YSENBRANDT,' Style of 'Adriaen' . . . . ,, 1151

ENTOMBMENT See DEPOSITION

FLAGELLATION

*EYCK, Jan van . . . . No. 186
*MASTER OF THE BRUGES PASSION SCENES . . . . . . ,, 1087

FLIGHT INTO EGYPT (Matthew ii. 13 sqq.)

S. Joseph should be present.

MASTER OF 1518, Studio of . . . . No. 1084
See also REST ON THE FLIGHT.

MARIES AT THE SEPULCHRE

The only reference in this index is according to Mark xvi. 1–5.

*WEYDEN, Follower of Rogier van der . . . . No. 1086

* An asterisk denotes that the figure or scene is not a principal part of the picture.

* An asterisk denotes that the figure or scene is not a principal part of the picture.

5. OTHER FIGURES OF THE NEW TESTAMENT PERIOD

* An asterisk denotes that the figure or scene is not a principal part of the picture.

* An asterisk denotes that the figure or scene is not a principal part of the picture.

S. LAZARUS

The brother of the Magdalen, raised by Jesus from the dead (John xi); said to have become the first bishop of Marseilles. Emblem here, a tomb or coffin, which seems a natural one. An example of a dressed figure of S. Lazarus (name inscribed) with one foot in a small tomb or coffin is in S. Léonard, Léau, Circle of D. Bouts (*Dieric Bouts* Exhibition, Brussels–Delft, 1957/8, No. 73, repr.). A print issued by A. Wierix (d. 1624 ?) shows according to the description a figure of S. Lazarus, name inscribed, holding a tomb or coffin; see L. Alvin, *Catalogue Raisonné de Œuvre des trois Frères Jean, Jérome et Antoine Wierix*, 1866, pp. 186/7, No. 1003.

'MARMION,' Style of 'Simon' . . . . No. 1939

S. LONGINUS

Identified with the soldier who pierced Christ's side on the Cross (John xix. 34); he was later said to have been literally or spiritually afflicted with blindness, but to have 'recovered his sight' on touching his eyes with blood from the spear. He is also identified with the centurion who believed (Mark xv. 39, etc.). The name may be simply derived from λόγχη (spear). He often appears (though not always clearly) at *Crucifixions* (see in Section 4)

S. LUKE

Evangelist. His symbol is an ox (Ezekiel i. 4–10); S.Jerome says the ox is an emblem of sacrifice, and adds for explanation that it is S. Luke who dwells chiefly on the priestly functions of Christ. He is said to have been a painter, and was the patron of painters' guilds.

MASSYS, Follower of Quinten . . . . No. 3902

MAGI

The legends concerning the Epiphany had an extraordinary development. 'Wise men' in Matthew ii., and the first Gentiles to honour Christ, they became after a time in number three, in title Magi, then Kings (cf. Psalm lxxi (lxxii), 10). Their names do not appear very early—they are called Melkon, Gaspard and Balthazar, Kings of Persia, India and Arabia, in the *Armenian Gospel of the Infancy* of dubious date. There seems to be a moderately old tradition that Balthazar was dark-skinned (fuscus), but it is only very rarely that he was represented as a black man before the fifteenth century. The Magi are said eventually to have been baptized in the Indies by S. Thomas, and to have been martyred; their relics were transferred to Constantinople, then Milan, then Cologne.

See in Section 4, *LIFE OF CHRIST:* ADORATION OF THE KINGS

MALCHUS

S. Peter cut off his ear at the moment of the Betrayal (John xviii. 10).

*EYCK, Jan van . . . . No. 186

MARIES

Referred to in the text as *Holy Women*, they appear at *Crucifixions* and in later scenes of the *Passion*. For the traditional identification of S. Mary Salome as one of the midwives of the Virgin, see under ZELOMI.

MARY See VIRGIN MARY

S. MARY MAGDALENE

Mentioned under this name several times in the Gospels; traditionally identified with Mary of Bethany, sister of Lazarus, who anointed Christ's feet in the house of Simon. According to Matthew xxvii. 56, and Mark xv. 40, she was present at the Crucifixion; painters often represent her embracing the foot of the Cross. She also appears at *Depositions* and *Entombments*; and (in accord with the Gospels) at the time of the Resurrection. She is said to have spent the last thirty years of her life in penitence at La Sainte-Baume,

* An asterisk denotes that the figure or scene is not a principal part of the picture.

S. MARY MAGDALENE—*continued*

near Toulon. She appears frequently as a single figure, nominally symbolizing repentance; there was even a fashion for women to have their portraits painted under the guise of the Magdalen (cf. the commentary to Netherlandish School, No. 2615). Her emblem is a pot; a secondary one a book, perhaps because she spent much of her time in Provence reading the Scriptures.

S. MATTHEW

Apostle and Evangelist. His normal emblem is an angel (cf. Ezechiel i. 4–10; four winged creatures with the faces, one of a man, one of a lion, one of an ox, one of an eagle); justification for associating S. Matthew with the first has been found in the fact that he begins his Gospel with the human generation of Christ. A halberd is also associated with him; it is often hard to distinguish S. Matthew with this emblem from other apostles with similar emblems.

S. NICODEMUS

According to John xix. 39, he assisted S. Joseph of Arimathaea in preparing Christ's body for burial; he appears in *Depositions* and *Entombments*.

S. PAUL

Apostle; author of many Epistles. His emblems are a sword and a book; the book symbolizes the Word of God, the sword his martyrdom by beheadal. He and S. Peter as the two principal Apostles are often associated.

S. PETER

Apostle, and first Pope. His most constant emblem, though not in the earliest representations, is one or more keys (Matthew xvi. 19). Among the historical scenes in which he appears is the *Capture of Christ*, at which he cut off the ear of Malchus (John xviii. 10).

* An asterisk denotes that the figure or scene is not a principal part of the picture.

6. SAINTS SINCE NEW TESTAMENT TIMES

* An asterisk denotes that the figure or scene is not a principal part of the picture.

S. AMBROSE

Bishop of Milan, and Doctor of the Church; died A.D. 397. His usual emblem is a scourge; he is said to have intervened thus armed at the battle of Parabiago (A.D. 1339), which ensured the power of the Visconti for nearly a century.

S. ANTHONY ABBOT

An Egyptian hermit, the founder of monasticism; died A.D. 356. His temptations by the Devil are often represented. Emblems, a crutch in the form of a Tau-Cross, a bell, a hog.

S. ANTHONY OF PADUA

A Franciscan from Lisbon; he spent the last years of his life in Padua, where he died A.D. 1231. One of his most frequent symbols is the Infant Jesus seated or standing on a book he holds.

S. AUGUSTINE

Bishop of Hippo and a Doctor of the Church; the *City of God* and the *Confessions* are his best known works. He died A.D. 430. His usual emblem is a flaming heart, sometimes pierced by an arrow; *sagittaveras tu cor nostrum caritate tua* occurs in the *Confessions*, Book IX, ii. 3. For the heart flaming, see the text quoted by G. Kaftal, *Iconography of the Saints in Central and South Italian Schools of Painting*, 1965, col. 128.

S. BARBARA

A Virgin; martyred probably A.D. 306. Her most constant attribute is a tower; this has no connection with her martyrdom. Her father, fearing that she would marry and leave him, shut her up in a tower.

S. BERNARDINO (OF SIENA)

A Franciscan; died A.D. 1444. One of his most frequent emblems is a book or tablet bearing the letters I.H.S. within the solar rays; he is said to have persuaded a maker of playing-cards to devote himself entirely to making such tablets, which became immensely popular.

S. BERTIN

Abbot of Sithiu (Saint-Bertin), near Saint-Omer; died about A.D. 709.

S. CATHERINE OF ALEXANDRIA

A Virgin of Royal Blood; martyred by being broken on a wheel, then beheaded; died about A.D. 310. In a vision, she was introduced by the Virgin into Heaven, where Christ plighted His troth to her, putting a ring on her finger; this subject frequently occurs in pictures as *The Marriage of S. Catherine*.

* An asterisk denotes that the figure or scene is not a principal part of the picture.

S. CHRISTOPHER

A giant; martyred in the fourth century. He set out in search of Christ, after learning that Christ was stronger than even the Devil. A hermit instructed him to carry wayfarers across a dangerous river; after a time, a Child asked to be carried across. S. Christopher was hardly strong enough, for the weight was that of the whole world and its Creator, the Child being Christ Himself. The legend has probably some connection with his name (Christ-Bearer); the writers who think he is merely a form of the Egyptian Anubis, who carried Horus across the Nile, do not seem to have proved their case.

MASTER OF THE FEMALE HALF-LENGTHS, Style of . . . . . No. 716
MEMLINC, Hans . . . . ,, 6275

S. CLEMENT, POPE

The third Bishop of Rome; died A.D. 100. He is said to have suffered martyrdom by being tied to an anchor and cast into the Black Sea.

'MARMION,' Style of 'Simon' . . . . No. 2669

S. DENIS

The First Bishop of Paris; martyred probably at the end of the third century. He appears here on the sculptures of the monument to Dagobert, which see in the commentary to the entry.

*MASTER OF S. GILES . . . . No. 4681

S. DOMINIC

A Spaniard, d. 1221. Founder of the Order of Preachers (Dominicans).

WEYDEN, Rogier van der . . . . No. 6265

S. DONATIAN

Bishop of Rheims; died about A.D. 389. The former cathedral of Bruges (now destroyed) was dedicated to him. His emblem is a wheel set with five tapers. According to a story suspected by the Bollandists (14 October, Ch. IV), he was thrown into a river by a servant; the Pope S. Dionysius placed a wheel with candles in the river. This stopped over the spot where S. Donatian was submerged, so that he could be brought to the surface and his life saved.

DAVID, Gerard . . . . No. 1045

S. FRANCIS OF ASSISI

Founder of the Franciscans; died A.D. 1226. He is often represented with the *stigmata*, or impressions of the five wounds of Christ, which he received on Mount Alvernia in 1224.

'MARMION,' Style of 'Simon' . . . . No. 1939

S. GEORGE OF CAPPADOCIA

Martyr; died about A.D. 303. From early times, legends collected round his name, many of them of Arian invention; so that Calvin and others could say that S. George never existed. In any case, the legend was very popular that he saved a Princess (variously identified) from a Dragon. He is said to have appeared, in armour, white with a red cross, at the Capture of Jerusalem (First Crusade, A.D. 1099); perhaps from this is derived the standard he frequently holds, a red cross on a white ground. Towards the thirteenth to fourteenth centuries he superseded S. Edward the Confessor as Patron of England, in which capacity he is usually shown with Dragon and no Princess.

MEMLINC, Studio of Hans . . . . No. 686

S. GILES

Patron of Edinburgh, etc. There is much chronological confusion about his legends. He appears to have been a hermit in the South of France, who founded the monastery of Saint-Gilles and died towards the beginning of the eighth century. For his two most popular scenes, the *Hind* and the *Mass of S. Giles*, see the entries in the text.

MASTER OF S. GILES . . . . Nos. 1419, 4681

* An asterisk denotes that the figure or scene is not a principal part of the picture.

S. GUDULA

Patroness of Brussels; died A.D. 712. The devil used to extinguish her lantern as she was going to church.

*WEYDEN, Follower of Rogier van der . . . . No. 783

S. HADRIAN See S. ADRIAN

S. HUBERT

First Bishop of Liège; died A.D. 727. When hunting the stag, he saw a Crucifix between its horns; the same miracle occurred to S. Eustace, who is sometimes hard to distinguish. The principal scene of the reference below is the translation of his relics.

WEYDEN, Follower of Rogier van der . . . . No. 783

S. JEROME

A Doctor of the Church, he fixed the text of the Bible according to the *Vulgate*; died 420. He is almost always represented in pictures with a lion; according to the legend, he domesticated one after extracting a thorn from its paw. (It seems probable that the lion is transferred from S. Gerasimus, another Palestinian recluse.) Some further adventures of the lion are described under the Patenier picture. He is usually represented as a Cardinal, although he was not.

DAVID, Studio of Gerard . . . . No. 2596
DAVID, Follower of Gerard . . . . . . (reverse) ,, 657
PATENIER, Ascribed to Joachim . . . . ,, 4826
WEYDEN, Rogier van der . . . . ,, 6265

S. LAWRENCE

A Deacon, who suffered martyrdom in Rome, A.D. 258, by being roasted on a grid-iron.

MEMLINC, Hans . . . . No. 747

S. LOUIS

Louis IX; died A.D. 1270. He took part in two Crusades, which explains why he is sometimes represented with a pilgrim's staff; and—if the identification is correct—with a cockle necklace in the picture No. 2606. This necklace may, however, be an ignorant reference to that of the French order of Saint Michel (founded in 1469).

COECKE, Ascribed to the Studio of Pieter . . . . . . No. 2606
*MASTER OF S. GILES . . . . (his monument) ,, 4681

S. LOUP

Lupus, Leu; Bishop of Sens, died A.D. 623. Protector of young children, and against epilepsy. Associated with S. Giles in Paris and the region.

MASTER OF S. GILES . . . . No. 1419

S. MARGARET

An Antiochian Virgin Martyr; died towards the beginning of the fourth century. Satan in the form of a Dragon is said to have swallowed her and burst; wherefore at her martyrdom she asked to be invoked by women in childbirth for their safe delivery. Alternative forms of the legend are that she conquered a Dragon by means of a Cross or by making the sign of a Cross, or even that she was the Princess saved by S. George from a Dragon.

*EYCK, Jan van . . . . No. 186
'MARMION,' Style of 'Simon' . . . . ,, 1939

S. MARTIN

Third Bishop of Tours; died towards A.D. 400. He shared his mantle with a beggar.

DAVID, Gerard . . . . No. 1045
*MASTER OF S. GILES . . . . ,, 4681

* An asterisk denotes that the figure or scene is not a principal part of the picture.

S. MAURICE

An officer in the Theban Legion, martyred at the end of the third century; the reference below is to his aid to Dagobert, revealed in a vision to a hermit Jean.

*MASTER OF S. GILES . . . . No. 4681

S. NICHOLAS

Bishop of Myra in Asia Minor; died towards the middle of the fourth century. His relics are preserved at Bari in Italy. One of the most popular legends concerning him tells how he dowered three impoverished girls; this is probably the origin of his most frequent attribute, three golden balls. According to another legend, he restored to life three children who had been salted down for food. He is the patron-saint of children, who call him Santa Claus.

DAVID, Follower of Gerard . . . . . (reverse) No. 657

* An asterisk denotes that the figure or scene is not a principal part of the picture.

INDEX OF PORTRAITS

Some of the doubtful and the impossible identifications have been omitted.

INDEX OF COLLECTIONS

NUMERICAL INDEX

LIST OF PAINTINGS ACQUIRED SINCE 1968

NETHERLANDISH School
16th Century

6412 PORTRAIT OF A MAN AGED 42, A MEMBER OF THE BOULENGE DE LA HAINIERE FAMILY

Wood, $29\frac{5}{16} \times 22\frac{1}{2}$ (74·5 × 57·2)
Presented by the Misses Rachel F. and Jean I. Alexander; entered the Collection in 1972.

Rogier van der WEYDEN
about 1399–1464

6394 SAINT IVO(?)

Wood, $17\frac{3}{4} \times 13\frac{3}{4}$ (45·1 × 34·8)
Purchased, 1971.